POPULAR FICTION BY WOMEN 1660–1730

Popular Fiction by Women 1660–1730

AN ANTHOLOGY

Paula R. Backscheider
John J. Richetti

CLARENDON PRESS · OXFORD

Oxford University Press, Great Clarendon Street, Oxford OX2 6DP
Oxford New York
Athens Auckland Bangkok Bogota Bombay
Buenos Aires Calcutta Cape Town Dar es Salaam
Delhi Florence Hong Kong Istanbul Karachi
Kuala Lumpur Madras Madrid Melbourne
Mexico City Nairobi Paris Singapore
Taipei Tokyo Toronto Warsaw
and associated companies in
Berlin Ibadan

Oxford is a registered trade mark of Oxford University Press

Published in the United States by
Oxford University Press Inc., New York

British Library Cataloguing in Publication Data
Data available

Library of Congress Cataloging in Publication Data
Popular fiction by women, 1660-1730 : an anthology / [edited by] Paula
R. Backscheider, John J. Richetti.
Includes bibliographical references.
1. English fiction—Women authors. 2. English fiction—Early
modern, 1500-1700. 3. Popular literature—Great Britain.
4. English fiction—18th century. I. Backscheider, Paula R.
II. Richetti, John J.
PR1286.W6P67   1996   823'.40809287—dc20   96-31093
ISBN 0-19-871137-9 (pbk)
ISBN 0-19-871136-0

10 9 8 7 6 5 4 3 2

Printed in Great Britain
on acid-free paper by
Biddles Ltd.
Guildford and King's Lynn

Acknowledgement

We would like to thank Hope Cotton, whose research skills, dedication, and good humour contributed abundantly to this anthology.

Contents

Introduction   ix

Chronology   xxv

Aphra Behn, *The History of the Nun* (1689)   1

Delarivière Manley, *The Secret History of Queen Zarah and the Zarazians*
    (1705)   45

Jane Barker, *Love Intrigues* (1713)   81

Penelope Aubin, *The Strange Adventures of the Count de Vinevil and
    His Family* (1721)   113

Eliza Haywood, *The British Recluse* (1722)   153

Eliza Haywood, *Fantomina* (1725)   227

Mary Davys, *The Reformed Coquet* (1724)   251

Elizabeth Singer Rowe, *Friendship in Death*, selections (1728)   323

Bibliography   335

Introduction

Two critical studies appeared in the 1950s that reinvigorated the study of the eighteenth-century British novel: A. D. McKillop's *The Early Masters of English Fiction* (1956) and Ian Watt's seminal *The Rise of the Novel: Studies in Defoe, Richardson, and Fielding* (1957). But the unspoken masculinist assumptions of both of these influential and powerful books are now embarrassingly apparent, since during the last twenty-five years or so numerous literary historians have begun to complicate the history of the novel in Britain in the late seventeenth and eighteenth centuries by reading beyond and around the works of the male masters on whom McKillop and Watt concentrated exclusively. What this revisionist history has recovered and re-evaluated is a mass of fiction by women during the eighteenth century that in actual fact dominated the production of the early novel in Britain. So that today no discussion of the subject or courses on the 'rise' of the British novel can afford to ignore the women writers in this anthology, most of whom may be said to be an important part of the history of the novel or, at least, form a set of rival or counter-traditions to the realistic and moral novel traced by older literary historians. Reading backwards from the perspectives and values of the nineteenth- and twentieth-century novel and imposing what we can now see is a falsely teleological line of evolution for the slow emergence of the novel in the early eighteenth century, critics like Watt and McKillop (and many others who followed in their path) tended to treat the extant narrative from those years (much of it by women) as the inchoate mass from which the masters triumphantly emerged. In this scenario, Richardson and Fielding were the originators of the modern novel because they revolutionized what they saw as the weak handling of narrative techniques and the diffuse arrangements of fictional materials by their inept predecessors and hapless contemporaries, taking the loose sense of plot, character, and setting they found all around them to create the extended narrative of complex moral and social characters and themes that we now think of as the standard recipe for the realistic novel. According to this story, in place of the faceless, formulaic repetitions of booksellers' hacks and financially distressed female authors, they produced individualized masterpieces of social observation and psychological depth which point the way to the great tradition of the modern novel in the centuries to come.

Although Richardson and Fielding did accomplish something like that, such an account of the development of the novel in Britain is misleading and radically incomplete. What we now think of as the main tradition of the novel as exemplified by the canonical male masters is, strictly speaking, the initiation and imposition as a culturally superior form of a certain kind of fiction. Both in terms of their numerical presence in the literary market-place and their influence upon the full-blown novel promulgated by Richardson and Fielding, women's fiction is the most important narrative produced from 1680 to 1740. With the revisionary books on the eighteenth-century English novel written in the 1950s and especially in the 1960s, a sustained effort to understand the place of fiction by women began and is today one of the major studies of those in eighteenth-century literature, the novel, and women's history and literature. Increasingly in recent years feminist critics and novel specialists have placed these writers and their texts in the contexts of their time and of literary history with illuminating results. The success of Aphra Behn rivalled or even surpassed that of all of her contemporaries except John Dryden by any measure—quality, popularity, longevity. Dryden passed over numerous male poets when he invited Behn to contribute to his edition of *Ovid's Epistles* (1680), and he praised her as a writer on several occasions.[1] Eliza Haywood's *Love in Excess* (1719) was one of the four best-selling books of the first half of the eighteenth century: only Daniel Defoe's *Robinson Crusoe* (1719), Jonathan Swift's *Gulliver's Travels* (1726), and Samuel Richardson's *Pamela* (1741) equalled it. Haywood, Aubin, and Defoe absolutely dominated prose fiction in the decade of the 1720s. The distinct varieties of narrative produced by the writers in this anthology point to the rich possibilities for fictional representation, many still very much alive and recognizable today, and to the active experimentation underway with traditional and new forms of fiction in those years.

Often entitled lives, 'lives and adventures', histories or secret histories, or novels, sometimes translated or adapted from the French *nouvelle* or the Spanish *novelas*, sometimes imitations or adaptations of continental or earlier English models, and sometimes original English inventions, the variety of sobriquets suggests both how rich the tradition was and how young the form that would be the English novel was. Recent books such as Ros Ballaster's *Seductive Forms*, Joan DeJean's *Tender Geographies*, and Linda Kauffman's *Discourses of Desire* have pointed out how important fictions in the development of the modern novel such as Marie-Madeleine de Lafayette's *La Princesse de Clèves* were and how English writers drew upon, popularized, and adapted the enormous French heroic romances of the seventeenth century, the multi-volume explorations of the moods of love with stylized aristocratic characters

[1] James Winn, *When Beauty Fires the Blood* (Ann Arbor: University of Michigan Press, 1992), 421–9.

and settings. The *nouvelles* and the romances such as Madeleine de Scudéry's *Artamène, ou le grand Cyrus* (1649–53) and *Clélie* (1656–60) were deeply concerned with contemporary politics, with the influence of a nation's history on its present, and in many ways were the successors of medieval and Renaissance romances in verse and prose in that they explored in stately, baroque prose with many interpolated stories and digressions the courtly ethos of love and honour that had been the obsession of European élites for centuries. Between 1685 and 1740 works of prose fiction moved away from the short forms related to the French romance and *nouvelle* with their inter-polated 'histories' of lives, and the Spanish and Portuguese tales like *Five Love Letters from a Nun to a Cavalier* and Cervantes's *Exemplary Novels*. They tended to become long narratives unified by a central character or two with some psychological depth who interacted in significant ways with society. Working within the often complicated, fantastic framework of older forms, they inscribe the beginnings of psychological realism. To a large extent, the development of the English novel is the history of the development of the psychological novel and of the working out of the means of constructing social commen-tary driven by moral judgement.

In addition, the market for fiction in these years in Britain clearly required something shorter and less elaborate, less stylized, more immediately appeal-ing to a wider range of taste, and more practical as well as affordable for a new generation of readers whose leisure time for reading and financial resources were not unlimited. Most of the writers in this anthology call these texts 'novels' in their prefatory manner. 'A small tale, generally of love,' is Samuel Johnson's definition of 'novel' in his 1755 *Dictionary of the English Language*, and what he had in mind was precisely the shorter fiction produced by Behn, Manley, Haywood, Aubin, Davys, Barker, and many others. Between 1680 and 1740, these women were, with Defoe, the most popular writers of fiction in England. And it is worth noting that Defoe shared some measure of their neglect (except for *Robinson Crusoe*) until the mid-1950s when Watt's and McKillop's studies appeared.

These texts continue to raise a number of important questions about the virtual disappearance from literary history of this body of fiction by women, and, inevitably, about the history of the English novel, about canon forma-tion, and about aesthetics.[2] One sociologically-oriented explanation is that such fiction, along with other parallel efforts in different modes and narrative forms, is essentially the precursor of modern mass market or popular fiction, highly readable and in effect disposable entertainment, often topically

---

[2] In 1979, Annette Kolodny wrote that reading the newly rediscovered texts by women writ-ers 'inevitably raised perplexing questions as to the reasons for their disappearance', 'Dancing through the Minefield', *Feminist Studies*, 6 (1980), 2. William Warner raises a variant on this question: 'How is the eclipse of an influential strain of popular fiction to be understood?', in 'Licensing Pleasure', in John J. Richetti (ed.), *The Columbia History of the British Novel* (New York: Columbia University Press, 1994), 13.

scandalous or sensational or pornographic or merely sentimental.[3] In this view, much of this material was aimed at readers conceived as having shorter attention spans and limited educational backgrounds (not just women, of course, but an expanding middle-class urban audience of literate but not formally educated consumers), and it offered simple and even cartoonish renditions of adventure in exotic places or of criminal careers, or more often of melodramatic, romantic, and erotic situations. As 'popular' fiction, these texts are necessarily ephemeral, limited in their appeal and effectiveness to the cultural and ideological moment that produced and marketed them, offered (often with crudely huckstering title-pages and advertisements) by opportunistic booksellers for a particular or targeted audience whose needs they served or hoped to please for profit.

But even from this critical approach and understanding, these texts are indeed significant and repay close study (if not of their textual details, for the patterns and formulas they display across a range of examples) precisely because, as popular literature, they initiate the specifically modern phenomenon of formula and mass market fiction, and in so doing dramatize the cultural fragmentation characteristic of modern life in which popular literature is a set of commodities targeted at what the producers hope are particular levels of the market who will respond in predictable ways. And like other forms of popular entertainment, such critics would insist, this fiction is at least superficially quite conservative, promoting current ideology and prevailing values. Women's fiction by these lights is amatory and appears as a species of escapist propaganda for the status quo, a form of ideological ratification of the myths of patriarchal culture about the special and redeeming weakness of the virgin-martyr who preserves moral order in her resistance to seduction and betrayal or illustrates the necessity of female rectitude in her tragic weakness and emotional vulnerability.[4] To be sure, such an approach fails to illuminate or to do full justice to self-consciously individualized works such as Manley's and Behn's, which add to popular scandal and easy eroticism an intellectual and political sophistication and a proto-feminist signature missing, for example, from the fictions of Aubin and some of Haywood; nor, many would say, to the importance of this fiction in the history of the novel. Indeed, one might argue that each of the fictions in this volume exploits popular formulas and bends or adapts those popular patterns for its own political, ideological, comic, or tragic purposes, which is precisely what on a different scale Richardson and Fielding sought to do in their novels.

---

[3] In *Factual Fictions: The Origins of the English Novel* (New York: Columbia University Press, 1983), Lennard Davis offered the provocative thesis that the novel emerges out of an intensified interest in contemporary happenings that he calls the novel/news discourse. And many early novels claim, however casually, that the events they offer are true and recent—news, in other words.

[4] See John J. Richetti, *Popular Fiction before Richardson: Narrative Patterns 1700–1739* (Oxford: Clarendon Press, 1969; repr. with new introduction by the author, 1992).

Nearly an entire generation of feminist critics would agree with this last statement, although they have offered other explanations for the reading experience that give rise to some of the objections to the texts as serious literature, and they ask us to realize as we read that our aesthetic criteria are culture-bound and socially constructed. Toni Bowers puts the current mood succinctly: 'Rather than denigrate (or praise) amatory fiction wholesale, critics might better ask why we define "good" literature as we do, how our assumptions about literary value still work to valorize some voices and exclude others, and how our capacities for pleasure might be augmented by respectful engagement with works we have been trained to resist or dismiss.'[5]

And this statement leads into the second most common feminist explanation: it may be the case that our inability to read some of these texts with pleasure or sympathy points to the inadequacy of traditional reading strategies and critical methods, which have made these texts 'unreadable', that is, both tedious and uninterpretable. Annette Kolodny puts it strongly when she says that the patriarchal critic 'enters a strange and unfamiliar world of symbolic significance' (5). For those who hold this view, then, these works are not repetitive or formulaic; such qualities are these writers' means of dramatizing the universal and replicated condition of women in the patriarchy. Haywood's work, for instance, is filled with doubled characters and thematically reinforcing reiterations; in *The British Recluse*, Bellamy is the phallic master signifier as it doubles Cleomira, then doubles her again and again in Melissa, Miranda, Belinda, and more.

This same generation of feminists has used the rich arsenal of sophisticated critical methodologies to reveal more than the sociological value of the texts. In looking at the plots and myths these women writers created and the influence they might have exerted on historical women and the literary marketplace, they have begun to explicate the forms they used and created. Joining the critics giving new attention to the non-realist novel, they have revealed unions of form and content and effective statements of personal and public engagement worthy of serious attention. They are arguing that, for instance, Eliza Haywood is a major contributor to the history of the early novel whose work is a sustained critique of her society, male–female relationships, and class politics, and that these characteristics should be recognized and integrated into studies of the eroticism and wild fantasies also typical of her texts.

From any of these perspectives, these texts reward close study. Not only did they initiate the specifically modern phenomenon of formula and mass market fiction, but they also helped shape the English novel form, introduced some of its major concerns and themes, and expanded the ways it participates in social debate. As many critics have noted of late, these fictions thereby stand in some sort of an essential or even an enabling relation to the canonical novels of mid-century, and serious attention must be paid to them.

---

[5] Toni Bowers, 'Sex, Lies, and Invisibility: Amatory Fiction from the Restoration to Mid-Century', *The Columbia History of the British Novel*, 70.

William B. Warner has asserted forcefully that Richardson and Fielding were aware of their dependence and their rivalry with women's novels and sought to occlude their adaptation of this popular or formula fiction. Warner sees the conflict between the new novel of Fielding and Richardson and the older tradition of racy female novels in rather stark and dramatic terms: 'by claiming to inaugurate an entirely "new" species of writing, Richardson and Fielding both seek to assert the fundamental difference of their own projects from these antagonists—the notorious trio of Behn, Manley and Haywood—who continue to circulate in the market as threatening rivals in a zero-sum struggle to control a common cultural space and activity.'[6] At the least, as Michael McKeon has argued, they help to create the novel as a set of generic possibilities and unspoken assumptions or expectations about fiction that displaced the older dominant patterns of romance and allegory. The new narratives of the 1740s and after can come into existence precisely because the novel itself now exists as what Karl Marx calls a 'simple abstraction', a 'quasi-objective category' in relation to which Richardson and Fielding can define themselves dialectically: separate from their precursors and contemporaries but dependent on them for defining their own particular complexity and independence, they simultaneously cancel and fulfil them.[7] The male masters needed the female producers of fiction, McKeon argues, if only to transcend them and bring fiction to a higher level of development.

To be sure, for feminist critics the kind of importance McKeon attaches to women's fiction, however complex and dialectical, is insufficient (even a bit condescending) and falls far short of evoking the special power and relevance (and pathos) of women's narratives. Critics like Ros Ballaster find in women's amatory fiction from these years a powerful articulation of female identity and self-consciousness available nowhere else in the culture of the time, an articulation which revises and subverts traditional masculinist constructions of the feminine. Ballaster argues that before the 1740s female amatory fiction offers a 'politically engaged and fantasy-oriented' fiction that is a powerful alternative to those 'naturalizing mechanisms' of human psychology projected by the realist novel.[8] Even the category of amatory fiction for critics like Ballaster has its own powerful *raison d'être* and is not simply or even dialectically important because it helps to provoke what becomes the main tradition of the novel. At its most compelling in the scandalous and amatory tales of Behn, Manley, and Haywood, in their bounding eroticism and emotionalism and their sometimes wild and fantastic intensities, amatory fiction by women forms a kind of deliberate counter-statement or alternative tradition to the measured social realism and moral analysis of the male novel.

[6] William B. Warner, 'The Elevation of the Novel in England: Hegemony and Literary History', *English Literary History*, 59 (1992), 577–96, quotation from 580.

[7] *The Origins of the English Novel 1600–1740* (Baltimore: Johns Hopkins University Press, 1987).

[8] Ros Ballaster, *Seductive Forms*: *Women's Amatory Fiction from 1684 to 1740* (Oxford: Clarendon Press, 1992), 10–11.

Many critics see how incomplete 'amatory' is as a descriptive term and how serious issues manifest themselves wherever we look. In these early novels women enter public discourse and, through narrative enactment and projection in fictional characters, publish their opinions on the most absorbing topics of the day: the intersections of religion and politics, the family and marriage, the nature of woman and female sexuality, the limits and abuse of authority, and the rights and obligations of monarchs. Jane Barker begins her *Love Intrigues* with the characters worrying about the personal consequences of yet another war; Delarivière Manley attacks the Duchess of Marlborough as a manipulative monster and sexual predator but places her and other women in Queen Anne's court at the centre of national affairs and the struggles for power;[9] in an apparently pious, other-worldly fiction, Elizabeth Rowe strikes out at the hypocrisy and materialistic values of the Church that had imprisoned her father. In the decades when Englishmen were required to take often contradictory vows or, in effect, lose their citizenship, many women writers joined in exploring and problematizing the binding nature of oaths. Aphra Behn's *The History of the Nun*, for instance, can easily be read as a troubling allegory about making and keeping vows that concludes with an absurdist Aesopian moral parodying the impractical commandment of successive governments: Never break a vow. Mary Davys includes Whig–Tory debates in her *Familiar Letters*, makes a patriotic comment in the dedication to *The Accomplished Rake*, and dedicates her plays to Princess Anne.

Feminist critics and even general readers have also embraced books by women as one of the few places in which women could speak for themselves, could represent women's experiences, could express their needs, their nightmares, and their utopian hopes, and escape the masculine myth of the female. The thin line between seduction and rape, the short interval between sexual arousal and surrender and then their aftermath in abandonment and betrayal speak, say feminist readers of these texts, to contemporary realities of abused and abandoned women, of 'date rape' and other routine dangers and humiliations that women still face every day and all the time. There is, in short, a disturbing and powerful contemporary resonance for many twentieth-century readers in these eighteenth-century fictions.[10] The relationship of these fictions to modern romances, 'gothics', and novels written for women is also apparent.

And yet even at their most wildly escapist and emotionally thrilling, these fictions can be said to partake of the moral and social functions narrative inevitably serves. As J. Paul Hunter has recently observed, the eighteenth-

---

[9] See Frances Harris, *A Passion for Government: The Life of Sarah, Duchess of Marlborough* (Oxford: Clarendon, 1991) for an intriguing portrait of Sarah and other women being bred to a 'career' in court life and influence.

[10] We are often reminded that sentences such as this must include men; as one of our male students commented, 'I have a wife, a mother, sisters, and a baby daughter—I have a stake in these issues and this literature.'

century novel is directed at problems or dilemmas that are specific to particular persons and social circumstances, and these fictions are often attentive to such situations. Hunter poses some typical questions that novels of the time seek to answer: 'How is an innocent servant girl to act when her wicked master decides it is his right to seduce her? [*Pamela*]'[11] Such practical and specific questions (and ostensible cautionary purposes) are at the heart of these fictions, and are sometimes exploited for subtle purposes as they are in Haywood's *Fantomina*. Although some would say that the emphasis in much of the fiction lies not so much in solving the problem or negotiating a way around it as in dramatizing in exciting and involving ways the internal and emotional effects, others would argue that closure tends to serve the dominant ideology, and these fictions by their very open-endedness highlight cultural issues in need of thought and address. Without falling into essentialist notions of gender, perhaps it is possible to say that male novelists of the period tend to dwell on problem-solving and a kind of pragmatic didacticism, whereas some women writers present a tragic absolutism at work in social and moral circumstances that pushes them to narrate the inevitable effects without possibility of satisfactory resolution. Like all generalizations, this one has its limits, and readers of this anthology will find that it hardly applies to political satire like Manley's *The History of Queen Zarah*, whose central figure is a strong and scheming self-promoter, to social comedy like Mary Davys's *The Reformed Coquet*, or to the erotic playfulness of Eliza Haywood's *Fantomina*, where sexual freedom and mastery of her male lover are temporarily and subversively achieved by the heroine's clever machinations.

To a greater or lesser degree, each of these texts displays the novel form's characteristic ability to move from interior consciousness to external forces and events, and protagonists come to know themselves and to change more than most earlier fictional characters. Each text explores forms of power, means of influence, and social mores, often with devastating explication of their implications. As such they are small steps toward the dilemma that the classic European novel has faced since its beginnings—the conflict between the free self who narrates and the confining or determining realities which that self both experiences and must employ to understand experience. The gendered experience of their authors may have determined that their plots often move by means of forces outside the character, such as a father's plans for his daughter's marriage, coincidences, or accidents rather than by the protagonist's psychology or initiatives.

In these texts and in many more like them during these years, women (in current critical parlance) write women and women's bodies. Women's ambitions, needs, emotions, aspirations, sexuality, and independence are often in this fiction quite different from what the main tradition of the British novel offers as their prevailing representation. Scrutinized as women's writing these

[11] J. Paul Hunter, *Before Novels: The Cultural Contexts of Eighteenth-Century English Fiction* (New York: W. W. Norton, 1990), 94.

texts point (sometimes by implication and negative example and sometimes quite explicitly) to how love might be experienced and expressed, of what fulfilment and happiness might mean in another moral and social order. In some cases, they dispute the patriarchal myth that volcanic emotion and irresistible sexual passion overwhelm weak woman's limited reason and give us instead women characters with self-possession, self-respect, intelligence, and courage; qualities which are most strongly marked, of course, in the authors themselves, whatever their characters may have to do within the patterns of fiction. Woman's sexuality and awakenings to sexual consciousness figure in all of them, and they complicate the stereotypical image of woman as the seduced, fallen woman who was 'swept away' by her treacherous body and tumultuous emotions. Eliza Haywood's Fantomina constructs an elaborate masquerade to enjoy in various disguises the sexual favours of Beauplaisir, and in so doing she exercises social and sexual privilege peculiar to her class but not to her sex. Comic and liberating, her plot cancels the usual pattern whereby the promiscuous male enjoys the monogamous woman and then abandons her when he is sated with her charms. For Fantomina, Beauplaisir is a sex object she manipulates for her pleasure.

While we might predict that one of Elizabeth Rowe's heroines would stand firm and say that she would 'never comply with any . . . Schemes' to compromise her virtue (Letter IV), even the pious Rowe gives us 'warm writing' in letters that depict attractions between men and women. In none of these fictions is the moment of loss of virginity the pivotal and definitional moment that gives meaning to a woman's life and character. These writers also open up the possibility of a respectable and fulfiling choice other than heterosexual marriage; while this is debated in *Love Intrigues*, discussion of celibacy and other arrangements is opened in the work of Aubin, Davys, Haywood, and Manley. Some feminists have argued that women's texts have a utopian urge and seek to portray the 'couple of the future' for whom sexual passion is a natural part of a companionate marriage. At the least, fiction such as we have selected complicates the stereotypes of female passion and sexual relationships, and this anthology has no repetitions but rather interesting variations on the kinds of short fiction women authors produced in this period.

We include the major women writers of the period and bring together prose fictions that are representative both of their work and of their versatility, texts that are revisionary in form and content, and yet have some common subjects, episodes, narrative strategies, and concerns. Some of the most striking examples of double vision—seeing themselves simultaneously from within and without—are in these sections. Galesia imagines murdering Bosvil, and embroiders the fantasy to imagine women building a statue to honour her, even as she notes her feelings of helplessness. At one point she responds to a change in Bosvil's behaviour by looking in a mirror 'to see if my person was changed in that fatal three weeks'. In a variety of entertaining, original ways they portray anger, always a vexed topic for women. Mary Davys has her heroine lament comically, 'what an assiduous creature is man, before enjoyment, and what a careless, negligent wretch after it.' In this text and several others, women write 'revenge fantasies', nearly a sub-genre in themselves. Several contemplate the retired life; incest figures into several, and a few take up such rarely opened topics as suicide.

Readers of this volume will notice that there is a noticeable shift in the construction of the feminine within these stories and of course beyond them into those novels by women such as Frances Sheridan, Sarah Fielding, Charlotte Lennox, and Frances Burney who write in the wake of Richardson and Fielding. Pious and deeply moral writers like Jane Barker, Penelope Aubin, and Elizabeth Singer Rowe represent both in their exemplary personal lives and in their fiction a distinctly separate idea of female writing and self-understanding and self-presentation. As Janet Todd has argued, between Aphra Behn at the end of the seventeenth century and Mary Wollstonecraft in the 1790s there is 'a century of sentimental construction of femininity, a state associated with modesty, passivity, chastity, moral elevation and suffering'.[12] As Todd, Jane Spencer, and others evoke it, female writers could not in the end afford to mimic male freedom like Behn, Manley, and Haywood or to create a subversive female plot in which subordination and submission became means of self-assertion and female glorification as they do in the texts by Aubin, Davys, Barker, and Rowe.

Indeed, although the stories in this collection can all be grouped in a number of ways, they are each distinct and particular to their authors. Our book begins with the woman writer of whom Virginia Woolf wrote, 'all women together ought to let flowers fall upon the tomb of Aphra Behn' and with Delarivière Manley, the other pioneer professional writer. The Behn and Manley selections are overt and explicit in their narrative purposes, and we might even say that as authors they lived under an earlier and less prudish dispensation when female wit and intelligence could express themselves more freely and openly than the generation of Frances Burney and Charlotte Lennox. Manley's *Queen Zarah* (1705) is short on plot, since it is simply a thinly fictionalized version of the nefarious schemes of the Marlboroughs and other Whig politicians she wished to vilify. But *Queen Zarah* sparkles with ferocious wit and bracing political hatred; it delights in Zarah's self-serving and inventive energy even as it denounces it, and Manley savours the erotic electricity of the corrupt court she evokes and attacks. *The History of the Nun* (1689) is a study of unfortunate Fate and unlucky Fortune, and the reader is invited to lament the chances and circumstances that lead to Isabella's transformation from female saint to double murderess. Like *Queen Zarah*, *The History of the Nun; or The Fair Vow-Breaker* offers readers an inside view of an exotic (and to English eyes) scandalous and corrupting milieu, a convent. Not

[12] Janet Todd, *The Sign of Angellica: Women, Writing and Fiction, 1660-1800* (New York: Columbia University Press, 1989), 4.

surprisingly given her Tory and Jacobite leanings, Aphra Behn's (and Eliza Haywood's) cloistered convent is not like the monasteries of later Gothic fiction, a scene of secret lust and corruption, but, as it was to their contemporary the Duchess of Mazarine and many others, a sanctuary and a decorous court where the outside world comes to chat and gossip at the visitors' grate with the daughters of the Flemish 'quality' who have chosen the religious life. Its chief interest lies in its analysis of the psychological and sexual effects on a young girl like Isabella of such an artificial and constricting existence. Drawn irresistibly to Henault and after anguished hesitation to break her vows, she is drawn just as compellingly some years later to acts of violent self-preservation when the long-absent and presumed-dead Henault returns and threatens the calm stability of her privileged life with Villenoys. The effects of Behn's wonderfully unjudgemental tale are nearly tragic and certainly painful, since Isabella is a victim of circumstances and her own fidelity to her instincts for virtue and for survival in a male world.

Jane Barker's *Love Intrigues* has already achieved nearly canonical status. Praised by modern critics for its artful composition and psychological turn, it is one of the first novels to move smoothly between the inner life of the heroine and the external world to which she is forced to respond. It takes as its subject the frustrations of trying to understand another human being, especially when social codes restrict the expression of honest feelings. As the heroine attempts to interpret Bosvil's words and actions, what others tell her about him, and what initiatives are open to her within courtship rituals, Galesia becomes a very early bearer of women's experiences, including self-consciousness about the body, the 'double vision' of seeing the self from within and without simultaneously, and the ambivalences associated with the writing life. Barker uses a variety of artful strategies to give heightened insight into Galesia's thoughts and feelings. Among them are her changes of dress, the poems included in the text, and allusions to plays and other kinds of literature. Anger, always a difficult emotion for women writers to convey acceptably, is well done. In one passage, she compares her experience to the cynical description of court promises being as worthless as whores' vows in a poem by John Wilmot, earl of Rochester.

Penelope Aubin's *The Strange Adventures of the Count de Vinevil* is the best example in this volume of popular fiction in the strict sense, of crudely imagined representations of good and evil opposed, in this case of Muslim treachery and lust versus Christian innocence and purity. Aubin's novels rehearse the edifying spectacle of Divine Providence coming to the rescue of beleaguered innocence, and their popularity points to a widespread need for such soothing certainties in what believers saw as an increasingly secular age. Ardelisa is a virginal innocent lusted after by Osmin, a merciless and martial Turk, who does succeed in killing her venerable father, the Count de Vinevil. Things look very dark for a time as treacherous Turks lurk around every corner, but her young lover the Count de Longueville is a capable young man who eventually, thanks to the lucky twists and turns of the plot, finds her alive and marries her (although not before she tests his constancy). In spite of the simplicity and general *naïveté* of the tale, Aubin was certainly shrewdly alert to the popularity of stories set in exotic places; and following the example of Defoe's recent bestseller, *Robinson Crusoe* (1719), she takes care to isolate her Christian refugees from their terrible sojourn in Turkey on a deserted island in the Mediterranean, where they survive by virtue of the foraging abilities of their faithful and devoted servants and are rescued by a Venetian ship that takes them back to Christian Europe and happy marriages all around.

Eliza Haywood may be the most controversial and most important writer in the collection. In a sense, as Margaret Doody has put it, her novels establish 'the seduction novel . . . and it is to this genre that Richardson's work ultimately belongs'.[13] But she is like all the writers in this collection a pioneer in her own right, the successor to Behn and Manley as the most prolific and successful woman writer of her day in Britain. Through the 1720s and 1730s her novellas dominated the market, and she was in terms of popularity nothing less than the Barbara Cartland or Danielle Steele of her day, or so at least her publishers tried to present her and to describe the effects of her work on willing readers. Certainly Haywood is the most revisionary of the writers in this collection, even in her uses of familiar plot lines. For instance, Fantomina's energy and passion are a marked contrast to the anguished submission to the feminine role, and her lack of remorse reveals the contradictions in definitions of 'woman'.

In their different ways, *Fantomina* and *The British Recluse* predict the remarkable adaptability Haywood would display in the post-Richardson era when she switched her narrative mode to the longer or 'dilated' and more sentimental novel then in fashion, producing books such as *The History of Miss Betsy Thoughtless* (1751) and *The History of Jemmy and Jenny Jessamy* (1753). Both of the short novels reprinted in this volume display a sharp, critical awareness of male tyranny and record female triumph of several sorts. Indeed, even in her more formulaic tales of tumultuous passion the corruption of the male establishment is a given. Taken all together, Haywood's novellas are as much a critique of patriarchal arrangements as they are often enough a celebration of female emotional intensity. Pathos and anger share the stage with erotic arousal and explorations of women's sexuality. To gain this effect, she sometimes creates the perspective of women watching men and construing them an alien, secret society. She can also meld class privilege with gender power in ways that have startling, contemporary resonance. When Miranda in *The British Recluse* is nearly kidnapped by a rake as she leaves church, she is doubly powerless. Not only is she seen by Bellamy as an available sex object, but the narrator remarks, 'Had such a piece of

---

[13] Margaret Anne Doody, *A Natural Passion: A Study of the Novels of Samuel Richardson* (Oxford: Clarendon Press, 1974), 149.

villainy been attempted by a meaner Man, he certainly had been secured; but his Quality made everybody unwilling. . . .'

Within the larger history of the English novel, *The British Recluse* can be used to explore a pivotal moment in the history of the novel. Traces of earlier fiction are obvious, as in the extravagantly emotional letters Cleomira writes, which seem modelled after *Five Love Letters between a Nun and a Cavalier*. Obviously related to the French *nouvelle* and romance, the text places Belinda in much the same position as the Princesse de Clèves in that she feels no passion for Worthly but slowly learns what ideal love would be. The nucleus of *The British Recluse* became the story of Betsy and Trueman in what is regarded as Haywood's best full-length novel and a major contribution to the fictional strain represented by Richardson and Burney, *The History of Miss Betsy Thoughtless* (1751).

Of all the texts in this anthology, the excerpt from Rowe's popular *Friendship in Death, or Letters from the Dead to the Living* (1728) may seem most strange to the reader. When Rowe wrote these little fictions, letters from the dead to the living were something of a literary fashion. John Dee's *A True and Faithful Relation of what passed for many years between Dr. John Dee . . . and Some Spirits* (1659) was still popular, and Thomas Brown's *Letters from the Dead to the Living* (1702) was successful enough for him to write several more volumes of them. Translations of such books by French intellectuals (Bernard Le Bovier de Fontenelle's *Dialogues of the Dead* {trans. 1708}, François de Salignac de La Mothé Fénelon's *Fables and Dialogues of the Dead* {trans. 1722}) sold alongside such humorous English books as *Sheppard in Egypt . . . Being a Letter from John Sheppard to Frisky Moll* (1725). The year before publication of her book, Daniel Defoe's *An Essay on the History and Reality of Apparitions* had included stories of appearances of spirits, including conversations held with them. Such books contributed to a larger effort mounted by religious believers in these years to defend religion against what they saw as a rising tide of irreligion and infidelity, deism and atheism. Religious publications outnumbered all other kinds at this time, and most types of writing offered advice. Rowe's little stories of warnings from the other side of the 'reality' of the afterlife were exceedingly popular, and, like popular fiction in other forms, they often turn on bizarre incidents, strange coincidences, or doomed love. In fact, in spite of the pious purpose, many of Rowe's epistolary fictions in *Friendship* are formula stories, familiar plots with conventional characters and predictable outcomes. One is from a nun, and another interweaves the eighteenth-century obsessions with babies switched at birth and with incest.

Mary Davys's *The Reformed Coquet* is a well-plotted, lively novel in which narrative devices that would remain popular throughout the century and highly original touches are integrated. Like so many novelists of the century, she explicitly points out the importance of the drama to her art, and heroine and narrator sometimes speak with the witty economy of Restoration drama. Some of her fops and other characters were still walking the boards of Drury

Lane and Covent Garden as she wrote. Her use of disguises is sophisticated; some characters use them for evil, some for benign, even idealistic purposes, and one, Altemira, to express her social position. Indeed all of the disguises are symbolic and are an original contribution to the novel's ability to convey internal states of mind within socially symbolic episodes. Davys also makes a significant contribution to novelistic style. Her narrator, as Henry Fielding's will be, has a firm, friendly relationship with the reader; she promises, for instance, that 'the Reader shall know by and by' what saves the heroine. She can sound Austenian, creating a combination of mock lament and serious accuracy that reminds us of *Emma* when she writes, 'What an unhappy Creature is a beautiful young Girl left to her own Management. . . .' Her characters echo each other, giving humour and nuance to observations about gender and human nature. A prowling rake can admire a ceiling painting of the rape of Helen. Quite early she had demonstrated considerable flexibility and effectiveness with combining comic, satiric, and narrative styles, and this novel adds strong unity and suspense. Just as *Miss Betsy Thoughtless* expands upon the story and characters in *The British Recluse*, Davys reworked the story of Lord Lofty and Altemira, deepening and exploring social and personal issues, in *The Accomplished Rake*.

Although we often think of romances and fictions such as these as having an almost exclusively female audience, they were read and enjoyed by both sexes in the eighteenth century. A testimonial poem ('By an unknown Hand') introduces Haywood's best-selling *Love in Excess* (1719) by depicting Haywood as a champion of her sex and a promoter of love's power:

> A Stranger Muse, an Unbeliever, too,
> That women's Souls such Strength of Vigour knew!
> Nor less an Atheist to Love's Power declar'd,
> Till you a Champion for the Sex appear'd!
> A Convert now, to both, I feel that Fire
> Your Words alone can paint! Your Looks inspire!
>
> .   .   .   .
>
> No more of Phoebus rising vainly boast,
> Ye tawny Sons of a luxurious Coast!
> While our bless'd Isle is with such Rays replete,
> Britain shall glow with more than Eastern Heat!

This panegyrist speaks as a man and describes the effects of these novels on a male sensibility, for Haywood's novels and those of the other writers we have gathered here were clearly intended for both men and women. Only Davys's novel has a specific, warm address to women, yet of all the stories we have selected, *The Reformed Coquet* has been treated by modern critics as the most traditional and the most clearly and smoothly linked to the 'mainstream' novel of mid-century and after. Amoranda, the coquette of the title, matures (albeit abruptly under the stress of the surprisingly violent and graphic incidents that make up the plot) and comes to value good sense as she falls in love with the man who delivers her from two sets of kidnappers. With a fine sense of comic control and with some of the sexual candour and near-violence of stage comedy, Davys has reminded some readers of Fielding, and her novellas have something of the qualities of his novels in the high spirits, the satiric edge, and the satisfyingly sentimental resolution of their plots.

Despite Davys's realism, many critics recognize that these fictions are fantasy machines; they see that as surely as one of the authors' goals was to give erotic pleasure, others were to figure a female Imaginary, a glimpse of the utopian hope of a new kind of man, a different model for marriage, and a better, more respected position for woman. We now see these women and their creations as scandalous not just because they dared to depict women's sexuality and some men's rapacious commodification of it but also because they created women who were economically independent, who had the capacity to protect themselves or even exact revenge, and whose characters or 'nature' deviated from the expected or socially sanctioned. In all of these texts, women show the unsettling ability to move from victimization to aggression. Women's texts use familiar paradigms and myths to express not only the social realities of women's position in eighteenth-century society but the larger ideological realities of the age. In doing so, they created new literary forms and invigorated old ones.

As *The Reformed Coquet* makes especially clear, part of the challenge for readers of this volume will be to judge whether there are any particular qualities in these fictions that mark them as distinctively by women and that separate them from the mainstream of British fiction in the eighteenth century. Do they constitute, taken together and separately, a counter-tradition or a rival and competing set of narrative choices to the male novel of mid-century? The diversity of these stories, their affinities with the mainstream in some cases and their clear differences from it in others, may make the answer difficult and complicated. Whatever the answer the reader settles on and whatever critical perspective one brings to reading this fiction, one thing is clear: fiction by women is a crucial part of the literary history of the British eighteenth century, and the dialogue about the issues these texts raise is far from over.

Chronology

1642   Aug. The Civil War begins in earnest.
1649   Jan. Trial and execution of the king.
      Mar. Acts pass to abolish the monarchy and the House of Lords.
      May Act declaring England a commonwealth passed by the Rump Parliament.
1651   Sept. Charles begins his exile on the Continent.
1660   25 Apr. Charles II invited to return to England by Convention Parliament.
      29 May Charles II arrives in London.
      Likely year of Daniel Defoe's birth.
1662   Chartering of the Royal Society.
1665   The Great Plague.
1666   2 Sept. Outbreak of the Great Fire of London.
1667   July Treaty of Breda ends Anglo–Dutch war.
      John Milton's *Paradise Lost* published.
1677   Mary, daughter of James II, marries William of Orange.
1678   John Bunyan's *Pilgrim's Progress* published.
1680   4 Nov. Reading of Exclusion Bill designed to exclude James, Duke of York from Britain and succession to the throne: rejected by House of Lords.
1685   Death of Charles II; succeeded by his brother, James II.
      Monmouth's Rebellion; Monmouth executed.
      Louis XIV revokes the Edict of Nantes; end of religious toleration in France.
1687   Isaac Newton's *Principia Mathematica* published.
1688   William of Orange invited to England.
      Dec. Escape of James II to France.
1689   Accession of William III and Mary.
      Samuel Richardson born.
1690   1 July The Battle of the Boyne: James II defeated by William III and escapes to France.

1690 Publication of John Locke's *An Essay Concerning Human Understanding*.
1694 28 Dec. Death of Queen Mary II.
      Founding of the Bank of England.
1700 John Dryden dies.
1702 England and allies declare war against France and Spain: War of Spanish Succession.
      Death of William III.
      Accession of Queen Anne.
1704 English capture Gibraltar; Duke of Marlborough defeats the French at Blenheim.
1707 Henry Fielding born.
      Union of Scotland and England ratified.
1710 Sarah Fielding born.
1711 Addison and Steele's *The Spectator* begins publication.
1713 Treaty of Utrecht signed with France, ending War of Spanish Succession.
1714 Death of Queen Anne.
      Accession of George I.
1715 Jacobite Rebellion.
      Death of Louis XIV of France.
1718 War with Spain declared.
1719 Daniel Defoe's *Robinson Crusoe* published.
1720 South Sea Company fails ('South Sea Bubble').
1721 Robert Walpole appointed First Lord of the Treasury and Chancellor of the Exchequer.
      Tobias Smollett born.
1723 Sarah Scott born.
1724 Frances Brooke born.
1726 Jonathan Swift's *Gulliver's Travels* published.
1727 Death of George I.
      Accession of George II.
1729 Charlotte Lennox born.
1731 Daniel Defoe dies.
1737 Theatrical Licensing Act passed.
1739 War of Jenkins' Ear with Spain.
      David Hume's *A Treatise of Human Nature* published.
1740 Samuel Richardson's *Pamela* (vols. i–ii) published.

THE
HISTORY
OF THE
NUN:
OR, THE
Fair Vow-Breaker.

Written by Mrs. A. BEHN.

LICENSED,
Octob. 22. 1688.   *Ric. Pocock.*

LONDON:

Printed for *A. Baskervile*, at the *Bible*,
the Corner of *Essex-Street*, against
St. *Clement*'s Church, 1689.

Aphra Behn
(1640?-1689)

PROLIFIC poet, playwright, and novelist, Aphra Behn was without question the most famous and successful woman writer of her time, but her origins are obscure and the details of a good deal of her life remain something of a romantic mystery. A memoir prefixed to the *Histories and Novels of the Late Ingenious Mrs. Behn* (1696) says that she was born in 1640 at Canterbury to John Johnson, a close relative of Lord Willoughby, Royal Patentee for the colony at Surinam (present-day Guyana in northern South America); recent studies, however, suggest that she was the daughter of Bartholomew Johnson, a Canterbury barber. Behn probably spent some time in Surinam in her early twenties, and she used that experience to great effect in the setting of her most popular work of fiction, *Oroonoko, The History of the Royal Slave* (1688). She served as an English spy in Antwerp during the Anglo–Dutch War in 1666, and in 1668 when she returned to England she spent time in a debtors' prison in London. On the way back from Surinam, she probably married Captain Johan Behn, a ship captain and slave trader, who died in 1665, leaving Aphra (who took as her pen name Astrea, from the French heroic romance of Honoré d'Urfé, *L'Astrée*) to earn her living by her pen, perhaps the first English woman to do so.

For the next twenty years she produced an astonishing variety of literary work, and she stands out with Dryden, Rochester, Wycherley, and Congreve as one of the major poets and playwrights of the Restoration. Her eighteen plays held the stage during the reflorescence of English drama in those years, and she moved in glittering literary and political circles that included the great wits and aristocratic patrons of the day. Her most popular play was *The Rover* (1677), but others such as *The Forced Marriage* (1670), *The Amorous Prince* (1671), and *The False Count; or, A New Way to Play an Old Game* (1682) were well received. She is best known today, however, for her prose fiction, especially *Oroonoko*, whose title character is a magnificent African prince who ends his days heroically and tragically as a rebellious slave in Surinam. In recent years there has been a revival of critical interest in all her dozen pieces of shorter fiction on amatory themes and, especially, in her longest narrative, the three-part *Love Letters between a Nobleman and His Sister* (1684-7), based on a contemporary sex scandal but also featuring

1

characters from the turbulent political events of those days, such as Charles II's rebellious illegitimate son, the Duke of Monmouth (executed in 1685 for attempting to overthrow his uncle, James II). Behn's fiction is elegant and stylish in its renditions of complicated and often forbidden passion, witty and irreverently knowing about the adulterous affairs and sexual betrayals which are her recurring theme. Her fiction mainly delivers an erotic world of aristocratic hedonism and often enough of sensational and even brutal violence. Emotional intensity and sexual variety are accompanied in her fiction by subtle psychological analysis, and her characters, both male and female, are more complex, more clearly rooted in the aristocratic ethos of love and military glory and honour than the conventional figures of much subsequent amatory fiction. *The History of the Nun* (1689) is rather more sentimental and melodramatic than her other fictions, and the lovely and tragic heroine, Isabella, is a wonderful study in the force of intertwining passion and self-interest that transforms her at length into a monster. Behn's story is an implicit critique of the distorting effects of the monastic life, but it is also a shrewd presentation of the powerful satisfactions such a life could offer and the selfish and powerful ego it could produce. It is also a dramatization of the traps and dead ends patriarchal society offers to beautiful and virtuous women, and Isabella is a sympathetic figure even when she murders two husbands.

Behn's works continued to be printed and remained in circulation through the eighteenth century, although for many readers she (and most of her heroines) became, as taste grew prim and sentimentally didactic, embodiments of scandalous female transgression, and her novels were labelled as morally dangerous for innocent readers. In the twentieth century, her status as a major literary figure has been fully restored, and she has become an exemplar of the woman writer for feminist critics, a pioneer of female literary accomplishment and independence.

J.J.R.

The History of the Nun; or, The Fair Vow-breaker

DEDICATION

To the Most Illustrious Princess,
The Duchess of Mazarine.[1]
Madam,

There are none of an illustrious quality who have not been made, by some poet or other the patronesses of his distressed hero, or unfortunate damsel;

---

[1] *Duchess of Mazarine*: Hortense Mancini, an Italian aristocrat, who married Armand-Charles de la Meilleraye, one of the richest men of the time. She left her husband in 1666 and eventually settled in London in 1675, where her great admirer, King Charles II, assigned her a pension. She lived a free and unconventional personal life and was (as Behn's flattery makes clear) a great patron of literature and the fine arts.

and such addresses are tributes due only to the most elevated, where they have always been very well received, since they are the greatest testimonies we can give of our esteem and veneration.

Madam, when I surveyed the whole tour of ladies at court, which was adorned by you, who appeared there with a grace and majesty peculiar to your great self only, mixed with an irresistible air of sweetness, generosity, and wit, I was impatient for an opportunity, to tell Your Grace, how infinitely one of your own sex adored you, and that among all the numerous conquests Your Grace has made over the hearts of men, Your Grace has not subdued a more entire slave; I assure you, Madam, there is neither compliment nor poetry in this humble declaration, but a truth which has cost me a great deal of inquietude, for that fortune has not set me in such a station as might justify my pretence to the honor and satisfaction of being ever near Your Grace to view eternally that lovely person and hear that surprising wit; what can be more grateful to a heart than so great and so agreeable an entertainment? And how few objects are there that can render it so entire a pleasure as at once to hear you speak and to look upon your beauty? A beauty that is heightened, if possible, with an air of negligence in dress wholly charming, as if your beauty disdained those little arts of your sex whose nicety alone is their greatest charm, while yours, Madam, even without the assistance of your exalted birth, begets an awe and reverence in all that do approach you and every one is proud and pleased in paying you homage their several ways, according to their capacities and talents. Mine, Madam, can only be expressed by my pen, which would be infinitely honored in being permitted to celebrate your great name for ever and perpetually to serve where it has so great an inclination.

In the mean time, Madam, I presume to lay this little trifle at your feet; the story is true, as it is on the records of the town where it was transacted; and if my fair unfortunate VOW-BREAKER do not deserve the honor of your Grace's protection, at least she will be found worthy of your pity, which will be a sufficient glory, both for her and Madam, Your Grace's most humble and most obedient Servant, A. BEHN.

The History of the Nun; or, The Fair Vow-breaker

Of all the sins incident to human nature, there is none of which Heaven has took so particular, visible, and frequent notice and revenge as on that of violated vows, which never go unpunished; and the Cupids may boast what they will for the encouragement of their trade of love that Heaven never takes cognizance of lovers' broken vows and oaths, and that 'tis the only perjury that escapes the anger of the gods. But I verily believe, if it were searched into, we should find these frequent perjuries that pass in the world for so many gallantries only, to be the occasion of so many unhappy marriages and the cause of all those misfortunes which are so frequent to the nuptialed pair. For not one of a thousand but, either on his side or on hers, has been perjured and broke vows made to some fond believing wretch whom they have abandoned and undone. What man that does not boast of the numbers he has thus ruined, and who does not glory in the shameful triumph? Nay, what woman, almost, has not a pleasure in deceiving,[2] taught, perhaps, at first, by some dear false one, who had fatally instructed her youth in an art she ever after practiced in revenge on all those she could be too hard for and conquer at their own weapons? For without all dispute[3] women are by nature more constant and just than men, and did not their first lovers teach them the trick of change, they would be doves that would never quit their mate and, like Indian wives, would leap alive into the graves of their deceased lovers, and be buried quick with 'em.[4] But customs of countries change even Nature herself, and long habit takes her place. The women are taught by the lives of the men to live up to all their vices and are become almost as inconstant; and 'tis but modesty that makes the difference and hardly inclination; so depraved the nicest[5] appetites grow in time by bad examples.

But as there are degrees of vows, so there are degrees of punishments for vows; there are solemn matrimonial vows, such as contract and are the most effectual marriage, and have the most reason to be so; there are a thousand vows and friendships that pass between man and man, on a thousand occasions. But there is another vow, called a *Sacred Vow*, made to God only; and by which we oblige ourselves eternally to serve him with all chastity and devotion. This vow is only taken and made by those that enter into Holy Orders, and of all broken vows these are those that receive the most severe and notorious revenges of God; and I am almost certain there is not one example to be produced in the world where perjuries of this nature have passed unpunished, nay, that have not been pursued with the greatest and most rigorous of punishments. I could my self, of my own knowledge, give an hundred examples of the fatal consequences of the violation of Sacred Vows; and whoever make it their business and are curious in the search of such misfortunes shall find, as I say, that they never go unregarded.

The young beauty, therefore, who dedicates her self to Heaven and weds herself for ever to the service of God ought, first, very well to consider the self-denial she is going to put upon her youth, her fickle, faithless, deceiving youth, of one opinion today and of another tomorrow; like flowers, which never remain in one state or fashion, but bud to day and blow by insensible degrees and decay as imperceptibly. The resolution we promise and believe we shall maintain is not in our power, and nothing is so deceitful as human Hearts.

---

[2] *almost, has not a pleasure in deceiving*: almost takes pleasure in deceiving.

[3] *without all dispute*: without any dispute.

[4] *Indian wives*: the practice known as suttee or sati whereby Hindu widows cremated themselves (*quick*: alive) on their husband's funeral pyre.

[5] *nicest*: discriminating, careful.

I once was designed an humble votary in the house of devotion, but fancying my self not endued[6] with an obstinacy of mind great enough to secure me from the efforts and vanities of the world, I rather chose to deny myself that content I could not certainly promise myself, than to languish (as I have seen some do) in a certain affliction; though possibly, since I have sufficiently bewailed that mistaken and inconsiderate approbation and preference of the false, ungrateful world (full of nothing but nonsense, noise, false notions, and contradiction) before the innocence and quiet of a cloister; nevertheless, I could wish for the prevention of abundance of mischiefs and miseries that nunneries and marriages were not to be entered into 'till the maid so destined were of a mature age to make her own choice; and that parents would not make use of their justly assumed authority to compel their children neither to the one or the other; but since I cannot alter custom, nor shall ever be allowed to make new laws, or rectify the old ones, I must leave the young nuns inclosed to their best endeavors of making a virtue of necessity; and the young wives to make the best of a bad market.

In Iper,[7] a town not long since in the dominions of the King of Spain and now in possession of the King of France, there lived a man of quality, of a considerable fortune, called Count Henrick de Vallary, who had a very beautiful lady by whom he had one daughter called Isabella, whose mother dying when she was about two years old to the unspeakable grief of the count, her husband, he resolved never to partake of any pleasure more that this transitory world could court him with, but determined with himself to dedicate his youth and future days to Heaven and to take upon him Holy Orders; and, without considering that, possibly, the young Isabella, when she grew to woman, might have sentiments contrary to those that now possessed him, he designed she should also become a nun. However, he was not so positive in that resolution as to put the matter wholly out of her choice, but divided his estate; one half he carried with him to the monastery of Jesuits, of which number he became one; and the other half he gave with Isabella to the monastery, of which his only sister was Lady Abbess, of the Order of St. Augustine; but so he ordered the matter that if at the age of thirteen, Isabella had not a mind to take orders, or that the Lady Abbess found her inclination averse to a monastic life, she should have such a proportion of the revenue as should be fit to marry her to a nobleman, and left it to the discretion of the Lady Abbess who was a lady of known piety and admirable strictness of life, and so nearly related to Isabella that there was no doubt made of her integrity and justice.

The little Isabella was carried immediately (in her mourning[8] for her dead mother) into the nunnery, and was received as a very diverting companion by all the young ladies, and, above all, by her reverend aunt, for she was

---

[6] *endued*: endowed.   [7] *Iper*: Ypres, a city in Flanders, western Belgium.
[8] *mourning*: mourning (black) clothes.

5

come just to the age of delighting her parents; she was the prettiest forward prattler in the world, and had a thousand little charms to please, besides the young beauties that were just budding in her little angel face. So that she soon became the dear loved favorite of the whole house; and as she was an entertainment to them all, so they made it their study to find all the diversions they could for the pretty Isabella; and as she grew in wit and beauty every day, so they failed not to cultivate her mind. And delicate apprehension in all that was advantageous to her sex, and whatever excellency any one abounded in, she was sure to communicate it to the young Isabella: if one could dance, another sing, another play on this instrument, and another on that; if this spoke one language and that another; if she had wit, and she discretion, and a third the finest fashion and manners; all joined to complete the mind and body of this beautiful young girl; who, being undiverted with the less noble and less solid vanities of the world, took to these virtues and excelled in all. And her youth and wit being apt for all impressions, she soon became a greater mistress of their arts than those who taught her; so that at the age of eight or nine years, she was thought fit to receive and entertain all the great men and ladies, and the strangers of any nation at the grate;[9] and that with so admirable a grace, so quick and piercing a wit and so delightful and sweet a conversation that she became the whole discourse of the town, and strangers spread her fame as prodigious throughout the Christian world; for strangers came daily to hear her talk, and sing, and play, and to admire her beauty; and ladies brought their children, to shame 'em into good fashion and manners with looking on the lovely young Isabella.

The Lady Abbess, her aunt, you may believe, was not a little proud of the excellencies and virtues of her fair niece and omitted nothing that might adorn her mind; because, not only of the vastness of her parts[10] and fame, and the credit she would do her house by residing there forever; but also, being very loath to part with her considerable fortune, which she must resign if she returned into the world, she used all her arts and stratagems to make her become a nun, to which all the fair sisterhood contributed their cunning. But it was altogether needless; her inclination, the strictness of her devotion, her early prayers, and those continual,[11] and innate steadfastness and calm, she was mistress of; her ignorance of the world's vanities, and those that unenclosed young ladies count pleasures and diversions being all unknown to her, she thought there was no joy out of a nunnery, and no satisfactions on the other side of a grate.

The Lady Abbess, seeing that of herself she yielded faster than she could expect, to discharge her conscience to her brother, who came frequently to visit his darling Isabella, would very often discourse to her of the pleasures of

---

[9] *grate*: cloistered nuns like these received visitors in a reception area divided by a lattice or grate, so that in theory at least they did not mix with the outside world.

[10] *parts*: abilities.   [11] *continual*: that is, her prayers were continual.

the world, telling her how much happier she would think herself to be the wife of some gallant young cavalier, and to have coaches and equipages;[12] to see the world, to behold a thousand rarities she had never seen, to live in splendor, to eat high, and wear magnificent clothes, to be bowed to as she passed, and have a thousand adorers, to see in time a pretty offspring, the products of love, that should talk, and look, and delight, as she did, the heart of their parents; but to all her father and the Lady Abbess could say of the world and its pleasures, Isabella brought a thousand reasons and arguments so pious, so devout that the Abbess was very well pleased to find her (purposely weak) propositions so well overthrown; and gives an account of her daily discourses to her brother, which were no less pleasing to him; and though Isabella went already dressed as richly as her quality deserved, yet her father to try the utmost that the world's vanity could do upon her young heart orders the most glorious clothes should be bought her, and that the Lady Abbess should suffer her to go abroad with those ladies of quality that were her relations and her mother's acquaintance; that she should visit and go on the Toore, (that is, the Hyde Park there[13]) that she should see all that was diverting, to try whether it were not for want of temptation to vanity that made her leave the world and love an enclosed life.

As the Count had commanded, all things were performed; and Isabella arriving at her thirteenth year of age, and being pretty tall of stature, with the finest shape that fancy can create, with all the adornment of a perfect brown-haired beauty, eyes black and lovely, complexion fair; to a miracle, all her features of the rarest proportion, the mouth red, the teeth white, and a thousand graces in her mien and air. She came no sooner abroad, but she had a thousand persons fighting for love of her; the reputation her wit had acquired got her adorers without seeing her, but when they saw her, they found themselves conquered and undone; all were glad she was come into the world of whom they had heard so much, and all the youth of the town dressed only for Isabella de Valerie, she rose like a new star that eclipsed all the rest, and which set the world a-gazing. Some hoped, and some despaired, but all loved, while Isabella regarded not their eyes, their distant, darling looks of love, and their signs of adoration; she was civil and affable to all, but so reserved that none durst tell her his passion, or name that strange and abhorred thing, Love, to her. The relations with whom she went abroad every day were fain[14] to force her out, and when she went 'twas the motive of civility, and not satisfaction, that made her go; whatever she saw, she beheld with no admiration, and nothing created wonder in her, though never so strange and novel. She surveyed all things with an indifference, that though it was not sullen was far from transport, so that her evenness of mind was

---

[12] *equipages*: the elegant equipment that went with a nobleman's carriage, such as caparisoned horses and liveried servants.

[13] *Hyde Park*: a London park where the rich and the fashionable promenaded.

[14] *fain*: willing.

infinitely admired and praised. And now it was that, young as she was, her conduct and discretion appeared equal to her wit and beauty, and she increased daily in reputation, insomuch, that the parents of abundance of young noblemen made it their business to endeavor to marry their sons to so admirable and noble a maid, and one, whose virtues were the discourse of all the world. The father, the Lady Abbess, and those who had her abroad were solicited to make an alliance; for the father, he would give no answer, but left it to the discretion of Isabella, who could not be persuaded to hear any thing of that nature; so that for a long time she refused her company to all those who proposed any thing of marriage to her; she said, she had seen nothing in the world that was worth her care or the venturing the losing of Heaven for, and therefore was resolved to dedicate herself to that; that the more she saw of the world, the worse she liked it, and pitied the wretches that were condemned to it; that she had considered it and found no one inclination that forbade her immediate entrance into a religious life; to which her father, after using all the arguments he could to make her take good heed of what she went about to consider it well; and had urged all the inconveniences of severe life, watchings,[15] midnight risings in all weathers and seasons to prayers, hard lodging, coarse diet, and homely habit,[16] with a thousand other things of labor and work used among the nuns; and finding her still resolved and inflexible to all contrary persuasions, he consented, kissed her, and told her, she had argued according to the wish of his soul, and that he never believed himself truly happy till this moment that he was assured she would become a religious.

This news, to the heart-breaking of a thousand lovers, was spread all over the town, and there was nothing but songs of complaint, and of her retiring, after she had shown herself to the world and vanquished so many hearts; all wits were at work on this cruel subject, and one begat another, as is usual in such affairs. Amongst the number of these lovers, there was a young gentleman, nobly born, his name was Villenoys, who was admirably made and very handsome, had travelled and accomplished himself, as much as was possible for one so young to do. He was about eighteen, and was going to the siege of Candia,[17] in a very good equipage, but, overtaken by his Fate, surprised in his way to Glory, he stopped at Ipers, so fell most passionately in love with this maid of immortal fame; but being defeated in his hopes by this news, was the man that made the softest complaints to this fair beauty, and whose violence of passion oppressed him to that degree that he was the only lover who durst

---

[15] *watchings*: periods of night wakefulness for religious devotions or vigils.

[16] *homely habit*: simple dress.

[17] *siege of Candia*: Candia was the capital city of Crete, then a colony of Venice. In an effort to end raids against the Ottoman coast and shipping, the Turks landed a large force on the island in 1645 and established Turkish domination. Venice retaliated with a Christian fleet made up of European supporters, and in 1647 the Turks began a long siege of Candia that lasted for years until Candia and all of Crete were captured by them. In 1669 a treaty was signed with Venice, which withdrew from Crete in exchange for trading privileges with the Ottoman empire.

himself tell her he was in love with her. He writ billets[18] so soft and tender that she had, of all her lovers, most compassion for Villenoys, and deigned several times in pity of him to send him answers to his letters, but they were such as absolutely forbad him to love her; such as incited him to follow glory, the mistress that could noblest reward him; and that, for her part, her prayers should always be that he might be victorious and the darling of that fortune he was going to court; and that she, for her part, had fixed her mind on Heaven, and no earthly thought should bring it down; but she should ever retain for him all sisterly respect and begged in her solitudes to hear whether her prayers had proved effectual or not, and if Fortune were so kind to him as she should perpetually wish.

When Villenoys found she was resolved, he designed to pursue his journey, but could not leave the town, till he had seen the fatal ceremony of Isabella's being made a nun, which was every day expected; and while he stayed, he could not forbear writing daily to her, but received no more answers from her, she already accusing herself of having done too much for a maid in her circumstances; but she confessed of all she had seen, she liked Villenoys the best; and if she ever could have loved, she believed it would have been Villenoys, for he had all the good qualities and grace that could render him agreeable to the fair. Besides, that he was only son to a very rich and noble parent, and one that might very well presume to lay claim to a maid of Isabella's beauty and fortune.

As the time approached when he must eternally lose all hope by Isabella's taking orders, he found himself less able to bear the efforts of that despair it possessed him with; he languished with the thought, so that it was visible to all his friends, the decays it wrought on his beauty and gaiety. So that he fell at last into a fever; and 'twas the whole discourse of the town that Villenoys was dying for the fair Isabella; his relations, being all of quality,[19] were extremely afflicted at his misfortune and joined their interests yet, to dissuade this fair young victoress from an act so cruel as to enclose herself in a nunnery, while the finest of all the youths of quality was dying for her, and asked her if it would not be more acceptable to Heaven to save a life and perhaps a soul than to go and expose her own to a thousand tortures? They assured her, Villenoys was dying, and dying adoring her; that nothing could save his life but her kind eyes turned upon the fainting lover, a lover that could breathe nothing but her name in sighs and find satisfaction in nothing but weeping and crying out, 'I die for Isabella!' This discourse fetched abundance of tears from the fair eyes of this tender maid; but at the same time she besought them to believe these tears ought not to give them hope she should ever yield to save his life by quitting her resolution of becoming a nun; but, on the contrary, they were tears that only bewailed her own misfortune in having been the occasion of the death of any man, especially a man who had so many excellencies as might have rendered him entirely happy and

---

[18] *billets*: love letters.   [19] *quality*: aristocratic, members of the highest social class.

glorious for a long race of years had it not been his ill fortune to have seen her unlucky face. She believed it was for her sins of curiosity and going beyond the walls of the monastery to wander after the vanities of the foolish world that had occasioned this misfortune to the young Count of Villenoys, and she would put a severe penance on her body for the mischiefs her eyes had done him; she fears she might, by something in her looks, have enticed his heart, for she owned she saw him with wonder at his beauty, and much more she admired him when she found the beauties of his mind; she confessed she had given him hope by answering his letters; and that when she found her heart grow a little more than usually tender when she thought on him, she believed it a crime that ought to be checked by a virtue, such as she pretended to profess, and hoped she should ever carry to her grave; and she desired his relations to implore him, in her name, to rest contented in knowing he was the first, and should be the last that should ever make an impression on her heart; that what she had conceived there for him should remain with her to her dying day, and that she besought him to live that she might see, he both deserved this esteem she had for him and to repay it her; otherwise he would die in her debt, and make her life ever after reposeless.

This being all they could get from her, they returned with looks that told their message; however, they rendered those soft things Isabella had said in so moving a manner as failed not to please, and while he remained in this condition, the ceremonies were completed of making Isabella a nun; which was a secret to none but Villenoys and from him it was carefully concealed, so that in a little time he recovered his lost health, at least so well as to support the fatal news, and upon the first hearing it, he made ready his equipage and departed immediately for Candia; where he behaved himself very gallantly under the command of the Duke De Beaufort, and with him returned to France after the loss of that noble city to the Turks.

In all the time of his absence, that he might the sooner establish his repose, he forbore sending to the fair cruel nun, and she heard no more of Villenoys in above two years; so that giving herself wholly up to devotion, there was never seen any one who led so austere and pious a life as this young votress; she was a saint in the chapel and an angel at the grate. She there laid by all her severe looks and mortified discourse, and being at perfect peace and tranquillity within, she was outwardly all gay, sprightly, and entertaining, being satisfied no sights, no freedoms, could give any temptations to worldly desires; she gave a loose to all that was modest and that virtue and honor would permit, and was the most charming conversation that ever was admired. And the whole world that passed through Iper, of strangers, came directed and recommended to the lovely Isabella; I mean those of quality. But however diverting she was at the grate, she was most exemplary devout in the cloister,[20] doing more penance and imposing a more rigid severity and task on herself

---

[20] *cloister*: that is, within the convent itself.

than was required, giving such rare examples to all the nuns that were less devout, that her life was a proverb, and a precedent, and when they would express a very holy woman indeed, they would say, 'She was a very "Isabella".'

There was in this nunnery, a young nun called, Sister Katteriena, daughter to the Grave[21] Vanhenault, that is to say an Earl, who lived about six miles from the town in a noble Villa; this Sister Katteriena was not only a very beautiful maid but very witty, and had all the good qualities to make her be beloved, and had most wonderfully gained upon the heart of the fair Isabella. She was her chamber-fellow and companion in all her devotions and diversions, so that where one was, there was the other, and they never went but together to the grate, to the garden, or to any place whither their affairs called either. This young Katteriena had a brother who loved her entirely and came every day to see her; he was about twenty years of age, rather tall than middle statured, his hair and eyes brown but his face exceeding beautiful, adorned with a thousand graces, and the most nobly and exactly made that 'twas possible for Nature to form; to the fineness and charms of his person, he had an air in his mien and dressing so very agreeable, besides rich, that 'twas impossible to look on him without wishing him happy, because he did so absolutely merit being so. His wit and his manner was so perfectly obliging, a goodness and generosity so sincere and gallant that it would even have atoned for ugliness. As he was eldest son to so great a father, he was kept at home while the rest of his brothers were employed in wars abroad; this made him of a melancholy temper and fit for soft impressions; he was very bookish and had the best tutors that could be got for learning and languages, and all that could complete a man; but was unused to action and of a temper lazy and given to repose, so that his father could hardly ever get him to use any exercise, or so much as ride abroad, which he would call losing time from his studies. He cared not for the conversation of men, because he loved not debauch, as they usually did; so that for exercise more than any design he came on horseback every day to Iper to the monastery and would sit at the grate, entertaining his sister the most part of the afternoon and in the evening retire; he had often seen and conversed with the lovely Isabella, and found from the first sight of her he had more esteem for her than any other of her sex. But as love very rarely takes birth without hope; so he never believed that the pleasure he took in beholding her and in discoursing with her was love, because he regarded her as a thing consecrate to Heaven, and never so much as thought to wish she were a mortal fit for his addresses; yet he found himself more and more filled with reflections on her which was not usual with him; he found she grew upon his memory, and oftener came there than he used to do, that he loved his studies less and going to Iper more; and that every time he went, he found a new joy at his heart that pleased him;

[21] *Grave*: the German title for count is *Graf*.

he found he could not get himself from the grate without pain; nor part from the sight of that all-charming object without sighs; and if while he was there any persons came to visit her whose quality she could not refuse the honor of her sight to, he would blush and pant with uneasiness, especially if they were handsome and fit to make impressions. And he would check this uneasiness in himself and ask his heart what it meant by rising and beating in those moments, and strive to assume an indifference in vain, and depart dissatisfied, and out of humor.

On the other side, Isabella was not so gay as she used to be, but on the sudden retired her self more from the grate than she used to do, refused to receive visits every day, and her complexion grew a little pale and languid; she was observed not to sleep or eat as she used to do, nor exercise in those little plays they made and diverted themselves with now and then; she was heard to sigh often, and it became the discourse of the whole house that she was much altered. The Lady Abbess, who loved her with a most tender passion, was infinitely concerned at this change and endeavored to find out the cause, and 'twas generally believed she was too devout, for now she redoubled her austerity; and in cold winter nights of frost and snow would be up at all hours and lying upon the cold stones before the altar, prostrate at prayers. So that she received orders from the Lady Abbess not to harass herself so very much but to have a care of her health as well as her soul; but she regarded not these admonitions, though even persuaded daily by her Katteriena, whom she loved every day more and more.

But one night when they were retired to their chamber, amongst a thousand things that they spoke of to pass away a tedious evening, they talked of pictures and likenesses, and Katteriena told Isabella, that before she was a nun, in her more happy days, she was so like her brother Bernardo Henault (who was the same that visited them every day) that she would, in men's clothes, undertake,[22] she should not have known one from t'other, and fetching out his picture she had in a dressing-box, she threw it to Isabella, who at the first sight of it turns as pale as ashes, and, being ready to swoon,[23] she bid her take it away, and could not for her soul hide the sudden surprise the picture brought. Katteriena had too much wit[24] not to make a just interpretation of this change, and (as a woman) was naturally curious to pry farther, though discretion should have made her been silent, for talking in such cases does but make the wound rage the more; 'Why, my dear Sister,' (said Katteriena) 'is the likeness of my brother so offensive to you?' Isabella found by this she had discovered too much, and that thought put her by all power of excusing it; she was confounded with shame, and the more she strove to hide it, the more it disordered her; so that she (blushing extremely) hung down her head, sighed and confessed all by her looks. At last, after a considering pause, she cried, 'My dearest sister, I do confess, I was surprised at the

22 *undertake*: venture to say.   23 *swoon*: to faint away.
24 *wit*: understanding, shrewdness.

sight of Monsieur Henault, and much more than ever you have observed me to be at the sight of his person, because there is scarce a day wherein I do not see that, and know beforehand I shall see him; I am prepared for the encounter and have lessened my concern, or rather confusion, by that time I come to the grate, so much mistress I am of my passions when they give me warning of their approach, and sure I can withstand the greatest assaults of fate, if I can but foresee it; but if it surprise me, I find I am as feeble a woman as the most unresolved; you did not tell me you had this picture, nor say you would show me such a picture; but when I least expect to see that face, you show it me, even in my chamber.'

'Ah, my dear sister!' (replied Katteriena) 'I believe that paleness and those blushes proceed from some other cause than the nicety of seeing the picture of a man in your chamber.'

'You have too much wit,' (replied Isabella) 'to be imposed on by such an excuse, if I were so silly to make it; but oh! my dear sister! it was in my thoughts to deceive you; could I have concealed my pain and sufferings, you should never have known them; but since I find it impossible, and that I am too sincere to make use of fraud in any thing, 'tis fit I tell you from what cause my change of color proceeds and to own to you, I fear 'tis love. If ever, therefore, oh gentle pitying maid! thou were a lover? If ever thy tender heart were touched with that passion? Inform me, oh! inform me, of the nature of that cruel disease, and how thou found'st a cure?'

While she was speaking these words, she threw her arms about the neck of the fair Katteriena and bathed her bosom (where she hid her face) with a shower of tears; Katteriena, embracing her with all the fondness of a dear lover, told her with a sigh that she could deny her nothing, and therefore confessed to her she had been a lover, and that was the occasion of her being made a nun, her father finding out the intrigue, which fatally happened to be with his own page, a youth of extraordinary beauty. 'I was but young,' (said she) 'about thirteen and knew not what to call the new-known pleasure that I felt; when e'er I looked upon the young Arnaldo my heart would heave, when e'er he came in view and my disordered breath came doubly from my bosom; a shivering seized me and my face grew wan; my thought was at a stand,[25] and sense itself for that short moment lost its faculties. But when he touched me, oh! no hunted deer, tired with his flight and just secured in shades, pants with a nimbler motion than my heart; at first, I thought the youth had some magic art to make one faint and tremble at his touches; but he himself when I accused his cruelty told me he had no art but awful passion, and vowed that when I touched him he was so; so trembling, so surprised, so charmed, so pleased. When he was present, nothing could displease me, but when he parted from me then 'twas rather a soft silent grief that eased itself by sighing, and by hoping that some kind moment would

---

[25] *at a stand*: at a standstill.

13

restore my joy. When he was absent, nothing could divert me, howe'er I strove, howe'er I toiled for mirth; no smile, no joy, dwelt in my heart or eyes; I could not feign, so very well I loved, impatient in his absence, I would count the tedious parting hours and pass them off like useless visitants, whom we wish were gone; these are the hours where life no business has, at least a lover's life. But, oh! what minutes seemed the happy hours when on his eyes I gazed and he on mine, and half our conversation lost in sighs, sighs, the soft moving language of a lover!'

'No more, no more,' (replied Isabella, throwing her arms again about the neck of the transported Katteriena) 'thou blowest my flame by thy soft words, and makest me know my weakness and my shame: I love! I love! and feel those differing passions.'[26]—Then pausing a moment, she proceeded—'Yet so didst thou, but hast surmounted it. Now thou hast found the nature of my pain, oh! tell me thy saving remedy?' 'Alas!' (replied Katteriena) 'though there's but one disease, there's many remedies. They say, possession's[27] one, but that to me seems a riddle; absence, they say, another, and that was mine; for Arnaldo having by chance lost one of my billets discovered[28] the amour and was sent to travel, and myself forced into this monastery, where at last time convinced me I had loved below my quality, and that shamed me into holy orders.' 'And is it a disease,' (replied Isabella) 'that people often recover?' 'Most frequently,' (said Katteriena) 'and yet some die of the disease, but very rarely.' 'Nay then,' (said Isabella) 'I fear you will find me one of these martyrs; for I have already opposed it with the most severe devotion in the world. But all my prayers are vain, your lovely brother pursues me into the greatest solitude; he meets me at my very midnight devotions, and interrupts my prayers; he gives me a thousand thoughts that ought not to enter into a soul dedicated to Heaven; he ruins all the glory I have achieved, even above my sex, for piety of life and the observation of all virtues. Oh Katteriena! he has a power in his eyes that transcends all the world besides. And to show the weakness of human nature and how vain all our boastings are, he has done that in one fatal hour that the persuasions of all my relations and friends, glory, honor, pleasure, and all that can tempt, could not perform in years; I resisted all but Henault's eyes, and they were ordained to make me truly wretched. But yet with thy assistance and a resolution to see him no more, and my perpetual trust in Heaven, I may, perhaps, overcome this tyrant of my soul, who, I thought, had never entered into holy houses, or mixed his devotions and worship with the true religion; but, oh! no cells, no cloisters, no hermitages are secured from his efforts.'

This discourse she ended with abundance of tears, and it was resolved, since she was devoted forever to a holy life that it was best for her to make it as easy to her as was possible; in order to it and the banishing this fond and use-

---

[26] *differing passions*: passions that make her different from what she thought she was.
[27] *possession*: giving in to the lover, being possessed sexually.
[28] *discovered*: revealed.

less passion from her heart, it was very necessary she should see Henault no more. At first, Isabella was afraid that in refusing to see him he might mistrust her passion; but Katteriena who was both pious and discreet and endeavored truly to cure her of so violent a disease, which must, she knew, either end in her death or destruction, told her she would take care of that matter, that it should not blemish her honor; and so leaving her a while, after they had resolved on this, she left her in a thousand confusions. She was now another woman than what she had hitherto been; she was quite altered in every sentiment, thought and notion; she now repented she had promised not to see Henault; she trembled and even fainted for fear she should see him no more; she was not able to bear that thought, it made her rage within, like one possessed, and all her virtue could not calm her; yet since her word was past, and as she was she could not without great scandal, break it in that point, she resolved to die a thousand deaths rather than not perform her promise made to Katteriena; but 'tis not to be expressed what she endured; what fits, pains, and convulsions she sustained; and how much ado she had to dissemble to Dame Katteriena, who soon returned to the afflicted maid. The next day, about the time that Henault was to come, as he usually did, about two or three a clock after noon, 'tis impossible to express the uneasiness of Isabella; she asked a thousand times, 'What, is not your brother come?' When Dame Katteriena would reply, 'Why do you ask?' She would say, 'Because I would be sure not to see him.' 'You need not fear, Madam,' (replied Katteriena) 'for you shall keep your chamber.' She need not have urged that, for Isabella was very ill without knowing it, and in a fever.

At last, one of the nuns came up and told Dame Katteriena that her brother was at the grate, and she desired he should be bid come about to the private grate above stairs, which he did, and she went to him, leaving Isabella even dead on the bed at the very name of Henault. But the more she concealed her flame, the more violently it raged, which she strove in vain by prayers and those recourses of solitude to lessen; all this did but augment the pain, and was oil to the fire, so that she now could hope that nothing but death would put an end to her griefs and her infamy. She was eternally thinking on him, how handsome his face, how delicate every feature, how charming his air, how graceful his mien, how soft and good his disposition, and how witty and entertaining his conversation. She now fancied she was at the grate, talking to him as she used to be, and blessed those happy hours she passed then and bewailed her misfortune that she is no more destined to be so happy, then gives a loose to grief; griefs at which no mortals but despairing lovers can guess, or how tormenting they are; where the most easy moments are those wherein one resolves to kill oneself, and the happiest thought is damnation; but from these imaginations, she endeavors to fly, all frighted with horror; but, alas! whither would she fly but to a life more full of horror? She considers well, she cannot bear despairing love and finds it impossible to cure her despair; she cannot fly from the thoughts of the charming Henault; and 'tis

15

impossible to quit 'em; and, at this rate, she found, life could not long support itself, but would either reduce her to madness, and so render her an hated object of scorn to the censuring world, or force her hand to commit a murder upon herself. This she had found, this she had well considered, nor could her fervent and continual prayers, her nightly watchings, her mortifications on the cold marble in long winter season, and all her acts of devotion abate one spark of this shameful fever of love that was destroying her within.

When she had raged and struggled with this unruly passion, 'till she was quite tired and breathless, finding all her force in vain, she filled her fancy with a thousand charming ideas of the lovely Henault, and, in that soft fit had a mind to satisfy her panting heart and give it one joy more by beholding the lord of its desires and the author of its pains. Pleased, yet trembling, at this resolve, she rose from the bed where she was laid, and softly advanced to the staircase, from whence there opened that room where Dame Katteriena was and where there was a private grate, at which she was entertaining her brother; they were earnest in discourse and so loud that Isabella could easily hear all they said, and the first words were from Katteriena, who in a sort of anger cried, 'Urge me no more! My virtue is too nice to become an advocate for a passion that can tend to nothing but your ruin; for suppose I should tell the fair Isabella, you die for her, what can it avail you? What hope can any man have to move the heart of a virgin so averse to love? A virgin whose modesty and virtue is so very curious, it would fly the very word, love, as some monstrous witchcraft, or the foulest of sins, who would loathe me for bringing so lewd a message and banish you her sight as the object of her hate and scorn; is it unknown to you how many of the noblest youths of Flanders have addressed themselves to her in vain, when yet she was in the world?[29] Have you been ignorant how the young Count de Villenoys languished, in vain, almost to death for her? And that no persuasions, no attractions in him, no worldly advantages, or all his pleadings, who had a wit and spirit capable of prevailing on any heart less severe and harsh than hers? Do you not know that all was lost on this insensible fair one, even when she was a proper object for the adoration of the young and amorous? And can you hope, now she has so entirely wedded her future days to devotion and given all to Heaven; nay, lives a life here more like a saint than a woman; rather an angel than a mortal creature? Do you imagine with any rhetoric you can deliver now to turn the heart and whole nature of this divine maid to consider your earthly passion? No, 'tis fondness[30] and an injury to her virtue to harbor such a thought; quit it, quit it, my dear brother! before it ruin your repose.' 'Ah, Sister!' (replied the dejected Henault) 'your counsel comes too late, and your reasons are of too feeble force to rebate[31] those arrows the charming Isabella's eyes have fixed in my heart and soul; and I am undone unless she know my pain, which I shall die before I shall ever dare mention to her. But you young

---

[29] *in the world*: that is, outside the convent, before she took her vows.
[30] *fondness*: foolishness.   [31] *rebate*: to dull or blunt a weapon.

maids have a thousand familiarities together, can jest, and play, and say a thousand things between raillery[32] and earnest that may first hint what you would deliver and insinuate into each others hearts a kind of curiosity to know more; for naturally (my dear sister) maids are curious and vain; and however divine the mind of the fair Isabella may be, it bears the tincture[33] still of mortal woman.'

'Suppose this true, how could this mortal part about her advantage you,' (said Katteriena) 'all that you can expect from this discovery (if she should be content to hear it, and to return you pity) would be to make her wretched, like yourself? What farther can you hope?' 'Oh! talk not,' (replied Henault) 'of so much happiness! I do not expect to be so blest that she should pity me, or love to a degree of inquietude; 'tis sufficient for the ease of my heart that she know its pains and what it suffers for her; that she would give my eyes leave to gaze upon her and my heart to vent a sigh now and then; and when I dare to give me leave to speak and tell her of my passion. This, this, is all, my sister.' And at that word the tears glided down his cheeks, and he declined his eyes and set a look so charming and so sad that Isabella, whose eyes were fixed upon him, was a thousand times ready to throw herself into the room, and to have made a confession how sensible[34] she was of all she had heard and seen. But, with much ado, she contained and satisfied herself with knowing that she was adored by him whom she adored, and with a prudence that is natural to her, she withdrew and waited with patience the event of their discourse. She impatiently longed to know how Katteriena would manage this secret her brother had given her, and was pleased that the friendship and prudence of that maid had concealed her passion from her brother; and now contented and joyful beyond imagination to find herself beloved, she knew she could dissemble her own passion and make him the first aggressor; the first that loved, or at least, that should seem to do so. This thought restores her so great a part of her peace of mind, that she resolved to see him and to dissemble with Katteriena so far as to make her believe she had subdued that passion she was really ashamed to own; she now with her woman's skill begins to practice an art she never before understood and has recourse to cunning and resolves to seem to reassume her former repose. But hearing Katteriena approach, she laid herself again on her bed where she had left her, but composed her face to more cheerfulness and put on a resolution that indeed deceived the sister, who was extremely pleased, she said, to see her look so well: When Isabella replied, 'Yes, I am another woman now; I hope Heaven has heard and granted my long and humble supplications, and driven from my heart this tormenting god, that has so long disturbed my purer thoughts.' 'And are you sure,' (said Dame Katteriena) 'that this wanton deity is repelled by the noble force of your resolution? Is he never to return?' 'No,' (replied Isabella) 'never to my heart.' 'Yes,' (said Katteriena) 'if you should see the lovely murderer of your repose, your wound would bleed anew.'

[32] *raillery*: joking, in fun. [33] *tincture*: trace or vestige.
[34] *sensible*: aware of, cognizant.

At this Isabella, smiling with a little disdain, replied, 'Because you once to love and Henault's charms defenseless found me, ah! do you think I have no fortitude? But so in fondness lost, remiss in virtue, that when I have resolved (and see it necessary for my after-quiet) to want the power of keeping that resolution? No, scorn me and despise me then, as lost to all the glories of my sex, and all that nicety I've hitherto preserved.' There needed no more from a maid of Isabella's integrity and reputation to convince any one of the sincerity of what she said, since in the whole course of her life she never could be charged with an untruth, or an equivocation; and Katteriena assured her she believed her and was infinitely glad she had vanquished a passion that would have proved destructive to her repose. Isabella replied, she had not altogether vanquished her passion, she did not boast of so absolute a power over her soft nature but had resolved things great,[35] and time would work the cure; that she hoped Katteriena would make such excuses to her brother for her not appearing at the grate so gay and entertaining as she used, and by a little absence she should retrieve the liberty she had lost. But she desired such excuses might be made for her that young Henault might not perceive the reason. At the naming him, she had much ado not to show some concern extraordinary, and Katteriena assured her, she had now a very good excuse to keep from the grate when he was at it; 'For,' (said she) 'now you have resolved, I may tell you, he is dying for you, raving in love, and has this day made me promise to him to give you some account of his passion and to make you sensible of his languishment. I had not told you this, (replied Katteriena) but that I believe you fortified with brave resolution and virtue, and that this knowledge will rather put you more upon your guard than you were before.'

While she spoke, she fixed her eyes on Isabella to see what alteration it would make in her heart and looks; but the masterpiece of this young maid's art was shown in this minute, for she commanded herself so well that her very looks dissembled and showed no concern at a relation that made her soul dance with joy; but it was what she was prepared for, or else I question her fortitude. But with a calmness which absolutely subdued Katteriena, she replied, 'I am almost glad he has confessed a passion for me, and you shall confess to him you told me of it and that I absent myself from the grate on purpose to avoid the sight of a man who durst love me and confess it; and I assure you, my dear sister!' (continued she, dissembling) 'You could not have advanced my cure by a more effectual way than telling me of his presumption.' At that word, Katteriena joyfully related to her all that had passed between young Henault and herself, and how he implored her aid in this amour; at the end of which relation, Isabella smiled and carelessly replied, 'I pity him.' And so going to their devotion, they had no more discourse of the lover.

[35] *resolved things great*: resolved these great things.

In the mean time, young Henault was a little satisfied to know his sister would discover his passion to the lovely Isabella; and though he dreaded the return, he was pleased that she should know she had a lover that adored her, though even without hope; for though the thought of possessing Isabella was the most ravishing that could be; yet he had a dread upon him when he thought of it, for he could not hope to accomplish that without sacrilege, and he was a young man, very devout and even bigoted in religion; and would often question and debate within himself that if it were possible he should come to be beloved by this fair creature and that it were possible for her to grant all that youth in love could require, whether he should receive the blessing offered? And though he adored the maid, whether he should not abhor the nun in his embraces? 'Twas an undetermined thought that chilled his fire as often as it approached; but he had too many that rekindled it again with the greater flame and ardor.

His impatience to know what success Katteriena had with the relation she was to make to Isabella in his behalf brought him early to Iper the next day. He came again to the private grate, where his sister receiving him and finding him with a sad and dejected look, expect what she had to say; she told him that look well became the news she had for him, it being such as ought to make him both grieved and penitent; for to obey him she had so absolutely displeased Isabella, that she was resolved never to believe her friend more. 'Or to see you,' (said she) 'therefore, as you have made me commit a crime against my conscience, against my order, against my friendship, and against my honor, you ought to do some brave thing; take some noble resolution worthy of your courage to redeem all; for your repose, I promised I would let Isabella know you loved, and for the mitigation of my crime, you ought to let me tell her you have surmounted your passion, as the last remedy of life and fame.'

At these her last words, the tears gushed from his eyes, and he was able only a good while to sigh; at last, cried, 'What! see her no more! see the charming Isabella no more!' And then vented the grief of his soul in so passionate a manner, as his sister had all the compassion imaginable for him but thought it great sin and indiscretion to cherish his flame. So that after a while, having heard her counsel, he replied, 'And is this all, my sister, you will do to save a brother?' 'All!' (replied she) 'I would not be the occasion of making a nun violate her vow to save a brother's life, no, nor my own; assure yourself of this and take it as my last resolution. Therefore, if you will be content with the friendship of this young lady and so behave yourself that we may find no longer the lover in the friend, we shall reassume our former conversation and live with you as we ought; otherwise, your presence will continually banish her from the grate and, in time, make both her you love and yourself a town discourse.'[36]

---

[36] *town discourse*: a subject of gossip.

19

Much more to this purpose she said to dissuade him and bid him retire, and keep himself from thence till he could resolve to visit them without a crime; and she protested if he did not do this and master his foolish passion, she would let her father understand his conduct, who was a man of temper so very precise that should he believe his son should have a thought of love to a virgin vowed to Heaven, he would abandon him to shame and eternal poverty by disinheriting him of all he could. Therefore, she said, he ought to lay all this to his heart and weigh it with his unheedy passion. While the sister talked thus wisely, Henault was not without his thoughts, but considered as she spoke, but did not consider in the right place; he was not considering how to please a father and save an estate but how to manage the matter so to establish himself as he was before with Isabella; for he imagined, since already she knew his passion and that if after that she would be prevailed with to see him, he might, some lucky minute or other, have the pleasure of speaking for himself, at least, he should again see and talk to her, which was a joyful thought in the midst of so many dreadful ones. And as if he had known what passed in Isabella's heart, he, by a strange sympathy, took the same measures to deceive Katteriena, a well-meaning young lady and easily imposed on from her own innocence. He resolved to dissemble patience, since he must have that virtue, and owned his sister's reasons were just and ought to be pursued; that she had argued him into half his peace, and that he would endeavor to recover the rest; that youth ought to be pardoned a thousand failings, and years would reduce him to a condition of laughing at his follies of youth, but that grave direction was not yet arrived. And so desiring she would pray for his conversion and that she would recommend him to the devotions of the fair Isabella, he took his leave and came no more to the nunnery in ten days; in all which time none but impatient lovers can guess what pain and languishments Isabella suffered, not knowing the cause of his absence nor daring to enquire; but she bore it out so admirably that dame Katteriena never so much as suspected she had any thoughts of that nature that perplexed her and now believed indeed she had conquered all her uneasiness. And one day, when Isabella and she were alone together, she asked that fair dissembler if she did not admire[37] at the conduct and resolution of her brother? 'Why!' (replied Isabella unconcernedly, while her heart was fainting within for fear of ill news). With that Katteriena told her the last discourse she had with her brother, and how at last she had persuaded him (for her sake) to quit his passion; and that he had promised he would endeavor to surmount it; and that, that was the reason he was absent now, and they were to see him no more till he had made a conquest over himself. You may assure yourself this news was not so welcome to Isabella as Katteriena imagined; yet still she dissembled with a force beyond what the most cunning practitioner could have shown and carried herself before people

---

[37] *admire*: wonder about, be surprised by.

as if no pressures had lain upon her heart; but when alone retired in order to her devotion, she would vent her griefs in the most deplorable manner that a distressed, distracted maid could do, and which, in spite of all her severe penances, she found no abatement of.

At last Henault came again to the monastery and with a look as gay as he could possibly assume, he saw his sister and told her he had gained an absolute victory over his heart; and desired he might see Isabella, only to convince both her and Katteriena that he was no longer a lover of that fair creature that had so lately charmed him; that he had set five thousand pounds a year against a fruitless passion, and found the solid gold much the heavier in the scale. And he smiled and talked the whole day of indifferent things with his sister, and asked no more for Isabella; nor did Isabella look or ask after him, but in her heart. Two months passed in this indifference, till it was taken notice of that Sister Isabella came not to the grate when Henault was there as she used to do. This being spoken to Dame Katteriena, she told it to Isabella and said, 'The nuns would believe, there was some cause for her absence if she did not appear again.' That if she could trust her heart, she was sure she could trust her brother, for he thought no more of her she was confident; this in lieu of pleasing[38] was a dagger to the heart of Isabella, who thought it time to retrieve the flying lover and therefore told Katteriena she would the next day entertain at the low grate as she was wont to do,[39] and accordingly as soon as any people of quality came, she appeared there, where she had not been two minutes but she saw the lovely Henault, and it was well for both that people were in the room, they had else both sufficiently discovered their inclinations, or rather their not-to-be-concealed passions; after the general conversation was over, by the going away of the gentlemen that were at the grate, Katteriena being employed elsewhere, Isabella was at last left alone with Henault. But who can guess the confusion of these two lovers, who wished, yet feared, to know each other's thoughts? She trembling with a dismal apprehension that he loved no more; and he almost dying with fear she should reproach or upbraid him with his presumption; so that both being possessed with equal sentiments of love, fear, and shame, they both stood fixed with dejected looks and hearts that heaved with stifled sighs. At last, Isabella, the softer and tender-hearted of the two tho' not the most a lover perhaps, not being able to contain her love any longer within the bounds of dissimulation or discretion, being by Nature innocent, burst out into tears, and all fainting with pressing thoughts within, she fell languishly into a chair that stood there, while the distracted Henault, who could not come to her assistance, and finding marks of love rather than anger or disdain in that confusion of Isabella's, throwing himself on his knees at the grate, implored her to behold him, to hear him, and to pardon him, who died every moment for her, and who adored her with a violent ardor; but yet with such an one as should

---

[38] *in lieu of pleasing*: instead of pleasing.   [39] *wont to do*: accustomed to do.

21

(though he perished with it) be conformable to her commands; and as he spoke, the tears streamed down his dying eyes that beheld her with all the tender regard that ever lover was capable of; she recovered a little and turned her too beautiful face to him, and pierced him with a look that darted a thousand joys and flames into his heart, with eyes that told him her heart was burning and dying for him; for which assurances, he made ten thousand asseverations of his never-dying passion, and expressing as many raptures and excesses of joy to find her eyes and looks confess he was not odious to her, and that the knowledge he was her lover did not make her hate him. In fine,[40] he spoke so many things all soft and moving, and so well convinced her of his passion that she at last was compelled by a mighty force, absolutely irresistible, to speak.

'Sir,' (said she) 'perhaps you will wonder where I, a maid brought up in the simplicity of virtue, should learn the confidence not only to hear of love from you but to confess I am sensible of the most violent of its pain myself; and I wonder and am amazed at my own daring that I should have the courage rather to speak than die and bury it in silence; but such is my fate. Hurried by an unknown force, which I have endeavored always, in vain, to resist, I am compelled to tell you, I love you, and have done so from the first moment I saw you; and you are the only man born to give me life or death, to make me happy or blest; perhaps had I not been confined and, as it were, utterly forbid by my vow, as well as my modesty, to tell you this, I should not have been so miserable to have fallen thus low as to have confessed my shame; but our opportunities of speaking are so few and letters so impossible to be sent without discovery, that perhaps this is the only time I shall ever have to speak with you alone.' And at that word the tears flowed abundantly from her eyes and gave Henault leave to speak. 'Ah Madam!' (said he) 'do not as soon as you have raised me to the greatest happiness in the world, throw me with one word beneath your scorn; much easier 'tis to die and know I am loved, than never, never, hope to hear that blessed sound again from that beautiful mouth. Ah, Madam! rather let me make use of this one opportunity our happy luck has given us and contrive how we may forever see and speak to each other; let us assure one another, there are a thousand ways to escape a place so rigid as denies us that happiness; and denies the fairest maid in the world the privilege of her creation, and the end to which she was formed so angelical.' And seeing Isabella was going to speak, lest she should say something that might dissuade from an attempt so dangerous and wicked, he pursued to tell her it might be indeed the last moment Heaven would give 'em, and besought her to answer him what he implored, whether she would fly with him from the monastery? At this word, she grew pale and started as at some dreadful sound, and cried, 'Hah! what is it you say? Is it possible you should propose a thing so wicked? And can it enter into your

---

[40] *In fine*: in short.

imagination, because I have so far forgot my virtue and my vow to become a lover, I should therefore fall to so wretched a degree of infamy and reprobation? No, name it to me no more, if you would see me; and if it be as you say a pleasure to be beloved by me, for I will sooner die than yield to what . . . Alas! I but too well approve!' These last words she spoke with a fainting tone, and the tears fell anew from her fair soft eyes. 'If it be so,' said he (with a voice so languishing it could scarce be heard), 'If it be so and that you are resolved to try, if my love be eternal without hope, without expectation of any other joy than seeing and adoring you through the grate; I am, and must, and will be contented, and you shall see I can prefer the sighing to these cold irons[41] that separate us before all the possessions of the rest of the world; that I choose rather to lead my life here, at this cruel distance from you forever, than before the embrace of all the fair; and you shall see how pleased I will be to languish here; but as you see me decay (for surely so I shall), do not triumph o'er my languid looks and laugh at my pale and meager face; but, pitying, say, "How easily I might have preserved that face, those eyes, and all that youth and vigor, now no more, from this total ruin I now behold it in. And love your slave that dies and will be daily and visibly dying, as long as my eyes can gaze on that fair object and my soul be fed and kept alive with her charming wit and conversation; if love can live on such airy food (tho' rich in itself, yet unfit, alone, to sustain life), it shall be forever dedicated to the lovely Isabella." But, oh! that time cannot be long! Fate will not lend her slave many days who loves too violently to be satisfied to enjoy the fair object of his desires no otherwise than at a grate.'

He ceased speaking, for sighs and tears stopped his voice, and he begged the liberty to sit down; and his looks being quite altered, Isabella found herself touched to the very soul with a concern the most tender that ever yielding maid was oppressed with. She had no power to suffer him to languish, while she by one soft word could restore him, and being about to say a thousand things that would have been agreeable to him, she saw herself approached by some of the nuns, and only had time to say, 'If you love me, live and hope.' The rest of the nuns began to ask Henault of news, for he always brought them all that was novel in the town, and they were glad still of his visits above all other, for they heard how all amours and intrigues passed in the world by this young cavalier. These last words of Isabella's were a cordial[42] to his soul, and he, from that and to conceal the present affair, endeavored to assume all the gaiety he could, and told 'em all he could either remember, or invent, to please 'em, tho' he wished them a great way off at that time.

Thus they passed the day till it was a decent hour for him to quit the grate, and for them to draw the curtain; all that night did Isabella dedicate to love; she went to bed, with a resolution to think over all she had to do and

---

[41] *cold irons*: the bars of the grate that separate visitors from the nuns.
[42] *cordial*: a restorative drink.

23

to consider how she should manage this great affair of her life. I have already said, she had tried all that was possible in human strength to perform in the design of quitting a passion so injurious to her honor and virtue and found no means possible to accomplish it. She had tried fasting long, praying fervently, rigid penances and pains, severe disciplines, all the mortifications, almost to the destruction of life itself, to conquer the unruly flame; but still it burnt and raged but the more; so, at last, she was forced to permit that to conquer her she could not conquer and submitted to her fate as a thing destined her by Heaven itself; and after all this opposition, she fancied it was resisting even Divine Providence to struggle any longer with her heart; and this being her real belief, she the more patiently gave way to all the thoughts that pleased her.

As soon as she was laid, without discoursing (as she used to do) to Katteriena, after they were in bed, she pretended to be sleepy, and turning from her settled herself to profound thinking and was resolved to conclude the matter between her heart, and her vow of devotion that night, and she, having no more to determine, might end the affair accordingly the first opportunity she should have to speak to Henault, which was to fly and marry him; or to remain for ever fixed to her vow of chastity. This was the debate; she brings reason on both sides. Against the first, she sets the shame of a violated vow and considers where she shall show her face after such an action; to the vow, she argues that she was born in sin and could not live without it; that she was human and no angel, and that, possibly, that sin might be as soon forgiven as another; that since all her devout endeavors could not defend her from the cause, Heaven ought to execute[43] the effect; that as to showing her face, so she saw that of Henault always turned (charming as it was) towards her with love, what had she to do with the world or cared to behold any other?

Some times, she thought, it would be more brave and pious to die than to break her vow; but she soon answered that as false arguing, for self-murder was the worst of sins and in the deadly number.[44] She could after such an action live to repent, and of two evils she ought to choose the least; she dreads to think, since she had so great a reputation for virtue and piety, both in the monastery and in the world, what they both would say when she should commit an action so contrary to both these she possessed; but, after a whole night's debate, love was strongest and gained the victory. She never went about to think how she should escape, because she knew it would be easy, the keeping of the key of the monastery, [was] often intrusted in her keeping, and was, by turns, in the hands of many more, whose virtue and discretion was infallible and out of doubt; besides, her aunt being the Lady Abbess, she had greater privilege than the rest; so that she had no more to do, she thought, than to acquaint Henault with her design as soon as she should get

---

[43] *execute*: to make valid, to legalize.
[44] *deadly number*: suicide is a mortal sin, enough to damn the offender.

an opportunity. Which was not quickly; but in the mean time, Isabella's father died, which put some little stop to our lover's happiness and gave her a short time of grief; but love, who while he is new and young can do us miracles soon wiped her eyes and chased away all sorrows from her heart and grew every day more and more impatient to put her new design in execution, being every day more resolved. Her father's death had removed one obstacle and secured her from his reproaches; and now she only wants opportunity, first, to acquaint Henault, and then to fly.

She waited not long, all things concurring to her desire; for Katteriena falling sick, she had the good luck as she called it then to entertain Henault at the grate oftentimes alone; the first moment she did so, she entertained him with the good news and told him she had at last vanquished her heart in favor of him, and loving him above all things, honor, her vow or reputation, had resolved to abandon herself wholly to him, to give herself up to love and serve him, and that she had no other consideration in the world; but Henault, instead of returning her an answer all joy and satisfaction, held down his eyes and sighing, with a dejected look, he cried, 'Ah, Madam! pity a man so wretched and undone as not to be sensible of this blessing as I ought.' She grew pale at this reply and, trembling, expected he would proceed: ''Tis not' (continued he) 'that I want love, tenderest passion, and all the desire youth and love can inspire. But, Oh, Madam! when I consider (for raving mad in love as I am for your sake, I do consider) that if I should take you from this repose, nobly born and educated as you are; and for that act should find a rigid father deprive me of all that ought to support you and afford your birth, beauty, and merits their due, what would you say? How would you reproach me?' He, sighing, expected her answer, when blushes overspreading her face, she replied in a tone all haughty and angry, 'Ah, Henault! Am I then refused, after having abandoned all things for you? Is it thus you reward my sacrificed honor, vows, and virtue? Cannot you hazard the loss of fortune to possess Isabella who loses all for you!' Then bursting into tears at her misfortune of loving, she suffered him to say, 'Oh, charming fair one! how industrious is your cruelty to find out new torments for an heart already pressed down with the severities of love? Is it possible you can make so unhappy a construction of the tenderest part of my passion? And can you imagine it want of love in me to consider how I shall preserve and merit the vast blessing Heaven has given me? Is my care a crime? And would not the most deserving beauty of the world hate me if I should, to preserve my life, and satisfy the passion of my fond heart, reduce her to the extremities of want and misery? And is there anything in what I have said but what you ought to take for the greatest respect and tenderness!'

'Alas!' (replied Isabella sighing) 'young as I am, all unskillful in love, I find but what I feel, that discretion is no part of it; and consideration inconsistent with the nobler passion, who will subsist of its own nature and love unmixed with any other sentiment. And 'tis not pure if it be otherwise. I know had I mixed discretion with mine, my love must have been less, I never thought of

living, but my love; and, if I considered at all, it was that grandeur and magnificence were useless trifles to lovers, wholly needless and troublesome. I
thought of living in some lonely cottage, far from the noise of crowded, busy
cities, to walk with thee in groves and silent shades, where I might hear no
voice but thine; and when we had been tired to sit us down by some cool
murmuring rivulet and be to each a world, my monarch thou, and I thy sovereign queen, while wreaths of flowers shall crown our happy heads, some
fragrant bank our throne, and Heaven our canopy. Thus we might laugh at
Fortune and the proud, despise the duller world, who place their joys in
mighty show and equipage. Alas! my nature could not bear it, I am unused
to worldly vanities and would boast of nothing but my Henault; no riches but
his love; no grandeur but his presence.' She ended speaking with tears, and
he replied, 'Now, now, I find, my Isabella loves indeed when she's content to
abandon the world for my sake; Oh! thou hast named the only happy life that
suits my quiet nature, to be retired has always been my joy! But to be so with
thee! Oh! thou hast charmed me with a thought so dear as has forever banished all my care but how to receive thy goodness! Please think no more what
my angry parent may do when he shall hear how I have disposed of myself
against his will and pleasure, but trust to love and Providence; no more! be
gone all thoughts but those of Isabella!'

As soon as he had made an end of expressing his joy, he fell to consulting
how and when she should escape; and since it was uncertain when she
should be offered the key, for she would not ask for it, she resolved to give
him notice, either by word of mouth or a bit of paper she would write in and
give him through the grate the first opportunity; and, parting for that time,
they both resolved to get up what was possible for their support, till time
should reconcile affairs and friends and to wait the happy hour.

Isabella's dead mother had left jewels of the value of £2000 to her daughter at her decease, which jewels were in the possession now of the Lady
Abbess, and were upon sale to be added to the revenue of the monastery; and
as Isabella was the most prudent of her sex, at least had hitherto been so
esteemed, she was entrusted with all that was in possession of the Lady
Abbess, and 'twas not difficult to make herself mistress of all her own jewels,
as also some £3 or 400 in gold that was hoarded up in her Ladyship's cabinet against[45] any accidents that might arrive to the monastery; these Isabella
also made her own and put up with the jewels; and having acquainted
Henault with the day and hour of her escape, he got together what he could
and waiting for her with his coach one night, when nobody was awake but
herself, when rising softly, as she used to do in the night to her devotion, she
stole so dexterously out of the monastery, as nobody knew anything of it; she
carried away the keys with her, after having locked all the doors, for she was
entrusted often with all. She found Henault waiting in his coach and trusted

---

[45] *against*: in case of.

none but an honest coachman that loved him; he received her with all the transports of a truly ravished lover, and she was infinitely charmed with the new pleasure of his embraces and kisses.

They drove out of town immediately, and because she durst not be seen in that habit[46] (for it had been immediate death for both) they drove into a thicket some three miles from the town, where Henault having brought her some of his younger sister's clothes, he made her put off her habit and put on those; and, rending the other, they hid them in a sand-pit covered over with broom[47] and went that night forty miles from Iper, to a little town upon the River Rhine, where, changing their names, they were forthwith married and took a house in a country village, a farm where they resolved to live retired by the name of Beroon and drove a farming trade; however, not forgetting to set friends and engines[48] at work to get their pardon, as criminals, first, that had transgressed the law; and, next, as disobedient persons, who had done contrary to the will and desire of their parents. Isabella writ to her aunt the most moving letters in the world; so did Henault to his father; but she was a long time before she could gain so much as an answer from her aunt, and Henault was so unhappy as never to gain one from his father, who no sooner heard the news that was spread over all the town and country that young Henault was fled with the so famed Isabella, a nun, and singular for devotion and piety of life, but he immediately settled his estate on his youngest son, cutting Henault off with all his birthright, which was £5000 a year. This news, you may believe, was not very pleasing to the young man, who though in possession of the loveliest virgin and now wife that ever man was blessed with, yet when he reflected he should have children by her and these and she should come to want (he having been magnificently educated and impatient of scanty fortune), he laid it to heart and it gave him a thousand uneasinesses in the midst of unspeakable joys; and the more he strove to hide his sentiments from Isabella, the more tormenting it was within; he durst not name it to her, so insuperable a grief it would cause in her to hear him complain; and though she could live hardly[49] as being bred to a devout and severe life, he could not but must let the man of quality show itself, even in the disguise of an humbler farmer. Besides all this, he found nothing of his industry thrive; his cattle still died in the midst of those that were in full vigor and health of other peoples; his crops of wheat and barley and other grain, though managed by able and knowing husbandmen were all, either mildewed, or blasted, or some misfortune still arrived to him; his coach horses would fight and kill one another, his barns sometimes be fired;[50] so that it became a proverb all over the country if any ill luck had arrived to anybody, they would say, 'They had Monsieur Beroon's luck.' All these reflections did but add to his

---

46 *habit*: her nun's dress.   47 *broom*: shrubs.

48 *engines*: literally, machinery, but here used in a wider sense as any means of securing their pardon.

49 *hardly*: sparely, simply.   50 *be fired*: that is, they catch fire.

melancholy, and he grew at last to be in some want, insomuch that Isabella, who had by her frequent letters and submissive supplications to her aunt (who loved her tenderly) obtained her pardon and her blessing; she now pressed her for some money and besought her to consider, how great a fortune she had brought to the monastery, and implored she would allow her some salary out of it, for she had been married two years and most of what she had was exhausted. The aunt, who found that what was done could not be undone, did from time to time supply her so, as one might have lived very decently on that very revenue; but that would not satisfy the great heart of Henault. He was now about three and twenty years old, and Isabella about eighteen, too young and too lovely a pair to begin their misfortunes so soon; they were both the most just and pious in the world; they were examples of goodness and eminent for holy living and for perfect loving, and yet nothing thrived they undertook. They had no children, and all their joy was in each other; at last, one good fortune arrived to them by the solicitations of the Lady Abbess, and the Bishop, who was her near kinsman, they got a pardon for Isabella's quitting the monastery and marrying, so that she might now return to her own country again. Henault having also his pardon, they immediately quit the place where they had remained for two years and came again into Flanders, hoping the change of place might afford 'em better luck.

Henault then began again to solicit his cruel father, but nothing would do; he refused to see him, or to receive any letters from him; but, at last, he prevailed so far with him as that he sent a kinsman to him to assure him if he would leave his wife and go into the French campagn,[51] he would equip him as well as his quality required, and that, according as he behaved himself, he should gain his favor; but if he lived idly at home, giving up his youth and glory to lazy love, he would have no more to say to him but race[52] him out of his heart, and out of his memory.

He had settled himself in a very pretty house, furnished with what was fitting for the reception of anybody of quality that would live a private life, and they found all the respect that their merits deserved from all the world, everybody entirely loving and endeavoring to serve them; and Isabella so perfectly had the ascendent over her aunt's heart that she procured from her all that she could desire, and much more than she could expect. She was perpetually progging[53] and saving all that she could to enrich and advance her, and at last pardoning and forgiving Henault loved him as her own child; so that all things looked with a better face than before and never was so dear and fond a couple seen as Henault and Isabella; but, at last, she proved with child and the aunt, who might reasonably believe so young a couple would have a great many children, and foreseeing there was no provision likely to be made them unless he pleased his father, for if the aunt should chance to die, all their hope was gone; she therefore daily solicited him to obey his father and go to the

---

[51] *campagn*: the military campaign or service.   [52] *race*: erase.
[53] *progging*: purveying, soliciting, foraging.

camp;[54] and that having achieved fame and renown, he would return a favorite to his father and comfort to his wife. After she had solicited in vain, for he was not able to endure the thought of leaving Isabella, melancholy as he was with his ill fortune; the Bishop, kinsman to Isabella, took him to task and urged[55] his youth and birth, and that he ought not to waste both without action when all the world was employed; and that since his father had so great a desire he should go into a campagn, either to serve the Venetian against the Turks, or into the French service, which he liked best;[56] he besought him to think of it; and since he had satisfied his love, he should and ought to satisfy his duty, it being absolutely necessary for the wiping off the stain of his sacrilege, and to gain him the favor of Heaven, which he found had hitherto been averse to all he had undertaken. In fine, all his friends and all who loved him joined in this design, and all thought it convenient, nor was he insensible of the advantage it might bring him; but love, which every day grew fonder and fonder in his heart, opposed all their reasonings, tho' he saw all the brave youth of the age preparing to go, either to one army or the other.

At last, he lets Isabella know what propositions he had made him, both by his father and his relations; at the very first motion, she almost fainted in his arms while he was speaking, and it possessed her with so entire a grief that she miscarried, to the insupportable torment of her tender husband and lover, so that, to re-establish her repose, he was forced to promise not to go; however, she considered all their circumstances and weighed the advantages that might redound both to his honor and fortune by it; and in a matter of a month's time with the persuasions and reasons of her friends, she suffered him to resolve upon going, herself determining to retire to the monastery till the time of his return; but when she named the monastery, he grew pale and disordered and obliged her to promise him not to enter into it any more, for fear they should never suffer her to come forth again; so that he resolved not to depart till she had made a vow to him never to go again within the walls of a religious house, which had already been so fatal to them. She promised, and he believed.

Henault, at last, overcame his heart, which pleaded so for his stay, and sent his father word he was ready to obey him, and to carry the first efforts of his arms against the common foes of Christendom, the Turks; his father was very well pleased at this and sent him two thousand crowns, his horses and furniture suitable to his quality, and a man to wait on him; so that it was not long e'er he got himself in order to be gone after a dismal parting.

He made what haste he could to the French army, then under the command of the Monsignor, the Duke of Beaufort, then at Candia and put

---

[54] *camp*: the army.

[55] *urged*: used his youth and birth as reasons why he should enter the army.

[56] *which he liked best*: to enter which ever service he liked better.

himself a volunteer[57] under his conduct, in which station was Villenoys, who you have already heard was so passionate a lover of Isabella, who no sooner heard of Henault's being arrived and that he was husband to Isabella but he was impatient to learn by what strange adventure he came to gain her, even from her vowed retreat, when he with all his courtship, could not be so happy, tho' she was then free in the world and unvowed to Heaven.

As soon as he sent his name to Henault, he was sent for up, for Henault had heard of Villenoys, and that he had been a lover of Isabella; they received one another with all the endearing civility imaginable for the aforesaid reason, and for that he was his countryman, tho' unknown to him, Villenoys being gone to the army, just as Henault came from the Jesuits' College. A great deal of endearment passed between them, and they became from that moment like two sworn brothers, and he received the whole relation from Henault of his amour.

It was not long before the siege began anew, for he arrived at the beginning of the Spring, and as soon as he came, almost, they fell to action; and it happened upon a day that a party of some four hundred men resolved to sally out upon the enemy, as when ever they could they did; but as it is not my business to relate the history of the war, being wholly unacquainted with the terms of battles, I shall only say, that these men were led by Villenoys, and that Henault would accompany him in this sally, and that they acted very noble and great things, worthy of a memory in the history of that siege; but this day, particularly, they had an occasion to show their valor, which they did very much to their glory; but venturing too far, they were ambushed, in the pursuit of the party of the enemies, and being surrounded, Villenoys had the unhappiness to see his gallant friend fall, fighting and dealing of wounds around him, even as he descended to the earth, for he fell from his horse at the same moment that he killed a Turk; and Villenoys could neither assist him, nor had he the satisfaction to be able to rescue his dead body from under the horses, but with much ado escaping with his own life got away in spite of all that followed him, and recovered the town[58] before they could overtake him. He passionately bewailed the loss of this brave young man, and offered any recompense to those that would have ventured to have searched for his dead body among the slain; but it was not fit to hazard the living for unnecessary services to the dead; and tho' he had a great mind to have interred him, he rested content with what he wished to pay his friend's memory tho' he could not. So that all the service now he could do him was to write to Isabella, to whom he had not writ, tho' commanded by her so to do, in three years before, which was never since she took orders. He gave her an account of the death of her husband, and how gloriously he fell fighting for

---

[57] *volunteer*: that is, without a commission as an officer but acting independently and voluntarily.
[58] *recovered the town*: returned to the town.

the Holy Cross,[59] and how much honor he had won, if it had been his fate to have outlived that great but unfortunate day, where with 400 men they had killed 1500 of the enemy. The General Beaufort himself had so great a respect and esteem for this young man, and knowing him to be of quality, that he did him the honor to bemoan him and to send a condoling letter to Isabella: how much worth her esteem he died and that he had eternized[60] his memory with the last gasp of his life.

When this news arrived, it may be easily imagined what impressions or rather ruins it made in the heart of this fair mourner; the letters came by his man,[61] who saw him fall in battle and came off with those few that escaped with Villenoys; he brought back what money he had, a few jewels, with Isabella's picture that he carried with him and had left in his chamber in the fort of Candia for fear of breaking it in action. And now Isabella's sorrow grew to the extremity; she thought she could not suffer more than she did by his absence, but she now found a grief more killing; she hung her chamber with black and lived without the light of day. Only wax lights that let her behold the picture of this charming man, before which she sacrificed floods of tears. He had now been absent about ten months, and she had learnt just to live without him, but hope preserved her then; but now she had nothing for which to wish to live. She for about two months after the news arrived lived without seeing any creature but a young maid that was her woman; but extreme importunity obliged her to give way to the visits of her friends, who endeavored to restore her melancholy soul to its wonted easiness; for however it was oppressed within by Henault's absence, she bore it off with a modest cheerfulness; but now she found that fortitude and virtue failed her when she was assured he was no more. She continued thus mourning and thus enclosed the space of a whole year, never suffering the visit of any man but of a near relation; so that she acquired a reputation such as never any young beauty had, for she was now but nineteen and her face and shape more excellent than ever; she daily increased in beauty, which joined to her exemplary piety, charity, and all other excellent qualities gained her a wondrous fame and begat an awe and reverence in all that heard of her and there was no man of any quality that did not adore her. After her year was up, she went to the churches but would never be seen any where else abroad, but that was enough to procure her a thousand lovers; and some who had the boldness to send her letters, which if she received she gave no answer to and many she sent back unread and unsealed. So that she would encourage none, tho' their quality was far beyond what she could hope; but she was resolved to marry no more, however her fortune might require it.

It happened that about this time Candia being unfortunately taken by the Turks, all the brave men that escaped the sword returned, among them Villenoys, who no sooner arrived but he sent to let Isabella know of it and to

---

[59] *Holy Cross*: the Christian cause against the Muslim Turks.
[60] *eternized*: made eternal.   [61] *his man*: his servant.

beg the honor of waiting on her; desirous to learn what fate befell her dear
lord, she suffered him to visit her, where he found her in her mourning a
thousand times more fair (at least, he fancied so) than ever she appeared to
be; so that if he loved her before, he now adored her; if he burnt then, he
rages now; but the awful sadness and soft languishment of her eyes hindered
him from the presumption of speaking of his passion to her, tho' it would have
been no new thing; and his first visit was spent in the relation of every circumstance of Henault's death; and at his going away, he begged leave to visit
her sometimes, and she gave him permission. He lost no time but made use
of the liberty she had given him; and when his sister, who was a great companion of Isabella's, went to see her, he would still wait on her; so that either
with his own visits and those of his sister's, he saw Isabella every day and
had the good luck to see he diverted her by giving her relations of transactions of the siege and the customs and manners of the Turks. All he said was
with so good a grace that he rendered everything agreeable; he was, besides,
very beautiful, well made, of quality and fortune, and fit to inspire love.

He made his visits so often and so long that at last he took the courage to
speak of his passion, which at first Isabella would by no means hear of, but
by degrees she yielded more and more to listen to his tender discourse; and
he lived thus with her two years before he could gain any more upon her
heart than to suffer him to speak of love to her; but that which subdued her
quite was that her aunt, the Lady Abbess, died and with her all the hopes and
fortune of Isabella, so that she was left with only a charming face and mien,
a virtue, and a discretion above her sex to make her fortune within the world;
into a religious house she was resolved not to go, because her heart deceived
her once and she durst not trust it again, whatever it promised.

The death of this lady made her look more favorably on Villenoys; but yet
she was resolved to try his love to the utmost and keep him off as long as
'twas possible she could subsist, and 'twas for interest[62] she married again,
tho' she liked the person very well; and since she was forced to submit
herself to be a second time a wife, she thought, she could live better
with Villenoys, than any other, since for him she ever had a great esteem and
fancied the hand of Heaven had pointed out her destiny, which she could not
avoid, without a crime.

So that when she was again importuned by her impatient lover, she told
him she had made a vow to remain three years, at least, before she would
marry again after the death of the best of men and husbands and him who
had the fruits of her early heart; and, notwithstanding all the solicitations of
Villenoys, she would not consent to marry him till her vow of widowhood was
expired.

He took her promise, which he urged her to give him, and to show the
height of his passion in his obedience, he condescends[63] to stay her appointed

---

[62] *interest*: self-interest, personal advantage.   [63] *condescends*: assents, gives in.

time, tho' he saw her every day, and all his friends and relations made her visits upon this new account, and there was nothing talked on but this designed wedding, which when the time was expired was performed accordingly with great pomp and magnificence, for Villenoys had no parents to hinder his design; or if he had, the reputation and virtue of this lady would have subdued them.

The marriage was celebrated in this house, where she lived ever since her return from Germany, from the time she got her pardon; and when Villenoys was preparing all things in a more magnificent order at his villa, some ten miles from the city, she was very melancholy and would often say she had been used to such profound retreat and to live without the fatigue of noise and equipage that, she feared, she should never endure that grandeur which was proper for his quality; and tho' the house in the country was the most beautifully situated in all Flanders, she was afraid of a numerous train[64] and kept him for the most part in this pretty city mansion, which he adorned and enlarged as much as she would give him leave; so that there wanted nothing, to make this house fit to receive the people of the greatest quality, little as it was. But all the servants and footmen, all but one valet and the maid, were lodged abroad, for Isabella, not much used to the sight of men about her, suffered them as seldom as possible to come in her presence, so that she lived more like a nun still than a lady of the world; and very rarely any maids came about her but Maria, who had always permission to come whenever she pleased, unless forbidden.

As Villenoys had the most tender and violent passion for his wife in the world, he suffered her to be pleased at any rate, and to live in what method she best liked, and was infinitely satisfied with the austerity and manner of her conduct, since in his arms, and alone, with him, she wanted nothing that could charm; so that she was esteemed the fairest and best of wives, and he the most happy of all mankind. When she would go abroad, she had her coaches rich and gay and her livery[65] ready to attend her in all the splendor imaginable; and he was always buying one rich jewel or necklace or some great rarity or other that might please her; so that there was nothing her soul could desire which it had not, except the assurance of eternal happiness, which she labored incessantly to gain. She had no discontent, but because she was not blessed with a child; but she submits to the pleasure of Heaven and endeavored by her good works and her charity to make the poor her children and was ever doing acts of virtue to make the proverb good, That more are the children of the barren than the fruitful woman.[66] She lived in this tranquillity, beloved by all for the space of five years, and time (and perpetual obligations from Villenoys, who was the most indulgent and endearing man in the world) had almost worn out of her heart the thought of Henault, or if she remembered him, it was in her prayers, or sometimes with a short sigh

[64] *train*: a staff of persons in attendance, a retinue.
[65] *livery*: servants dressed in livery or uniforms.   [66] Isaiah 54: 1.

and no more, tho' it was a great while before she could subdue her heart to that calmness; but she was prudent and wisely bent all her endeavors to please, oblige, and caress the deserving living and to strive all she could to forget the unhappy dead, since it could not but redound to the disturbance of her repose to think of him; so that she had now transferred all that tenderness she had for him to Villenoys.

Villenoys of all diversions loved hunting and kept at his country house a very famous pack of dogs, which he used to lend sometimes to a young lord who was his dear friend and his neighbor in the country, who would often take them and be out two or three days together where he heard of game, and oftentimes Villenoys and he would be a whole week at a time exercising in this sport, for there was no game near at hand. This young lord had sent him a letter to invite him fifteen miles farther than his own villa to hunt and appointed to meet him at his country house in order to go in search of this promised game. So that Villenoys got about a week's provision of what necessaries he thought he should want in that time; and taking only his valet who loved the sport, he left Isabella for a week to her devotion, and her other innocent diversions of fine work at which she was excellent and left the town to go meet this young challenger.

When Villenoys was at any time out, it was the custom of Isabella to retire to her chamber and to receive no visits, not even the ladies, so absolutely she devoted herself to her husband. All the first day she passed over in this manner, and evening being come, she ordered her supper to be brought to her chamber, and because it was washing-day the next day, she ordered all her maids to go very early to bed that they might be up betimes, and to leave only Maria to attend her; which was accordingly done. This Maria was a young maid that was very discreet and of all things in the world loved her lady, whom she had lived with ever since she came from the monastery.

When all were in bed and the little light supper just carried up to the lady, and only, as I said, Maria attending, somebody knocked at the gate, it being about nine of the clock at night; so Maria snatching up a candle went to the gate to see who it might be; when she opened the door, she found a man in a very odd habit and a worse countenance, and asking, Who he would speak with? He told her, her lady. 'My lady' (replied Maria) 'does not use to receive visits at this hour. Pray, what is your business?' He replied, 'That which I will deliver only to your lady, and that she may give me admittance, pray, deliver her this ring.' And pulling off a small ring, with Isabella's name and hair in it, he gave it Maria, who shutting the gate upon him went in with the ring. As soon as Isabella saw it, she was ready to swoon on the chair where she sat, and cried, 'Where had you this?' Maria replied, 'An old rusty fellow at the gate gave it me, and desired it might be his passport to you; I asked his name, but he said you knew him not, but he had great news to tell you.' Isabella replied (almost swooning again) 'Oh, Maria! I am ruined.' The maid, all this while, knew not what she meant, nor that that was a ring given to

34

Henault by her mistress, but endeavoring to recover her only asked her what she should say to the old messenger? Isabella bid her bring him up to her (she had scarce life to utter these last words) and before she was well recovered, Maria entered with the man; and Isabella making a sign to her to depart the room, she was left alone with him.

Henault (for it was he) stood trembling and speechless before her, giving her leisure to take a strict survey of him; at first finding no feature nor part of Henault about him, her fears began to lessen, and she hoped, it was not he, as her first apprehensions had suggested; when he (with the tears of joy standing in his eyes and not daring suddenly to approach her for fear of increasing that disorder he saw in her pale face) began to speak to her and cried, 'Fair creature! is there no remains of your Henault left in this face of mine, all o'rgrown with hair? Nothing in these eyes, sunk with eight years absence from you and sorrows? Nothing in this shape, bowed with labor and griefs, that can inform you? I was once that happy man you loved!' At these words, tears stopped his speech, and Isabella kept them company, for yet she wanted words. Shame and confusion filled her soul, and she was not able to lift her eyes up to consider the face of him whose voice she knew so perfectly well. In one moment she run over a thousand thoughts. She finds by his return she is not only exposed to all the shame imaginable; to all the upbraiding, on his part, when he shall know she is married to another; but all the fury and rage of Villenoys and the scorn of the town, who will look on her as an adulteress. She sees Henault poor and knew she must fall from all the glory and tranquillity she had for five happy years triumphed in; in which time, she had known no sorrow or care, tho' she had endured a thousand with Henault. She dies to think, however, that he should know she had been so lightly in love with him to marry again; and she dies to think that Villenoys must see her again in the arms of Henault; besides, she could not recall her love, for love like reputation once fled never returns more. 'Tis impossible to love and cease to love (and love another) and yet return again to the first passion, tho' the person have all the charms or a thousand times more than it had when it first conquered. This mystery in love, it may be, is not generally known but nothing is more certain. One may a while suffer the flame to languish, but there may be a reviving spark in the ashes, raked up, that may burn anew; but when 'tis quite extinguished, it never returns or rekindles.

'Twas so with the heart of Isabella; had she believed Henault had been living, she had loved to the last moment of their lives; but, alas! the dead are soon forgotten, and she now loved only Villenoys.

After they had both thus silently wept, with very different sentiments, she thought 'twas time to speak; and dissembling as well as she could, she caressed him in her arms, and told him she could not express her surprise and joy for his arrival. If she did not embrace him heartily or speak so passionately as she used to do, he fancied it her confusion and his being in a condition not so fit to receive embraces from her; and evaded them as much as 'twas possible for him to do, in respect to her till he had dressed his face and put himself in order; but the supper being just brought up when he knocked, she ordered him to sit down and eat, and he desired her not to let Maria know who he was, to see how long it would be before she knew him or would call him to mind. But Isabella commanded Maria, to make up a bed in such a chamber without disturbing her fellows and dismissed her from waiting at table. The maid admired what strange, good, and joyful news this man had brought her mistress that he was so treated and alone with her, which never any man had yet been; but she never imagined the truth, and knew her lady's prudence too well to question her conduct. While they were at supper, Isabella obliged him to tell her how he came to be reported dead; of which she received letters, both from Monsieur Villenoys and the Duke of Beaufort, and by his man the news, who saw him dead? He told her that after the fight, of which, first, he gave her an account, he being left among the dead, when the enemy came to plunder and strip 'em, they found he had life in him and appearing as an eminent person, they thought it better booty to save me (continued he) and get my ransom than to strip me and bury me among the dead. So they bore me off to a tent and recovered me to life; and after that I was recovered of my wounds and sold by the soldier that had taken me to a Spahee,[67] who kept me a slave, setting a great ransom on me, such as I was not able to pay. I writ several times to give you and my father an account of my misery but received no answer and endured seven years of dreadful slavery. When I found, at last, an opportunity to make my escape, and from that time resolved never to cut the hair of this beard till I should either see my dearest Isabella again or hear some news of her. All that I feared was that she was dead; and at that word he fetched a deep sigh; and viewing all things so infinitely more magnificent than he had left 'em, or believed she could afford; and that she was far more beautiful in person and rich in dress than when he left her. He had a thousand torments of jealousy that seized him, of which he durst not make any mention but rather chose to wait a little and see whether she had lost her virtue. He desired he might send for a barber to put his face in some handsomer order and more fit for the happiness 'twas that night to receive; but she told him, no dress, no disguise could render him more dear and acceptable to her, and that tomorrow was time enough, and that his travels had rendered him more fit for repose than dressing.

So that after a little while they had talked over all they had a mind to say, all that was very endearing on his side and as much concern as she could force on hers; she conducted him to his chamber, which was very rich and which gave him a very great addition of jealousy. However, he suffered her to help him to bed, which she seemed to do with all the tenderness in the world; and when she had seen him laid, she said she would go to her prayers and come to him as soon as she had done, which being before her usual custom, it was

---

[67] *Spahee*: a Turkish cavalry officer.

not a wonder to him she stayed long, and he, being extremely tired with his journey, fell asleep. 'Tis true, Isabella essayed[68] to pray, but alas! it was in vain, she was distracted with a thousand thoughts what to do, which the more she thought, the more it distracted her; she was a thousand times about to end her life, and, at one stroke, rid herself of the infamy that she saw must inevitably fall upon her; but Nature was frail, and the Tempter[69] strong. And after a thousand convulsions, even worse than death itself, she resolved upon the murder of Henault, as the only means of removing all obstacles to her future happiness; she resolved on this, but after she had done so, she was seized with so great horror that she imagined if she performed it, she should run mad; and yet, if she did not, she should be also frantic with the shames and miseries that would befall her; and believing the murder the least evil, since she could never live with him, she fixed her heart on that; and causing herself to be put immediately to bed, in her own bed, she made Maria go to hers, and when all was still she softly rose and taking a candle with her, only in her nightgown and slippers, she goes to the bed of the unfortunate Henault with a penknife in her hand; but considering, she knew not how to conceal the blood should she cut his throat, she resolves to strangle him or smother him with a pillow; that last thought was no sooner borne but put in execution; and as he soundly slept she smothered him without any noise or so much as his struggling. But when she had done this dreadful deed, and saw the dead corpse of her once-loved lord lie smiling (as it were) upon her, she fell into a swoon with the horror of the deed, and it had been well for her she had there died; but she revived again and awakened to more and new horrors, she flies all frighted from the chamber and fancies the phantom of her dead lord pursues her; she runs from room to room, and starts and stares, as if she saw him continually before her. Now all that was ever soft and dear to her with him comes into her heart, and she finds he conquers anew, being dead, who could not gain her pity while living.

While she was thus flying from her guilt, in vain, she hears one knock with authority at the door. She is now more affrighted, if possible, and knows not whither to fly for refuge; she fancies they are already the officers of justice and that ten thousand tortures and wrecks[70] are fastening on her to make her confess the horrid murder; the knocking increases and so loud that the laundry maids, believing it to be the woman that used to call them up and help them to wash, rose, and opening the door let in Villenoys, who having been at his country villa, and finding there a footman instead of his friend, who waited to tell him his master was fallen sick of the small pox and could not wait on him, he took horse and came back to his lovely Isabella; but running up, as he used to do, to her chamber, he found her not, and seeing a light in another room, he went in but found Isabella flying from him out at another door with all the speed she could; he admires at this action, and the

---

[68] *essayed*: attempted.   [69] *Tempter*: the Devil.
[70] *wrecks*: racks, instruments of torture that stretched the body.

more because his maid told him her lady had been a bed a good while; he grows a little jealous, and pursues her, but still she flies; at last he caught her in his arms, where she fell into a swoon, but quickly recovering, he set her down in a chair and kneeling before her implored to know what she ailed and why she fled from him, who adored her? She only fixed a ghastly look upon him, and said she was not well. 'Oh!' (said he) 'put not me off with such poor excuses. Isabella never fled from me when ill but came to my arms and to my bosom to find a cure; therefore, tell me, what's the matter?' At that, she fell a weeping in a most violent manner and cried she was for ever undone. He, being moved with love and compassion, conjured her to tell what she ailed: 'Ah!' (said she) 'thou and I, and all of us, are undone!' At this, he lost all patience and raved and cried, 'Tell me, and tell me immediately, what's the matter?' When she saw his face pale and his eyes fierce, she fell on her knees and cried, 'Oh! you can never pardon me, if I should tell you, and yet, alas! I am innocent of ill, by all that's good, I am.' But her conscience accusing her at that word, she was silent. 'If thou art innocent,' said Villenoys, taking her up in his arms, and kissing her wet face, 'By all that's good, I pardon thee, whatever thou hast done.' 'Alas!' (said she) 'Oh! but I dare not name it, till you swear.' 'By all that's sacred,' (replied he) 'and by whatever oath you can oblige me to, by my inviolable love to thee, and by thy own dear self, I swear, whate'er it be, I do forgive thee; I know thou art too good to commit a sin I may not with honor pardon.'

With this and heartened by his caresses, she told him that Henault was returned; and repeating to him his escape, she said she had put him to bed, and when he expected her to come, she fell on her knees at the bedside and confessed she was married to Villenoys. 'At that word' (said she) 'he fetched a deep sigh or two and presently after, with a very little struggling, died; and, yonder, he lies still in the bed.' After this she wept so abundantly that all Villenoys could do could hardly calm her spirits; but after consulting what they should do in this affair, Villenoys asked her who of the house saw him? She said, 'Only Maria, who knew not who he was.' So that, resolving to save Isabella's honor, which was the only misfortune to come, Villenoys himself proposed the carrying him out to the bridge and throwing him into the river, where the stream would carry him down to the sea and lose him; or, if he were found, none could know him. So Villenoys took a candle and went and looked on him, and found him altogether changed, that nobody would know who he was; he therefore put on his clothes, which was not hard for him to do, for he was scarce yet cold, and comforting again Isabella, as well as he could, he went himself into the stable and fetched a sack, such as they used for oats, a new sack whereon stuck a great needle with a pack-thread[71] in it; this sack he brings into the house and shows to Isabella, telling her he would put the body in there, for the better convenience of carrying it on his back.

---

[71] *pack-thread*: a strong, two- or three-ply twine for tying packages or bundles.

Isabella all this while said but little, but filled with thoughts all black and hellish, she pondered within while the fond and passionate Villenoys was endeavoring to hide her shame and to make this an absolute secret. She imagined that could she live after a deed so black, Villenoys would be eternal[ly] reproaching her, if not with his tongue at least with his heart, and emboldened by one wickedness, she was the readier for another and another of such a nature as has, in my opinion, far less excuse than the first; but when Fate begins to afflict, she goes through stitch with her black work.[72]

When Villenoys, who would, for the safety of Isabella's honor, be the sole actor in the disposing of this body, and since he was young, vigorous, and strong, and able to bear it would trust no one with the secret, he having put up the body and tied it fast set it on a chair, turning his back towards it, with the more conveniency to take it upon his back, bidding Isabella give him the two corners of the sack in his hands; telling her they must do this last office for the dead, more in order to the securing their honor and tranquillity hereafter than for any other reason, and bid her be of good courage till he came back, for it was not far to the bridge, and it being the dead of the night, he should pass well enough. When he had the sack on his back and ready to go with it, she cried, 'Stay, my dear, some of his clothes hang out, which I will put in;' and with that, taking the pack-needle with the thread, sewed the sack with several strong stitches to the collar of Villenoy's coat without his perceiving it and bid him go now. 'And when you come to the bridge,' (said she) 'and that you are throwing him over the rail (which is not above breast high), be sure you give him a good swing, lest the sack should hang on any thing at the side of the bridge and not fall into the stream.' 'I'll warrant you,'[73] (said Villenoys) 'I know how to secure his falling.' And going his way with it, love lent him strength, and he soon arrived at the bridge, where, turning his back to the rail and heaving the body over, he threw himself with all his force backward, the better to swing the body into the river, whose weight (it being made fast to his collar) pulled Villenoys after it, and both the live and the dead man falling into the river, which being rapid at the bridge soon drowned him, especially when so great a weight hung to his neck; so that he died without considering what was the occasion of his fate.[74]

Isabella remained the most part of the night sitting in her chamber without going to bed to see what would become of her damnable design; but when it was towards morning and she heard no news, she put herself into bed, but not to find repose or rest there, for that she thought impossible after so great a barbarity as she had committed. 'No,' (said she) 'it is but just I should forever wake, who have in one fatal night destroyed two such innocents. Oh!

[72] *through stitch with her black work*: once Fate begins to weave a web or knit the fabric of an individual's destiny, she doesn't stop till she finishes the work.

[73] *warrant you*: I assure you, promise you.

[74] *without considering what was the occasion of his fate*: without realizing what Isabella had done.

what Fate, what destiny, is mine? Under what cursed planet was I born that Heaven itself could not divert my ruin? It was not many hours since I thought myself the most happy and blest of women, and now am fallen to the misery of one of the worst fiends of Hell.'

Such were her thoughts and such her cries till the light brought on new matter for grief; for about ten of the clock news was brought that two men were found dead in the river, and that they were carried to the town hall, to lie there till they were owned.[75] Within an hour after, news was brought in that one of these unhappy men was Villenoys; his valet, who all this while imagined him in bed with his lady, ran to the hall to undeceive the people, for he knew if his lord were gone out he should have been called to dress him; but finding it as 'twas reported, he fell a weeping and wringing his hands in a most miserable manner. He ran home with the news; where, knocking at his lady's chamber door and finding it fast locked, he almost hoped again he was deceived; but Isabella rising and opening the door, Maria first entered weeping with the news and then brought the valet to testify the fatal truth of it. Isabella, tho' it were nothing but what she expected to hear, almost swooned in her chair; nor did she feign it but felt really all the pangs of killing grief and was so altered with her night's watching and grieving that this new sorrow looked very natural in her. When she was recovered, she asked a thousand questions about him and questioned the possibility of it. 'For' (said she) 'he went out this morning early from me and had no signs in his face of any grief or discontent.' 'Alas!' (said the valet) 'Madam, he is not his own murderer, some one has done it in revenge.' And then told her how he was found fastened to a sack with a dead strange man tied up within it; and everybody concludes that they were both first murdered and then drawn to the river and thrown both in. At the relation of this strange man, she seemed more amazed than before, and commanding the valet to go to the hall and to take order about the coroner's sitting on the body of Villenoys, and then to have it brought home. She called Maria to her, and after bidding her shut the door, she cried, 'Ah, Maria! I will tell thee what my heart imagines; but first,' (said she) 'run to the chamber of the stranger and see if he be still in bed, which I fear he is not.' She did so and brought word he was gone. 'Then' (said she) 'my forebodings are true. When I was in bed last night with Villenoys' (and at that word, she sighed as if her heart strings had broken), 'I told him I had lodged a stranger in my house, who was by when my first lord and husband fell in battle; and that after the fight, finding him yet alive, he spoke to him and gave him that ring you brought me last night; and conjured him if ever his fortune should bring him to Flanders to see me and give me that ring and tell me' (with that, she wept, and could scarce speak), 'a thousand tender and endearing things, and then died in his arms. For my dear Henault's sake' (said she) 'I used him nobly and dismissed you that night

---

[75] *owned*: recognized, identified.

because I was ashamed to have any witness of the griefs I paid his memory. All this I told to Villenoys, whom I found disordered; and, after a sleepless night, I fancy he got up and took this poor man and has occasioned his death.' At that she wept anew, and Maria, to whom all that her mistress said was Gospel, verily believed it so without examining reason; and Isabella conjuring[76] her, since none of the house knew of the old man's being there (for old he appeared to be) that she would let it forever be a secret, and to this she bound her by an oath; so that none knowing Henault, altho' his body was exposed there for three days to public view. When the coroner had set on the bodies,[77] he found, they had been first murdered some way or other and then afterwards tacked together and thrown into the river.

They brought the body of Villenoys home to his house, where, it being laid on a table, all the house infinitely bewailed it; and Isabella did nothing but swoon away, almost as fast as she recovered life; however, she would to complete her misery be led to see this dreadful victim of her cruelty, and coming near the table, the body whose eyes were before close shut now opened themselves wide and fixed them on Isabella, who, giving a great shriek, fell down in a swoon, and the eyes closed again; they had much ado to bring her to life, but at last they did so and led her back to her bed, where she remained a good while. Different opinions and discourses were made, concerning the opening of the eyes of the dead man and viewing Isabella; but she was a woman of so admirable a life and conversation, of so undoubted a piety and sanctity of living that not the least conjecture could be made of her having a hand in it, besides the improbability of it; yet the whole thing was a mystery, which they thought they ought to look into. But a few days after, the body of Villenoys being interred in a most magnificent manner, and by will all he had was long since settled on Isabella, the world, instead of suspecting her, adored her the more, and everybody of quality was already hoping to be next, tho' the fair mourner still kept her bed and languished daily.

It happened not long after this there came to the town a French gentleman, who was taken at the siege of Candia, and was fellow slave with Henault for seven years in Turkey and who had escaped with Henault, and came as far as Liège[78] with him, where having some business and acquaintance with a merchant, he stayed some time; but when he parted with Henault, he asked him where he should find him in Flanders. Henault gave him a note, with his name, and place of abode, if his wife were alive; if not, to inquire at his sister's or his father's. This Frenchman came, at last, to the very house of Isabella, inquiring for this man and received a strange answer, and was laughed at. He found that was the house and that the lady; and inquiring about the town, and speaking of Henault's return, describing the man, it was quickly discovered to be the same that was in the sack. He had his friend

---

[76] *conjuring*: entreating, requesting emphatically.
[77] *set on the bodies*: examined the bodies.   [78] *Liège*: a city in eastern Belgium.

taken up[79] (for he was buried) and found him the same, and causing a barber to trim him, when his bushy beard was off, a great many people remembered him; and the Frenchman affirming he went to his own home, all Isabella's family and herself were cited before the magistrate of justice, where, as soon as she was accused, she confessed the whole matter of fact, and, without any disorder delivered herself in the hands of justice as the murderess of two husbands (both beloved) in one night. The whole world stood amazed at this; who knew her life a holy and charitable life, and how dearly and well she had lived with her husbands, and every one bewailed her misfortune, and she alone was the only person that was not afflicted for herself; she was tried and condemned to lose her head; which sentence she joyfully received, and said Heaven and her judges were too merciful to her and that her sins had deserved much more.

While she was in prison, she was always at prayers and very cheerful and easy, distributing all she had amongst and for the use of the poor of the town, especially to the poor widows; exhorting daily the young and the fair that came perpetually to visit her never to break a vow; for that was first the ruin of her, and she never since prospered, do whatever other good deeds she could. When the day of execution came, she appeared on the scaffold all in mourning but with a mien so very majestic and charming and a face so surprising fair, where no languishment or fear appeared but all cheerful as a bride, that she set all hearts a flaming even in that mortifying minute of preparation for death. She made a speech of half an hour long, so eloquent, so admirable a warning to the Vow-Breakers that it was as amazing to hear her as it was to behold her.

After she had done, with the help of Maria she put off her mourning veil and, without anything over her face, she kneeled down, and the executioner at one blow severed her beautiful head from her delicate body, being then in her seven and twentieth year. She was generally lamented and honorably buried.

[79] *taken up*: exhumed.

THE
Secret History
OF
Queen *ZARAH,*
AND THE
Zarazians;
BEING A
Looking - glaſs
FOR

In the Kingdom of
ALBIGION.

Faithfully Tranſlated from the *Italian* Copy
now lodg'd in the *Vatican* at *Rome,* and
never before Printed in any Language.

Albigion, Printed in the Year 1705.

Price Stitch'd 1 s. Price Bound 1 s. 6 d.

Delarivière Manley
(c. 1672–1724)

DELARIVIÈRE MANLEY, named after a relative, was probably born in Portsmouth, the daughter of Sir Roger Manley, then the lieutenant governor of the isle of Jersey. When her father died in 1687, she and her sisters may have been put in the care of their cousin, John Manley. According to her own account of her life, he seduced her into a bigamous marriage, and then after she was pregnant abandoned her. For several years afterwards, Manley was a retainer of the Duchess of Cleveland and lived for another few years in the country, where she wrote two plays and came to London in 1696, where they were produced without much success: *The Lost Lover; or The Jealous Husband*, a comedy, and *The Royal Mischief*, a tragedy. During these years in London, she was the mistress of a married man, John Tilly, the warden of the Fleet Prison.

Her first great success was *The Secret History of Queen Zarah and the Zarazians* (1705), which was so popular that she quickly produced a second part the same year. Published around the time of the parliamentary elections of 1705, it is a vigorous satirical attack on Sarah and John Churchill, Duke and Duchess of Marlborough, Sidney, Earl of Godolphin, and various other Whig politicians who dominated the cabinet formed by Queen Anne on her accession to the throne in 1702 on the death of her brother-in-law, William III. The Tory opposition and popular rumour had it that the Duke and Duchess, the Queen's old friends when she was an unhappy princess and estranged from her brother-in-law, King William, manipulated her for their advantage. And indeed after Anne ascended the throne Sarah became First Lady of the Bedchamber and Groom of the Stole, and the Tories saw in this friendship a case of petticoat government and domination by a royal favorite. *Queen Zarah* capitalized on such political accusations and is an early example in English of what in French is called a *roman à clef* (and subsequent editions had a Key identifying the real names of the characters). Tory political satire is also the main purpose of her next and most popular work, the book with which her name would be associated far into the century: *Secret Memoirs and Manners of Several Persons of Quality, of both Sexes, From the New Atalantis, an Island in the Mediterranean* (1709). An extension and amplification of *Queen Zarah*, *The New Atalantis* was even more popular, and all London, including figures like Lady Mary Wortley Montague, clamoured to read it. And more than topical scandal was clearly the source of its popularity, since it was reprinted many times well into the eighteenth century. Still attacking the Whigs and her old enemies the Marlboroughs, Manley now manages a satiric and consistently sensationalized panorama of scandalous doings in ruling class Whig circles. This book is less political than its shorter predecessor, emphasizing sexual scandal and moral irregularity of every conceivable sort, from seduction and adultery to incest and homosexuality as well as financial corruption. So effective was *The New Atalantis* that the Whig government attempted to suppress it. Manley was thrown into prison in October 1709, but she was soon released when the authorities found they had no case. The fictional pretext of the book protected her from prosecution.

A sequel to *The New Atalantis*, *The Memoirs of Europe* (1710, 2 volumes, like its predecessor) features much the same attractions, scandalous stories about the Whigs with some basis in fact and a good deal in popular rumour and court gossip. As a political satirist, Manley was very good, so effective that in 1711 she succeeded Jonathan Swift as the chief writer of the Tory political periodical, *The Examiner*. She was nothing less than the principal woman of letters of Queen Anne's England. According to Swift, she became in these years of her success the mistress of John Barber, who had printed *The New Atalantis*. In 1714 she published her autobiographical novel, *The Adventures of Rivella*, from which scholars have extracted some of the more obscure aspects of her life. She seems to have written very little in her last years, although her play *Lucius, the First Christian King of Britain* was produced at Drury Lane in 1717. She died in 1724, her brand of ironic political satire and scandalous eroticism, popular narrative elements in those years, giving way to more sentimental and strictly amatory fiction.

J.J.R.

The Secret History of Queen Zarah and the Zarazians: Being a Looking-glass for — — — In the Kingdom of Albigion

INTRODUCTION

To the Reader[1]

The romances in France have for a long time been the diversion and amuse-

---

[1] Long considered an original and characteristically English landmark statement about changing tastes for prose fiction, Manley's preface turns out to be an almost literal translation of a French essay by the Abbé Morvan de Bellegarde (1648-1734) contained in the 1702 courtesy book, *Lettres curieuses de litterature*, and is itself a paraphrase of the second part of Sieur de Plaisir's *Sentiments sur les lettres et sur l'histoire* (1683). Bellegarde's book was translated into English and published in London in 1705. For a full discussion of Manley's translation, see the article by the scholar who discovered this interesting fact, John L. Sutton, Jr., 'The Source of Mrs. Manley's Preface to Queen Zarah', *Modern Philology*, 82 (1984), 167-72.

46

ment of the whole world; the people both in the city and at court have given themselves over to this vice, and all sorts of people have read these works with a most surprising greediness. But that fury is very much abated, and they are all fallen off from this distraction. The little histories of this kind have taken place of romances, whose prodigious number of volumes were sufficient to tire and satiate such whose heads were most filled with those notions.

These little pieces which have banished romances are much more agreeable to the brisk and impetuous humor of the English, who have naturally no taste for long-winded performances, for they have no sooner begun a book but they desire to see the end of it. The prodigious length of the ancient romances, the mixture of so many extraordinary adventures, and the great number of actors that appear on the stage, and the likeness which is so little managed—all which has given a distaste to persons of good sense and has made romances so much cried down as we find 'em at present. The authors of historical novels, who have found out this fault, have run into the same error, because they take for the foundation of their history no more than one principal event and don't overcharge it with episodes, which would extend it to an excessive length; but they are run into another fault, which I cannot pardon, that is, to please by variety the taste of the reader, they mix particular stories with the principal history, which seems to me as if reasoned ill. In effect, the curiosity of the reader is deceived by this deviation from the subject, which retards the pleasure he would have in seeing the end of an event. It relishes of a secret displeasure in the author which makes him soon lose sight of those persons with whom he began to be in love. Besides, the vast number of actors who have such different interests embarrasses his memory and causes some confusion in his brain, because 'tis necessary for the imagination to labor to recall the several interests and characters of the persons spoken of, and by which they have interrupted the history.

For the reader's better understanding, we ought not to choose too ancient accidents nor unknown heroes which are sought for in a barbarous country and too far distant in time, for we care little for what was done a thousand years ago among the Tartars or Ayssines.

The names of persons ought to have a sweetness in them, for a barbarous name disturbs the imagination; as the historian describes the heroes to his fancy, so he ought to give them qualities which affect the reader and which fixes him to his fortune. But he ought with great care to observe the probability of truth, which consists in saying nothing but what may morally be believed.

For there are truths that are not always probable, as for example 'tis an allowed truth in the Roman history that Nero put his mother to death, but 'tis a thing against all reason and probability that a son should imbrue his hand in the blood of his own mother. It is also no less probable that a single captain should at the head of a bridge stop a whole army, although 'tis probable that a small number of soldiers might stop in defiles[2] prodigious armies because the situation of the place favors the design and renders them almost equal. He that writes a true history ought to place the accidents as they naturally happen without endeavoring to sweeten them for to procure a greater credit, because he is not obliged to answer for their probability. But he that composes a history to his fancy, gives his heroes what characters he pleases, and places the accidents as he thinks fit without believing he shall be contradicted by other historians; therefore he is obliged to write nothing that is improbable. 'Tis nevertheless allowable that an historian shows the elevation of his genius when advancing improbable actions he gives them colors and appearances capable of persuading.

One of the things an author ought first of all to take care of is to keep up the characters of the persons he introduces. The authors of romances give extraordinary virtues to their heroines, exempted from all the weakness of human nature and much above the infirmities of their sex. 'Tis necessary they should be virtuous or vicious to merit the esteem or disesteem of the readers, but their virtue ought to be spared and their vices exposed to every trial. It would in no wise be probable that a young woman fondly beloved by a man of great merit and for whom she had a reciprocal tenderness finding herself at all times alone with him in places which favored their loves could always resist his addresses. There are too nice occasions, and an author would not enough observe good sense if he therein exposed his heroine. 'Tis a fault which authors of romances commit in every page; they would blind the reader with this miracle, but 'tis necessary the miracle should be feasible to make an impression in the brain of reasonable persons. The characters are better managed in the historical novels which are writ nowadays; they are not filled with great adventures and extraordinary accidents, for the most simple action may engage the reader by the circumstances that attend it. It enters into all the motions and disquiets of the actor when they have well expressed to him the character. If he be jealous, the look of a person he loves, a mouse, a turn of the head, or the least complaisance to a rival throws him into the greatest agitations which the readers perceive by a counter blow. If he be very virtuous and falls into a mischance by accident, they pity him and commiserate his misfortunes. For fear and pity in romance as well as tragedies are the two instruments which move the passion. For we in some manner put ourselves in the room of those we see in danger; the part we take therein and the fear of falling into the like misfortunes causes us to interest ourselves more in their adventures because that those sort of accidents may happen to all the world. And it touches so much the more because they are the common effects of nature.

The heroes in the ancient romances have nothing in them that is natural; all is unlimited in their character; all their advantages have something prodi-

---

[2] *defiles*: narrow passes or valleys that restrict the lateral movements of troops.

gious, and all their actions something that's marvelous. In short, they are not men. A single prince attacked by a great number of enemies is so far from giving way to the crowd that he does incredible feats of valor, beats them, puts them to flight, delivers all the prisoners, and kills an infinite number of people to deserve the title of a hero. A reader who has any sense does not take part with these fabulous adventures, or at least is but slightly touched with them because they are not natural and therefore cannot be believed. The heroes of the modern romances are better characterized; they give them passions, virtues or vices, which resemble humanity; thus all the world will find themselves represented in these descriptions, which ought to be exact and marked by traits which express clearly the character of the hero to the end we may not be deceived and may presently know our predominant quality, which ought to give the spirit all the motion and action of our lives. 'Tis that which inspires the reader with curiosity and a certain impatient desire to see the end of the accidents, the reading of which causes an exquisite pleasure when they are nicely handled. The motion of the heart gives yet more, but the author ought to have an extraordinary penetration to distinguish them well and not to lose himself in this labyrinth. Most authors are contented to describe men in general. They represent them covetous, courageous, and ambitious, without entering into the particulars and without specifying the character of their covetousness, valor, or ambition. They don't perceive nice distinctions which those who know it remark in the passions. In effect, the nature, humor, and juncture give new postures to vices; the turn of the mind, motion of the heart, affection and interests alter the very nature of the passions, which are different in all men. The genius of the author marvelously appears when he nicely discovers those differences and exposes to the reader's sight those almost unperceivable jealousies which escape the sight of most authors because they have not an exact notion of the turnings and motions of human understanding and they know nothing but the gross passions from whence they make but general descriptions.

He that writes either a true or false history ought immediately to take notice of the time and sense where those accidents happened that the reader may not remain long in suspense. He ought also in few words describe the person who bears the most considerable part in his story to engage the reader; 'tis a thing that little conduces to the raising the merit of a hero to praise him by the beauty of his face. This is mean and trivial. Detail discourages persons of good taste. 'Tis the qualities of the soul which ought to render him acceptable, and there are those qualities likewise that ought to be discouraged in the principal character of a hero. For there are actors of a second rank who serve only to bind the intrigue, and they ought not to be compared with those of the first order nor be given qualities that may cause them to be equally esteemed. 'Tis not by extravagant expressions nor repeated praises that the reader's esteem is acquired to the character of the hero's; their actions ought to plead for them. 'Tis by that they are made known and describe themselves;

although they ought to have some extraordinary qualities, they ought not all to have 'em in an equal degree. 'Tis impossible they should not have some imperfections, seeing they are men, but their imperfections ought not to destroy the character that is attributed to them. If we describe them brave, liberal, and generous, we ought not to attribute to them baseness or cowardice, because that their actions would otherwise belie their character and the predominant virtues of the heroes. 'Tis no argument that Sallust,[3] though so happy in the description of men, in the description of Cataline[4] does not in some manner describe him covetous also; for he says this ambitious man spent his own means profusely and raged after the goods of another with an extreme greediness. But these two motions which seem contrary were inspired by the same wit; these were the effects of the unbounded ambition of Cataline and the desire he had to rise by the help of his creatures on the ruins of the Roman republic. So vast a project could not be executed [but] by very great sums of money, which obliged Cataline to make all sorts of efforts to get it from all parts.

Every historian ought to be extremely uninterested; he ought neither to praise nor blame those he speaks of; he ought to be contented with exposing the actions, leaving an entire liberty to the reader to judge as he pleases without taking any care not to blame his heroes or make their apology. He is no judge of the merit of his heroes, his business is to represent them in the same form as they are and describe their sentiments, manners and conduct. It deviates in some manner from his character and that perfect uninterestedness when he adds to the names of those he introduces epithets either to blame or praise them. There are but few historians who exactly follow this rule, and who maintain this difference from which they cannot deviate without rendering themselves guilty of partiality.

Although there ought to be a great genius required to write a history perfectly, it is nevertheless not requisite that a historian should always make use of all his wit, nor that he should strain himself in nice and lively reflections. 'Tis a fault which is reproached with some justice to Cornelius Tacitus, who is not contented to recount the feats but employs the most refined reflections of policy to find out the secret reasons and hidden causes of accidents; there is nevertheless a distinction to be made between the character of the historian and the hero, for if it be the hero that speaks, then he ought to express himself ingeniously, without affecting any nicety of points or syllogisms because he speaks without any preparation, but when the author speaks of his chief he may use a more nice language and choose his terms for the better expressing his designs. Moral reflections, maxims and sentences are

---

   [3] *Sallust*: Gallius Sallustius Crispus (86–34 BC), Roman historian and politician.
   [4] *Cataline*: Lucius Sergius Catilina, an ambitious Roman aristocrat who rose to power in the 60s BC. Led an unsuccessful rebellion, famously denounced by Cicero, in 63 BC against the senatorial establishment.

more proper in discourses for instructions than in historical novels, whose chief end is to please. And if we find in them some instructions, it proceeds rather from their descriptions than their precepts.

An acute historian ought to observe the same method at the ending as at the beginning of his story, for he may at first expose maxims relating but a few feats, but when the end draws nigher the curiosity of the reader is augmented, and he finds in him a secret impatience of desiring to see the discovery of the action. An historian that amuses himself by moralizing or describing discourages an impatient reader who is in haste to see the end of intrigues. He ought also to use a quite different sort of style in the main part of the work than in conversations, which ought to be writ after an easy and free manner. Fine expressions and elegant turns agree little to the style of conversation, whose principal ornament consists in the plainness, simplicity, free and sincere air which is much to be preferred before a great exactness. We see frequent examples in ancient authors of a sort of conversation which seems to clash with reason, for 'tis not natural for a man to entertain himself, for we only speak that we may communicate our thoughts to others. Besides, 'tis hard to comprehend how an author that relates word for word the like conversation could be instructed to repeat them with so much exactness. These sorts of conversations are much more impertinent when they run upon strange subjects which are not indispensably allied to the story handled. If the conversations are long, they indispensably tire because they drive from our sight those people to whom we are engaged and interrupt the sequel of the story.

'Tis an indispensable necessity to end a story to satisfy the disquiets of the reader, who is engaged to the fortunes of those people whose adventures are described to him; 'tis depriving him of a most delicate pleasure when he is hindered from seeing the event of an intrigue which has caused some emotion in him, whose discovery he expects, be it either happy or unhappy. The chief end of history is to instruct and inspire into men the love of virtue and abhorrence of vice by the examples proposed to them. Therefore the conclusion of a story ought to have some tract of morality which may engage virtue; those people who have a more refined virtue are not always the most happy, but yet their misfortunes excite their readers' pity and affects them. Although vice be not always punished, yet 'tis described with reasons which show its deformity and make it enough known to be worthy of nothing but chastisements.

The Secret History of Queen Zarah

Of all the kingdoms in the world, Albigion is now reckoned the fullest of adventures, there being scarce any nation in the habitable earth but what it hath some commerce or communication with, insomuch that the people are become as famous abroad for politics as the Muscovites are at home for love and gallantry. The youth of that country, encouraged by their parents' examples, aspire to be privy counsellors before they get rid of the rod of their schoolmasters, and prentice boys assume the air of statesmen e'er yet they have learned the mystery of trade.

Mechanics[5] of the meanest rank plead for a liberty to abuse their betters and turn out ministers of state with the same freedom that they smoke tobacco. Carmen and cobblers over coffee draw up articles of peace and war and make partition treaties at their will and pleasure; in a word, from the prince to the peasant everyone here enjoys his natural liberty. Whether it proceed from the nature of the climate or the temper of the people I cannot resolve you; I rather think such subjects are such as the rules and laws of the government make them.

This renowned Lady Zarah[6] (though of obscure parents) was born in the reign of Rollando, King of Albigion,[7] one of the most gallant princes the world ever had when gallantry was so much in vogue that it was almost natural to be a gallant as to live. In those happy days it was she first received the breath of life common to all other creatures as well as her, but which none has improved to that vast advantage. Her mother's name was Jenisa, a woman who moved in a low sphere but had a large occupation, was one who knew the world well and was studious of her own interest. And though she was not admired for her wit, that defect was supplied by some little arts she had peculiar to some sort of women, by which means she gained the hearts of all the men who conversed with her.

In a few years Zarah grew up to the admiration of all that knew her birth and education, for her mother had instructed her in every art that was necessary to engage and charm mankind, so that she soon became the object of their wishes and desires as well for the excellency of her wit as the agreeableness of her beauty. About that time there was one Hippolito, a handsome gentleman, well born, young and vigorous, who had pleased other women and was reputed to make his fortune that way. She had twice or thrice seen him at the ball, which were frequently made in those days for the diversion of the ladies. Hippolito was excellent at dancing and always came off with applause and admiration; every step he took carried death with it and made all the company praise him, which sensibly touched Zarah's heart. 'Tis not unusual to find women affected with a man's merit upon occasions of that nature. She was deeply sensible of the applause and honor bestowed by the company on Hippolito; when she came from the ball she could not forbear being melancholy and pensive, even before her mother. She could neither eat, drink, nor sleep. This troubled extremely the indulgent Jenisa, who was so inquisitive after the least concern of the health and pleasure of her daughter

---

[5] *Mechanics*: manual labourers.

[6] *Zarah*: Sarah Jenyns (1660-1744) was a childhood friend of Princess Anne and married John Churchill (later Duke of Marlborough) in 1677.

[7] *King of Albigion*: King Charles II, who reigned from 1660 to 1685.

that she was more in pain than her to see her languish as she did. She could not imagine what it should be that she should hide it from such a mother and was so much concerned at it she could not rest for thinking of it. Zarah was more and more love sick, which by degrees grew so upon her it altered her quite. The good mother redoubled her care and if it had been possible would have redoubled her love. She prayed her every moment if she was in love to tell her the cause and protested she would not stick at anything for her satisfaction, so tender a regard had the old woman for her daughter's passion.

Zarah perceiving her mother's fondness and how pleasantly she flattered her most passionate desires cried out with a surprising tenderness, 'Hippolito is the man, the most charming in my eyes and the most accomplished on earth; but alas he loves and is beloved again by Clelia.[8] And you know,' continued she, 'what disadvantages a lover lies under to have a rival that is both proud and handsome. Besides the title of chief mistress to the king gives her both power and favor to oblige him and affords him the greater pleasure and ambition to be obliged. For Clelia is wholly possessed with a passion for Hippolito; she loves the king as most mistresses of that kind use to do, that is, as far as the power of a monarch could make her love a man who raised her above all other women.' She reigned in all outward splendor imaginable, but amidst all her glories she was troubled with a passion for a man she could love for his own sake. A woman subject to such reflections as these is hardly kept within the bounds of her duty; thus Clelia found it too hard a task not to transgress a little when she had cast her eyes upon Hippolito.

The king's bounties she thought were but her due, or at least sufficiently requited in the superficial acknowledgments she made him; and that if she loved him not heartily 'twas not her fault but his, who knew not how to gain her affection. Such is the fortune of monarchs in love; when they are with their mistresses they commonly lay aside that majesty which dazzles the eyes and affects the hearts of mankind. They go undressed into their chambers and make themselves so familiar with their mistresses they afterwards use them as other men.

As glorious as it is for an ambitious woman to see at her feet every day a person who commands all others, yet monarchs are deceived if they think their mistresses are always true. No passion but that of extraordinary love can fix a woman's heart. Ambition alone is too weak a gage for their fidelity. It frequently happens princes owe their amorous conquest more to their quality than merit; and accordingly they extend only to what is external and gross, when love and inclination, frustrated of their expectation from them and not satisfied with pomp and show, goes in search of satisfaction elsewhere.

'If this be all' (said Jenisa, the kind mother), 'trouble not your self about it; this is but a small matter in respect of what I have performed in my time of the like nature. For as Hippolito is a brave man, he will scorn to be obliged

---

[8] *Clelia*: Barbara, Duchess of Cleveland, who was for a time the mistress of Charles II.

long to a woman, who having first forfeited her honor to her royal master, will cancel the obligation of honor he otherwise owed to her and be glad of the pretence to bestow her favors on another woman in whose beauty and fidelity he can place his heart as well as his interests. For 'tis natural for men that love pleasure to love that which is of their own procuring. And 'tis easy,' continued she, 'to think of such measures as will bring about what is very agreeable both to your wishes of love and my desires of ambition.'

Accordingly as Jenisa had laid the plot the next time Zarah went to court Clelia saw her, grew violent fond of her, and invited her to her apartments, little thinking she was her rival, which Zarah was so far from denying that she willingly accepted of the favor. Night drawing on, Hippolito came as usual to pay Clelia a visit, but how was Zarah confounded when she saw the man she loved next heaven best approach her with all the advantages and opportunities of a happy lover, not knowing how he should come there. For Clelia was absent, being sent for suddenly by the king. Hippolito, who saw her in surprise, gazed on her beauty for a while, was charmed with the sight of it, and could not express his joy for the transport of his love. But at last recollecting himself and observing Zarah's countenance, he broke silence thus: 'Madam, I confess my surprise, but it is altogether owing to your beauty, for I can scarce satisfy myself that what I [see][9] is real, though my heart would willingly flatter me it is. Pray resolve me, Madam, is this place enchanted?' (For it was very spacious and made on purpose for a cooling room in the heats of summer and had in it several beds of turf very prettily made, with pots of jessamine flowers and other sweets all about; in a word it was a place picked out for the king's pleasure.) Here Zarah was in bed, and as there is nothing so handsome as a beautiful woman in bed, he was so charmed at the sight of her he was as much disordered as she and knew not what she did. At last Zarah got the liberty of her tongue, which at other times was voluble enough, and answered, 'I believe, Sir' (said she) 'you have mistaken the object of your passion, for I am not ignorant Clelia is her, the happy she, for whom those soft and tender things were meant.' 'I confess, Madam,' said he, 'Clelia is my mistress but deserves not to possess a heart whose eyes have seen a lady so beautiful as you are. And nothing but a passion equal to that I have for you could prevail upon me to think less of her. Nothing but the extremity of your beauty, whose charms are irresistible, could excuse me. But let a man value himself never so much on his integrity yet a passion raised in him by a person so amiable as you will be proof against all batteries of duty or interest.'

We may easily guess these passionate expressions of Hippolito were not a little pleasing to Zarah, who replied that she believed he was a generous and brave man but that his heart was its own master and would love one today and another tomorrow, that his sentiments were subject to change as other

---

[9] The text reads 'said', which must be a misprint for 'see'.

things, that love like nature was not charming to him but in its variety. 'For example,' says she, 'today you are for me but three or four days hence you will be for another. And you would think it injustice in me to expect that you should be truer to me than you are to Clelia.'

It may be admired[10] perhaps that two persons so little acquainted should in so few minutes become so familiar, but we must know love in those countries makes far quicker progress than in ours, where the winds, and the snow, and the rain spoil his wings and hinder his flight; for it is the custom of the grandees of that country when they have not a particular inclination for any woman to take this today and another tomorrow. And having lost the taste of love, to search for pleasure in change and variety.

Thus while the two lovers were wholly engaged in their amours, Hippolito used all the gallantry of a courtier and all the endearments of a passionate lover. Jenisa, who had contrived this interview, had likewise procured Clelia's absence, and resolving to strike while the iron was hot goes directly to Clelia's apartments, on purpose not so much to surprise the lovers as to compass the design which she was then carrying on of marrying her daughter to Hippolito. They heard a noise at the door: 'What should be the meaning of all this?' said they one to another, having a thousand fears upon them, though they could not imagine that any person in the apartments could make the least discovery of an intrigue which was so accidental that neither of them was the contriver of, or could have imagined to happen. But at last Jenisa breaks open the door, comes in quite out of breath, and throws herself half dead (as she pretended) into the arms of her daughter. What frightful fancies had Hippolito then in his head? He presently imagined they were utterly undone and that it was by Clelia's contrivance, not suspecting Jenisa's designs in the least.

'Blast my eyes,' said she, 'what is this I see?' (And then she let fall a shower of tears.) 'Hippolito and alone in your company? For heaven's sake, my daughter, tell me how he came hither? And for what design?' Zarah not knowing what to answer or reply continued mute, while she loaded Hippolito with a thousand false reproaches for his unworthiness in undertaking such a base attempt. This was a well managed scene on the part of Jenisa, who not so much as let her daughter into the secret but fell upon her with that pretended fury that Hippolito interposed and used all his endeavors lest he should be ill handled. He was sensibly touched to the quick at this outrage, and no consideration of life or duty could have prevented him from doing violence to Jenisa had not the fear of losing Zarah prevailed more upon him than her resentment.

The scuffle was no sooner over but Hippolito before the mother's presence took Zarah and embracing her tenderly: 'Madam,' said he, 'the dangers you have gone through on my account and the cruel assault you have now endured will make me for the future study your repose and satisfactions more

---

[10] *admired*: marvelled at, wondered about.

than my own love, though it is no easy matter to be disengaged from a passion like mine.' This declaration answered not Jenisa's intentions so full as she desired, for she was afraid by this his passion of warm love would dwindle into cold friendship and respect but that Zarah's reply relieved her doubting fears. 'Sir,' said she, 'I am satisfied you have a value for me by the kindness of your expressions and the concern I observed you in at this rencounter, but I can never have the vanity to hope you can so easily quit your passion for Clelia as to think of loving any other.' 'But you shall find, Madam,' answered Hippolito, 'that all the passion I can have for her will never hinder the tenders of love I offer here; I will quit all my pretensions to Clelia that I may prevent all dispute with a person to whom I am so deeply obliged; that there is nothing so dear to me but I will part with it for your sake.'

At this Jenisa smiled to perceive the good effects of her policy, while Hippolito made a thousand oaths he would keep within the bounds of that respect and discretion she might expect from the severest virtue and protested he desired only till tomorrow that he might have an hour's discourse with Clelia. Jenisa, who knew too well the fickleness of men and all the seducing arts the women are mistresses of, reproached him for such a thought, while he requested it of Zarah with all the kindest words and the most tender and passionate expressions imaginable. Zarah answered she owed that duty to her mother and that virtue to herself she would not betray for the whole world, and since he had professed such a passion for her, and her mother was now become a witness of it, she did not know how he could part from her without giving her such satisfaction as parents in those cases expected. 'I have honor and virtue too,' said he, 'as you have, and the precepts of 'em perhaps as severe as yours; but love is stronger than all the precepts in the world.'

This began to nettle Jenisa, who was not very well pleased to think of any thing that might delay their being immediately married, and therefore she told Hippolito there was but one of these two things that ought presently to be resolved on, either that Clelia be made privy to this affair (and then he might easily guess what would be the consequence, both as to himself and Zarah) or else to marry her, which might preserve both his honor and his interest. For the king would be better satisfied to have his rival married, and Clelia, said she, could not reproach you with a dishonorable action. Hippolito was silent for a time, as if he studied what to say; but Jenisa pressing him to declare what he would do, looking with a melancholy air, he told her with some trouble, 'Madam,' said he, 'I am the most unfortunate of men, especially in love. Zarah,' added he sighing, 'the unkind Zarah, hath not the least tenderness for me, no, not the least pity for the torments she sees me suffer for her; and unless you will be a little kinder to me I know not what will become of me. Let me but know what you desire of me, and what it is you'd have me do?' 'I would have you resolve,' said Jenisa, 'instantly to marry Zarah. I have a priest attends without ready to perform the ceremony.' This proposal astonished him on the sudden so extremely that having blushed at it very much he knew not what answer to make; while Jenisa observing the disorder he was in went directly and fetched in the priest, who without more hesitation performed his office and pronounced them man and wife.

As soon as this was effected to Jenisa's great satisfaction and Zarah's desires, Hippolito to both their amazements left the room and made a thousand reflections on his ill fortune that had drawn him into such a fatal snare. Not but he was passionately pleased with Zarah's beauty and persuaded some considerable greatness would attend her, but the consideration of being outwitted and as it were forced into such a compliance grated upon him exceedingly and seemed to be the chief thing that troubled him the most.

But Zarah finding him leave the chamber so abruptly and fearing lest what had then passed might occasion Hippolito to do some rash act immediately followed him into the next chamber, where finding him in a passion almost beyond the power of reason to manage and enough to put him on the most desperate enterprise, she fell at his feet with all the agonies of a despairing lover. 'Am I then despised already?' said she, and with tears in her eyes continued. 'Do you insult over your conquest because it was so easily gained? You have already too cruelly wounded me not to pity me a little.' More she would have said, but the excess of her passion stifled all her endeavors to proceed and she sunk down under the conflict between her love and resentment. Hippolito snatched her from the ground, raised her up into his arms and clasped her round with all the tenderness possible, for the transports of his love had banished the extravagance of his fury and he melted into all the softness of a happy lover. It is beyond imagination to conceive the joy Zarah was in at this sudden change of Hippolito, and being about to return his passion an equal fire after having given him some looks that discovered her inclination, she had time to say no more than 'Heaven and my Hippolito support me, for I'm ravished with excess of pleasure,' when Clelia in a desperate frenzy occasioned by what had happened that night entered the room where these two lovers seemed so happy. But hearing a voice she knew and Hippolito's name, she had not conduct enough to stay and observe them but hastened forward and rushed upon them, when she was too well satisfied 'twas Zarah and Hippolito she saw. 'Ah traitor,' cried she, 'is it possible you should be thus ungrateful? Have you the confidence to make my own lodging the scene of your villany? Could you find no other way for revenge but to make me witness of your infidelity? Barbarous man,' continued she, 'is this the way you repay my former services to you?' 'Madam,' said he with a coolness of temper and great presence of mind peculiar to him, ''tis fit you should hear us speak for ourselves, and if you please we will send for those who shall justify us, and you shall see how we will defend ourselves.' What a rage, what a fury did this put her in? 'Good Heavens!' said she, 'to what will this impudence arise?' At that she seized the sword he had on, not knowing which of the two to begin with first, being both equally perfidious. She thought at last Zarah as most criminal was first to be sacrificed to her revenge, and just as she was going to stab her Hippolito interposed and received a slight wound upon himself by staying of her hand, when she threw herself upon him. 'Traitor,' said she, 'this blow was not reserved for thee, thou shalt not have the power of being first revenged.'

At these words and the bustle that was made, Jenisa and the priest not being yet gone, entered into the room. But Heavens! What confusion and a trembling seized Clelia when she saw them? This was a scene more shocking than what her thoughts and jealousies could ever have suggested to her. 'Gods!' she cried (with all the rage and fury that despair could raise). 'What mean these Apparitions here? Why that old hag? And why that bawding priest? What have you robbed me? And what have you done with my Hippolito?' And then she ran round the room like a distracted woman, seeking in every place, but the noise continuing all the servants awaked and came running in to their lady's assistance, supposing some misfortune had happened. But when they saw Hippolito was there, they readily withdrew again, knowing the disorders the family had been sometimes subject to upon his account. And he perceiving Clelia's passion too violent to harken to anything he could say at that time committed her to the care of her woman and with the rest of the company retired.

In a few days this action was noised all over the court, and at last it came to the king's ears, who seemed to be pleased with the news that Hippolito was married and that he now should be quit of the rival that had alienated from him the affections of a woman he loved the best in the world. For the king was no stranger to Clelia's unfaithfulness, notwithstanding he continued to dote of her charms. Upon this he sent for Hippolito to court, gave him joy of his new bride and repeated assurances of his continued favor to him. This so much surprised Hippolito that he knew not whether to thank his majesty for those expressions of his bounty or no, thinking it could not be real but that Clelia had told the king all that had happened and that this was to mock him. But you may guess the surprise was very agreeable to him when the king continued in this good humor and told him he was sorry he was not so happy to know the lady that he had made his choice, for she could not choose but be very handsome, since he knew very well he had a good taste in what was beautiful or agreeable. He desired to see her and reproached Hippolito very handsomely in telling him not to be concerned if she was as fair as he believed her, for he would moderate his desires and not think of invading any man's property again, since Clelia had shown him what he had to expect from the most charming of her sex. This put Hippolito into some concern lest the king should tax him with his former love to Clelia, but instead of that he, being a personage of admirable wit and pleasantry, he began to be very facetious and rally him:[11] 'What would become of men and women of gallantry,' says he, 'if when they engage in kindness with one another they should absolutely sell

---

[11] *rally*: to rail, to banter or joke with.

themselves and not be allowed to change when they grow weary or have a greater inclination for another. 'Tis a natural right to bestow our affections where we please and revoke them where we please. They are wretched who enjoy not that liberty. And you know, Hippolito,' continued the king, 'I glory in these maxims; for if Clelia had not been of my humor I fancy I should not have loved her so well, and perhaps I love her for nothing more than that she loves inconstancy. I once endeavored to engage her to be false to me, insomuch that I told her one day I dreamed I had seen her in your arms, and it was not long e'er I found it true. Now, Hippolito, would you take it ill the king should do as much for you as you did then for him?' 'Yes, without doubt,' says he, 'Sir, for I did it not for that purpose that you should do as much for me.' 'Well,' answers the king prophetically, 'if I do not another may.' This pleasant dialogue was soon interrupted by one less entertaining, for Clelia who had heard of Hippolito's being there, who had free admittance always to the king's presence, entered very majestically with that haughty air natural to her temper when provoked and thus accosted the king: 'Is it thus you love me, Sir, to entertain and countenance the man that has abused me? And you, perfidious traitor,' says she to Hippolito, 'how durst you approach your royal master you have injured?' 'tis hard to represent the astonishment, the fear, and the confusion of Hippolito when he heard these words, knowing how apt the king was to be seduced by this fair flatterer. For pleasant as he was with railing before, he was made to hear what was spoken and without examining any farther into the reason of Clelia's resentment cries out to her, 'You false one, without honor or truth, do you reproach me? Is this your requital of the obligation I put upon you in making you what you are?' There was harsher language in the case, which I shall forbear repeating; however Hippolito came off with flying colors and left the king and Clelia to make up the breach between themselves.

Jenisa all this while was overjoyed to think she had married her daughter so well, considering all circumstances, for Hippolito was a gallant soldier and one that had the favor of the court, for he had served in the armies of a neighboring prince who was famous for the best generals and the best troops then in the world, and he was looked upon at that time as one that was the likeliest to be preferred whenever the nation had occasion to make use of his services that way. However it was, he increased in his esteem both with the king and court so that Zarah and he lived very great and splendid and began to draw the eyes of envious people upon 'em, who stood gazing with admiration to behold their sudden rise and successful proceedings, while Hippolito insensibly[12] wound himself into the favor of Duke Albanio,[13] the king's brother and next heir to the crown, who was a warlike prince and gave encouragement to all gentlemen about court who had been bred in the field[14] or had a genius to arms. For having been educated in his younger years with drums and trumpets, though he was forced from their noise at home by a

---

[12] *insensibly*: by degrees; in a slow and subtle manner.
[13] *Albanio*: The Duke of York, later King James II.   [14] *the field*: the battlefield.

fatal necessity of relinquishing his own country to embrace a long and tedious exile, he had still a strong inclination to war as hoping to make a better security if ever he came to the crown of Albigion by the use of arms than his father had done, who lost it through the ill conduct of his soldiers.[15]

But now Zarah (for so I shall call her still) was introduced to attend upon the princess Albania,[16] who was the second daughter of the duke and afterward became Queen of Albigion. By this means she had the opportunity of improving the interest of Hippolito with Albanio's family, who were sure to succeed to the crown, and likewise to ingratiate herself with the young princess, who was then about the age that women settle their affections upon those they like best with the most lasting impressions of love and friendship. About this time it was Albania discovered a secret inclination she had to Mulgarvius,[17] a nobleman of the greatest gallantry, wit and address about the court. This passion, for so it was, Albania had stifled in her breast for some time before she could meet with one to whom she could commit an amour of such importance. But finding Zarah a woman every way qualified for a confidante, by the observation she had or the account she gave of her own life and the variety of accidents that had attended her to that time, she then made no scruple to entrust her with the narration of her love to Mulgarvius, which to that time had been a secret to all the world beside.

But Zarah, whom fortune had cut out purely for the service of her own interest, without any regard to the strict rules of honor or virtue, soon resolved within herself how she might make the best advantage of this every way, both to the satisfaction of her ambition in having the opportunity of communicating an affair of this consequence to the king and Albanio, and next in gratifying her pleasure with Mulgarvius, who was one she greatly admired and who she was glad she could appear to be as his most particular friend, when at the same time she had taken measures to frustrate any success he could pretend to gain by means of those promised hopes she designed to flatter him with about Albania.

This was a treacherous part as was ever acted by woman filled with love and ambition, for though she was resolved to gain the last, she was one who left no stone unturned to secure to herself the first, which has always made her life one continued scene of politic[18] intrigue.

No sooner was the princess retired but Zarah filled with her intended treachery hastes away to the king's apartments, where the first person she met was Mulgarvius, then in waiting,[19] who was very inquisitive what affair had brought her at that time of night to court and if he could serve her. Zarah was puzzled and knew not which way to dissemble her infidelity, but at last

[15] The second phase of the English Civil Wars began in 1648 and ended with the defeat of Charles II at Worcester in 1651. In the first phase of the Wars (1642–6), Charles I was forced to surrender and was eventually executed for treason in 1649 by the Parliamentary party.

[16] *Albania*: Princess, later Queen, Anne, who reigned 1702–14.

[17] *Mulgarvius*: John Sheffield, Duke of Buckingham. [18] *politic*: political.

[19] *in waiting*: that is, Mulgarvius is one of the courtiers who attends upon the king.

with a flattering smile answered, 'You little think, my Lord, how much the thoughts of you employ my time. Don't mistake me, you are a happier man than you think yourself; the princess loves you, ask no questions now. I have business with Albanio, and they say he is with the king.' She had no sooner done speaking but the duke came into the gallery where they were, which Zarah perceiving soon followed him and desired to speak a word in private with him, which as soon as he knew it was concerning his daughter he ordered her to go along with him back again into the king's closet.[20] Mulgarvius, who saw this interview, was very uneasy and could not imagine what mighty business Zarah could have to be closeted at that time of night with the king and Albanio. In the mean time Zarah was busily employed to acquit herself handsomely to the king, lest he should suspect she was guilty of any treachery. 'Sir,' said she with a feigned story in her mouth, 'the princess herself does not know or suspect that I am privy to the amour betwixt Mulgarvius and her, nor had I been capable of doing your majesty this piece of service by discovering an affair that may be of so great moment to the royal family in particular or to the nation in general, had not I accidentally met with Mulgarvius as your highness saw me,' said she, turning to Albanio.

'I must confess,' continued she, 'I have lately observed the princess very pensive and melancholy but never could obtain from her the cause, which increased in me a suspicion that she was in love; but I must own I had never known with whom had not Mulgarvius himself confessed it to me.' 'What,' said the king with a great deal of passion, 'would Mulgarvius own that Albania loved him, or was it only that he loved the princess? The last speaks him what I always thought him, an ambitious man, but the first declares him impudent, impolitic, and a fool.' This heat of the king put Zarah into a trembling, knowing what a falsity she had forged; she would have given the world to have withdrawn, but the duke, who was less passionate and more thoughtful, increased her fears upon her by asking how Mulgarvius durst commit such a secret to her, considering the little intimacy that appeared betwixt them two and the great confidence the king and he had placed both in her and Hippolito. This put Zarah to her wit's end for an excuse, which in this confusion she must certainly have failed of, had not the king interrupted Albanio from taking her answer by the excess of his rage. 'Sir,' said she, turning to Albanio, 'I cannot trifle with this matter; therefore I lay my commands upon you that Mulgarvius be instantly banished the court and such farther care be taken of the princess as may put me out of all fears and jealousies of this nature.'

In this disorder of the king and Albanio, Zarah found an opportunity to retire, which she could not do without tears in her eyes and the utmost confusion in her face, which Mulgarvius soon discovered as she came out of the closet, for he had waited all the time with the last impatience to guess at the

---

[20] *closet*: a private chamber.

meaning of this close cabal[21] betwixt the king, the duke, and Zarah. Having this opportunity, he was resolved not to let it slip without knowing something of this grand affair before he let her go. 'Madam,' said he, 'with all the tenderness of a lover I conjure you if you have any honor, if you have any pity or compassion for a man upon the wrack of despair, satisfy me in this point only: was not I the subject of your discourse when in the king's closet? And have you not betrayed the princess to her father and the king? Answer me, I entreat you, for my boding heart foretells me it is true. Was it not barbarous and cruel to tell me that the princess loved me when you designed to ruin me? Could you not have kept that secret from my breast?' At this rate, he went on, exclaiming against the perverseness of his stars and reproaching Zarah so passionately as if he had been rather her lover than Albania's. She all the while, though she had been confounded with vexation, listened to the music of his melting numbers and found her breast soon warmed with a relenting pity for the usage she had treated him with. Nor was she able any longer to keep on the mask which veiled her passion from Mulgarvius but cried out as in the ectasy of love, 'You are undone, my Lord, and I have made myself unhappy!' At these words she would have left him, but he used all means possible to stay her. 'For heaven's sake, Madam,' said he, 'tell me what you have done or said to my prejudice or your own that I may be able to vindicate myself if innocent or sue for mercy if guilty.' 'You are guilty,' answered she, 'for you love the princess, and I am doubly guilty, for I have betrayed both her, myself, and you.' And with that she broke out of his arms and ran down the backstairs with such violence, he was left in the greatest surprise imaginable, not knowing what to think or do. Sometimes he fancied one thing, sometimes another; now he imagined this the effect of some sudden passion of love in Zarah's breast and then again he thought this might proceed from something that Albanio had spoke against him to the king, and thus agitated betwixt hope and fear, he took as little rest as we may suppose Zarah did that night.

Next morning a message from the king was sent him, in which he was forbid the court till further orders. But good God! What confusion was he in when he received it? 'Is it possible,' said he, 'that any person much less that Zarah should be so wicked without any reason or provocation to expose me to the king's anger? It is a thing I cannot believe, I cannot penetrate into, but 'tis a thing I can never pardon.' Zarah in the mean time, being sensible what she had done would reflect upon her without[22] she found out some way to divert the storm, instanced[23] Hippolito all that night to go to the king next day and give him such an account of the matter as might entirely alter his measures against Mulgarvius, for the king was easy to believe anything that might free himself from trouble and therefore thanked Hippolito for his infor-

---

[21] *cabal*: a conspiratorial group or plot.
[22] *without*: unless.   [23] *instanced*: insisted that.

mation and was glad he had an opportunity now of showing the esteem he had for Mulgarvius, whom he caused to be called to court again very suddenly. This created many speculations abroad as well as at court to know what the secret of the king's sudden displeasure was against Mulgarvius and his as suddenly being reinstated into the king's favor again. But at last it got wind and publicly talked by everybody that Mulgarvius had made love to Albania, that she really approved of his addresses, and that Zarah was confidante to the amour, that the king had been informed of it, and that this was the cause of Mulgarvius' sudden disgrace. So that being no secret it presently blew over, and there was an end of that hurricane. But our heroic lover could never forget this treachery of Zarah's all his life after, though she courted him to her favor by all the arts and endearments proper for a woman now in her rank and station. For she had always a double plot upon him; the one was to oblige herself by his conversation, and the next was to oblige him by maintaining him in the good graces of the princess, whom he had always the vanity to believe had a kindness in reserve for him. And therefore notwithstanding he could never heartily forgive her, he carried a fair outside to her to show that either his politeness or his good manners, or however, both together were able to surmount his ill nature.

In a short time after this, Rolando dies, and Albanio succeeds to the crown, when Hippolito became one of the greatest favorites of his court. And now there was no longer need to make use of Mulgarvius for any designs they had in view, but Hippolito and Zarah's interest was sufficient to obtain what they could reasonably desire. The king, first of all, as his future merits showed he deserved advanced him to one of the chief commands of his army, and afterwards made him a grandee of Albigion.[24] Zarah at the same time was not wanting to establish the interest of her family firm[25] as well as that of her own. And though her sister had good assurance of all the favors Albanio's queen[26] could bestow upon her, yet her assistance was not wanting to make Onelio[27] viceroy of Iberia. And notwithstanding this had not all the good effects they expected from so great a design, they made still sure work against all accidents that might happen hereafter to engage the princess Albania, who was certain in herself or posterity to succeed her father. So that they took two strings to their bow and were resolved whenever either of them broke they would still have something to trust to.

But it was not long e'er Zarah herself grew jealous of some powers at court growing too great for her or the princess either to master. She did not like the

[24] In 1665 John Churchill became a page of the Duke of York (later King James II) and in 1667 he entered the army, where he rose rapidly under York's patronage and in 1685 helped crush the rebellion led by the Duke of Monmouth, for which he was promoted to major-general.

[25] That is, to establish firmly the interest of her family.

[26] Albanio's queen: James's first wife, Anne Hyde, died in 1671, and his queen was Mary of Modena, whom he married in 1673.

[27] Onelio: Richard Talbot, Duke of Tyrconnel, second husband of Frances Jenyns, Sarah's sister, appointed Viceroy of Ireland by James II in 1685.

queen taking upon her so much, and particularly her intimacy with Volpone,[28] who was her creature, and she saw the queen had entirely gained him to her lure by some arts she was sensible no ambitious or covetous man could resist. Therefore, she presently raised a misunderstanding betwixt Albania and the queen, being continually near the persons both of one and the other, in which controversy she influenced both Hippolito and Volpone, pretending there was a great deal in it that concerned the good of the nation and the succession of Albanio to the crown. Indeed, there was such just apprehensions of danger as she spoke of, but they proceeded not from that cause she wanted them to pique the queen for but from a private grudge the queen had against Zarah, who she observed influenced Albania in all her actions. And therefore she could never have any intimacy with her but what immediately was communicated to Zarah and so of course came to Hippolito and Volpone, both whom were always on the watch lest the queen by her subtle insinuations should alienate the affection of Albania from those private friends of hers and procure her other acquaintance of her own interest, which was necessary to persuade her into a good opinion of the queen and the indulgent fondness of the king her father, who at the same time were contriving to deprive her of her hopes of succession to the crown and only wanted to make her an instrument in her own ruin.

This matter was long in agitation to bring Albania into the interest of the king's designs, but their measures were always broke or interrupted by Zarah, Hippolito, or Volpone, who still counterplotted all the stratagems laid by the court till they were let into the secret and rewarded liberally by the king for their wise management of Albania, whom they were directed to keep in ignorance from the great designs they had in view. All this time there was one Solano,[29] a perfect Machiavel,[30] and one who was secretly in the interest of Zarah but had not at that time declared himself. This subtle statesman the king employs, caresses, and in short opens to him all the secrets of his heart, so that nothing was done now without Solano. He governed the king as absolutely as Zarah did Albania; no designs were set on foot but what he was first made privy to, and none were executed without his particular direction. He was a man of Zarah's principles and Volpone's politics, *would sell his Master for a groat, change his religion for policy, and betray his country for nought*, and therefore had this gentleman been subject to revenge, having shown us what wonders he was capable of performing, what might not his enemies have expected from him? But as it was not sufficient for the legislators of the Greeks only to understand philosophy but also to put it in practice, so it was his pleasure to

[28] *Volpone*: Sidney, first Earl of Godolphin (1645-1712) was a close ally of Marlborough and a trusted financial adviser of Charles II, who made him First Lord of the Treasury in 1684.

[29] *Solano*: Charles Spencer, third Earl of Sunderland, who married Marlborough's daughter in 1700 and was made a secretary of state in 1706.

[30] *Machiavel*: after the Italian political philosopher, Niccolò Machiavelli (1469-1527), whose name because of the policies described in his treatise on statecraft, *The Prince* (1532), became synonymous with unscrupulous and ruthless politics.

profess the precepts of the Stoics,[31] and particularly that of taming his passions before he would sit at the helm to prescribe the rules of government.

The obligations which Albigion owes to this great man render her incapable of acknowledgement, and the thanks they owe his policy are much greater than the satisfaction they receive from it, though he made a bold attempt to purchase the benedictions of the kingdom and by the productions of strange and unheard of revolutions to furnish the rest of the world with matter both for envy and admiration. For without being anything less than a barbarian, no man ought endeavor to blemish the fame of his politics who has made Albigion flourish so much in policy as it has done of late.

But to proceed: Solano was the very creature both of the king and queen, so that all foreign princes made their court to him as they did afterwards to Hippolito. This uncommon favorite of the king's being so entirely master of all the transactions at the council board and everywhere else and not making the least court to Albania, by which means Zarah might pry into some of his mysterious doings, perplexed her very much and she could no longer bear the torment of living ignorant amidst the variety of cabals that were then carried out without her privity.[32] For Volpone and Hippolito were both ignorant of the designs Solano was advancing, in which he acted with such refined subtlety that he made even the king himself a stalking horse[33] to his dexterous treachery. Zarah on the other hand, perceiving to what a height things were carried and how Albania was now like to become no other than a pensioner to that crown she had expectations to wear, resolves with all her might and power to thwart the designs of Solano, which she by this promoted to the last degree.

Away she hastes to Albania with all the speed revenge and jealousy could make in an enraged woman. 'Madam,' said she to the princess, 'prepare to hear the dismal news I am obliged in duty to tell you: that you are undone, and Solano has contrived your ruin; I cannot doubt but you must understand the fatal consequence of what is now transacted by the king your father, who has at most excluded you from hopes to the crown of Albigion. There was never so notorious a thing done in the world as is now advised by Solano. The king asks counsel no more of Salopius,[34] Volpone, or Hippolito. Therefore, Madam, for heaven's sake, see the queen no more; I'll spread it then abroad that she has insulted you since Prince Cambrio's[35] birth. The nation then will pity and protect you. Then leave the court, give it out as if the king had slighted you and fly to some popular place for safety; the court will be

---

[31] *Stoics*: school of philosophy founded by Zeno of Citium (in Cyprus) *c.*300 BC. A materialistic philosophy, stoicism was best known for advising control of the passions.

[32] *privity*: knowledge of secrets shared with others.

[33] *stalking horse*: one trained to conceal the hunter while stalking; any device used to cover one's real purpose.

[34] *Salopius*: Charles Talbot, twelfth Earl and first Duke of Shrewsbury.

[35] *Prince Cambrio*: James Stuart (1688–1766), the son of James and Mary of Modena. There were rumors at his birth that he was not actually their son.

too much embarrassed to take notice of your journey if it be true as 'tis reported that Prince Aurantio[36] is marching with an army to oppose the king's designs.

'Zarah,' answered the princess, 'what danger is there for me to fear that I should fly the court? Is not the king infinitely fond and kind to me? And has he not this day ordered me two hundred thousand florins out of his treasury?' 'But Madam,' said Zarah, 'what is that to the depriving you of a crown? Besides, it is dangerous to stay when the nation appears in a disposition to revolt and forsake your father.' 'And therefore,' says Albania, 'would you have me forsake him and become the first rebel against my father, to set Aurantio my brother on the throne, and so lest I be thus deprived by my father, run on headlong and by this means deprive myself? But why do you persuade me to forsake the king, since Hippolito is obliged both by his command and duty to attend him? And gratitude should tie you closely to his interest, since he always generously promoted yours.' 'I own you have convinced me of my duty and allegiance,' answered Zarah, 'but consider, Madam, the zeal you have expressed for the religion of your country, which you must leave without[37] you leave the king. You know, Madam,' continued she, 'I hate Aurantio nor do I love the love the princess, but 'tis for your sake alone that I advise this counsel. I'll instantly go to Hippolito, Volpone, and Salopius, see to persuade 'em all to leave the king now when he least expects it.' 'Can you prevail on them, think you, to act such base ingratitude?' said Albania, 'and would you persuade your husband to be a treacherous villain to his master and a traitor to this king? As for Volpone and Salopius, I always took 'em for statesmen, politicians, gamesters, and consequently *****,[38] but for Hippolito he is a soldier and should have more honor than to betray his prince.' 'Well, Madam,' says Zarah, 'if you depend upon honor I hope you never expect to succeed to the crown of Albigion.'

Upon this they parted, and the next news that was heard was that Hippolito had forsaken the king and sent him a letter of excuse wherein it plainly appeared he did not leave him for interest or honor but purely as Zarah had told the princess out of a principle of religion. This soon was made public and became the subject of discourse and admiration of all the court. Everybody wondered to hear of Hippolito's defection; some thought it was only a feint to try how the army stood affected to the king, others supposed he had taken some private disgust against Duraceo the general. But at last all the world was satisfied he had deserted his master and embraced the interest of Prince Aurantio. Good Heavens! What exclamations did the king's friends make

[36] *Prince Aurantio*: William of Orange and Stadtholder of the United Provinces of the Netherlands. Married in 1677 to James II's Protestant daughter, Mary, he was invited in 1688 by the opposition to James to assume the British throne. Landing in England with his army, he marched unopposed to London and became king.

[37] *without*: unless.

[38] *****: thus in Manley's text; as Princess Albania says something too strong to print?

against him, the army cursed him, and everybody despised him so that he was forced to retire a time for fear of enraging the populace, who though they were embittered against his master they could not forgive this treachery of the servant.

On the other hand, Zarah was far enough out of the reach of the tumult, having with much persuasion drawn Albania along with her. And now the spirits of the people being on the ferment, occasioned partly by the mismanagement of state affairs directed by Solano and partly by the advance of Aurantio's army, flocked in great numbers to Albania as another assertor of their liberty and freedoms. Zarah all this time pleased herself to think how she had obtained her ends by ruining all the designs of Solano, hearing every day how he was cursed by the people and what grievous crimes were laid to his charge; that the whole turn of affairs that were prejudicial to the king were laid at his door. So that a great many good people there began to pity the king and thought he had been too wretchedly abused by his ministers and particularly by those that appeared at last to slight him. But this touching too near upon Zarah, notwithstanding she could with pleasure hear Solano reflected on, she thought it was high time to interpose and let the world know how barbarous Albano and his queen had been to the whole nation in general and how unkind they had been in particular to Albania then amongst them. This succeeded as she could wish, for the whole country expressed their value and esteem for the princess by paying her all the honors and respect due to her birth and character. In a little time they heard Albanio almost distracted with the infidelity he met with among those in whom he most entirely confided, fled from the hasty advances of Aurantio after he had endeavored to consult Solano without so much as suspecting him false, or however not in the least imagining that he was the person that had designedly betrayed him to Aurantio. But yet e'er he could leave his country he was resolved to try Hippolito, but as he was inquiring for him a fatal letter soon informed him he was miserable beyond redemption. This stroke left him no room for thought but made him precipitate his flight and banished him from Albigion forever.

And now the time was come when Zarah found a happy opportunity of flattering Albania. 'Madam,' says she with dissembled tears, 'your royal father, just as he was, and kind to you, has been obliged to quit his throne. Solano, whom you suspected always, has been the author of his misfortunes. Aurantio, your hateful brother, revels in his palace at Lodunum and all the people's voices crown him king.' 'You ought not, Zarah,' says the princess, 'to reflect since you might have well foreseen the consequence that would ensue when you advised me hither.' 'Madam,' answered she, 'I dreamed not that Aurantio would be king, or that Albanio would be forced to fly, but only that he might be brought to reason and your just right asserted to the crown.' During this discourse a messenger came in and told Albania that Solano, who was supposed by everybody to have been the king's sincerest friend as he was his secret counsellor, was the chief instrument that betrayed him to Aurantio, with whom he was at present and declared himself publicly in the prince's interest. At this narration, Zarah (who was disappointed in what she had done to oppose Solano) fell down in a violent rage and cursed herself a thousand times. The princess, surprised at what had happened and not being able to guess the cause, left the room and Zarah to her passion, thus exclaiming against her own mismanagement, 'Weak woman,' cried she, 'and unfit for those designs thou art surely born for that could not penetrate into Solano's treachery. I might have known a man like him, bred up in all state craft, could never design what he pretended or was so shallow as to make pretensions of any thing that he designed. Poor fool, is it for this Hippolito betrayed his benefactor? Is it for this Volpone has lost his royal bubble?[39] Is it for this I have ruled Albania? And is it for this at last I must repent? I hate myself for such a thought but worst of all I hate Aurantio who occasions it.' In this way she spent the remaining part of the day.

By this time Aurantio had settled himself at Lodunum, and Albania was invited to the court again, where Zarah had the daily mortification to see her rival in dissimulation and state politics flourish and carressed by the very man she most abhorred. She could have killed herself for spite, but finding that disquietude was vain, she resolved to attempt whatever statesmen she could meet withal fit for a competitor to Solano to try if she could counterplot and frustrate all the designs laid by Aurantio. But still to increase the misfortunes of Zarah and make more work for her intriguing brain, Aurantia (sister to Albania) was sent for to be crowned with the prince her husband king and queen of Albigion. This was a stroke beyond the rack of her invention to have thought of and now beyond the power of her malice to prevent, so that she imagined herself miserable beyond redress. But being of a restless and indefatigable spirit, she was resolved never to sit still till she had eased herself of this oppression by satiating her revenge either on herself or enemies, to favor which design the new king takes into his council Salopius, a man every way as well qualified to betray him as Solano was his predecessor. This gave new life to Zarah, who knew Salopius was a man of wit and intrigue, that he had formerly been very amorous upon her, and that she thought such a spark once kindled could not be so soon extinguished in one that she knew had a great deal of love in him and very little *****.[40] Besides he still retained a secret kindness for Albanio, which she understood how to improve to the best advantage.

It happened about this time there was a great design on foot to penetrate into Picardia by the way of Dunecclesia,[41] a place of vast importance to the king of Albigion as well upon the account that he was at war with the prince

---

[39] *bubble*: a dupe or victim of a plot.

[40] *****: Perhaps Manley means by these asterisks that Salopius is impotent.

[41] *Picardia . . . Dunecclesia*: Picardy is a region and at that time a province in northern France, although Manley's Picardia seems to refer to all of France; Dunecclesia is the port town of Dunkirk in northern France, which withstood a bombardment by Anglo-Dutch forces in 1694.

of that country[42] as that he was a friend to Albania in the recovery of his own dominions. This affair was carried on with great secrecy and nobody thought fit to be entrusted with it but Salopius and Hippolito, who by his interest was introduced to Aurantio as a proper person to execute the design or at least to advise with about it, by reason he was allowed to be a good soldier and a man of great conduct. Hippolito was now reckoned to be as firm in the interest of Aurantio as any officer employed about his person and in his service, and accordingly the whole plan of the design was communicated to him, with strict instructions to divulge it to no person living upon any pretence whatsoever; but Zarah, who was always upon the watch to take advantage, observed something a doing more than usual by the daily attendance of Hippolito at court and therefore having the ascendant over him was resolved if possible to penetrate into the bottom of this affair. And accordingly she laid a train for him which succeeded, otherwise he had run the risk of a perpetual noise in his ears, which to free himself from he was resolved to venture the displeasure of his prince and the forfeit of honor.

Zarah by this means having gained her point, away she hastes to Salopius, being assured she could work upon him to give her the opportunity of transmitting this account to Onolia,[43] her sister, at Albanio's court; she had no sooner met with him[44] but with a flattering smile: 'My Lord,' says she, 'how glad am I to meet with a person of your merit, so happily placed at the helm of the state, whereby you have the opportunity of showing your large acquirements to all the world and your known affabilities to your particular friends. Your lordship has had always the character of a gallant kind-natured man, that I am sure you cannot think it flattery in me who have made trial of it to tell you so.'

'Madam,' answered he to Zarah, 'the only way to convince me that you do not flatter me is to try how far I would extend that good nature you are pleased to compliment me with to your service.' ''Tis but a trifle,' says she, 'I would ask of you, but I know 'tis contrary to the trust reposed in you to grant me a conveyance of some little domestic occurrences to Onolia, my sister at Albanio's court; though I am confident you cannot but retain some small respect for that unhappy prince, if you could imagine without a fault that I could be guilty of giving any intelligence to that court I helped to banish hence. But I know, my lord, you are sensible my interest is so firmly knit to Albania and hers to the present disposition of affairs here, that it would be impossible in me to have a thought tending that way.' Zarah pressing this argument so very affectionately gave Salopius reason to suspect there was something more in her request than he at first apprehended, he therefore made some excuses to try her a little further. But finding she grew warmer in her request, he was then confirmed in his suspicion and was not a little glad

---

[42] *prince of that country*: Louis XIV of France.
[43] *Onolia*: Frances Talbot Tyrconnel (née Jenyns), sister of Sarah Jenyns Churchill.
[44] *him*: that is, Salopius.

to find one of her management had undertaken to do something that he was unwilling however she should know, pleased him to have performed. Upon this he consented to her desires, and immediately dispatched her intelligence, all the while being tickled with a secret pleasure to think he had discovered this without running the hazard of letting her know it was agreeable to his inclinations, for nobody knew her character better than he, and he was resolved never to trust her with any secret but what was indispensably necessary to the maintaining both her honor and her interest; for though she might be prevailed with to sacrifice one to the service of the other, yet she would never part with the last without it was to gratify that noble passion of revenge, which is the darling vice of her sex and was not a stranger to Zarah's breast.

It was not long after this e'er Aurantio had notice his well-laid stratagem was discovered, he betrayed, and his expedition frustrated. Away he sends for Salopius and Hippolito, both [of] whom persisted in their innocence and that they were ignorant of any discovery that had been made by them; though at the same time Hippolito could not but be conscious of what he had said, and Salopius of what he had done. Aurantio was galled at the very soul to think such a great design should miscarry through treachery, and he be thought so little a statesman as not to know the men better that he entrusted; never was prince so perplexed with ministers, nor knew he how to help himself, for still as he changed he was but in a worse condition. Sometimes he thought to please the friends of Albanio by employing them, but they betrayed him. Then he took the sworn foes both of him and their country, but they were true to nothing but their interest. Hippolito was vexed within himself to think what a strange opinion the king would entertain of him after such a betraying of his trust and therefore went to Zarah with all the passion of a man justly provoked to anger. 'Madam,' said he, 'What fury has possessed you to seek my ruin by your base designs? Did you not study it to satisfy your foul revenge when I forsook Albanio, and now you have contrived this to bring disgrace upon me from Aurantio? 'tis you have done it, no other could; no other durst but you. Has not Aurantio advanced me to honor as Albanio did? And will you bury it while fresh and green? Good Heavens, contain me that I act not some rash deed to make us both forever infamous.' With that he flung away and left her to her own melancholy reflections, which however prevailed not upon her to alter her disposition; but she cursed her ill fortune which had reduced Hippolito to the extremity of serving Aurantio, yet was mad to think he should be taken for a villain, though she was glad of the cause that gave the prince that occasion, notwithstanding she had betrayed him so basely. Hippolito's anger was not the thing which troubled her, but the thoughts of his being no more employed by Aurantio whereby she would be deprived of the opportunity of giving intelligence.[45] For she would not but have done what she did for all the world, and therefore that she might be sure to know what was always in agitation, she resolved how contrary soever it might be

---

[45] *intelligence*: here and elsewhere this means news or information about secret political affairs.

to her present inclinations to strike up a friendship with Solano, in order to which she had made an appointment that evening with Aranio[46] his friend, where love as well as politics was to be the subject of their conference.

While Salopius, being sensible of the favor he had bestowed on Zarah so lately, resolved she should serve his ends in a proposal that included as much treachery in it as that he had transacted and therefore proposed immediately to go and see her that night in disguise. He had not patience to stay long, but as soon as 'twas night he went away in such a disguise as proved like that Aranio was to come in and being come to the apartment he found only an old Moor[47] at the door whom he sent to Zarah to tell her a particular friend of her acquaintance desired to speak with her in the chamber of repose. He made choice of this chamber as the most proper for his design. The old Moor innocently told her there was a particular friend of her acquaintance desired to speak with her in the chamber of repose. Zarah hearing of this made no question at all but Aranio was the man and without farther inquiring what kind of man he was or any other consideration, she goes to the place of assignation. Had she made the least reflection on the message, she could not have been so deceived, nor have exposed herself so easily. It was not the custom of her gallant to use her thus, or to see her usually in this chamber. But those who are in love, as Zarah was, are subject to greater oversights than these; she knew Aranio was not to see her till late at night, yet she apprehended nothing in this amorous expectation which tantalized her extremely and kept her in a moral inquietude whether he came or came not. There needed no help to hurry her away when the time drew near. Women who have been in love will easily confess there is nothing so hard as to be prudent on such occasions, and that the name of their lover when expected has made them start up for joy and run to meet him e'er they know whether he were come. The passionate Zarah having given up herself to be led blindfold where she thought love waited for her borrowed wings of that god to carry her the sooner into that chamber where the Moor had first conducted Salopius. There was not any light there, but this did not surprise her, it not being usual to place any there when Aranio came.

Our gallant who waited for her took her by the hand and led her to the farther end of the chamber, where he was so loath to lose time for making use of the occasion that embracing her with some transport he had almost put it out of her power to defend herself. Zarah thinking this action too violent to be Aranio's began to mistrust, and having given him his liberty till then, she did the utmost in her power to resist him. This resistance she made after the kindness she expressed at the first was observed by Salopius and made him then sensible he was taken for some other; so that having no hopes to succeed any other ways, or at least not venturing to fortune without further dallying

---

[46] *Aranio*: uncertain just who is meant here, although Patricia Köster speculates that it may be either Charles Butler, Earl of Arran in Ireland, or James Douglas, fourth Duke of Hamilton, referred to at the time as the 'Scotch Earl of Arran'.

[47] *old Moor*: probably meant to indicate a black servant.

71

he made his last efforts and rendered those of Zarah so useless that she lay at his mercy. But it was not long e'er this transported lover had allayed his passion, when he would have withdrawn without saying a word. But the lady, who was resolved to know who had been so bold with her honor, held him fast and refused to let him go till he discovered himself. When Salopius spoke: 'Madam,' said he, 'I hope you don't regret this happy moment I have had, though I own it equal to the hazard of my life and honor, both which I ventured to oblige you.' At those words Zarah trembled, partly from the confusion of what had happened and partly from the words that were spoken, fearing lest Salopius had made a discovery of her intelligence. However, she resolved to dissemble it a little further that he might not think she understood him in this hurry of her spirits. 'For God's sake, who e'er you are,' answered she, 'don't continue to fright a helpless woman whom you have thus injured by surprise!' 'I thought, Madam,' said he with all the softness love could inspire him with to soothe her up for the violence he had offered, 'I am happier than e'er you designed me; though I have ever been your lover, I am now your slave, your devoted Salopius; accept therefore, I beseech you, Madam, the sacrifice I here make you.' 'Bless me!' cries Zarah, 'is this you, my lord? And could you find no other way to wrest a favor from me but this unprecedented one?' 'Madam,' answered he, 'if all the passion man can have for a woman is not capable to justify the crime I committed against you, you ought to pardon me at least, having suffered that for you which still fills my soul with grief and confusion. Though yet to serve you I will not spare the doing myself any violence I am capable of; and if I have wronged you, I know how to punish myself for it,' attempting to go.

'I should be heartily sorry,' said she, 'so extraordinary a person as you should part with an ill opinion of me, and that I know not how to value your friendship.' Salopius, extremely surprised at this answer so full of respect, cried out, 'I love you, Madam, and love you with a passion as tender as it is lasting. And though I committed an innocent treason, it was the power of your charms provoked me to it. However, I am more in love than any man living, and what will become of me unless you pity me?' This dialogue continued for some time, till Zarah recovered her surprise so far as to make inquiries after what was doing afresh at court, while Salopius was fond to discover to her all that was consulted. He told her the king resented the last discovery so heinously that he was resolved to oblige Albania to discard her, else to forfeit his displeasure and so incur the danger of being thought a public enemy to the state by countenancing one that had betrayed it. This nettled Zarah so it disturbed all the pleasure she could otherwise have taken in Salopius's company at that time, since he was a person so likely to be serviceable to her in her future designs.

It was now the king sent Aurantia to her sister on purpose to persuade her not to employ Zarah any farther in her service and to give her the secret reasons why. But Zarah had so managed the matter with Albania as to prepossess her with the thoughts that her sister was come on a private message from the king to prevail with her to relinquish her future title to Albigion, or at least to do something that would be prejudicial to her and her posterity, and in order to that they designed to engage her highness to turn her out of her service upon some pretensions or other she heard they had formed against her to facilitate their designs. So that when the queen was arrived at the gates of Albania's palace, which was then in the country, which she had chose on purpose to be retired from court, she had a message ready prepared for her, that Albania was not in a disposition to receive visits, though it was from the queen her sister. This you may be sure could not but afflict the good queen, who was full of love and affection to Albania, being a woman that was always compassionate and showed a tender regard to all her subjects. But the king, who was naturally passionate in himself, though he governed it more than most men were capable of doing in the public administration of affairs, yet he took such notice of this carriage to Aurantia that he scarce forgot it all his reign after. And since he could not reach Zarah, whom he never thought innocent, he showed visible marks of his resentment to Albania, and neglected Hippolito a long time after. Though it was not so long e'er Zarah remembered the king again, when he had laid a second stratagem to penetrate into the enemy's country by the way of Briescia;[48] but this succeeded worse than the first, and was so well known to the enemy that the whole nation began to take notice of it as a miscarriage that redounded much to the dishonor of Aurantio, who had more people about him, some said, than Zarah that studied to confound all his devices and render him odious to the people, who then began to murmur grievously against his reign. Others there were that extolled those very persons the court thought instrumental to all the treacheries that happened in the public counsels of the nation.

At last Aurantio saw there was no good to be done without employing those persons who appeared to thwart his counsels; not but he saw at the same time they were persons fitly qualified for public business, being men of discerning parts and quick judgments. Besides, Salopius began now to appear backward and refuse every thing the king would have put upon him, for he never suspected him at all, notwithstanding his treachery, because he deceived him by his indifference and shyness to be employed, when his chief reasons were he loved his pleasure too much to serve any prince, and he loved Albanio too much to serve Aurantio to any purpose. Another thing was, [that] Solano, who transacted all affairs behind the curtain, was now become as one person by his strict alliance with Hippolito and therefore recommended him to the king's favor, who saw in him everything he could desire to his designs and therefore received him again, both into the counsel and the army. Nor was it long e'er Volpone, who had likewise allied his family to Zarah's, was employed in the most secret counsels, so that she had no room left now

---

[48] *Briescia*: the city of Brest, a seaport in western France.

to entertain envy or revenge; yet still she had not what she chiefly wanted, Aurantio's absence. For though the queen was gone, her fears were greater still lest any accident should intervene to cross Albania of the crown, for there were all her hopes; and Fortune, which had pursued her close in every adventure of her life, resolving not to keep her long in suspense, now made way for all her expectations to succeed by the sudden death of Aurantio and Albania's accession to the throne of Albigion.[49]

Now the whole scene of affairs was turned to Zarah's will and pleasure; she could look nowhere round her without tempting objects of grandeur, riches and ambition; everything that she saw flattered her, everybody made their court to her, while the formality of Albania's state hindered her of the secret pleasure Zarah enjoyed among crowds of fawning courtiers.

The government of the kingdom was in a manner in her hands, and whoever expected favors or rewards must apply themselves to Zarah by whom all was granted as the pipe that conveyed the royal bounty to the subject. Past ages have furnished us with examples of this nature, and posterity may see the like but not equal to this, for it may be said without exaggerating upon the subject too much Albania took the crown from her own head to put it on Zarah's. This great rise of hers and her power at court gained her the title of Queen Zarah among foreigners, who knew not the constitution of Albigion where it has been a usual thing for kings to uncrown themselves and place it on their favorites. This raised her many enemies among the ambitious grandees, who envied her greatness; yet she had a particular way with her of monopolizing all perquisites to her self that gained her more hatred from the court followers. But the most considerable and dangerous enemies she had were Rossensis[50] and Mulgarvius, the last of which retained still a relish of her old grudge to him.

Statesmen and favorites of this kind are seldom known to agree, the first aiming at the good of the state and the felicity of their monarch, the last only striving to enrich themselves though upon the ruin of their country, are opposites to one another. And consequently when favorites flourish the state languishes, for persons of their characters being rivals to one another generally go cunningly to work and interrupt all other business going forward but their own.

These persons, though they were all of great spirits, they were too prudent to declare open war against one another and let the world see their blind side and who had the apparent advantage over the other. Albania, on the other hand, was very wise and of a peaceable disposition, too cautious as yet to side with either to the prejudice of the other; but having a kindness for both Rossensis and Mulgarvius and knowing Zarah had a secret distaste against them as persons that were only capable of influencing her, she never gave Zarah the encouragement of speaking anything to the prejudice of either of them.

[49] William III died after a fall from his horse while hunting in March 1702 and Anne became queen.
[50] *Rossensis*: Laurence Hyde, third Earl of Rochester.

And now we must suppose Hippolito advanced to the highest pinnacle of honor he was capable of having bestowed upon him as a subject; and indeed none could be too great for his services, considering all their circumstances. He merited a just esteem both from the court and country; everybody now admired the queen, that she had confirmed the wise choice of Aurantio, for all the world spoke well of Hippolito and extolled his gallantry. He was looked upon abroad as if he had been sovereign of Albigion from which he had been sent; and the same honors were paid him in the army as they use to crowned heads. Thus laden with honors at home and victory abroad, he fought, he conquered, and he triumphed over all the heroes of his age, nor was he less in his family than in himself. Volpone, his nearest ally, was absolute at home as he abroad; under his administration the nation flourished in wealth and riches. Soldiers turned usurers in their tents, and sailors in their cabins; the merchant went no more abroad for gain but traded safer with the government. The queen sat easy in her throne nor felt the weight that crowns do give, and all the people wondered at the tranquillity the nation felt in those blest days of Zarah and Volpone's reign.

But there was still one obstacle to all their flattering felicities, for what human happiness has yet been without a 'but?' The ecclesiastics of Albigion were very restless and uneasy at this tide of government, which like a torrent threatened the destruction of their constitution, which as all wise men of the nation thought was the foundation of Albigion's future peace and tranquillity. The priests began now, as they had all the reason in the world, to exclaim against the modern invasion of their rights and privileges from the pulpit and to admonish their audience boldly to adhere to the principles of religion their forefathers had taught 'em and purchased for 'em as an inheritance, at the price of their precious blood. They were daring enough at all times and in all places, even in their public assemblies, to point out, as we may say in plain English, the persons whom they saw were the authors and promoters of those mischiefs that were then brought upon their function and daily like to increase to the prejudice of the present establishment.

This management, which was thrown upon Zarah and Volpone, caused great alterations in the ministry, and no small feuds among the people, whose heats rise to that degree they were ready to knock those on the head who appeared to vindicate the religion of the state which the others were endeavoring to laugh out of countenance and stigmatize all those that were its faithful assertors with infamous nicknames to render them odious to the populace. But this hellish stratagem so far failed of its designed success that it produced quite contrary effects, and those very persons whose fame and reputations they designed to ruin became the darling patriots of all the wise, disinterested, and unprejudiced people of Albigion and may in future times become a scourge to those impolitic statesmen who now envy them the honor that they themselves have established upon them throughout their country, and it is not unlikely they may prove a thorn in the sides of those men who thought to stab them to the quick.

If Mulgarvius and Rossensis be thrown out of the ministry, who knows but Volpone and Fuimus[51] may be drawn into the mire? Obornius[52] was as great in the days of Rolando, who loved him as tenderly as e'er Albania could Volpone; but yet this wise and just favorite minister durst not be trusted by his master through the streets of Lodonum for fear of the enraged multitude. 'Tis a happiness a statesman knows not how sufficiently to value not to be too popular. Hippolito has managed this beyond example; he never made himself the people's idol and consequently the people will never make him their sacrifice.

What though Danterius[53] was made a stalking horse to the state? They were forced to part with him before they could catch the game Volpone was hunting for; and though the Cambrian[54] be a tamer beast, he's but an ass at best whose ears will scare the partridge before they can drive them to their nets. Solano, the beardless legate, will return well fraught with long experience, and then the state will have no further use for making shifts.

But after all this while these intricate affairs of church and state perplexed the good Queen Zarah; for though her royal mistress was still living and reigned absolute queen o'er all her subjects' hearts, yet the weight and burden of the government pressed heavy on Zarah's shoulders, which she like a second Atlas kindly sustained without the least return of thanks from that ungrateful country of Albigion, that country that could never speak well of her protectors and deliverers but like an untamed horse was always apt to kick those that dared to ride her.

Nothing grieved Zarah like this ungovernable spirit of the Albigionois, who would not bear to think of being rid with side saddle, having had their backs galled so much before in the female reign of Rolando.

But notwithstanding all these difficulties, Zarah was resolved to mount on the stirrup of Hippolito's fame and conduct and drive her beasts forward by the help of Volpone's rod; for though it would not smart as some other rods do it had a strange faculty in it of tickling such cattle as were froward into the most pleasant gentle paces imaginable. By this means she got on the backs of the most able pads in the whole kingdom of Albigion, some of which she rid to death, others she jaded, and some she rides still.[55]

There were two very serviceable black nags she would gladly have rid and used all the gentle means she could think of to manage, but they would never submit to be backed; they had been too long used to run at their own liberty. It was not in her power ever to get 'em bridled with either curb or snaffle.[56] There was a milk-white steed that was thought would have made one of the usefulest beasts about the court; this she managed so dexterously as to be able to mount him. But setting forward of a journey where she designed to ride

[51] *Fuimus*: Charles Montagu, Earl of Halifax (1661–1715).
[52] *Obornius*: Thomas Osborne, first Duke of Leeds.
[53] *Danterius*: Daniel Finch, second Earl of Nottingham.
[54] *Cambrian*: Robert Harley, first Earl of Oxford.
[55] *pad*: a horse with a plodding gait; *jaded*: from jade, a broken down or useless horse.
[56] *curb or snaffle*: a chain or strap that serves with a bit (a snaffle) to restrain a horse.

him, he kicked her highness off at the court gate, which so disgraced her she never could endure a white horse since; and some say it had such an effect upon her that she begins to hate every thing that is white, will scarce bear clean linen, and cannot endure lawn sleeves.[57]

A small time after these little disgraces which Zarah met with, the great esteem Mulgarvius gained among the patriots of Albigion did not a little perplex her, for he had now both the ear of Albania and the affections of the people, and nature and merit both had furnished him with a capacity fit for authority. And that which vexed Zarah worst of all was that they had given him so much independency; for had he been one that would have suffered himself to be carried away by the persuasions of flattery, he would easily become a prey to her alluring arts.

This was so insupportable to her that she could not rest till she had communicated her resentments to Volpone of continuing Mulgarvius still about the court to be an eyesore to her and spy upon all her actions. Volpone submissively told her all things should be according to her mind in a short time; but as yet she ought to wait a few days, saying that great politicians (such as himself undoubtedly) had found by precedents that peace and union preserves a state, that love maintains it, that ambition and novelty destroys it, that moderation banishes hatred and quarrels, that suavity suppresses envy. 'Besides,' continued he, 'amongst so many illustrious qualities as we have observed in Albania, I will not omit the supreme virtue of moderation wherewith she favors her friends and even her very enemies too, and which we both know by experience she possesses in the highest measure; and that her irascible part hath never been able to surmount it. Wherein I take much more notice of their good luck who have the benefit of it than of their own deserts; and of the influences which come from her than of the subject which makes her lay aside severity and show herself favorable and merciful. I mean her clemency, which is the judge of vengeance and the moderatrix of power when there is question of lessening the punishments, which a person of authority may inflict upon such as are under her obedience.'

'This virtue is a gift of piety, a sweetness of spirit; for clemency is of an heroic essence, and the defection of that active and unbridled passion which oppugns[58] it, and seems to check it, is the most wonderful effect that they who exercise this virtue are able to produce and the victory gotten over it is much more glorious than that which is won by force of arms.'

Here Zarah interrupted him, saying, 'Sir, you put me in mind of an act of this virtue which she exercised some days since at my request in the behalf of ——.' 'Therefore it was that I spoke of it,' answered Volpone, 'because I was present when you begged that person's pardon, and when the addresses of your eloquence easily obtained what you desired of a soul already disposed

---

[57] *linen . . . lawn sleeves*: undergarments, and lace cuffs made of cotton or linen worn by both men and women.

[58] *oppugns*: to oppose, contradict, call into question.

thereto by virtue; and for this cause it is I told you clemency favors as well enemies as friends; and that we must hold ourselves happy when fortune makes us meet with more necessary motions to pardon in them whom we petition than merit in the offenders. Not but that your discourse might have wrought the same effect even upon barbarians because you took Albania upon a good advantage, but that with another you would not have succeeded so well.'

'Sir,' said Zarah, 'I will only tell you for what reason I undertook this affair, which was accidental, for finding him alone in the ante-chamber I began to discourse with him about the cause of his disgrace; whereupon I observed in him a great moderation of spirit and much serenity of mind, and as he was going into the council chamber I took occasion to speak more freely to him. Upon which I undertook his peace with Albania after this manner. "Madam," said I, "it is a human accident to have an advantage over one's enemies; but to pardon when we overcome is a divine virtue. Whence it comes that we prefer clemency before rigor. Pardon him, therefore, Madam, and if you will not grant it for his sake who hath offended you nor for mine who deserves not this favor, yet do it for your own honor, which will be much more glorious for you than to free yourself from a weak enemy. An enemy! I style him false, for I protest to you he has as many good wishes for you as you can think of ways to destroy him, and he hath already received punishment sufficient from the sense of his fault and from the terror you have given him. Break therefore the neck of your indignation and by forbearing to punish him show that your hatred is not immortal." '

LOVE INTRIGUES:
Or, The
HISTORY
OF THE
AMOURS
OF
BOSVIL and *GALESIA*,

As Related to

LUCASIA, in St. *Germains* Garden.

A
NOVEL.

Written by a Young LADY.

Omne tulit punctum qui miscuit utile dulci. *

LONDON:

Printed for E. CURLL, at the *Dial* and *Bible*
against St. *Dunstan*'s Church in *Fleetstreet* ;
and C. CROWNFIELD, at *Cambridge*.
M DCC XIII.

* 'By mixing the useful and agreeable you will gain every heart,' Horace, *Ars Poetica*, 1. 343.

Reproduced courtesy of The British Library (11646 cc17).

Jane Barker
(1652-1732)

JANE BARKER was baptized at Blatherwicke, Northamptonshire, on 17 May 1652. Her father had been employed by Charles I, fought for him, and suffered financially for it. An uncle may have died fighting against the Protestant rebel, the Duke of Monmouth, and another uncle fought for James II against William; a nephew died in battle in 1704. After her parents died, she spent some time in France during James II's exile; she was back in London by 1704. She died at St Germain-en-Laye on 29 March 1732.[1] A manuscript of her poems, 'A Collection of Poems Refering to the Times,' explains her conversion to Catholicism during the reign of James II, includes attacks on William, and states strong opinions about specific political events. Her published collection of poems, *Poetical Recreations* (1688), includes poems by literary friends, several in a Cambridge University circle; by two poets not completely forgotten today, Charles Cotton and Charles Sedley; and twelve by Benjamin Crayle, the somewhat disreputable publisher who was fined that same year for the 'lascivious' publishing of *The School of Venus*.[2] One of these poems provides evidence that she was already working on prose fiction. The poetry in *Love Intrigues* is her own, and earlier and later revisions of some of them survive.

Love Intrigues, her novel as she calls it in the dedication, was published by Edmund Curll in 1713, included in the collected *Entertaining Novels* (1715), and was revised and published as *The Amours of Bosvil and Galesia, As Related to Lucasia in St. Germain's Garden* in the second edition of *Entertaining Novels* (1719). There were four editions of *Entertaining Novels*. Barker's other novels, *Exilius* (1715), *A Patchwork Screen for the Ladies* (1723), and *The Lining of the Patch-work Screen* (1726) are less unified than *Love Intrigues*, and the tales in them may have been written or translated at widely spaced intervals.

Love Intrigues is a tightly unified book with an allusive richness that shows wide reading. The Aesopian fables Barker mentions, for instance, have strong connections to each other and are theme bearing. They and references to such images as the Tower of Babel contribute to the central story of the difficulties men and women have in understanding each other, especially during courtship when personal

---

[1] I am grateful to Carol Shiner Wilson for this date and the documentary evidence for it.

[2] See Kathryn R. King, 'Poetical Recreations and the Sociable Text,' *English Literary History*, 61 (1994), 551-70. I am grateful for Professor King's additional suggestions.

insecurities and social rules of conduct complicate communication. Perhaps the first English novel by a woman writer about a woman with inclinations to be a writer, it provides a glimpse of society's mixed opinion of such a choice and of the competing demands all writers, especially women, face. Galesia tries on a number of roles for women, and Barker without self-consciousness has made her an intelligent woman. Galesia can master many things yet finds Bosvil her most frustrating study. *Love Intrigues* gives the courtship novel new depth.

P.R.B.

Love Intrigues; or, The History of the Amours of Bosvil and Galesia, as Related to Lucasia, in St. Germains Garden[1]

DEDICATION

To the Honourable
The Countess of Exeter

May it please Your Ladyship,
To send abroad the composure of leisure Hours, as at first I was very timorous, so (had not the Sweet Reflections of Your Ladyship's experienced Goodness emboldened me to screen this little Novel under your auspicious Protection) it had for ever lain Dormant; and which indeed, now it does humbly prostrate itself before you, can have no other Pretensions, than to be Half an Hours Amusement to Your Ladyship; I wish I could say, any Improvement to those ripening Graces which shine so conspicuously in my Young Lady,[2] whilst they pattern Your Ladyship's, and so may justly be esteemed Hereditary from Your truly Noble Blood; who, as she is the Darling of Your Ladyship's Heart, and the Delight indeed of all who behold her, so that she may never entangle her Noble Person in those Levities and Misfortunes the ensuing Treatise describes me unhappily to have struggled with, shall always be the hearty Wish of,
Your Ladyship's
Most Obedient,
Humble Servant,
J. B.

---

[1] James II made his residence at St Germains (Saint-Germain-en-Laye), a town on the Seine a few miles from Paris, after he fled England in December 1688. By locating her story here, Barker implies her characters are Jacobites, supporters of the deposed James.

[2] Elizabeth Brownlow was the second wife of John Cecil, sixth Earl of Exeter; her daughter was also named Elizabeth and could not have been more than 13 years old.

INTRODUCTION

It was in the Heat of Summer, when News is daily coming and hourly expected, from the Campaigns;[3] which, as it employs the Heads of the Politicians, and Arms of the Heroes, so it fills the Hearts of the Fair with a thousand Apprehensions, in Consideration of their respective Friends and Relations therein concerned. This induced *Galesia* to an early walk in St. *Germains* Garden; where meeting her Friend *Lucasia*, they took a Turn or two by the little Wood, entertaining themselves on the Several Adventures of the former and late War,[4] and what they had to hope or fear from the Success, or Overthrow of either or both Parties;[5] their dearest and nearest Relations being equally engaged on both Sides. King James's Affairs having so turned Things in *Europe*,[6] that the War between *France* and the Allies was almost like a Civil War: Friend against Friend, Brother against Brother; Father against Son, and so on. After divers Disquisitions and Turns of Discourse on these Occurrences, *Lucasia*, being willing to quit this melancholy Theme, desired *Galesia* to recount to her the Adventures of her early Years, of which she had already heard some Part, and therefore believed the whole to be a diverting Novel; wherefore seating themselves, *Galesia* related as follows.

Love Intrigues

THE HISTORY OF GALESIA

My Father (said *Galesia*) and all his Family being of the Loyal Party, in the Time of King CHARLES the First,[7] is a sufficient Demonstration of the Non-

---

[3] *Campaigns*: The War of Spanish Succession (1702–13), fought to establish a balance of power, began as an effort by the Allies (Austria, England, United Provinces, Portugal, Prussia, Savoy, and the Holy Roman Empire) to prevent the accession of Philip, grandson of Louis XIV, the French king, from ascending to the throne of Spain.

[4] *former and late War*: the women had many wars to discuss as 'former and late'. The Third Dutch War, fought for trade advantages, ended in 1674; England and France had been allies against the Dutch. The Nine Years War, variously called King William's War and the War of the Grand Alliance, began because of French territorial aggression; the Treaty of Ryswick ended the war temporarily in 1697. They could also have been talking of the English Civil War, which established a republic and led to the beheading of Charles I or to the campaign against the Jacobites in Ireland (1688–91). Barker had relatives who fought there.

[5] *both Parties*: the reign of Queen Anne (1702–14) was plagued by vicious party warfare; after the death of her only surviving child in July 1700 and as her health declined, political manœuvring increased. Upon her death, the Tories were largely displaced, and Whigs came to power.

[6] *King James's Affairs . . . in Europe*: upon James's death in 1701, King Louis XIV recognized the son as 'James III', heir to the British throne; this action further embroiled the French in England's internal disputes over who would succeed King William.

[7] Charles I, king of England, was beheaded in January 1649. Many of the Royalists (the loyal party) who supported or fought with the king lost their positions, estates, or even lives.

existence of Riches among them; for some were in Battle slain, and some in Prison died; some were ruined in their Estates, some in their Persons, so that most of the Adherents to the Royal Cause were unhappy. My Father, with the rest, lost a very honourable and profitable Place at Court; after which he retired into the Country, leading a very private, or rather obscure Life, just above the contempt of Poverty, and below that Envy which attends Riches, of which he laid aside all Hopes, only contenting himself to give his Children an Education that might fit them for a more plentiful Condition of Life if Fortune should ever make them her Favourites.

I was about ten or eleven Years old when my Mother took me from *Putney-School*;[8] finding those Places the Academies of Vanity and Expense; no ways instructive in the rudiments of a Country Gentlewoman's Life, for which, in all Probability, I was destined; therefore reasonably judged her own House a fitter Class to prepare me for that Station.

Here I had not been long e'er there came to our House a young Gentleman of our Neighbourhood, one Mr. *Brafort*, a School-fellow and particular Companion of my Brother's. This Gentleman took such a Liking to Miss, (for I was not yet past that Title) that he resolved to have no other Wife, though he was already a Man, and I but a Child; which he not only said but demonstrated, in refusing all Proposals of that kind, always alleging that he would stay for *Galesia*; and accordingly frequented our House, dispensed with my Follies and Humours, making himself my Companion even in my childish Recreations.

I cannot but reflect on this Part of Life as the Happiest Time we are born to know, when Youth and Innocence tune all things, and render them harmonious; our Days pass in Play and Health, and our Nights in sound Sleep; our Pillows are not stuffed with Cares, nor our waking Hours encumbered with Passions: We reflect not on what is past, nor take a Prospect of what is to come: we toss our Shuttlecock[9] while weary, and then at our Tutor's Beck cheerfully go to our Lecture: thus we pass our happy Days till Reason begins to bud in our Actions; then we no sooner know that we have a Being and rejoice that we are the noblest Part of the Creation, but Passion takes Root in our Hearts, and very often outgrows and smothers our Rational Faculties. This I experienced; for I was scarce arrived to those Years in which we begin to distinguish between Friendship and Affection; but I became sensible of the latter towards a Kinsman of ours, one Mr. *Bosvil*, who came to our House, and notwithstanding I had armed my Thoughts with a thousand Resolutions against Love, yet the first Moment I saw this Man I loved him; though he had nothing extraordinary in Person or Parts, to excite such an Affection;

---

[8] *Putney-School*: Putney, a London suburb, was the location of several fashionable boarding schools for young women; they learned dancing, music, writing, languages, needlework, and other subjects suitable for cultured women.

[9] *toss our Shuttlecock*: the player bounced the shuttlecock, made of cork and feathers, on a battledore or light racket as many times in succession as possible without dropping it.

nevertheless, the Moment that his Eyes met mine, my Heart was sensible of an Emotion it had never felt before.

I was now about the age of fifteen, at which time my Mother thought fit to send me to *London*, to remain under the Government of my aunt, my Lady *Martial*, a virtuous Matron, under whose prudent Conduct, I might learn a little of the Town Politeness; its Civilities without its Vanities; its Diversions without its Vices, etc. This Journey was extremely pleasing to me, which is usual to any young Country Creature. *London!* the Idol of all the World, might naturally create Longings in a young female Heart: It was also pleasing to Mr. *Brafort*, my reputed Lover: He supposing this Voyage would ripen my Understanding and Knowledge of the World, which was yet very green, want-ing Experience and Conversation to ripen, and bring to Maturity those Parts wherewith Nature had endued me. In the meantime declaring to his Relations, that he intended to marry me at my Return; not doubting (I sup-pose) my Parents' Consent whenever he should ask it; his Estate rendering the Demand too advantageous to be refused; his Person not disagreeable; therefore concluded he had nothing to fear, having always found a kind reception at our House, not only as a Neighbour, but my Brother's Friend and particular Acquaintance.

The Satisfaction I took, was not only that I should enjoy a little Ramble and Diversions of the Town, always agreeable to Youth, but knew I should there see my Cousin *Bosvil*, who was then a Student at the Inns of Court.[10] But alas how was I nonplused when at the first Visit he made me, he let me know he was informed that my coming to *London* was to buy me Clothes, in order to be married to Mr. *Brafort!* This he affirmed with such an Air as left me no Room to suppose it Jest or Banter, letting me know his Authors, one of which was Mr. *Brafort's* Man; insomuch that I really began to fear that it was so at the Bottom, and that such an Affair might have been transacted between him and my Parents. However, I assuring him that I knew nothing of any such Intention, he believed me with a great Pleasure and Satisfaction; and from Time to Time made me understand by his Looks and Gestures that his Visits proceeded rather from Passion than Friendship; and that he was drawn to my Aunt's House by other Cords than those of consanguinity to me, or Respect to her Ladyship; which my vigilant Aunt soon perceived, but (as the Proverb is) looked through her Fingers;[11] and under the Cloak of a Kinsman, gave the Lover just so much Opportunity as served to blow up his Flame, without too far engaging my young and unexperienced Heart; she knowing that his Estate, besides his Pretensions to the Law, rendered him an advantageous Party.

[10] *Inns of Court*: Lincoln's, Middle, Inner, and Gray's were technically houses for barristers and students; they were set up to educate students in English common law, which was not taught at the universities. In the early eighteenth century, the students were not known for their seriousness.

[11] *looked through her Fingers*: to overlook or wink at small faults; a popular ballad included the line, 'Not an officer under the sunne but does looke through his fingers'.

By this discreet Proceeding of my aunt, he had very little Opportunity to testify his Affection; still he found some Moments to assure me of an everlasting Love, and to sue for the same of me. I, young and unexperienced as I was, had nevertheless the Cunning to conceal my Passion and pretend not to believe his. The Truth is, I had heard so ill a Character of the Town Amours, as being all Libertinism, and more especially the Inns of Court that I dreaded to launch on so dangerous a Sea, thinking each sigh a Storm to overset one's Reputation; which too often proves true in Fact, especially if the Amour be secret, or without Parents' Consent, that good Pilot which conducts young Lovers to the safe Harbour of Matrimony. Without which, we can hope for little but Shipwreck of our Fortunes and Quiet.[12] This consideration made me pretend to take all he said for Banter, or youthful Gallantry. In fine,[13] I put him off with one little Shuffle, or other, which he pretended to hope was only the Effect of Modesty, till such time as we should come into the Country; and there be authorized by our Parents to make him happy. In the interim he resolved to demean himself so as to merit their Consent. All which pleased not only my amorous, but my haughty Inclination; for I disdained to be courted thus in hugger mugger.[14] Thus Crimes, or Folly, mix themselves with our Virtues, Pride with Honour, Dissimulation with Modesty, etc. However as the World now rolls, we are under a kind of Constraint to follow its Bias.

Now as Pride agitated my Thoughts in regard of *Bosvil*, so did Revenge a little in regard of *Brafort*; for I pleased myself to think how he would be balked, who, I thought, had been very remiss in his Devoirs towards such a Goddess, as the World's Flatterers had made of me. Seven or eight Months being past in this manner, my Mother sent for me home into the Country, and my Brother, who was to be my Convoy, carried me by *Oxford*, to show me the Glory of the University at the time of the Act,[15] when it shines with greatest Splendor. The Compliments and Civilities I received there from the Townsmen of all Ranks were so many and so much above my Merit, that it would look like a Fiction for me now to repeat them. Therefore (with *Friar Bacon's* speaking Head)[16] I will only say, *Time is past*, and for ever keep Silence on that Subject; for the very naming those bright Encomiums then given to my Youth, would be like dressing up a Death's-Head in Curls, Point,[17] and Ribbons: However, all this Vanity did not sequester my Thoughts one Moment from my beloved *Bosvil*, but I returned home into the Country, full of Longings for his Arrival.

---

[12] *Quiet*: peace of mind.   [13] *In fine*: in short.

[14] *in hugger mugger*: secret, clandestinely.   [15] *the Act*: commencement.

[16] *Friar Bacon*: a character in Robert Greene's *The Honourable History of Friar Bacon and Friar Bungay* (1594) who uses magic to make a Brazen Head that speaks three times. The last time it says, 'Time is past!' A hand from Heaven breaks it with a hammer and Friar Bacon's hopes of hearing important philosophical truths are destroyed.

[17] *Point*: lace, ribbon, or lacing with a tip or tag used to close garments or to attach one piece of clothing to another.

In the meantime, our Neighbour Mr. *Brafort* had got some little Hint of this Amour; resolved speedily to accomplish his intended Marriage with me: but Almighty Providence ordered it so, that immediately after my Arrival into the country, he fell sick of a continued Fever, which in the space of ten Days carried him into his Grave, instead of his Nuptial Bed, to the great Grief of all his Relations. Thus we see that Human Projects are mere Vapours, carried about with every Blast of cross Accidents; and the Projectors themselves pushed by the Hand of Death into the Abyss of Oblivion.

This unlooked for Death of *Brafort* was no way afflicting to me, more than as a Friend and Neighbour; for all my tender Thoughts were bound up in *Bosvil*, whose Absence made my life tedious, and every Minute seemed a Year till his Arrival. But ah my *Lucasia!* what are our Hopes when founded on anything but Heaven? My longed for *Bosvil* came, and instead of bringing with him the Caresses of an overjoyed Lover, or at least the Addresses of a fond Admirer, nothing accompanied his Conversation but a certain cold Respect, scarce surmounting common Civility. Instead of engaging my Parents to intercede on his Behalf with me their Darling Child, he, in my Presence, consulted my Father about a certain Neighbouring Gentlewoman, who was proposed him in Marriage. This Discourse I heard with seeming Tranquility, and praised the young Lady, wishing she might be so sensible of his Merit, as to make him speedily happy. Here, my *Lucasia*, Truth and Sincerity were supplanted by a certain Tincture of Modesty, and Pride; for no Mouth spoke more directly against the Sentiments of a Heart, than mine did at that time; but this is one of the finest spun Snares wherewith the Devil entraps us; when he makes us abandon one Virtue to idolize another: As when the Learned Casuists contend for Faith, to the Breach of Charity; and the Enthusiastics, in their fantastic Raptures, neglect the common Duties of Human Life.[18] Thus I, silly Maid, set up a pretended Indifferency, to which false Idol I sacrificed all my Satisfaction.

Now, tho' in *Bosvil's* Presence I made a shift to keep up this Outside of a seeming Insensibility of Love; but interiorly I was tormented with a thousand Anxieties, which made me seek Solitude where I might without Witness or Controul, disburden my overcharged Heart of Sighs and Tears. This Solitude I sought was not hard to be found, our Habitation being situated in a remote Country Village; where one had full Opportunity, to soothe and cajole Melancholy; till it becomes rampant, and hardly to be restrained. Sometimes I endeavoured to divert my Chagrin, by contemplating in these shady Walks the wondrous Works of the Creation. In the Spring methought the Earth was dressed in new Apparel, the soft Meadow Grass was as a Robe of green Velvet,

---

[18] Anglicans condemned both casuistry and enthusiasm as religious *faux pas*. Casuistry was a way of deciding difficult cases of conscience and was associated with devious, ingenious reasoning; today it might be called 'situational ethics'. Enthusiasm was rapturous intensity of religious feeling and was often considered delusionary, hypocritical, or even hysterical.

embroidered with Pearls and Diamonds, composed of the Evening Dew, which the sun's Morning Rays made bright and sparkling; all the Borders curiously laced, by the checkered Work of Sun and Shade, caused by the Trees and Hedges. It was in some of these solitary Walks that my rolling Thoughts turned themselves in to these Verses.[19]

Methinks these Shades, strange Thoughts suggest,
Which beat my Head, and cool my Breast;
And mind me of a Laurel Crest.[20]

Methinks I hear the Muses sing,
And see 'em all dance in a Ring;
And call upon me to take wing.

We will (say they) assist thy Flight,
Till thou reach fair ORINDA's Height,[21]
If thou can'st this World's Follies slight.

We'll bring thee to our bright Abodes,
Amongst the Heroes and the Gods,
If thou and Wealth can be at odds.

Then gentle Maid cast off thy Chain,
Which links thee to thy faithless Swain,
And vow a Virgin to remain.

Write, write thy Vow upon this Tree,
By us it shall recorded be;
And thou enjoy Eternity.

Looking behind me, I saw a very smooth-barked Ash, under which I sat; and in the midst of melancholy Whimsies, I wrote those Lines on the Body of the Tree, having commonly a little Pen and Ink in my Pocket. This Fancy joined with what I had lately read in a little Book of my Lord *Bacon's*, that a wise Man ought to have two Designs on foot at a time, or according to the Proverb, *two Strings to one's Bow*:[22] So I, finding myself abandoned by *Bosvil*, and thinking it impossible ever to love again, resolved to espouse a Book, and spend my Days in Study: This Fancy having once taken Root, grew apace, and branched itself forth in a thousand vain Conceits. I imagined myself the

[19] *Verses*: all of the poetry unless otherwise identified is by Barker. This one is entitled 'The contract with the muses writ on the bark of a shady ash-tree' in a manuscript of her poems in Magdalen College, Oxford.

[20] *laurel*: sacred to Apollo, god of poetry, music, and the arts, and awarded for victory and merit.

[21] *Orinda*: Katherine Philips's poems were published posthumously as *Poems by the Most Deservedly Admired Mrs. Katherine Philips, The Matchless Orinda* (1667) by her friend Charles Cotterell. By 1696, Philips was established as a model for aspiring women writers.

[22] 'It is always good to have two stringes to a bowe', John Heywood, *Proverbs* (1546). That would provide the archer with a second string should the first break. The proverb is as old as Terence and has always carried the meaning of having two possibilities, not putting all one's eggs in one basket.

Orinda or *Sapho* of my Time,[23] and amongst my little Reading, the Character of the Faithful Shepherdess in the Play pleased me extremely; I resolved to imitate her, not only in perpetual Chastity, but in learning the Use of Simples for the Good of my Country Neighbours. Thus I thought to become *Apollo's* Darling Daughter and Maid of Honour to the Muses. In order to this I got my Brother (who was not yet returned to *Oxford*) to set me in the way to learn my Grammar, which he willingly did, thinking it only a Vapour of Fancy, to be blown away with the first Puff of Vanity or new Mode; or a Freak without Foundation, to be overthrown with the first Difficulty it should meet with in the Syntax; knowing it to be less easy to make Substantive and Adjective agree, than to place a Patch,[24] Curl, or any other additional Graces on a young Face; so as to render it, if not more charming, more gallant: He not knowing the Foundation of my Enterprize laughed at my Project, though he humoured me out of Complaisance: for I had not let him know anything of this Amour, supposing an Affront of this kind might produce some fatal Accident; beside, my Pride would not permit me to let this contempt of my Youth and Beauty be known; these Considerations made me keep this a Secret from my Brother and all the world; though otherwise, he was the confidant of all my poor Heart was able to conceive; for he was dear to me, not only as a Brother, but a Friend; the Bands of fraternal Love were strengthened, by those of Choice, and Inclination, and both united by Reason; for never was Man fitter for an Election of this kind, where Prudence might have the casting Voice, which indeed ought to be in all our Actions. But to return from whence I digressed.

I followed my Study close, betook myself to a plain kind of Habit: quitted all Point, Lace, Ribbons, and fine Clothes; partly (I suppose) out of Melancholy, not caring to adorn that Person slighted by him I loved; and partly out of Pride, vainly imagining that the World applauded me, and admired that a Person, in the Bloom of Youth, should so perfectly abdicate the World with all those Allurements, which seldom fail to please our Sex, in all the Stages of our Lives, but much more in the juvenile part of our time: but thus it was, I sought vain Glory through differing Paths, I seemed to scorn (what I really courted) popular Applause; and hid a proud Heart under an humble Habit. The Consideration of this makes me see how difficult it is to draw a Scheme of virtuous Politics whereby to govern this little Microcosm but by that Model of all Perfection, *Deny thy self*, etc.[25] and that not only in Deeds, but in the most secret Intentions: for whilst I strove to cast out the Devil of Love, I made room for Pride, with all its vile Adherents.

[23] Katherine Philips became known as 'the Matchless Orinda', a platonic pseudonym she had used in some of her poems and which her editor put in the title of the posthumous edition of her poems. She was reputed to be the finest English woman poet. Sappho was the Greek poet whose name became a metaphor for the best woman poet of a generation.

[24] *Patch*: small, adhesive beauty marks made of silk or court-plaster, often cut in decorative shapes (stars, hearts, flowers) pasted on the face to highlight the complexion, attract attention, or cover blemishes. Although worn primarily by women, fashionable young men wore them, too.

[25] *Deny thy self*: Jesus to his disciples, Matt. 16: 24.

However, I thought I had set myself in a good, and convenient Road, to pass on my Life's Pilgrimage; but this my designed Tranquility was disturbed by the frequent Visits of *Bosvil*, who, as a Kinsman and a Friend, had free Access to our House; and though he made no formal or direct Address to me, yet his Eyes darted Love, his Lips smiled Love, his Heart sighed Love, his Tongue was the only part silent in the Declaration of a violent Passion: that between his cold Silence and his Sunshine Looks, I was like the Traveller in the Fable;[26] the warm Rays of his Eyes made me cast away that Garment of firm Resolution, which the Coldness of his Silence had made me to wrap close about my Heart.

But why my *Galesia* (said *Lucasia*) did you not consult your Parents, and in particular your Mother, whose Care and Prudence might have adjusted the Business to all your Satisfactions? I considered much on that Point (replied *Galesia*) but I concluded if I discovered it to my Mother, she would discourse him about it, and he perhaps might put it off with a Laugh, and say, he had only rallied with his young Cousin during her Residence in *London*, to try how her Heart was fortified against such-like Assaults. So by this means I should have passed for an ignorant Country Girl, not capable of judging between Jest and Earnest; which would have grated hard upon my proud Humour. Wherefore I resolved (that as long as he remained silent towards my Parents) to take all he said or did as Raillery, or little Efforts of Gallantry. Thus, Fool as I was! I concealed from my dear Mother the thing in which I had greatest need of her Counsel and Conduct: And as most young People have too great an Opinion of their own Wisdom, so I (no doubt) thought myself as capable to make, or use a Conquest, as any Town Lady armed *Cap a pee*,[27] with all sorts of Embellishments, and who had served divers Campaigns under *Venus's* Banner; but too late I found my Weakness and Folly, in this my opinionated Wisdom.

Bosvil frequently came to our House, where he made the outward Grimaces of a Lover, with an indifferent Interiour; whilst I bore up an outside Indifferency, with a Heart full of Passion: Thus a Mask is put on, sometimes, to conceal an ill Face, and sometimes to preserve a good one: And the most part of Mankind are in reality different from what they seem, and affect to be thought what they are not; Youth affects to be thought older, and they of ripe Years, younger; the sober young Gentleman affects to talk like a Rake, and the Town-Miss to pretend to Modesty. Therefore I wonder not, that I, silly Country Girl, assumed to myself a Discretion, which time and want of Experience had denied me. But things were on this footing, when Mr. *Brafort*, Cousin to my dead Lover *Brafort*, cast his Eyes on me with greater Esteem

---

[26] In an Aesop fable, the sun and the wind bet on which would be able to make the traveller remove his cloak. The wind went first, and blew repeatedly on the traveller, but he wrapped his cloak tighter and tighter around him. Then the sun shone directly on him, and the traveller removed his cloak.

[27] *Cap a pee*: cap-à-pie, from head to foot.

than I merited; and as if he had been destined to choose the Devil for his Confessor, he chose my Cousin *Bosvil* for his Confidant, desiring him to introduce him to me, and make his Proposals to my Parents. *Brafort* knew nothing of *Bosvil's* pretended Inclinations for me, but addressed to him as my near Relation and intimate Friend. To this *Bosvil* freely replied that he could not serve him, saying, that he designed his Cousin *Galesia* for himself; and was so far from introducing any body to her on that score, that he should be very careful to keep off all Pretenders. Upon which Mr. *Brafort* remained satisfied, and laid all Thoughts of me aside.

> To an exact Perfection he had brought
> The Action Love, the Passion be forgot.

This Transaction, though coming to me by a third hand, gave me a strong Belief of *Bosvil's* Sincerity and made me interpret every little dubious Word, which he sometimes mixed with his fond Actions, to be Demonstrations of a real Passion; not doubting but a little time would ripen the same into an open Declaration to my Parents, as well as formerly to me, and now lately to young *Brafort*. In the mean time attributing this Delay to his Prudence in acquainting himself with my Humour and Inclinations before he gave himself irrevocably to me; which made me regulate my Behaviour with the discreetest Precautions my poor unexperienced Thoughts could dictate. My Grammar Rules now became harsh Impertinences, for I thought I had learned *Amo*, and *Amor*, by a shorter and surer Method; and the only syntax I studied, was how to make suitable Answers to my Father, and him, when the longed-for Question should be proposed; that I might not betray my Weakness in a too ready Compliance, nor ruin my Satisfaction in too rigid an Opposition.

In the meantime, a Friend of mine that had married a Sister of my dead Lover, *Brafort*; and for that Reason he and his Wife always called me Sister, This Gentleman, whether out of Kindness, or Curiosity, or because their Cousin the young *Brafort* had discovered his Inclinations for me, had a great Desire to inform himself of the Secret between me and *Bosvil*; for he and his Wife being much in our Company, could not but remark something in his Carriage towards me: and being very intimate with *Bosvil*, told him, that he wondered that he being an only Child, and Heir to a considerable Estate, beside his growing Practice in the Law, did not fix on a Wife; thereby to establish his Family, and make his aged Parents happy. That Affair is not undone, replied *Bosvil*, till this time of Day, for I am fixed on my Neighbour Mr. *Lowland's* Daughter; and hope shortly to enjoy your good Company, with the rest of my Friends and Relations, at the Celebration of our Marriage. This Answer my Friend little expected to receive: however believing it concerned me nearly, took the first Opportunity to tell me, which he did, in a frank, jocose manner, not seeming to suspect how great my concern was, which indeed was the greatest in the World. The Notes of a stuttering Cuckoo are not half so disagreeable, though they sing the spring's Obsequies, and proclaim Silence to the whole choir of chirping Musicians. The Edifice I had so lately built on the foundation of that Discourse between *Bosvil* and young *Brafort*, proved a mere airy nothing, serving only to make my Fall the greater, by how much I had raised my Hopes on its Battlements. I spent my Days in Sighs and my Nights in Tears; my Sleep forsook me, and I relished not my Food; nor had I made any Friend or Confidant into whose Bosom I might discharge my Griefs or receive Consolation. My dear Brother was then at *Paris*, to improve his Studies in that University, where, complaining of his Absence, I also hinted this other Original of my Sorrows.

> Nothing at present wonted Pleasure yields,
> The Birds, nor Bushes, nor the gaudy Fields;
> Nor *Osier* Holts,[28] nor Banks of *Glenn*[29] are seen,
> Nor the soft Meadow crowned with tufted Green,
> Are half so pleasant now, or half so fair
> As when we mused together kindly there,
> And thought each Blade of Corn a Jem[30] did bear!
> Instead of this, and thy Philosophy,
> Nought but my own false *Latin* now I see,
> False Verse, or Lover falsest of the three.

Thus I walked on in Sorrow and Desolation, without reflecting, that my Vanity deserved a greater Punishment; for in our Youth we commonly dress our thoughts in the Mirrour of Self-Flattery, and expect Heaven, Fortune, and the world should cajole our Follies, as we do our own; and lay all Faults upon others, and all Praise on our selves: how far I was guilty of this, I know not; but whatever I deserved from the Hand of just Heaven, I deserved nothing but well from *Bosvil*, whose Scorn (the Cause of my Afflictions) I endeavoured to conceal, yet spite of my Industry, this Melancholy, together with my plain Dress, was taken notice of; and it was believed I mourned for *Brafort*. My Parents fearing this might prove a Hindrance to my Fortune, commanded me to quit that plain Dress, and endeavour to forget *Brafort*. This their Fancy of my Affection for Mr. *Brafort* I did not much contradict, it being a proper Curfeu[31] to that Flame I had for *Bosvil*. Thus we see how easily we are deceived by outward Appearances, and what Care we ought to take of censuring, judging, or condemning Things, or Persons without knowing the true and genuine Cause of Contingencies; which are often very hard to be understood; for according to the Fable, the Ass seems valiant in the Lyon's Skin, and the Crow glorious in her borrowed Plumes.[32] We often give undeserved applause where

---

[28] *Osier Holts*: a grove where osiers, a kind of willow, are grown. They were used in basket-making, and Galesia will weave a garland from them.

[29] *Glenn*: river in Lincolnshire.   [30] *Jem*: a new leaf bud.

[31] *Cur-feu*: ending, time to cease.

[32] Allusion to two Aesop fables. In the first, an ass found a lion's skin that hunters had left in the sun to dry. He put it on and scared the men and animals in the village. In his delight, he brayed, and everyone recognized him. His master beat him for frightening people. In the second, the bird finds peacock feathers lost as they molted and ties them to his tail. He struts around, but the peacocks recognize that he is not one of them, peck him, and pluck away the borrowed feathers.

Fortune makes a Fool her Favourite; and on the other side, condemn the wisest Designs when not attended with Success. We are Fortune's Machines, and the Alarm of popular Applause must run off, as she is pleased to turn the Key of our Affairs. But pardon (*Madam*) this Digression, and give me leave to return.

After my foresaid Discourse with my Friend, that he had told me of *Bosvil's* intended Marriage with Mrs. *Lowland*, there passed many weeks that I neither saw nor heard from him; he keeping close at his Father's House (which was about twenty Miles from us) where I thought he passed his time at the Feet of his fair Mistress *Lowland*, who lived in his Father's Neighbourhood: But the Truth is, he was detained by a light, but a lingering Sickness; in which time I gained much upon my distempered Mind, and thought myself so perfectly cured, as never more to relapse by the Infection of any Lover, how contagious soever Youth, Gallantry, or Riches, might render him. But alas! I had not yet passed the Dog days of *Bosvil's* hot Pursuits, but at his return he entertained me in another manner than ever; for if before he admired, esteemed, or had a Passion for me, he now doted, adored, and died for me! Vowed a thousand times, that he could not live without me, that his Passion had been the Cause of his late Indisposition and would be of his Death, if he did not apply the Salutary Remedy of *Hymen's* Rites.[33] In order to which he had brought a License with him; and therewithal took it out of his Pocket, and showed it to me. All which so astonished, pleased, and confounded me, that I knew not what to reply! But, with Tears in my Eyes, told him, that I was wholly nonplused, and knew not what Interpretation to make of all that had passed between him and me! 'Tis true, replied he, I have been extremely remiss in my Devoirs towards you; for which I deserve the utmost Punishment your Scorn can inflict, nor should I dare to ask Pardon of a Goodness less perfect: Be not cruel then to your Penitent, but forgive him who now asks it with all Submission; him, who vows never to offend you; him, who swears to suffer any thing, rather than deserve your Anger; him, who dedicates every Action of his Life to love, please, and serve you. Cease, said I, these Asseverations;[34] I never pretended to be displeased with you; and as you have done nothing to offend me, so I have done nothing to deserve your Love, beyond that of a Kinswoman or a Friend; which I hope I shall never lose; but as such I shall and will forever love you. If you love me as a Kinswoman, or a Friend, replied he, testify the same in saving my Life, which as a wretched Criminal I beg; and as a faithful Lover hope to receive from your Goodness, in consenting to a speedy Marriage: for, without that, you cannot pretend to either Friendship, Love, or Charity itself; my Life, and Love being now inseparable. Sure, dear Cousin, said I, (with a Tone wholly confused) you forget in whose Company you are, and believe yourself with fair Mrs. *Lowland*: If such an amorous

---

[33] *Hymen's Rites*: marriage. Hymen, a beautiful youth carrying a bridal torch and veil, in Greek myth was the personification of marriage.

[34] *Asseverations*: solemn or emphatic declarations.

Slumber has cast you into this *delirium*, pray awake, and behold before you, your Cousin *Galesia*. I need no Monitor (replied he) to tell me it is my Cousin *Galesia*, with whom I converse at present: Her reserved Behaviour, with which she treats me her faithful Lover, is a sufficient Demonstration, that it is the prudent, virtuous, chaste *Galesia!* It is this reserved Mien, Madam, which has often deterred me, and commanded my Tongue to a respectful Silence; whilst my poor Heart, over-charged with Passion, only eased itself with Sighs, and my Looks were the only Language whereby to express my interiour Thoughts. How far your Silence has been guilty of your suffering (replied I) is not easy for me to penetrate; but I believe the Insincerity of this Declaration, might prove very obnoxious to my Quiet, if my preengaged Resolution of a single Life, did not secure me from those Dangers, to which my Youth, and your Merit might betray me. Ah Madam! replied he, and is it possible you should doubt the Sincerity of what I now assert? The great God of Heaven that created us, knows what I say is true, when I say I love you above all things in the World! That I will never marry any Woman but your-self; that I never did, can, or will, place any Beauty or Interest in competition with you; that I have thought of nothing but you since the Moment I beheld you; that I denied myself all the Diversions of the Town for your sake; and when I tugged the Oar of *Coke upon Littleton*[35] and other harsh Studies, it was to arrive safe at the Harbour of your Embrace! This Heaven knows to be true, and not Heaven only, but there is not a Person on Earth, with whom I have conversed, that has not been entertained with *Galesia's* Perfections, and my Passion; there is not a Person of my Acquaintance but has heard that I love *Galesia*. Ah Madam! this is true, Heaven that inspired me with this vir-tuous Affection, knows it to be true! Earth which adores you, knows it to be true! And even you yourself know it to be true! Look into your own con-science, and it will bear witness to this Truth, that I have loved you since the first Moment that I saw you. Remember (Madam) how, after the first Salutations, I sat and gazed on you with such a deep Surprize, that there was little Difference between me and a Statue, except sometimes a stolen Sigh, which called the Blood into your Cheeks and made me know (that young as you were) you understood that Language. Moreover, Madam, that when I sat at Table I could not eat for looking on you, insomuch that your charitable Mother thinking me indisposed, sent to her Closet for a Cordial: Then it was I gazed that Life away, you now refuse to save, and have ever since laboured under deadly Pangs; and after thus suffering Martyrdom, to have the Truth of what I profess called in Question, is downright Tyranny. Those (replied I) who have once swerved from the Faith they profess, ought always to be sus-pected; you have loved Mrs. *Lowland*——and so stopped with a stolen Sigh.

---

[35] *Coke upon Littleton: The First Part of the Institutes of the Laws of England; or, A Commentary upon Littleton* (1628), a compendium of property law, by Edward Coke was the standard source for Restoration and early eighteenth-century lawyers and the principal law textbook. It was based on Thomas Littleton's *New Tenures* (1482).

With that he called to mind what he had said to my Friend; and told me that all he had then said, was only to put a stop to his Curiosity, not thinking it proper to name me as the Object of his designed Espousals, without my Leave; and then, again and again, called Heaven to witness that he loved me above all terrestrial Beings: And if you believe me not (continued he) I hope you will believe my Father, who intends to be here next week, to bear witness of this Truth: He will tell you how often I have avowed it to him, when he has proposed Matches to me; telling him nothing but my fair Cousin, the virtuous *Galesia* could make me happy. My fond Mother also, when she hears me sigh, knows it is for you, and then blames your Cruelty. If you persist in this Rigor, you will not only cause my Death, but theirs also, whose Lives are bound up in mine. When my Father comes, I hope you will compassionate his Years, when he courts you for his only Child; think how much your tender Mother loves you, and then consider mine; and as your Tenderness extends to them, 'tis hoped you shall have little Beauties of your own to do the same one day by you.

In this kind of Discourse, my *Lucasia*, we passed some Hours, and it was with great Difficulty that I restrained my foolish Tongue from telling the Fondness of my Heart; but the restraint was with such broken Words, stolen Sighs, suppressed Tears, that the merest Freshman in Love's Academy could not but read and understand that Language; much more he, that had passed Graduate amongst the Town Amours. What Interpretation he made I know not, but I thought myself safe landed on Love's Shore, where no cross Wind, unseen Accident, could oppose my Passage to *Hymen*'s Palace, or wreck me in this Harbour of true Satisfaction: For since he assured me of his Parents' Consent, I knew him to be too advantageous a Party to be refused by mine: Now my Thoughts swam in a Sea of Joy, which meeting with the Torrent of the foresaid Vexations, made a kind of a dangerous Rencounter, ready to overset my Reason. I passed some Nights without Sleep, and Days without Food, by reason of this secret Satisfaction. At last, being overcome with a little Drowsiness, I fell asleep in a Corner of our Garden, and dreamed, that, on a sudden, an angry Power carried me away and made me climb a high Mountain: at last brought me to that Shade where I had heretofore written those Verses on the Bark of an Ash, as I told you, in which I seemed to prefer the Muses and a studious Life, before that of Marriage and Business. Whereupon,

> ——My uncouth Guardian said,
> ——Unlucky Maid!
> Since, since thou hast the Muses chose,
> Hymen, and Fortune are thy Foes.
> For Thou shalt have *Cassandra's* Fate,
> In all thou say'st, unfortunate,
> The God of Wit gave Her this Curse,
> And Fortune sends Thee this, and worse.

In all thou dost, tho' ne'er so good,
By all the World misunderstood!
In best of Actions, be despised!
And Fools, and Knaves above thee prized!
Foes like Serpents hiss and bite thee,
All thy Friends agree to slight thee!
Love and Lovers, give thee Pain,
For they, and thou shalt love in vain!
Either Death shall from thee take 'em,
Or they thee, or thou forsake 'em!
Thy Youth and Fortune vainly spend,
And in thy Age have not a Friend!
Thy whole Life pass in Discontent,
In Want, in Woe, and Banishment!
Be Broken under Fortunes Wheel,
Direct thy Actions ne'er so well.
A thousand other Ills beside ⎫
Fortune does still for them provide, ⎬
Who to the Muses are allied. ⎭
    At this Harangue, my Grief was so extreme,
    That I awaked all Joy it proved a Dream.[36]

But it has proved so true in the Event, that I think one can hardly call it so but a real Vision, as may appear by the Sequel of my Story, to which I return.

Many Days and Weeks passed; and several Visits he made me, with repeated Assurances of his Passion: still expecting the coming of his Father. How far my Looks, or Gestures, might betray my Thoughts, I know not; but I kept my Words close Prisoners, till they should be set at Liberty by the Desire of his Father or the command of mine or at least conveyed into the Mouth of my prudent Mother. Thus I thought I planted my Actions in a good Soil, in the Ground of Virtue; and watered them with the Stream of Discretion: But the worm of Pride, and Self-esteem was at the bottom and gnawed the Root: I did not enough reflect on the author of all Good; but thought perhaps I trod the Path of Virtue, by the clue of my own Wisdom, and without due Reflection and Thanks to the Donor. Which is, as if one should daily wind up a Watch, and keep it clean, but never set it to the Hour: By which means the little Machine is useless, though it go never so well; so if we perform all moral Virtues, without directing them to Heaven, they prove little available to our Happiness.

Whether *Bosvil* knew, or was informed that his Father would not come, or was impatient of his Delay, I know not; but he disposed himself to go to his Father, who lived twenty Miles from us, as before remarked; though my Lover

---

[36] Echoes the end of John Bunyan's *The Pilgrim's Progress*; Christian and Hopeful watch from Heaven while Ignorance is cast into Hell.

had established himself in our Neighbourhood, both for his Health, it being a more serene Air, and more convenient for his Practice, being nearer *London*. When he took his Leave of me, he begged me a thousand times to remember him when absent. How is it possible (said he) that I shall pass this tedious time without you. Every Minute that I am from you, seems an Age; nothing is grateful, nothing satisfactory without you; my Senses take Pleasure in nothing but you, even Reason loses her Regency; and I rave on nothing but my absent *Galesia*. Ah! that I might call you truly mine: However, let me flatter myself, that I am so far yours; that you will not quite forget me when absent; but pity my Banishment; pity, and promise to think on me; promise but that, and I shall consolate myself with that Thought; our Souls have subtle ways of corresponding, they will converse, when these terrestrial Organs know nothing of the Matter: Then breathe a Sigh, and bid it go to your *Bosvil*, it will meet whole Legions of mine, which will surround it, and bring it safe to my Heart unmixed with common air; and, when you are in your solitary Walks, whisper that you want your *Bosvil's* Company, and some little waiting Spirit appointed by my good Genius, to attend you, shall quickly bring it to his Master, and I shall in a Moment, by a secret Inspiration, know my *Galesia's* Desires; and so be happy at a Distance! Then promise me, my Sweet, my Fair, my Bright Charmer! this small Consolation; this is the way by which Souls converse, independent of these heavy Tenements in which they are imprisoned: Promise this, and your *Bosvil* shall not be quite unhappy in this three Weeks Absence; which otherwise will be a *Tedium* to me. In this manner he took his leave of me. All which I answered with alternate Smiles, Sighs, and broken Words, scarce containing common Sense.

When he was gone, I thought on him perpetually; I sighed every Moment, I counted the whiling Hours and Moments of his Absence; wished this tedious three Weeks cut out of the Records of Time, often repeating to myself his Vows and Assurances of everlasting Love, resolving to be no longer cruel to myself and him; but let him know what mighty Sums of Love I had been hoarding up for him, since the Moment of our first Interview. O my *Bosvil* (said I to myself) I will let thee know, how true a Master thou hast been of my Affections; I will beg thy Pardon for the Pains I have made thee feel, by my seeming Indifference; and kindly reproach thee for thy feigned Negligence; and then repair all with infinite Testimonies of everlasting Fidelity: Tie myself to thee in Nuptial Bands, and ratify all by a constant Obedience. Thus, a thousand rambling Thoughts, a thousand fond Fancies agitated my poor young Head and Heart! Sometimes I busied myself with thinking what I was to say to his Father, whom I concluded he would bring along with him. I said, and unsaid a thousand things. This Speech I feared betrayed too much Fondness, that too little Kindness: This seemed too submissive to the Son, that not respectful enough to the Father. Now I studied what Excuse to make to my Mother, for having so long concealed from her a Matter of such Importance; then what to say to my Father, for being so ready to leave him for a Husband.

Thus I passed my Hours in perpetual Agitation of Mind, part of which was what Clothes, what Friends, what Ceremonies should be at this my approaching Marriage.

The tedious three Weeks being elapsed, *Bosvil* arrives, but not my Lover: He came with greater Coldness and Indifferency than ever! No Ray of Love darted from his Eyes, no Sigh from his Heart, no Smile towards me, nothing, nothing, but a dusky cold Indifferency, as if Love had never shined in his Hemisphere! The Truth is, I took it for Disguise, but could not imagine what should make him put it on; I thought the *Mumming* went too far, when the Masqueraders murdered those they pretended to divert;[37] but to convince me that this was no feigned Indifference, he stayed several Days at our House, acting this Scene of Inconstancy to Perfection. Much I studied, but could think of nothing that could have disobliged him; I examining my Words to find if I had said anything that might have been affronting at his Arrival. I consulted my Glass to see if my Person was changed in that fatal three Weeks: I reflected on all things, from the beginning, to the end; but could find nothing whereof to accuse myself; sometimes in my Thoughts I confronted his past Kindness, with his present Coldness; his passionate Speeches, Looks, and Gestures, with his Neglect, Coldness, and Indifferency; one raised my Hopes above *Ela*, the other cast my Despair below *Gamut*.[38] Thus I ran divisions in my Fancy, which made but harsh Music to my Interiour: Methoughts I resembled the Sisters in Hell, whom the Poets feign to catch Water in a sieve.

Now whether this Affliction was laid on me by the immediate Hand of Providence, or that Fate, or my Constellations produced it by secondary Causes, I knew not; but Innocence was my Consolation; for I had nothing wherewith to reproach myself; I had acted justly and honourably towards him; he could not upbraid me either with Coyness or Kindness; for though I had squared my Actions by the exact Rules of Virtue and Modesty; yet I did not exclude Civility and good Nature; for I always stayed in his Company, heard him, laughed, fooled, and jested with him; yet not so freely as to transgress good Manners or break Respect on either side; all which might assure a Person less judicious than himself, that neither his Person, nor Proposals, were disagreeable. All these considerations served to render his Coldness the more surprizing; but it pleased God to have it thus; *Bosvil* perhaps was my Idol, and rivaled Heaven in my Affections, that I might say to him, as *Cowley* to his *Mistress*.

[37] Allusion to *The Revenger's Tragedy* (1607) in which Vindice, Hippolito, and two others come in masquerade and murder the late duke's son Lussurioso and three others, *or* to Thomas Durfey's *The Famous History of the Rise and Fall of Massaniello*, Part II (1699), in which the Viceroy's wife treats the usurping plebeians to a masque and has them seized and killed.

[38] *Eia . . . Gamut*: the highest and lowest notes on the medieval musical scale.

Thou even my Prayers dost steal from me, ⎫
For I with wild Idolatry, ⎬
Begin to God, and end 'em all in Thee.[39] ⎭

This Vicissitude in my Affairs, made me reflect on those Verses, or Vision, which said, Hymen *and Fortune are thy Foes*, etc. In which I endeavoured to be resigned, saying, 'It is the Lord's doing, tho' marvelous in my Eyes.'[40] Though nothing could be harsher than to be thus abandoned in the Flower of my Youth, and that by my own Relation, who ought to have sustained me against any false Pretender: I endeavoured to detach my Thoughts from him; or if it was so that I must needs think on him, I resolved it should be on his Crimes, Falsehood, and Cruelty.

Thus by degrees his Company became troublesome, and his Presence ungrateful. Yet could I not avoid either, for I had no Reason to quarrel with him, unless for not courting me, as formerly: And that was turning the Tables, and making myself the Lover, instead of the Person beloved; which was not only contradictory to my haughty Humour, but seemed in a manner to invert Nature; nevertheless I forced myself to bear it, with a seeming Equality of Mind, till a fit Occasion would offer itself to my Revenge. Like the Quaker that is smitten on the one Cheek, turns the other also; but after that having (as he thinks) fulfilled the Law, can beat his Adversary as well as any carnal Man: so I waited but for a left Cheek-blow; some ungrateful Action, that might give at least a seeming just Cause to quarrel, so as to take occasion to banish him; his Presence being as disagreeable to me as a Specter; for it's natural enough, that the Cause of Grief, should be the Object of Aversion.

I remained full of this Wish many Months; at last Fortune was a little propitious to my Desires, at least I wrested an Occasion to my Caprice, which was thus.

Bosvil and another young Gentleman his Friend met my Father at a certain Place over a bottle; here *Bosvil* proposed his Friend to my Father as an Husband for me, all Conditions of Portion[41] and Jointure[42] were there proposed, and approved on both sides, and the Day appointed on which the Gentleman should come to visit me, which was to be the Week following. This my Father told me with Satisfaction, withal minding me, how much I was obliged to my Cousin *Bosvil*: To which my Answers were few, dubious, and

---

[39] 'The Thief' from *The Mistress, or Several Copies of Love-Verses* (1647) by Abraham Cowley (1618–67). Cowley's lines read, 'Thou, even my prayers thou hauntest me; | And I, with wild Idolatry. | Begin, to God, and end them all, to Thee,' ll. 3–6. Barker may have quoted from memory.

[40] Matt. 21: 42 and Mark 12: 11.

[41] *Portion*: the share of a parent's estate established for a daughter or younger son by the parents' marriage settlement. For daughters, it was usually expressed as a fixed amount of money.

[42] *Jointure*: part of a marriage settlement designed to support the wife should she be widowed, usually a provision of land or income from property or investments.

obscure; which passed with my good Father, for a little Virgin Surprize; which Discourses of this nature are apt to raise in the Hearts of young Creatures. But, O my *Lucasia!* I cannot tell you what I suffered when I was alone, Rage and Madness seized me; Malice, and Revenge were all I thought on: I inspired an evil Genius, resolved his Death, and pleased myself in the Fancy of a barbarous Revenge: I shall delight myself to see the Blood pour out of his false Heart: In order to accomplish this detestable Freak, I went towards the Place of his Abode, supposing a Rapier in my hand, and saying to myself; The false *Bosvil* should now disquiet me no more, nor any other of our Sex; in him I will end his Race, no more of them shall come to disturb, or affront Womankind; this only Son, shall die by the hands of me an only Daughter; and however the World may call it Cruelty or barbarous I am sure our Sex will have reason to thank me and keep an Annual Festival, on which a Criminal like him is executed: the Example perhaps will deter others, and secure many from the Wrongs of such false Traitors; and I be magnified in future times; for it was for ridding the World of a Monster, that *Hercules*[43] was esteemed so great a Hero, and *George* a Saint.[44] Then sure I shall be ranked in the Catalogue of Heroines, for such a Service done to my Sex: for certainly the Deserts of *Arabia* never produced a more formidable Monster than this unaccountable *Bosvil*. Behold what Sophisms one can find to justify any mad Attempt, and how for the gratifying our Fancy, we are able to affront, if not quite reverse the Laws of Nature: that, if the Feebleness of our Hands did not moderate the Fury of our Heads, Woman sometimes would exceed the fiercest Savages; especially, when affronted in her Amours: which brings into my Mind a Verse or two on such an Occasion.

> `A slighted *Woman* oft a *Fury* grows,
> And for Revenge quits her Baptismal Vows,
> Becomes a *Witch*, and does a *Fiend* espouse.

In these wild Thoughts I wandered, till Weariness made me know my own weakness and Incapacity of performing what Fury had inspired and forced me to seek Repose under the first Shade; where my flowing Tears mitigated the Heat of my Rage, washing away those extravagant Thoughts, and made me turn my Anger against myself, my wretched self, that woeful and unworthy thing; the Scorn of my Kinsman, Lover, Friend, etc. A thousand times I wished that some kind Serpent would creep out of its Hole and sting me to Death, or that Thunder would descend, and strike me into the Earth; and so at once perform my Death, and Funeral! O no (said I) that would render *Bosvil* too happy. I must go home and write the whole Scene of his Treachery, and

---

[43] *Hercules*: this hero of Greek myth had superhuman strength; he killed the Lernean hydra as one of the twelve Labours of Hercules. The hydra had nine heads, and, each time Hercules cut one off, two grew in its place.

[44] *George*: the patron saint of England, who killed a dragon that ate villagers; his story became an allegory for the victory of a Christian hero over evil.

then on myself act the last part of the Tragedy. With these Thoughts I bubbled my froward Fancy,[45] and so returning home very weary, I threw myself
on my Bed, where all my resentment became a Prey to gentle Slumbers;
which much refreshed my weary Body and more weary Mind, rendering me
a little capable of acting according to the Dictates of Reason; but not without
a large Mixture of Passion; that when I awaked, I wrote to him after this
Bizarre manner.

Cousin;

*I thought you had been so well acquainted with my Humour, touching a Married
Life, as to know it to be my Aversion, therefore wonder you should make such a
Proposal to my Father on your Friend's Behalf: perhaps you will say it was but in
jest, and I believe it was no more; but I beg you to make something else the Subject
of your Raillery, and leave me out, till Misbehaviour render me the proper Object
of ridicule, which has not hitherto; for I have done nothing dishonourable to myself,
nor disobliging to you; therefore ought rather to be the Object of civility than
Banter, which perhaps, Distance and Absence may accomplish; therefore I beg you
will see me no more, till Fortune commission you by the Change of your condition;
in the meantime I shall remain,*

Your Kinswoman,
and humble Servant,

GALESIA.

In the simplicity of these Words were a great deal of cunning, and under
the Shadow of Frowardness, lay covered much Kindness, which I knew he
must discern, if he had any real Affection for me in his Heart; for Love is like
Ghosts, or Spirits that will appear, to those to whom they would speak, and
to others are quite invisible. I pleased myself I had taken this Occasion, at once
to command his Absence, and in a covert manner testify my Affection; for I
knew that was the natural Interpretation of these Words, *See me no more.* For
nothing but a real Mistress could pretend to use them; and nothing but a fond
Mistress could pretend to be displeased at the Presence of a Kinsman, or a
Friend, for having offered an advantageous Marriage in the Person of his
Friend. Here was now no Medium left, no Space between open Lover, and
open Enemy; here was now no more Love-Frolics to be acted under the
Disguise of a Friend, or Kinsman; if he came to me after such a Prohibition,
he must come upon the Pikes of my Anger, which he could not pretend to
appease by any other Atonement, but that of his everlasting Love in Marriage-
Vows. If he stayed away, I had my Ends I had long sought, the being rid of
one that gave me so much Disquiet. Thus I satisfied myself in expectation of
his Answer, which came next Day in these Words.

Madam,

*I am extremely astonished, to find you so displeased at what passed the other
Day, which was no way meant to your Prejudice, but on the contrary, much to*

---

[45] *With these Thoughts . . . froward fancy:* deluded with insubstantial fantasies her eager hopes.

your Advantage. However, Madam, I shall not justify what you are pleased to condemn; but add also the Testimony of my Obedience, in submitting to your Prohibition, and not presume to see you more, tho' in it I sequester myself from those Charms I have so long adored; and only at a Distance admire what your rigor forbids me to approach, and so rest,

Madam,

Your Kinsman,

and humble Servant,

BOSVIL.

This his complying with seeing me *no more* gave me the same Satisfaction that a Patient has when his Limbs are cutting off, the Remedy, and the Disease being both grievous; however, I know now what I had to trust to, and therefore studied to make a Virtue of this Necessity, and consolate myself with patient suffering what I could no ways avoid. I experienced amply the Word of the Sage, that all was Vanity and Vexation of Spirit, and every Act of our Lives Folly, except offered to the Glory of God.[46] I reflected on my late extravagant Rage, when I designed his Death, and knew I ought to cry earnestly to be delivered from Blood-Guiltiness. I retired into myself, and returned to my Studies, the Woods, Fields, and Pastures had the most part of my time; by which means I became as perfect in rural Affairs as any *Arcadian* Shepherdess;[47] insomuch, that my Father gave me absolute Power and Authority over his Servants and Labourers; it was I that appointed them their Work, and paid them their Wages; I put in and put out who I pleased; and was as absolute over my Rustics, as the great *Turk* over his Subjects; and though this was a great Fatigue, yet it gratified my Vanity, that I could perform things above my Age and Sex; and though it was an impediment to my Studies, yet it made amends, it being itself a Study, and that a most useful one: the rules to sow and reap in their proper Seasons, to know what Pasture is fit for Beeves, and what for milched Kine, with all their Branches, being a more useful Study than the exactest Grammar-Rules, or Longitude, or Latitude, Squaring the Circle, etc. The Farmer, according to the Utility of his Occupation, deserves to hold the first Rank amongst Mankind: that one may justly reflect with Veneration on those times, when Kings and Princes thought it no Derogation to their Princely Dignities. The Nobles in ancient times, did not leave their Country Seats, to become the Habitation of Jackdaws, and the Manufactory of Spiders, who in reproach to their Mistress, prepare Hangings to supply those the Moth has devoured, through her

[46] Summary of a major theme of Ecclesiastes, see ch. 1.

[47] *Arcadian shepherdess*: Arcadia is a bleak and mountainous district in the central Peloponnese in which Virgil set the idealized world of the pastoral in his *Eclogues*. Philip Sidney's *Arcadia* (1581; 1583–4; combined 1593) is composed of poems, pastoral eclogues, and tales. Numerous English writers used Arcadia as the setting for literature about the lives and loves of romanticized shepherds.

Negligence, or Absence. But to return from whence I digressed. This Rural Business was so full of Employment, that its continual Fatigue contributed very much to the Ease of my Thoughts touching *Bosvil*. The constant Incumbrance which attended this Station, left no space for Love to agitate my Interior. The Labour of the Day was recompensed with sound Sleep at Night: Those silent Hours being passed in Sleep's Restorative, the Day provided new Business for my waking Thoughts, whilst Health and wholesome Food repaid this my Industry. Thus in a Country Life we roll on in a circle, like the heavenly Bodies, our Happiness being seldom eclipsed, unless by the Interposition of our follies, or Passions. Now finding myself daily to get ground of my sickly Thoughts, I doubted not of a perfect Recovery. I reflected on those Words of the Poet,[48] and with good Reason made their Application.

> *Fac monitus fugias otia, etc.*
> Ovid Remed. Amoris.
> Fly Sloth if thou wilt *Cupid* overthrow,
> Sloth points his Darts, but Business breaks his Bow,
> Employment to his Flames is Ice and Snow.
> *Cupid* and *Venus* are to Sloth inclined,
> From both, in Business, thou may'st safety find,
> For Love gives place, when Business fills the Mind.

Moreover, that which contributed much to this Victory over myself, was the return of my Brother from *France*; his dear Company which I had long wanted, filled my Heart with Joy, and exterminated that Melancholy, which had too long perplexed me: the little Rarities he brought adorned my Person and garnished my Closet; he frequently entertained me with the Description of Places and Customs of *France*, in particular Convents, and their way of living, which I so admired, that I wished for such Places in *England*, which if there had been, 'tis certain I had then become a Nun, and under a holy Veil buried all Thoughts of *Bosvil*. In this my Brother's dear Company I daily improved my Studies, so as to begin to understand an Author, and none pleased me more than those of Physic,[49] all which served to fill my Head with Notions, and perhaps my Heart with Pride, at best but a misspending of time; Learning being neither of use nor Ornament in our Sex. Some counting a studious Woman as ridiculous as an effeminate Man; and learned Books as unfit for her Apartment, as Paint, Washes,[50] and Patches for his. In fine, the Men will not allow it to be our Sphere; so consequently, we can never be supposed to move in it gracefully: but like the Toad in the Fable, that affected to swell

---

[48] *the Poet*: the works of the Roman poet Publius Ovidius Naso (48 BC–AD 17 or 18) were popular in the early eighteenth century; the *Heroides* and the *Metamorphoses* were especially familiar. The line from *Remedia Amoris* translates thus: 'Obey my counsels and shun leisure,' l. 136.

[49] *Physic*: the art and science of healing, practised with plants and other remedies.

[50] *Paint, Washes*: make-up and treatments for the complexion. Both were ridiculed and even dangerous. Make-up was often lead-based, and washes were made out of such ingredients as mercury and asses' milk.

itself as big as the Ox, and so burst in the Enterprize:[51] But let the World confine, or enlarge Learning as they please, I care not; I do not regret the time I bestowed in its company, it having been my good Friend, to bail me from *Bosvil's* Fetters, though I am not so generous, by way of return, to pass my word for its good Behaviour in our Sex always, and in all Persons.

Now *Bosvil* having been sometime absent, our Family, Friends, and Neighbours, began to take notice of it; and more especially at my Brother's Return, when everybody came to bid him welcome, not only the Gentlemen, but even the Ladies, at least to congratulate my Mother, on his safe Arrival.

Now it was that his pretended Mistress, the fair *Lowland* was married, which you will believe was a certain Satisfaction to me, as Mischief is to Witches, though they get nothing by it; much I longed to banter, and insult him on this Occasion; but his constant Absence deprived me of that Pleasure. However, I could not pass over such a Field of full ripe Content without cropping some few Ears.[52] Wherefore I wrote him a Letter in a counterfeit Character, and withal sent him a willow-Garland,[53] to crown the forsaken Lover, which indeed was so well made of Gumwork, that one might take it for a real Branch of that forsaken Tree. This, with divers other Emblems and Mottos, I sent him to *London* by the Carrier.

How he received this, I know not, neither did I care; but I was told afterwards that he laughed, and told his Friends what a pretty Present he had received from an unknown Hand; and withal that he would secure himself from the like Attacks by his speedy Marriage; and accordingly proceeded with a young Gentlewoman at *London*: And at his Return acquainted his Friends, and in particular, a young Gentlewoman of our Relation, who, with many others, mistrusted him of an Amour with me; but I not having told her of it, who was in all things else my Confident, she laid aside that Thought, especially now since he declared to her this his approaching Nuptials. However, she and everybody of our Acquaintance was amazed at his long Absence from our House, and asked him the Cause; to which he answered indirectly, and with divers shuffles; but the virtuous *Towrissa* (our said Cousin) pressed him from time to time, till he, no longer able to resist her Importunities, told her, that his Cousin *Galesia* had forbid him; at which she was much surprized, but

---

[51] *Toad in the Fable*: an Aesop fable in which a little frog told its father that it had seen a terrible monster, 'as big as a mountain', and the father said it was only a farmer's ox. He puffed himself up and asked if the monster was that big. The little frog said, 'Much larger'. The father puffed himself up larger and asked the little frog if it was that big. The little frog said bigger, and the father swelled and swelled. The little frog said that the ox was not that big, but the father frog burst.

[52] *Ears*: the metaphor is to ears of corn.

[53] *Willow-Garland*: traditional symbol of grief for an unrequited love or mourning for a lost or dead lover, an allusion in numerous early ballads. English poets depicted Dido carrying a willow branch, and Thomas Dekker's *Patient Grissill*, a play to which Barker refers later, has the line, 'A wreath of willow for despised Grissill', V.ii.109. Fredson Bowers lists Henry Chettle and William Haughton as co-authors of the play in *The Dramatic Works of Thomas Dekker*, vol. i (Cambridge: Cambridge University Press, 1953).

said it should not rest so; for (said she) I will have you go to her with me this very Day, that I may obtain the Blessing of a Peacemaker. He complied with her, and came to make me a Visit; our Interview, after a whole Year's Absence, was surprizing to us both, for we trembled, blushed, and flattered in our Words; that it was with utmost difficulty we performed the Civilities of the Occasion. After being seated, I remember he gazed with all the Eagerness, or rather Distraction of youthful Eyes, instigated by a tender Passion; which so dazzled and confounded me, that I was every moment afraid that I should sink down in the midst of the company, who sat talking of things indifferent. Having for some time thus planted the Batteries of our Eyes against each other's Hearts; he gave the first Shot by a deep sigh, saying, O cursed Love, that will never leave a Man; and rose from his Seat, as it were, to disperse those Vapours which seemed to oppress him; to which I replied (foolishly enough, with a feigned Laugh, to stifle a real Sigh) that I hoped he had no reason to complain of Love's Tyranny; yes, yes, said our cousin *Towrissa*, know you not, that our Cousin *Bosvil* is shortly to be married, so thinks every Moment a Martyrdom till the Day arrives; therefore, dear Cousin (continued she) get your self Dancing-Shoes, if you mean to be a Bridesmaid, etc. to which my Mother gravely answered, that it must needs be a great Satisfaction to his Parents, to see him their only Child well settled.

What a Shock this Discourse gave me I cannot describe, but 'tis certain I never felt anything like it; behold now, my *Lucasia*, what was become of all my Resolutions, and fancied Indifferency; see what all my Anger, Fury, Scorn, Revenge, prohibiting him to see me, the fancied Satisfaction I took in his Absence, behold, I say, what all this came to, even just as much as the Lord *Rochester* says of Court Promises, and Whores Vows, which all *End in Nothing*;[54] so these my Resolutions were all mere Gossamers, composed of Vapours, and carried about with airy Fancy, and next Day reduced to Nothing; but thus it is in most things of Human Life, we know not ourselves, nor our own Incapacity; we think ourselves able to perform this or that, or look even Death in the Face; and when we have most need of our imaginary Fortitude, we find ourselves most destitute, and feeble, as I experienced in this Rencounter: for I was ready to die in the place, but durst not remove, fearing my Legs should fail me; which I perceived all in convulsions, and trembling; I was like a Horse in a Stable on fire, burnt if he stays, yet dares not go out; at last holding by the Tables, and the Chairs, with feigned Smiles in my Face, and jocose Words in my Mouth; I made a shift to pass this Gauntlet, and get into my Chamber, where God only was witness of my Complaints and Succour. In the midst of my Sighs and Tears, I threw myself on my Bed, rolled on the floor, hoped that every Cramp I felt would be my Death's Convulsion, uttered a thousand Imprecations against him, and my

---

[54] *End in Nothing*: 'Upon Nothing' (1679), 'Kings' promises, whores' vows—towards thee [Nothing] they bend,' l. 50.

hard Fortune; and contrary to that Philosopher, who thanked the God that had made him a Man, and not a Beast;[55] I say quite contrary to him;

> I wished myself unsprung of Human Race,
> Rather than feel so piercing a Disgrace;
> For what is more disgraceful to a Maid,
> What Pangs so sharp her tortured soul invade,
> As this sad Curse——*Deserted and betrayed.*
> Thou Heav'n alone my Innocence can'st know,
> The World will ne'er believe that I am so,
> 'Tis contradictory to Human Thought,
> That Love from virtuous Principles is wrought,
> That nobler Passions are from Sense refined,
> And Reason over-rules the Youthful Mind.
> But Heav'n knows all, and knows my higher Soul,
> Did ev'ry meaner end of Love controul,
> Knows the just Schemes of my intended Life,
> The Chaste, the Cheerful, and the Virtuous Wife.
> To be a Matron, to my Household Good,
> A helpful Neighbour in my Neighbourhood,
> With hospitable Table, open door,
> One for my Friends, the other for the Poor:
> Then teach my Family to lead good Lives,
> And be a Pattern unto other Wives;
> In doing which a general Good I do,
> When Wives are good, they make good Husbands too,
> Thus by degrees might all Mankind be so.
> But Fate, or Fortune, call it what you please,
> Takes cruel Sport in baffling Schemes like these;
> Thus all my secret Plots and Mines are crost,
> The *Babel*[56] ruined, and the Builder lost;
> The tow'ring Notions from their airy Height,
> Are fall'n, and Scorn is added to the Weight.
> Methinks I hear the People pointing say,
> That, that's the fond, but scorned *Galesia.*
> That's she whose Beauty once the Youth inspired,
> She whom the gazing Scholars eyes admired,
> For whom the flutt'ring Gallants of the Gown,
> Despised their Idol Beauties of the Town.
> Behold her now abandoned and forlorn,
> The idle Object of each Rustic's Scorn;
> O thus to live, what Female Heart can bear,
> No, no, I'll first myself in pieces tear,
> And first begin with this disheveled Hair.

[55] Unidentified, but perhaps a witty paraphrase of Luke 18: 11.

[56] *Babel*: men built a tower in the Babylonian city of Babel in an attempt to reach Heaven and 'make a name for' themselves; God made them speak different languages, they gave up the tower, and scattered over the earth, Gen. 11: 1-9.

After this Hurricane and divers Gusts of Sighs and Tears, I began to flatter my Fancy, that all this might be a Composition, like that of *Lowland,* and no more of Truth in this his *London* Mistress, than in that of Mistress *Lowland;* who was now actually married to another Man: And when by this means the torments of my distorted Mind was a little appeased, I endeavoured to clear my Countenance, washed my Face, took Air at the window, and so went down again to the Company; some time passed in Discourse of things indifferent; then *Bosvil* took leave, and went that Night to his Father's House.

Towrissa stayed to bear me company, and was my Bed-fellow that Night, the greatest part of which we passed in discourse of *Bosvil,* she relating to me how seriously he had told her and her Mother of his intended Marriage, together with all the circumstance of Portion and Jointure, Description of the Lady's Person, and Family, etc. that there was no place left for doubt, for any one but me, who had the Eyes of my Understanding shut, and sealed up by the former Farce he had acted about Mrs. *Lowland.* Nevertheless, I suffered great Distractions in my Mind; and when length of Prattle had lulled *Towrissa* asleep, I only refreshed my weary Spirits with weeping.

After two or three Days, the News arrived that *Bosvil* was sick of a continued Fever, even so bad, that all despaired of his Life. This was a new Stroke of Fortune, and she was armed with a Weapon, against which I had never contended; and at the same time was angry at myself for grieving. Ah foolish *Galesia* (said I to myself) ah silly Girl, to grieve for him who deserves thy Scorn and Hatred, for him that has robbed thee of thy quiet three whole Years, for him that swore to love thee, that languished, and died at thy Feet, expressly to make thee miserable; for him that obstructed the Amours of the first and second *Brafort,* that thy Ruin might be the more complete; for him that was treated by thy hospitable Parents, more like their own Child than an adventitious Guest, by which the traitor had Opportunity to steal away the Heart of their only daughter! and is it possible that thou shouldst grieve for such a Wretch as this? one that Heaven has now marked with its just Vengeance, and *has sent this Sickness as a Scourge for his Falsehood.* But not withstanding all this, I must grieve and pray for him, which I am sure I did with more Eagerness than ever I prayed for my own Soul; in which I did but pay a Devotion which he had advanced, for he has often assured me, that he offered me daily in his Prayers. The Consideration of which holy Kindness made me redouble my Request to Heaven to spare his Life; though at the same time I had much rather he should have died than not live mine: However, I did not pretend to capitulate with the Almighty, but asked his Life in general Terms, without including or excluding his Person, which by Intervals, I hoped might yet one Day be mine; for I still bubbled my Fancy that he loved me, and that the Sight of me, after so long Absence, was the genuine Cause of this his Illness, and then made wild Resolutions to visit him, fancied myself there, figured to myself the Transports of Joy he would be in to see me so kind, imagined his Father and Mother, embracing me as their proper Child; then immediately drawing the curtain, behold myself rejected by them as the Plague of their Family, perhaps refused, and slighted by him, rebuked and wondered at for my coming, scorned and laughed at by all the World, severely treated by my Parents, or perhaps out of hopes of ever seeing them again; for I very well believed there was no Medium after such an Exploit, between being received by his Parents, and abandoned by my own; and for me to have proposed this Visit to them, I knew was vain, having no Pretence to justify the request, the whole Amour having been one continued Act of Folly on the one side, and Treachery on the other; and the last Scene a Declaration of Scorn instead of Kindness; he having owned in presence of my Mother, and other Friends, his Design of marrying another. And then repeat in my Thoughts all his Crimes, and with my best Malice enlarge upon his Treachery, Falsehood, Cruelty, etc. look upon him Dead by the Hand of Heaven, just and good in taking him away, from a Possibility of accomplishing his Perjury in his pretended Marriage; then in an instant, turn over the Leaf, and read him dead as my faithful Lover, recount all the tender Words and Actions that had passed in our three Years Conversation; blame all my feigned Indifference, and forced Coldness towards him; I fancy he thought on me in his Agony, and named me with his dying Breath; conceit[57] I saw his much grieved Parents cursing me as the Author of their Affliction; and after a thousand of these tragical Notions, which presented themselves to my distracted Imagination, my Fancy would open another Scene, and make me think I saw him alive, and happy in the Arms of his *London* Mistress, living in all the Felicities that a happy Espousal could procure. Thus my Thoughts played at Racket,[58] and seldom minded the Line of Reason, my Mind laboured under a perpetual shaking Palsy of Hope and Fear, my whole Interiour was nothing but Distraction and Uncertainty. At last I resolved to send a Messenger secretly to see how he did, in which I did a vast Penance for all the proud Actions of my Life; for nothing could be harder, than to be obliged to such a Person, in making him the Confident of my Affection. However, at this time I did Violence to my Nature, and ordered one of my Father's Men to go secretly on this Errand; but first I ordered him to go to my Cousin *Bosvil's* own Dwelling, which was near us, and there enquire after his Health, and if there he heard of his being better, then to go no farther, otherwise, to go on his way to *Bosvil's* Father's House. The Man performed my Orders exactly, and hearing at this Place that he was somewhat better, went no farther; with which I remained satisfied, till time brought him to our House perfectly recovered. But ah! this Recovery was a Death to all my Hopes, for the first Use he made of his new restored Health,

---

[57] *conceit:* imagined.
[58] *Racket:* game played by two people with rackets, who take turns hitting a ball that they hope to keep rebounding from a wall.

was to go marry his Mistress at *London*, making our House in the way, and me the Auditor of that horrid News, which at first shocked me; but I had been so often put upon by false Alarms, that I was now grown like the countrymen to the Shepherds in the Fable, who, when the Wolf really came, stirred not, having been often deluded by the Shepherds, and called without Occasion;[59] for I thought it impossible that he could come to tell me such News to my Face. But what is most astonishing, I have been told since, that in his Sickness he gave all he had to me, and recommended me to his Parents as their proper Child; and they promised him to receive me as such. Now after all this, to go directly after his Sickness and be married to another, is a Transaction most unaccountable. However, I knew nothing of this at that time, for I was told it afterwards, and that he had been extremely concerned on my Account in this his Sickness. However, ignorant as I was of these Circumstances, I did not in the least believe, that his going to *London* (when he passed by our House) was to be married, but looked upon it as a mere Jest or Banter, such as was that of Mrs. *Lowland* and others; wherefore I could not pass over this Subject of Frolic or Mirth, without adding to the Jest; and as I had sent him a Willow-Garland upon the Marriage of his pretended Mrs. *Lowland*; so now I sent him a pretty Pair of Horns, neatly made of Bugles,[60] by which I meant to joke and banter him on this his pretended Marriage; but alas! it proved more than a Pretence, and the Horns came to him just upon his Wedding-Day, in the Presence of his Bride, and all the Guests; as also several roguish Emblems and Mottos, the Horns being fastened to a Headband, as a most sovereign Remedy for the Headache, to which married Men are often very subject, especially those that are wedded to Coquets; and all which, I protest, was without the least Design of Malice, of thinking in the least, that he was really to be married, but thought I only rendered Jest for Jest, believing his Discourse of Marriage had only been a Banter or Amusement, such as that of Mrs. *Lowland*, and the rest beforementioned.

Now though all this came from an unknown Hand, no Question but he believed it came from me; and by his Behaviour I concluded as much, for he always avoided my Presence, and shunned my Company as much as possible, almost to the Breach of common Civility; by which I fancied I was the Object of his Aversion, but a Confident of his assured me the contrary, and that *Bosvil* had told him, that Love had taken such firm Root in his Soul, that in spite of all his Efforts, even Marriage itself, he could not eradicate it; and therefore avoided my Presence, because he could not see me with Indifferency. Moreover, he told him what Conflicts he underwent during his

---

[59] *Shepherds in the Fable . . . without Occasion*: in Aesop's fable, the shepherd boy cried 'Wolf,' to summon the villagers several times for his amusement. When a wolf came and he cried out, no one came.

[60] *of Bugles*: from wild oxen.

Sickness; but at his Recovery, finding that I had taken no notice of him, he resolved to shake off his Fetters and abandon one who had never showed any Kindness to him, but treated him always with such an Air of Indifference, as was rather the Effect of Prudence than Affection; and that he had invented that Story of Mrs. *Lowland* to try if Jealousy would work upon me; but all my Conduct had been with so much Caution and Circumspection, quite different from Passion or Tenderness, that he thought (with others) that all amorous Inclinations were buried with *Brafort*, and that he could never hope farther than for a second Place in my Affections. How far all this was sincere or pretended, I know not, I rather think he made it a Handle for his own Falsehood for Love is apt to interpret things in its own Favour; and Men believe Women to be forwarder than they really are, taking even complaisance and Civilities for Affection; but he thought fit to take hold of another Handle, the better to stifle his own Falsehood and hide it from the sight of my Friends, by laying the Blame on me. But to return; he was married at *London*, and brought home his Bride. Now it was that I was forced to act the Part of Patient *Grizell*,[61] and go with other Relations to bid her welcome, throw the Stocking, eat Sackposset,[62] and perform all the Farce of a well-pleased Kinswoman; invite her to our House, prepare Dinners and Treats for her, and in all things seem easy and satisfied; all this I was constrained to do, or lay my Disgrace open to all the World.

Thus, my *Lucasia*, I have brought you to the confines of my Story; how far I stand justified or condemned in your Thoughts, I know not, but I remember nothing in which I can accuse myself, even now that I am free from Passion and capable to make a serious Reflection.

The only thing (replied *Lucasia*) that I blame you for is that you did not consult your Mother, whose Wisdom might have found out a way to have accommodated things to all your Satisfactions. Alas (answered *Galesia*) I often reflected on that, but thought it his Business, or his Parents, to discover it to mine and always expected such an Address; for if I had told my Father and Mother, I should but have embarrassed them in a disagreeable Business, for it ill befitted them to proffer their Daughter in Marriage; however, I now believe it the safest and most commendable way in any the like Case, and if I was to act the Part over again, I should certainly proceed on that footing, and in so doing my Duty, find a good Event from the Hand of Providence; for I believe wiser Heads than mine would have been nonplused in a Case so Bizarre, and found enough to do to pass through such a Labyrinth as *Bosvil's*

---

[61] *Patient Grizell* dramatized the traditional story of the wife subjected to numerous tests designed by her husband to assure himself of her devotion. Petrarch, Boccaccio, Chaucer, and others wrote versions of the story. See n. 53.

[62] *throw the Stocking, eat Sack-posset*: on the wedding night, the bride threw her stocking, and, according to legend, the guest who was hit would be the next to marry. The wedding guests enjoyed sack posset, a delicacy made of curdled milk, sack (a white wine from Spain or the Canary Islands), sugar, and spices.

subtle Turnings had composed. Thus I have impartially pointed out to you this unhappy Scene of my Life, which the Bell now ringing to Prayers[63] shall put a Period to.

FINIS.

[63] *Prayers*: mass, which was then held twice between dawn and dusk at regular hours; bells called people to church.

The Strange

ADVENTURES

OF THE

Count *de Vinevil*

And his Family.

Being an Account of what happen'd to them whilst they resided at *Constantinople*.

And of Madamoiselle ARDELISA, his Daughter's being shipwreck'd on the Uninhabited Island *Delos*, in her Return to *France*, with VIOLETTA a *Venetian* Lady, the Captain of the Ship, a Priest, and five Sailors. The Manner of their living there, and strange Deliverance by the Arrival of a Ship commanded by VIOLETTA's Father.

ARDELISA's Entertainment at *Venice*, and safe Return to *France*.

By Mrs. *AUBIN*.

Si Genus Humanum, & mortalia temnitis Arma,
At sperate Deos memores fandi atque nefandi. *
                                                    VIRGIL.

LONDON,
Printed for E. BELL, J. DARBY, A. BETTESWORTH, F. FAYRAM, J. PEMBERTON, J. HOOKE, C. RIVINGTON, F. CLAY, J. BATLEY, and E. SYMON. M. DCC. XXI.

* The Aenied, I. 542–43: 'If men and mortal arms arouse your scorn, | Look unto the gods who will remember right and wrong.'

Reproduced courtesy of The Bodleian Library, University of Oxford (Douce.P.795(3)).

Penelope Aubin
(c.1658–1731)

VERY little is known about Penelope Aubin, and most of that comes from a satire written by the French novelist, the Abbé Prévost, who lived in London at the time she was active as a writer. Aubin was born in London of French parents, her father according to Prévost an impoverished French army officer who had emigrated to England. In the early years of the eighteenth century, she produced several topical political poems, including in 1708 'The Welcome: A Poem to his Grace the Duke of Marlborough', celebrating the Duke's military triumphs against the French in the War of the Spanish Succession. She also published a number of translations from the French and late in her career a play, *The Merry Masqueraders, or, The Humorous Cuckold* (1730). After her early poetic efforts, she published nothing during the next thirteen years, but clearly sensing a popular narrative trend and possibly under financial stress, she turned to writing novels in the early 1720s, the first of which were *The Strange Adventures of the Count de Vinevil and His Family* and *The Life of Madame de Beaumont, a French Lady* (1721). These were followed in quick succession by similar novels through the decade: *The Life and Amorous Adventures of Lucinda, an English Lady* (1722), *The Noble Slaves; or, The Lives and Adventures of Two Lords and Two Ladies* (1722), *The Life of Charlotta du Pont, an English Lady* (1723), *The Life and Adventures of the Lady Lucy* (1726), and *The Life and Adventures of Young Count Albertus, the Son of Count Augustus by the Lady Lucy* (1728).

As the publication of a collected edition of her novels in 1739 would seem to indicate, Aubin's novels were very popular. Although formulaic and repetitive, and awkward in execution much of the time, they shrewdly and effectively combine two major trends in the best-selling fiction of the time: the amatory novella as practised most expertly by Eliza Haywood in the 1720s and the travel adventures exemplified in Defoe's phenomenally popular *Robinson Crusoe* (1719). Most of Aubin's novels feature travel to exotic places, from Turkey and China to Mexico and Peru, and they are transparently structured to appeal to popular taste by offering thrilling moral simplicities where lustful infidels menace pure female innocence. As melodramatic and exciting as they aspire to be, however, Aubin's novels throw a discreet veil over lubricious and sensational particulars, and her pious purposes in her fiction are always explicit. As in *The Count de Vinevil*, her virtuous characters exemplify in their persistence and steady faith in the face of external calamities a trust in the power of

Providence to reward the just and punish the wicked. Her happy endings are designed to make readers feel good about God's Providence and to affirm what she sees as the beleaguered truths of the Christian religion, and to that extent her fiction is part of traditional believers' protest against a world more and more experienced in the early eighteenth century as secular and materialistic. In her last novel, *The Adventures of Young Count Albertus* (1728), this is how she justifies her fiction: 'Since religion is not a jest, death and a future state certain; let us strive to improve the noble sentiments such histories as these will inspire in us; avoid the loose writings which debauch the mind; and since our heroes and heroines have done nothing but what is possible, let us resolve to act like them, make virtue the rule of all our actions and eternal happiness our only aim.'

J.J.R.

The Strange Adventures of the Count de Vinevil and His Family

PREFACE TO THE READER

Since serious things are in a manner altogether neglected by what we call the gay and fashionable part of mankind, and religious treatises grow moldy on the booksellers' shelves in the back shops; when ingenuity is for want of encouragement starved into silence and Toland's[1] abominable writings sell ten times better than the inimitable Mr. Pope's Homer;[2] when Dacier's[3] works are attempted to be translated by a hackney writer, and Horace's Odes turned into prose and nonsense; the few that honor virtue and wish well to our nation ought to study to reclaim our giddy youth; and since reprehensions fail, try to win them to virtue, by methods where delight and instruction may go together. With this design I present this book to the public, in which you will find a story where Divine Providence manifests itself in every transaction, where virtue is tried with misfortunes, and rewarded with blessings. In fine, where men behave themselves like Christians, and women are really virtuous, and such as we ought to imitate.

---

[1] *Toland*: John Toland (1670–1722), deist and author of *Christianity not Mysterious* (1696), a book that scandalized many Christians by espousing a natural religion divorced from specific religious revelations or teachings.

[2] *Pope's Homer*: Alexander Pope (1688–1744) published his translation of Homer's *Iliad* in six volumes from 1715 to 1720, and of Homer's *Odyssey* in five volumes in 1725–6.

[3] *Dacier*: Anne LeFèvre Dacier (1651–1721), critic, woman of letters, and translator. Her *Les Poésies d'Anacréon et de Sapho* made her one of the most respected Hellenists of her time.

As for the truth of what this narrative contains, since Robinson Crusoe has been so well received,[4] which is more improbable, I know no reason why this should be thought a fiction. I hope the world is not grown so abandoned to vice as to believe that there is no such ladies to be found, as would prefer death to infamy; or a man that for remorse of conscience would quit a plentiful fortune, retire, and choose to die in a dismal cell. This age has convinced us that guilt is so dreadful a thing that some men have hastened their own ends, and done justice on themselves. Would men trust in Providence and act according to reason and common justice, they need not to fear any thing; but whilst they defy God and wrong others they must be cowards, and their ends such as they deserve, surprising and infamous. I heartily wish prosperity to my country and that the English would be again (as they were heretofore) remarkable for virtue and bravery, and our nobility make themselves distinguished from the crowd by shining qualities for which their ancestors became so honored and for reward of which obtained those titles they inherit. I hardly dare hope for encouragement after having discovered that my design is to persuade you to be virtuous; but if I fail in this, I shall not in reaping that inward satisfaction of mind that ever accompanies good actions. If this trifle sells, I conclude it takes, and you may be sure to hear from me again; so you may be innocently diverted, and I employed to my satisfaction. Adieu.

The Strange Adventures of the Count de Vinevil and His Family

In the year 1702, the Count de Vinevil, a native of France born of one of the noblest families in Picardy,[5] where he had long lived possessed of a plentiful estate, being a widower and having no child but the beautiful Ardelisa, his only daughter, finding his estate impoverished by continued taxations, and himself neglected by his sovereign and no ways advanced, whilst others less worthy were put into places of trust and power, resolved to dispose of his estate, purchase and freight a ship, sail for Turkey, and there settle at Constantinople to trade: being induced so to do from the perfect knowledge he had of those parts, having been in his youth for above ten years with an uncle of his who was consul there for the French factory[6] and carried him

---

[4] *Robinson Crusoe*: Daniel Defoe's *The Life and Strange Surprizing Adventures of Robinson Crusoe, of York, Mariner: Who lived Eight and Twenty Years, all alone in an un-inhabited Island on the Coast of America, near the Mouth of the Great River of Oroonoque; Having been cast on shore by Shipwreck, wherein all the Men perished but himself. With An Account how he was at last as strangely delivered by Pyrates* had been published in 1719 and had achieved a great success. Aubin in this novella and in other works sought to follow along this profitable path by offering tales of adventures in exotic places.

[5] *Picardy*: a region of northern France extending from the English Channel to the border with Belgium.

[6] *factory*: an establishment for commercial agents (factors) in a foreign country.

along with him to show him the world. Accordingly, he turned all into ready money, except some lands, which being entailed[7] he could not sell; and those he entrusted in the hands of the Count de Beauclair, his sister's son.

Having thus ordered his affairs, he purchased a ship called the Bon Avanture; and having loaded it with goods proper for the Levant,[8] he went aboard with the fair Ardelisa and a youth, who being an orphan and heir to a considerable estate in Picardy, was left to his care. This youth was Count of Longueville, then about seventeen years of age, a young gentleman of extraordinary parts and beauty: he was tall, delicately shaped, his eyes black and sparkling, and every feature of his face was sweet yet majestic; he was learned beyond his years, and his soul was full of truth and ingenuity. He had received from the best education the best principles, was brave, generous, affable, constant, and incapable of any thing that was base or mean. These qualities rendered him dear to the Count de Vinevil, who looked on him as his own son, and was pleased to find that Ardelisa and he grew together in affection as they grew in age. She was then fourteen, and the most charming maid nature ever formed; she was tall and slender, fair as Venus, her eyes blue and shining, her face oval, with features and an air so sweet and lovely that imagination can form nothing more completely handsome or engaging. Her mind well suited the fair cabinet that contained it; she was humble, generous, unaffected, yet learned, wise, modest, and prudent above her years or sex, gay in conversation, but by nature thoughtful, had all the softness of a woman with the constancy and courage of a hero: in fine,[9] her soul was capable of every thing that was noble. There needed nothing more than this sympathy of souls to create the strongest and most lasting affection betwixt this young nobleman and lady; they loved so tenderly and agreed so well that they seemed only born for one another.

The evening before the Count de Vinevil left his castle to go for Turkey, he called the young Count of Longueville into his closet, and spoke to him after this manner: 'My Lord and son,' said he, 'I am, you see, going to quit my native country, and to trust the faithless seas with myself and all that is mine. I am going amongst Mahometans to avoid the seeing those who have been my vassals lord it over me; but, my dear child, I am most unwilling to hazard your life, or involve you in whatever misfortunes may befall me. You have a noble fortune to enjoy, great relations, such as can with ease procure you such an honorable post at court or in the army as may give you opportunities of using to your King and country's glory those admirable qualifications heaven has bestowed upon you, which I have not been wanting to improve in you, nor omitted any thing that could make you such as I desired to see you. And, believe me, no news will be more grateful to me in my exile from France than to hear that you are great and happy. Now then, my dear child,

---

[7] *entailed*: limited to a specified succession of heirs.
[8] *Levant*: those countries bordering on the eastern Mediterranean.
[9] *in fine*: in short, to sum up.

let me prevail with you to consent to our separation. Stay here and be as blessed as I wish you; and if I die in Turkey and leave Ardelisa an orphan, let her returning find in you such a friend as you have found in me.' Here he stopped.

The young Count, whom respect had till now kept silent, throwing himself at his feet and embracing his knees with tears replied, 'My Lord and father! What have I done to merit your displeasure that you should propose such a thing to me? Can you believe me capable of an action so base as to abandon you and Ardelisa, to whom my soul is devoted, out of whose presence I would not live to gain the empire of the eastern world? No, my father, your fortune shall be mine; we will live and die together, nothing but death shall ever separate us. Ardelisa shall be my charge, and I will be to her a lover, husband, and father, and to you a son in the strictest and most tender sense. Urge me no more to leave you. My soul is filled with horror at the thought.' The old Count taking him up in his arms embraced him with transport. 'Forgive me, my son,' said he, ''twas the excess of my affection made me fear to hazard the life of what I loved so well; may Heaven prosper our voyage and reward you with a long life and safe return to France when I am gone to rest. And may Ardelisa make you just returns and be to you as great a blessing as you are to me. Let us now go to take our repose, and with the rising sun we'll set out. All things are ready, the wind is fair, and in another country we will try to improve that fortune we shall never be able here to better.'

The next morning the good old Count, young Longueville, and the fair Ardelisa left the castle, attended with many friends who accompanied them to the ship, where they were all handsomely treated with a dinner, after which they took leave with many tears and good wishes. The old Count's servants expressed themselves in so moving a manner that it would have drawn tears from the most savage heart; nor was there one of them but did beseech him to let them go with him, though he had taken care to recommend and provide for every one of them, having left pensions to those who were grown old in his service. He thanked them tenderly and dismissed them all but four, which were Nannetta, a maid who had brought up Ardelisa and governed his house ever since he had been a widower; Bonhome, his old Steward and Secretary; Manne and Joseph, a young maid and boy who had been bred up in his family. And now with a fair wind that evening, they hoisted sail on the 12th day of March in the year 1702/3[10] and having a prosperous voyage, reached the desired port, arriving at Constantinople May the 1st.

So soon as they came to an anchor, the old Count, who best knew the customs of the place, taking the captain of the vessel, went ashore to visit some

---

[10] Until 1752 England used the Julian or 'Old Style' calendar in which the year began on March 1, while the rest of Europe followed the Gregorian or 'New Style' calendar. So Aubin's dates reflect those different arrangements.

French merchants to whom he brought letters, and to pay the usual compliments to the Bassa[11] of the port and [to the] French Consul, leaving the young Count with Ardelisa, whom the disorder of a sea voyage had so much indisposed that she was scarce able to rise off the bed. 'Now my charming dear,' said the lover, 'we are arrived at a strange country where we shall no more see Christian churches, where religion shows itself in splendor, and God is worshipped with harmony and neatness, but odious mosques, where the vile impostor's name is echoed through the empty choirs and vaults, where cursed Mahometans profane the sacred piles once consecrate to our Redeemer, and adorned with shining saints and ornaments rich as piety itself could make them. Alas! Alas! Dear Ardelisa, what will our father's ambition and resentments cost both him and us? My boding soul seems to forewarn me that we here shall meet some dire misfortunes. The wealth we have brought with us may, perhaps, occasion our undoing; but, more, your beauty should some lustful Turk, mighty in slaves and power, once see that lovely face, what human power could secure you from his impious arms and me from death! Let me entreat you, as you prize your virtue and my life, show not yourself in public; let the house conceal you till Divine Providence delivers us from hence.'

Ardelisa, who was from his discourse made too sensible of what she had to fear, shedding some tears, replied, 'My dear lord, I did not dare to tell my father what I thought of his design; but I like you have had a dread ever since we left our native land. I shall be wholly governed by you in all things and rather choose to confine myself from all conversation than give you the least disquiet. But, alas! should my father's new undertakings, his tradings, occasion your absence from me, what must I do? Or who shall protect me from the infidels' insolence?' At these words, she remained silent, a flood of tears interrupting; whilst he folding her in his arms sighed deeply and just as he was going to speak was prevented by Bonhome's entering the cabin to inform him that the boat was returned with a message from his master that they should come ashore and that he only should stay aboard to see the cargo of the ship unloaded. 'My lord likewise,' continued he, 'desires that you, Madam, will take care to bring in your own hand the little cabinet of jewels; you will find him at a French merchant's house, where you are to continue till my lord has taken a house.'

Nannetta and the young lord assisting, Ardelisa arose and was led to the side of the ship, and he (descending into the boat) received his mistress into his arms and with the faithful Nannetta and Joseph landed. They were by the seamen conducted to the merchant's house, where they found the Count de Vinevil and were received and entertained with all the kindness and magnificence imaginable. Here they continued for about a month, in which time a

---

[11] *Bassa*: or 'bashaw', an earlier form of the Turkish title given to military and civil officials, 'pasha'.

handsome house was taken and furnished, all the goods got out of the ship, brought ashore, and safely put into warehouses, the greatest part of which goods were quickly sold to the Turks by means of the French Consul and merchant.

The Count de Vinevil at their leaving his house made handsome presents to Monsieur de Joyeuxe, his Lady, and servants, and he and she had conceived the highest esteem and friendship that is possible for him, his daughter, and the young Lord. And now the Count settled and thus acquainted and assisted began to be extremely pleased with his voyage and success and to resolve upon continuing in this place the rest of his days. Ardelisa carefully avoided going abroad, whilst her father and lover visited, managed, and dispatched all the affairs with the merchants. But so many Bashaws and persons of quality came to her father's to traffic for European goods that she could not avoid being sometimes seen. Amongst these, Mahomet, the captain of the port's son, a chief officer in the Sultan's guards, was so charmed with her beauty that he became passionately in love with her; and knowing that her father (being a Christian) would never consent to her being his, he concealed his affection, resolving to wait for an opportunity to steal her away or take her by force. In the mean time, he sent her several presents of considerable value by a slave whom he ordered to watch the young Count's going home at noon and to ask for her before him, and in case he was refused the sight of her to deliver the present and letter to the Count for her. This he did to render the Count and her uneasy, having been informed that he was to marry Ardelisa. These letters had no name to them, but were very amorous and contained all the passionate expressions in which a lover could declare his passion. This rendered both the old Lord and young very uneasy, but above all Ardelisa, who foresaw her ruin approaching.

One day the same slave comes as usual, bringing a letter in a silver basket of choice sweetmeats, in the midst of which was placed a gold box under the letter: this he delivered to the old Lord for his daughter, who now kept in her chamber and would no more be seen by strangers. Longueville offered the slave a large reward if he would reveal his master's name and quality. The slave surlily answered, 'Do you take me for a Christian, that I should betray my trust? A true believer keeps his word. My master when he thinks fit will take what he is pleased to love. Ardelisa shall then know her happiness. Till he reveal it himself, not all the wealth, the damning gold, that would procure a set of courtiers great enough to depose a Christian king or to create two new ones should seduce me to reveal his secret; though I am sure to fall a victim by his hand whenever he is displeased or would divert himself with dooming me to die. Farewell Christian, take care and blush to think we both despise your faith and you.'

He left them much amazed; they went to Ardelisa in her chamber, and there opening the gold box they found enclosed the picture of a young Turk set round with diamonds of great price. Just at this instant the old Lord was called by Nannetta to the French Consul, who wanted to speak with him. He leaving the room, the young Count throwing himself at his mistress's feet said, 'Now my Ardelisa, my prophetic fears are verified, now what course shall we take? Why does Christianity forbid me to prevent your ruin and my own by a noble death? Where shall we fly to? Oh! now deny me not one last request. This night, this hour, prevent my dishonor and let us marry. Stay not for a foolish modesty till you are ravished from me. Then we may with honor go together wherever cruel fate shall drive us.' Here he embraced her tenderly, and she replied, 'My dear Lord, I am at my father's and your dispose. I will no longer deny you any thing. May Heaven prosper our virtuous union and preserve my person always yours.' At these words the old Lord entered the room to inform them what the Consul was come about: 'He tells me,' said he, ' that he is secretly advertised that there is some design of seizing our ship as it lies in the harbor by means of some Turkish Bassa, but he can't yet discover who; and counsels me to send you, my son, immediately aboard with what goods we have proper for the Spanish trade, and that you sail for the first port there or in Italy, which you may reach in few days, and stay there till and I and my daughter can secretly get off with the remainder of our effects, which he will dispose of for us as his own. Now therefore, my dear children, let us resolve what to do; too late I see my rashness, for which I know you must condemn me. But forgive me, and reproach me not, say what's best to be done.' The young Lord answered, 'My honored father, first make Ardelisa mine, send for the Consul's priest, and marry us, that I may not be so wretched to lose her unenjoyed. Next let us go abroad in the dead of the night, and leave this fatal place.' 'Alas!' answered the Count, 'my son, that is impossible. Your first request is just, and shall be instantly complied with; but what you last advise is impracticable. You know no ship can go into this port or out but must first pass examination; they will not stop you, but rather will be pleased with your absence. You therefore can with safety carry off what is most valuable of our effects and stay at some port, to which we will follow you. From thence we will return to France.' 'No, my father,' said the young Lord, 'I can't consent to leave you; the consequence of that must be her ruin and your death. But this I will do, I will this night go on board the ship with our best effects, under pretense of going to trade. Thus I shall pass safely out of the port, at some distance from which I will lie at anchor, till you and Ardelisa come to me, which you shall do in this manner. Tomorrow in the afternoon you shall borrow the Consul's boat, pretending you are going to take the air on the water for pleasure, so you may get an opportunity of escaping to me.' This the old Count agreed to, and the same evening the priest made the lovely Ardelisa wife to the generous Longueville, the time and circumstances requiring haste and secrecy. After supper the servants packed up what was least cumbersome and most valuable. The Consul accompanied the young Lord to the Bassa of the port's house, who easily granted them the passports proper for Longueville's departure with the ship and goods. In the night he took leave of his bride and father with much concern and disorder. 'Now,' said he, 'my charming Ardelisa, whom heaven has this happy day made mine, I am going from you for some tedious hours, which I shall pass with an impatience and concern which words cannot express. May angels guard you and conduct you to my longing arms again; but if some dreadful chance prevents our meeting, remember both your duty to yourself and me. Permit not a vile infidel to dishonor you, resist to death, and let me not be so completely cursed to hear you live and are debauched. My soul is filled with unaccustomed fears. Forgive me, Ardelisa, I know your virtue's strong, though you are weak, but force does oft prevail. We are now on the crisis of our fate. 'Tis a bold venture that I run to leave you here; but if I stay, we are sure of ruin. To keep you, I must leave you; in Providence is all my hope. If we do meet no more, to God I'll dedicate the wretched hours I shall survive you and never know a second choice.' At these words he took her in his arms, whilst she, all drowned in tears, said, 'Why, my dear Lord, do you anticipate misfortunes? Why doubt that Providence which has preserved us coming hither and will, I hope, prevent our ruin? Fear not my virtue. I'm resolved never to yield whilst life shall last. I applaud your resolution, and shall prove I'm worthy you. Go, since there is no other way to save us, and by these fond delays waste not the time fate points out for our escape before the vicious infidel gets knowledge of our design.' At this he loosed her from his arms and, turning from her, wiped the falling drops from his eyes, whilst the old Count embraced him with all the tenderness of friendship and such affection as fathers have for only sons, saying, 'A thousand blessings follow you, my son, and prosper what we do.' At these words the young Lord bowed and went to the boat, followed by the boatswain only, the captain and part of the men being gone before on board. He arrived safe into the ship and fell down at break of day, passing the castles into the road, where he cast anchor.

CHAPTER II

And now the sun rising the young Lord began to count each minute, still looking out to see if the wished for boat appeared; but Providence that was resolved to try his faith and virtue determined to separate him and Ardelisa. A dreadful storm arose at noon, so violent that cables could no longer hold the laboring vessel. The anchors broke their hold, the ship was drove into the open seas, and in few hours lost sight of all the Turkish coast. Eighteen days they sailed, and then got sight of Leghorn, into which they gladly put to get refreshments and repair the shattered vessel, which had lost all her masts and rigging.

Here they were constrained to stay to refit fourteen days more; and then contrary to the captain's advice Longueville, whose uneasy state of mind it is impossible for words to describe, commanded them to return to

Constantinople, leaving here with the French Consul the money and goods they had brought from Turkey, for which place they again set sail, where we shall leave them pursuing their voyage and return to the old Count and Ardelisa.

No sooner was the young Lord gone aboard, but the Count de Vinevil reflecting upon their danger told Ardelisa he did not think it advisable for her to stay that night in the house. So he called Nannetta and Joseph and bid them go with her to the Consul's, whither he would come in the morning to consult how to accomplish what they designed. She much entreated her father to go with her, but he answered, 'No, my dear child, it is no ways safe for me to leave the house, for should the Bassa of the port send spies my presence would prevent their suspecting our design of going away. If you are asked for, I can plead your being in bed as a just excuse for your not appearing; me they have no reason to hate.' These reasons made her (though with great reluctance) consent to go without him. Shedding a flood of tears, she embraced him, saying, 'Adieu, my dear Lord and father, may the attending angels keep us and blast our enemies' bad designs against us.' He blessed her, and they parted, never, alas! to meet again, for Fate had so decreed. The Count and servants busied in packing up what yet remained in the house, Ardelisa having carried only the small cabinet of jewels with about a thousand pistoles in hers and the maid's pockets. They shut all the doors and windows fast to avoid discovery; but it was not long before somebody knocked with such fury at the gate that they all stood looking with amazement on one another. At last the Count bid them go see what was the matter. The servant who went to the gate demanded civilly who was there, thinking it might be the young Lord returned or Ardelisa; but he was soon answered by the enraged Mahomet, who having been informed by his slave of what had passed between Longueville and him was resolved to gratify his love and revenge together. In order to which he designed the seizing the ship to prevent their escape and then caused this rumor to be spread in hopes it would drive Longueville to fly with her, that so he might have a just pretense to seize them. But finding he went alone and that the lady and her father stayed behind, he resolved to give them this visit in the dead of the night, not doubting to find them defenseless. And besides whatever violence he should then commit would be better concealed, being not willing to occasion a quarrel betwixt his Emperor and France; or what was more certain lose his own life by the bow-string if justice were required by the French ambassador. To prevent all which fatal consequences, he determined to kill the old Lord and servants, carry off the lady, and leave none in the house to betray him. With this villainous intent he came, attended with his bloody vassals, whom the fear of death had so possessed that they dared not fail to act whatever villainy he commanded. Mahomet bid the servant open the gate that moment, or he would force his way in with fire and sword.

At these words the poor boy fled into the house to give his Lord notice; but the fatal message had scarce passed his trembling lips when they heard the gate broke open and saw the merciless Turks enter the house, Mahomet crying, 'Secure the Christian dogs. By Mahomet! if one escapes alive besides the lady, your forfeit lives shall answer it.' At these words they laid hands on the amazed servants, with their drawn scimitars in hand. The old Lord, whose noble soul disdained to shrink, stepped boldly to him, saying, 'Insolent Lord! what have we done to injure thee? Why are we treated thus? Natives of France and friends to your great emperor and you. If I or mine have injured you, you have a right as well as we to procure justice on us. Speak, what is our crime?' Mahomet, clapping his dagger to his breast, replied, 'Do you ask questions, fool? Show me to your daughter's bed, and with her honor buy that life which I on any other terms won't spare. Make me happy in her arms and silently conceal all that shall pass this night, or I will plunge this dagger into your heart, leave nothing here but speechless ghosts and murdered carcasses. Then with Ardelisa I'll return to my own palace and there force her to give all her treasures up to me and glut myself in her embraces.' The Count de Vinevil, with a look that spoke disdain and rage, replied, 'No, Villain! Ardelisa never shall be thine; not empires or the dread of any death thy cursed fury could invent should make me but in thought consent to such a deed. Life is a trifle weighed with infamy; the God I serve shall both preserve her virtue and revenge my death. My daughter is not educated so and will, I know, prefer a noble death to such dishonor.' Mahomet, enraged, cried 'Slaves! go search the chambers and bring her naked from her bed that I may ravish her before the dotard's face and then send his soul to hell.' At this the old Lord smiled, and lifting up his hands to heaven, cried, ''Tis just, my God, that I who have thus exposed my child should first feel the misery my rashness merits, but do not let her perish here. Preserve her, great creator, from the lust and rage of these vile infidels and let thy angels guide her home again. Let my blood expiate all my sins and give me courage in this great extremity.' At these words the Turks, who had in vain searched all the house, assured their Lord that Ardelisa was not there: 'Die then,' said he to the old Count, 'here I'll begin my vengeance.' At these words the cruel Mahometan plunged his dagger into his breast; at which the old Lord fell, crying, 'Mercy, my Savior!' The slaves soon dispatched the innocent servants, who in vain implored their pity. Then they proceeded to plunder the house, after which they shut the doors after them and departed, Mahomet swearing he would find Ardelisa or destroy all the Frenchmen in Constantinople.

CHAPTER III

Whilst this tragic scene was acting, the innocent Ardelisa, having recommended herself to heaven, was sleeping in her bed and dreamt her father called her, in a distant room, to come to him. She fancied she ran thither and saw him all over blood and wounds, at which he vanished from her; then found herself with strangers in a wild, desolate place, where they were in great distress for food and knew not where to go. She starting, waked, and in much disorder finding it was day, she rose, calling Nannetta, who was up already. 'Oh, Nanon,' said she, 'I've had a dismal dream, make haste and send Joseph to see if my dear father's stirring yet.' The maid was going, when the Consul's lady entering the chamber all in tears said, 'Dear Ardelisa, I have news to tell you that a virtue less than yours could not support. Now summon all your reason and religion to your aid and to that God submit who has this dreadful night preserved you.' 'Alas! Madam, I too well understand you,' she replied, 'my father's murdered.' She at these words fell into a swoon, out of which with difficulty they recovered her. Returning to life, she fell into such moving lamentations, such extreme though modest sorrow that would have made even the cruel infidels, could they have seen her, melt and feel remorse. The lady comforted her all she could, telling her she must now think of her own preservation, in order to which the boy and maid must not be seen to stir abroad. Says she, 'Monsieur de Joyeuxe, who living near your father first heard the dreadful news, just now sent a servant to acquaint us that your father and you were murdered, with all the servants, and the house plundered; but that nobody could tell by whom. Those that have done this hellish deed will doubtless lie in wait for you. Let us permit this report of your death to spread that we may get you secretly conveyed to some distant port, from whence you may get off safely.'

'Alas! Madam,' said she, 'your goodness will expose you and your family to ruin; were I so ungrateful as to accept it, my staying in your house would undo you. No, Madam, God forbid I should involve you in my unhappy fate; it is my ruin the fierce villain seeks, my fatal face has been our destruction. Had I not left my father, we had nobly died together. The only favor I can ask of you, with honor, is to let me depart ere I am discovered. Procure me but the habit of a man, the boy and I will venture to feign ourselves belonging to some ship that now lies in the road. If we are taken, we can only die; if we escape, money shall bribe the captain, where we may get aboard, to put us safe into my dear Lord's ship.' 'No, Madam,' replied the lady, 'your life's too precious to be risked in such a manner. We have a country house within thirty miles of this city, at a village called Domez-Dure; thither I will this night send you and your servants. You and Nannetta shall be dressed like men, and Joseph shall black his face and hands like Domingo our slave. So you shall feign yourself very sick, and in our horse-litter shall be conveyed thither; there you may continue in safety till a fit opportunity presents to get you off. Our boat shall about noon go off and acquaint your Lord with all that has happened and bid him put off to sea and make away for some other port, where he may some days hence drop in with his boat and receive you. Perhaps by that time, he whom we suspect to have done this villainy, the Bassa Ibrahim's son, who it seems was seen last night attended with his slaves late in the streets may be commanded hence to the army, and then you may go away safely.'

This offer Ardelisa accepted of with many acknowledgments, and the Consul's lady left the room to acquaint the Consul what they had determined to do, leaving Ardelisa on her bed overwhelmed with grief. The maid soon packed up the things, men's habits were brought, and she and her lady, who seemed half dead, dressed and put into the litter with Joseph walking by the side, so black that he appeared a perfect Moor. They arrived safe at the country house, where Ardelisa fell sick and remained much longer than she expected. The same day she went from Constantinople the storm prevented the Consul's boat from giving the Lord Longueville notice of what was past, and he was drove out to sea, as is before recited.

CHAPTER IV

Many spies were employed by Mahomet to get intelligence of Ardelisa; and the same evening of the day she went away the Consul's house was searched under pretense of his servants having concealed a Turkish slave whom the Bassa of the port pretended his son had lost. So that it was a great Providence for her and the family, she was not there. Whilst she lay sick at Domez-Dure, Joseph the fictitious black, used frequently to go about the town for provisions and became well acquainted with all the country thereabouts. It chanced one day that as he was going to a village near the sea he saw some troops of Turks going along the road, and fearing to be questioned he retired into a thick wood, which viewing well, he thought he perceived something like a house, but so covered with trees and bushes that he could scarce discern it. Curiosity made him venture to go farther, and coming into the midst of the wood he saw a small cottage, into which he entered by a door that stood ajar. He stopped a while to hear if any creature moved in it; but finding all things in silence, he entered and there found two little but convenient rooms, with a little table, three low stools, a fire place, some earthen dishes, a knife, fork, and spoon of silver, and a little pot; and in the inner room a mattress laid on some rushes with a quilt and sheets, a box in which he found some linen and some books of devotion in the Latin tongue with a crucifix. But no person being there, he concluded some Christian slave had escaped and lived there concealed. The soldiers, as he supposed, being now gone, he returned to the road, pursued his journey, and went home, relating to his lady and Nannetta what he had seen in the wood, adding, 'My honored Lady, should we be pursued hither, it were a most safe retreat for you to fly to.'

Some days they continued undisturbed, Joseph frequently going to the Consul's to learn news of his Lord, but in vain. Sometimes Ardelisa tormented herself with thinking he perished in the dreadful storm; but on reflection thought again some token of the wreck would sure have appeared, being so near the shore. Then she concluded he was drove to sea. But at length Joseph, going to the Consul's, chanced to overtake a slave who was going the same way; with whom falling in talk asked him whither he was going and from whence he came? 'From Domez-Dure,' said he, 'where I have been to view a Frenchman's country house and have found what I wanted, for which my lord will pay me nobly.'

I don't doubt these words struck Joseph like a thunderbolt. He recollecting himself said, 'Friend, will you drink a dram with me? Here,' said he, pulling out a little bottle full of good wine out of his pocket, 'come let us sit down under this trees and rest a while.' The Turk suspecting nothing and tempted with the opportunity of drinking wine consented, and Joseph as he lifted the bottle to his head stabbed him to the heart with his knife. 'Go, dog,' said he, 'go bear thy message to the Prince of Hell, there look [for your] reward.' The Turk cried, ''Tis just, Great Prophet! Youth, I envy thee the deed. So should the fool be served that tells his master's secret. Much Christian blood I've spilled, and thou hast punished me. Tell Ardelisa, if you do as I suppose belong to her, she is not safe at Domez-Dure; I can no more.' He in a few minutes died; whilst Joseph turning back fled to forewarn his lady to be gone.

He had no sooner told the story but a deathlike paleness overspread her face, and poor Nannetta could not speak. 'Dear God,' cried Ardelisa, 'where shall I fly? What must I do?' 'Madam,' cried the faithful boy, 'this night fly to the cottage in the wood; the slave prevented from delivering his message gains us time.' 'But, alas!' said she, 'whom may we find in that sad place?' 'None but a Christian,' he replied, 'for such I'm sure he must be by what I saw, if anybody lives there now. I will go hide myself in the wood and wait to see if any one come in or out, and speak to the person; and if I see any then return to let you know what is best to be done. Here we must not stay much longer, the dead slave will be found and some other sent; it is enough that this place is suspected and God by my hand has given us this time to think and escape.'

Having eat something, he departed, leaving Ardelisa much distracted in her thoughts. He had not waited long in the wood before he saw a man come forth of the cottage in the habit of a Santoin, or religious Turk, with sandals on his feet, his face pale and meager. He had in his hand a piece of bread; he lift[ed] up his eyes to heaven, sighed deeply, crossed his breast and began to eat. Joseph, who at first feared he had been a Mahometan, was now over-joyed; and stepping from behind the tree where he had stood concealed threw himself at his feet, saying, 'Christian and friend, fear me not, but let us go in and talk, and I will show you a way to preserve lives that may be of great use to you.' At these words the hermit viewed him with much attention; and though greatly surprised to hear him speak, yet as a man to whom death itself would not be terrible answered, 'Speak on.'

'Father,' said the boy, ''tis dangerous for us to talk here.' At this they entered the house, where he told the hermit that a Christian lady, a maid servant, and himself begged to be sheltered there till they might find means to get off at a sea port to return to France. 'To France,' said the hermit, 'Moor, for why?' 'Because we are all natives of that place,' replied the boy. 'Your lady's name?' said the hermit. 'My dear Lord was de Vinevil,' the youth replied, 'and I a luckless lad who here have lost him.' At these words he wept. 'Alas! sweet boy,' said he, 'I knew him well; all that are his I love and will refuse no kindness to.'

The boy, at these words, looking earnestly on him, knew him to be a priest born in Picardy who went a missionary to Japan about ten years before. 'Father Francis,' said he, 'how blessed am I to see you, though in this sad place? How came you here? And by what Providence preserved?' The joyful priest embracing him perceived he was no black and said thus, 'A cruel storm in our return to France drove our vessel on this coast, where a few of us were preserved from death but not from cruel usage. We were but five, and soon were separated; three died, I and my brother James a Turk brought to Constantinople under pretense of kindness, then demanded a ransom most exorbitant, which we protesting that we could not pay he loaded us with chains, threw us into a nasty vault, where we remained, sustained with bread and water till he feared our deaths. Then he removed us to his gardens in the country, where he made us work as slaves; till weary of our lives we resolutely leaped the wall and fled. And meeting with this wood in our way, stayed here to rest, not being able to go farther. My brother, stripping off his coat, even naked, entered the village begging to prevent our perishing for food, pretending sanctity and vows to Mahomet. The charitable villagers supplying his wants with food and raiment, he returned loaded to me. Thus were we encouraged to erect this homely cell with boughs and boards we begged to shield us from the winter rains and cold. Thus we lived three months together when he fell sick and died; for six months since I've lived by begging as before, but never discovered where I dwell. I go each morning forth and roam about, or sometimes sit under some tree to rest but don't return hither till night.'

The boy thus satisfied told all that related to his lady, telling him withal they had much treasure and that he might with less suspicion than they visit the next port and find a way both to deliver himself and them, and that he expected his Lord in a ship belonging to them, of which he should have intelligence from Constantinople. He answered, 'Child, you need not urge these reasons, since God who has preserved me here so long requires that I should assist others in distress. Go, bring your lady hither, and may the angels guide and keep us whilst we stay and give us opportunity to escape from hence. Be gone; I must as usual go my round and shall be back at night.' He gave his blessing to the youth, and so they parted.

CHAPTER V

Joseph returning home gave his lady an account of the surprising things he had met with in the wood; and she lifting her hands to heaven said, 'Now, my Great Deliverer whose Providence has provided me this retreat keep me and mine; guided by thee I cannot be unfortunate.' At night they left the house, taking their money and jewels and getting safely to the wood found the good father, waiting at his cottage door, who received them with a joy and civility suiting the polite education he had received. He embraced Ardelisa with a concern that called the blood into his pale cheeks and showed how dear her father was to him. 'Welcome,' said he, 'daughter of my dearest friend; this place and the poor master of it is devoted to your service.' Leading her in, he seated her, having a poor lamp burning. He had decked his little cell as well as he could, having in one corner of the out-room laid a bed of rushes for the boy and him to lie on, and made a door to the inner room of plaited rushes to render it more private that she and her maid who wore their men's clothes might undress and rise without being seen. He then reached a bottle of wine which he had kept there with some bread (for fear he should fall sick and not be able to go out some days); with a cup they drank, and after some discourse the lady retired to rest.

The next morning the boy and priest went forth early. At noon the lad returned, bringing provisions for three days. They buried their gold in a hole under their bed in the inner room; and their jewels behind the cottage in a hollow tree, covering the box so carefully with leaves and earth which they filled up the hollow with, that it was almost impossible for others to find them. And in the evening the boy set out for Constantinople to see if there was any news of his Lord and the ship, as also to inform the Consul of their departure from his country house and new habitation.

The lady and her maid thus left alone passed the time in prayer and discourse, wherein they conversed so piously and expressed themselves so excellently that it is pity the world is not favored with a recitation of all they said. For Nannetta was a maid whose education had been noble, her birth not mean, and indeed Ardelisa owed to her in great part the exalted principles and sentiments she possessed, she having had the care of her in her infancy. They eat together, and Ardelisa forgot all distinctions, only Nannetta's respect increased with her mistress' favor. At night they were glad to see the good father return home; he told them he had learned what ought to fill their souls with fresh acknowledgments to God who had that day miraculously preserved them. 'So soon,' says he, 'as I entered the village, I found the people all in an uproar and their eyes and steps were all directed to the house you left, where a band of Turkish soldiers were rifling and searching all the rooms and gardens, headed by a man who by the respect they showed him seemed of no small quality. I stayed at some distance to observe what passed, and after some time saw them depart in much disorder, and he in the utmost rage, swearing by Mahomet he would destroy the village if he found you not soon. The people stared upon one another and separated. I asked no questions, but as usual walked forward, seeming to mumble my orisons and receiving the alms of those who called me. I would advise you, Madam,' continued he, 'not to stir forth of the house some days. I will go to the next sea port to see if any ship be there belonging to Spain, France, Holland, or England, in either of which we may escape after Joseph is returned.' Ardelisa then besought him to take pieces of gold to serve his necessities. 'No, my child,' said he, 'the Providence of God shall provide for me. Money would render me suspected; this habit is my passport here. I pray God to keep you in my absence and prosper my journey.' They supped, prayed, and went to repose, and before day the hermit departed.

CHAPTER VI

At the end of three days Joseph returned to his lady and related the unhappy news he brought after this manner. 'My dear Lady,' said he, 'the Consul and his lady are in health, are much transported at your safety, and send you word my Lord was well some days ago and is so still, they hope.' 'Is he then alive and here?' she cried; 'then I am happy.' 'He was well,' replied the boy, 'and was here but is departed, Madam. His ship was drove so far out to sea in the storm that he was obliged to make the first port, which proved Leghorn, where the ship was repaired and victualed again. Thence he returned to Constantinople but entered not the port, fearing discovery. At evening he sent his boat ashore, ordering the crew to report when asked that he was dead and that the captain of the ship came there only to trade. The coxswain was ordered to go to Monsieur de Joyeuxe's house to inquire for my old Lord and you. They there informed him that he, you, and all the family were murdered the same fatal night he left you and that he counseled my Lord to get off the coast immediately and return to France, where Monsieur de Joyeuxe and his family hoped e'er long to see him, [they] designing to return thither next year. The coxswain returned to the ship with this message, upon which they set sail and are doubtless gone home to France. The Consul heard nothing of the ship's arrival till Monsieur de Joyeuxe sent him this account. The Consul has sent a letter by the ambassador's packet, which he hopes will meet him in Picardy to inform him that you are living, and the Consul will take care to inform you of the first opportunity to get off for France. Mean time, he is ready to serve you in all things, and hopes it will not be long before he shall be able to send you word that your enemy is gone to the army and you may safely return to Constantinople.'

'Alas! my God,' answered Ardelisa, 'when will my sorrows end? Thankful I am that my dear Lord still lives, but why did he depart without me? That he lives, said I! Alas! Grief has perhaps e'er this finished his life and sorrows, and I have little or no hopes of ever seeing him again.' Here tears stopped her from proceeding, and poor Joseph and Nannetta strove to comfort her all they were able.

The same night the good priest returned but brought no news of any ship. To him they related what the boy had learned at the city. He counseled

Ardelisa to trust in Providence and rest satisfied: 'My dear children,' said he, 'this life is attended with nothing but uncertainties and full of sorrows; the enjoyments of it are short and transitory. In all our affections and friendships here with one another we should have a future view and manifest that love by being instrumental to one another's eternal welfare. Our wise Creator inclined us to love one another so tenderly with a more glorious design than that of only propagating mankind. It was to render us useful to each other in the greatest concern of life, that of obtaining eternal happiness. Whilst this is our aim, no separation can be grievous, nor the death of what we love cast us down. He that leads the person he pretends to love into sin acts the devil's part and is his greatest enemy. I remember my dead friends as my greatest treasures, which I hope to enjoy when we wake together. So you, Ardelisa, must do, and if Heaven denies you the sight of a loved husband here, consider in a little while he will be restored to you so improved that your joy and friendship shall be eternal. This those of us who live as and are Christians are certain of.' 'What heavenly sounds are these?' said Ardelisa. 'Your words convey a balm into my sickly wounded soul, have stilled my passions, and cured my frailty. Yes, father, I submit and death itself will, I hope, find me well prepared.' These heavenly conversations they continued daily, and betwixt the pious father and the boy were well supplied with necessary food. Ardelisa and the maid ventured not out at any distance from the house. One evening they were surprised with hearing a hollowing in the wood. They looked upon one another as persons apprehensive of some great misfortune; but the noise coming nearer, the good father being not returned home, the boy went boldly out and saw something like a man on horseback. He went up to him, saying, 'In the name of God, what would you have?' This he spoke in the Turkish language, but the man replied in French: 'Are you not Joseph? If so, bring me to your lady.' The boy said, 'Who do you belong to?' 'The Consul,' said he. At these words he knew him and said, 'Domingo, you're welcome.' The horseman taking his hand said, 'How fares your lady? Mahomet her enemy is gone for the army, a French ship is in the harbor, and I have brought the horse litter to our country house with horses for the good father, you, and I. Bring your lady thither presently and tomorrow we'll return to Constantinople.'

By this time they came to the house, from whence the servant returned to the village, and the little family packing up what they had brought, designing to leave one of the Consul's servants to wait the father's return and bring him to them at Constantinople, departed soon after, leaving the lucky mournful cottage destitute of inhabitants where they had lived three months without disturbance.

CHAPTER VII

Full of joy and hopes, they cheerfully walked towards Domez-Dure, but nothing is to be depended on in this world. A great Turkish general named Osmin, who was going to Constantinople with many attendants, chose the coolness of the night to travel, as is very customary in the heat of summer, met these poor travelers, ordered them to be stopped and seized. They told him they were two poor French lads and the black, who were cast ashore in a boat coming from a ship for provisions and were making their way to Constantinople, where their ship was sailed for to go in search of her, or apply to the French Consul to be sent home, if the ship was lost or sailed thence. This Ardelisa, who was orator for the rest, said; but the charms of her face and the eloquence of her tongue so enchanted Osmin that he resolved to secure her for himself. He told them they were slaves, run away from their owners, he supposed; however, he would carry them to Constantinople and there see the truth of what they said. So ordered they should be chained together and walk in the middle of his troop, commanding that no violence should be offered to them, or that any thing they had about them taken away.

They had not gone far before Ardelisa fainted, being unable to support her inward grief and the fatigue of the march. At which the general was alarmed, and seeing the concern her companions were in guessed her to be the most noble of the three. He therefore ordered her to be put in a horse litter that attended him. So before day they arrived at his palace, which was at the entering into the city. She, and the boy and maid were brought in and locked into a room, where they could only sigh and look upon one another but dared not talk for fear of being overheard and discovered.

In few moments after they were thus left, the general entered and addressing himself to Ardelisa said, 'Lovely boy, or maid, I know not which as yet to call you, fear not the treatment I shall give you. My heart is made a captive to your eyes. I will enjoy and keep you here, where nothing shall be wanting to make you happy. If you are a man, renounce your faith, adore our prophet, and my great emperor and I will give you honors and wealth exceeding your imagination. If you're a woman, here are apartments where painting, downy beds, and habits fit for to cover that soft frame, gardens to walk in, and food delicious, with faithful slaves to wait upon you, invite your stay where I will feast each sense and make you happy as mortality can be.' At these words he clasped her in his arms and rudely opening her breast discovered that she was of the soft sex. She, trembling, strove and, falling at his feet, begged him to kill or let her go. 'You doubtless are,' said he, 'the beauteous maid who fled my friend Mahomet's pursuit, for whom he killed your slaves and father. How blessed am I to find you? Your maid, whose tears and blushes [have] discovered her to me, shall bear you company awhile. I must this moment to the emperor, and shall soon return to sleep within those lovely arms.'

At these words he left the room, and two eunuchs entered, who did lead her and the maid into the garden, and there opening the doors of a beautiful apartment conducted them in; after leaving them in a lovely room, departed, and soon returned with sherbets of delicate taste, preserved and cold meats, telling them they should refresh themselves and showing a rich bed chamber with closets full of women's clothes, bid them shift and dress in any of those rich Turkish habits they liked best, none should disturb them. At these words the eunuchs withdrew. Now the distracted maid and her lady, looking upon one another, wept, unable to express their thoughts in words. At length Ardelisa broke silence in this manner: 'Just God! What wilt thou do with us? Direct me now, and help me in this great distress. Oh Nannon! advise me. Shall this bold hand destroy the villain when he enters? Sure it can be no sin to save my virtue with his blood? Yes, I am resolved to do it, though I perish. Let his slaves revenge his death on me and torture me with all their fury can invent. Death's but a trifle in comparison of infamy. Yes, my dear Lord commanded me to suffer death rather than yield to lustful infidels, and Christianity enjoins it. Come, let us eat and, thus resolved, fear nothing. You, my faithful friend, they'll doubtless spare, as being neither young nor beautiful. Pray for me, and if ever you are so happy to see France and my dear Lord again, tell him I have obeyed him and behaved myself as does become a Christian and his wife.' She then sat down, looking with such serenity and calmness as one prepared for all events. They ate and prayed together and passed the night in pious talk, where we shall leave them.

CHAPTER VIII

We now return to Osmin to show what care Almighty Goodness takes of those who trust in him. The Turk had brought a packet from the Grand Vizier to the Sultan, the contents of which did so displease him that according to the barbarous customs of that nation he wrecked his rage upon the luckless Osmin, commanding him a prisoner to the Seven Towers, where chained we leave him to curse his false prophet and his destiny.

The news of his disgrace soon reached his home, and now the slaves no longer were so careful to watch the doors of his seraglio, but in the morning left them open, telling the lady she might have the liberty of the gardens to walk. This was pleasing news to Ardelisa because she and Nannetta hoped by this means to find some way to escape. They thanked the eunuchs who had brought in chocolate for their breakfast, and when they were gone Ardelisa and Nannetta ventured into the garden, which was such as showed that art and nature had there done their utmost and made it one of the most delightful places eyes ever saw: fountains and groves and grottoes where sun could never enter, long walks of orange and myrtles, with banks, where flowers of the most lovely kinds and fragrant scents stood crowded, with pleasure houses built of Parian marble, and within so wrought and painted that it appeared an earthly paradise. Nor did there want large terrace walks, from whence the eye might be entertained with the full view of that great city and the noble port which is one of the most lovely prospects in the world.

They had not walked long here before they perceived Joseph running towards them; he made a sign to them to retire into one of the grottoes whither he followed. And so soon as he could recover his breath, he embraced his lady's knees, saying, 'My soul is transported, my dear Lady, to see you safe; I have news will overjoy you. Last night the villain Osmin was sent by the Sultan to the Black Tower. Amongst the servants I have learned all, and this night will deliver you. I find the servants are very careful of the out-doors and gates, therefore in the night I will set fire to the house, which will put them all into confusion. Be you ready to follow me, and I doubt not to conduct you safe to the Consul's.' Ardelisa admired the boy's zeal and love, and said, 'My God, I thank thee; and if I live to see France again, Joseph, you shall know how much I esteem your fidelity.' They thought it not convenient to talk longer, so Joseph hasted back to the house, being taken little or no notice of by the servants, who were in the greatest concern, expecting their lord's ruin and consequently a new master, who might perhaps prove more cruel than their old; for it is customary for the Sultan when he puts one favorite to death to give his estate, house, and slaves to another.

The day growing hot, Ardelisa and her maid thought of returning to their apartment to pass the day, when they perceived a lady in Turkish habit, tall, delicately shaped, and a face perfectly beautiful yet looked melancholy. She started at the sight of them, being in men's clothes and dressed like Europeans, yet she stood still. At which Ardelisa hasted towards her, and bowing spoke to her in French, supposing her some Christian lady who had, like her, been forced thither. 'Madam,' said she, 'fear not to speak to me. I am like you a woman, and if you are a Christian tell me of what nation and how brought here?' At these words the lady looking on her attentively answered, 'Yes, stranger, I am a Christian, and by birth a Venetian, made captive with many others of our wretched nation, noble virgins who like me have lived too long, being now made slaves to the wild lusts of cruel infidels, from which nothing but death can deliver us.' At these words, Ardelisa embracing her said, 'Yes, God by me will I doubt not this night free us; come with me into that apartment, where I will tell you news that will not be unwelcome to you.' They went together, followed by Nannetta, and being seated Ardelisa told her of Osmin's disgrace, bid her stay with her that day, and at night she hoped they should be showed a way to escape. 'And now,' said she, ' to make the day seem less tedious, oblige me with the recital of your misfortunes.' To which the lady willingly condescended and thus began her story.

CHAPTER IX

'My name is Violetta. I was born in Venice of a family ancient and noble. My father's name was Don Manuel, who did then and I hope does still command a man of war for the republic, being honored with the order of St. Mark for his great services. My mother is a lady of great goodness and beauty and descended of one of the most illustrious families of the Venetian Senators. It pleased God to give them no other children but myself and one son, who lost his life in that unfortunate day when I was taken. He commanded the forces on the coast, and the Turks landing, after a bloody dispute, getting the better by numbers, ravaged the coast. And entering the churches and convents in one of which my father had placed me to secure me, as most of our nobility had their daughters, they carried us all aboard their ships, with all the treasure their sacrilegious hands had pillaged, and here divided the spoils, presented those of us whom they liked best or believed most noble to the Grand Seignior and his favorites. It was my lot to be given to Osmin, and here I have had the misfortune to be kept these two years, being too much esteemed by him.'

Ardelisa interrupting her, cried, 'Alas! Madam, are there no more ladies here?' 'No,' replied Violetta, 'not at present; there are here sometimes at least ten more of different nations, some of which are noble as myself and in my opinion more worthy to be loved, but they are all gone into the country to a house of pleasure during Osmin's absence. But as for my part whether it be that he loves me as he pretends more than the rest or that he fears to trust me hence, I know not; but I was never removed from this place. I have had one son by him, which I secretly baptized and which it pleased God to take to himself since Osmin went to the army, which is about three months. This is my unfortunate history. I pray heaven it may end more happily.' The ladies passed the day with much satisfaction to each other, longing for the approaching night.

CHAPTER X

Let us now make enquiry after the good priest, who returned not to his cottage till the day after Ardelisa and her servants had left it, being prevented from returning home by the following accident. As he was passing by a wood in his way home from the sea side, which he frequently visited to look out for a ship, he saw a troop of Turks at the head of which was the treacherous Turk who had used him so cruelly when he made him and the other good priest his gardeners. He stepped out of the road to avoid being seen, which immediately gave some suspicion to the eagle-eyed Turks who presently made up to him. This occasioned him to fly from them into the wood, where looking out for a place to hide himself he perceived in the side of a small rising of the ground a hole big enough for a man to go in at, and looking curiously into it saw steps cut in the earth to go down. His fears inclined him to venture into this place. Descending, he came to a door, which was put to but not fastened. Opening it, he entered into a cave where nature seemed to have played the part of art: it was spacious and clean, a lamp was burning on a table; there stood a large trunk locked, and on a bed of rushes lay a man in a rude habit of beasts' skins, and by him stood an earthen pitcher full of water. He appeared very sick and weak. The good father drew near to him; at which the man, turning his head, said with a weak voice in the Turkish language, 'Stranger, disturb me not, leave me to die in peace.' The good father, moved with compassion answered, 'God forbid I should injure you; I would much rather assist you in all I am able.'

At these words the dying man replied, 'Alas! Turk, thou canst give me no assistance, my Savior must assist me.' 'Are you then a Christian?' said the priest. 'I myself am so; and what is more a priest. God has doubtless sent me here to you.' 'Then I am happy,' said the penitent; and straight besought him, saying 'Father, there is bread in that trunk; take it, hear my confession, and make me blessed. Let my Lord but visit my soul, and I shall die joyfully.'

The good priest willingly consented and prepared him for death, as well as the time and place would permit, giving him wine out a bottle he carried in his pocket, after which he seemed much revived. Then he desired the penitent to relate to him, if he was able, how he came there, and who he was. He answered, 'Father, my strength and life are deficient; in that trunk you'll find a paper which contains what you desire to know; take that and what else you will find with it. I thank my God a Christian has it.' Here he returned to prayer, his agonies growing strong, in which he continued till six in the morning when he died. The good father finished his good work with saying the burial service over him, and covering him up in his rude habit and some of the rushes of his bed went to the trunk, which opening with a key he had given him he found some very rich linen, and choice books, and a cabinet of great value; which opening, there was a great quantity of gold and jewels with a crucifix, all diamonds, and in a corner of the trunk some church plate. In the same cabinet a large paper which, with the help of the lamp, he read, though by his confession he had been partly informed of his life past. The paper contained these words.

CHAPTER XI

My name was Don Fernando de Cardiole. I was by birth a noble Spaniard, and was commander of a galleon. I fell in love with a lady whose name was Donna Corinna, a maid of honor to the Queen. She seemed to favor me above all the other pretenders, of which she had many, being a lady of great fortune and beauty, till a young nobleman who came to court, just returned from his travels, whose name was Don Pedro de Mendoza, made love to her. She grew cold to me, and he rude and insolent, at which, incensed, I watched an opportunity and had him assassinated. Then putting out to sea with my vessel and not daring to return steered my course for Turkey, telling the slaves if they would consent to set me and my treasure, which I had brought on board, safe on the coast of Turkey, I would deliver the ship into their hands to go where they pleased, which they willingly consented to.

So soon as I came ashore at Gallipoli, I went to the Bassa of that place, declaring myself a Turk and offering to discover great secrets to the Grand Vizier of the designs of the Christian princes. I was circumcised and treated splendidly, sent with great attendance to Constantinople and there so ingratiated myself with the Grand Vizier that I was soon intrusted with the command of a ship against the Venetians. There with the fleet I did all the mischief I was able, entered and plundered the churches, deflowered noble virgins, and returned much commended and highly pleased. Neither did I fail of reward, being permitted to take what I pleased of my plunder.

I had now a palace of my own, a pension, and a seraglio of women, and lived in the enjoyment of all earthly delights. But God who had till now suffered me to go on and continue insensible awakened my conscience, and I felt such bitter remorse in my soul that I could take no rest or pleasure. All those things that I before took delight in were now hateful to me. After long debates in my own thoughts, I resolved upon what to do. To Spain I could not return; justice would meet me there. Shame and guilt forbad me to fly to any Christian country; here my conscience would not let me stay. I determined therefore to leave all my fortune, house, and family, and to retire to some lonely place where I might spend my days and nights in solitude and prayer, where I might with penitence, tears, fasting, and prayers reconcile myself to my offended God. I had a trusty slave named Ibrahim, who I acquainted with my design of retiring. He found this wood and contrived the cave you here do find me in, and one evening he brought me hither with what wealth you here will find, which I reserved to provide for me if should live to weak old age. Once in five days he comes to me, for I have given him his freedom and enough to live at ease. My fortune and command a favorite Turk enjoys. This servant brings me food, such as will keep, cordials, and dried fruits, for flesh I never taste, nor wine. 'Tis now a month since he was here, by which I guess him sick or dead. It is now ten days since I was seized with a fever and ague; I find myself so weak that I am apprehensive I shall die. I therefore write this that if any Christian finds me here he may be warned of sinning as I have done and may be enabled by the wealth herewith to procure a happier condition for himself than I can ever hope for in this world.

> Christian, remember you must one day die
> And unto judgment come as well as I.

CHAPTER XII

Father Francis read this paper with great concern and taking the cabinet left the dismal place, not doubting but his pursuers were gone and the coast clear, in which he was not deceived. For they having sought for him some time in vain desisted and pursued their journey to Constantinople. He got safe to the cottage, but was much surprised to find Ardelisa and her servants gone. One while he imagined they were discovered and seized, but upon second thoughts that seemed very improbable. Then he began to think they were gone for Constantinople. He passed the day in much anxiety and sat musing all night. At last, he resolved to go for Constantinople to the Consul's where he thought if any where he should hear of them.

Accordingly, early in the morning he set out, carrying with him the cabinet he found in the Spaniard's cave and arrived safely at the Consul's house, where having related the cause of his coming and name he was kindly received. But neither the Consul nor his servants could tell what was become of Ardelisa, Nannetta, or the boy. Domingo and the servants with the horse litter were returned from Domez-Dure, having waited there till they were weary; Domingo having first gone back to the cottage and not found them. 'We conclude,' said he, 'that some mischief has befallen them going from the wood, but what we are yet to learn.'

The priest entertained the Consul and his lady with an account of all the tragical passages of his life. They spent the evening much pleased with his conversation, but remembering how fatigued he must be with his journey, they broke off the conversation, and the Consul waited on him to his chamber, begging him to accept of some linen and habit suiting his birth and more commodious, which he modestly received with the most handsome acknowledgments. After which the Consul retired, leaving him to his devotions.

And now, left alone, he sat down and reflected on the goodness of God, which had at last delivered him from a life of misery, attended with continual fears from cold and hunger, and had brought him safe to Christian conversation, plenty, and a retreat where he might sleep securely. After returning the due thanks, he shifted and entered a bed easy and sweet, a comfort his tired limbs had long been strangers to. He wished for nothing now so much as for Ardelisa and the faithful maid and boy. 'Now my God,' said he, 'show yet more the wonders of thy mercy in preserving them, if living.' After that he fell into a profound sleep, sweet as the peace of his good conscience.

About midnight he and all the family were waked by some persons knocking at the gate in a manner that spoke the utmost haste or fury; they all left their beds and one of the servants called to know who was there. Joseph answered, 'It is I, open the gate quickly, I am Joseph.' At these words the servant unbarred the gate and saw Ardelisa, Violette, Nannetta, and Joseph. Shutting the gate, they went in, where they were received with a joy words can't express. Ardelisa said, 'Ask no questions, but put out the lights, for we have left the place we were confined in all in flames, and should any noise be heard in this house when the city is alarmed, it might render us suspected. Whereas now they will conclude us burned and that will prevent all reports of our escaping.'

The Consul consented, and Violetta was with Ardelisa conducted to a chamber; and the Consul, his lady, and Father Francis denied themselves the pleasure of knowing their adventures till the morning. All the family went to bed but not to sleep; that was impossible for the great noise in the streets, which was occasioned by the fire, for the city of Constantinople had been so many times almost destroyed by that merciless element that the people are very much alarmed with any thing of that nature. Osmin's palace was large and noble and flamed dreadfully in the garden, and the seraglio being fired at the same time by Ardelisa, who left it burning, their departure put the servants in such distraction that they ran through the streets crying 'Fire! Fire!' It raised almost all the city. The Consul and his family were early up, and then Ardelisa gave them a full relation of all that had befallen her since her departure from the wood with an account of all her friend Violetta's misfortunes, whose beauty and wisdom charmed all the company.

A general joy now spread itself through all the family, and Providence seemed to smile. The ladies, priest, Nannetta, and Joseph stirred not forth, and in a few days a French ship being freighted was ready to sail for France. The Consul waited on the French ambassador to inform him of all and obtained of him to assist him in procuring for them a safe passage home. In the Consul's boat, accompanied with the Consul and his lady, the two ladies in men's habits, with the priest, maid, and boy, got safe to the ship with the jewels, gold, and habits they carried with them. And there the Consul and his lady took leave of them with all demonstrations of love and respect on both sides. This ship was called the St. Francis, the captain's name was Monsieur de Feuillade, a fine, accomplished gentleman, young, brave, and of a noble, sweet disposition. The ladies, so soon as the ship was under sail, laid aside their men's habits and put on such as became their sex and quality, in which they appeared so charming that the unfortunate captain soon gazed away his liberty, becoming passionately in love with Violetta. He entertained them with such civility and respect as showed the esteem he had for them and spoke the gentleman and the lover.

They set sail the 20th of August, 1705, it being more than three years since Ardelisa came to Turkey, six months of which time she spent in the melancholy cottage in the wood and near a whole year since she saw her Lord; and now she doubted not of soon seeing again her dear native country, friends, and relations. But above all things, him whom she preferred to all things. They passed the time the most agreeably that was possible, in which the good father shared, who was so pious, useful, and modest, that not only they but all the sailors thought themselves happy in having such a man with them. He was physician to the sick, having great skill in physic and surgery, and could apply fit remedies to both soul and body. Violetta only seemed melancholy; the loss of her honor and the dismal impression the way of life she had led with Osmin had made in her soul no change of condition could perfectly efface. She thought only of retiring to a religious house to weep for a sin of which she was in reality altogether innocent. The good priest observed her sadness, and one day took an opportunity when Ardelisa was gone with the captain and Nannetta to take the air upon the deck to speak to her in this manner: 'Madam, why do you abandon yourself thus to grief at a time when you are returning to Christians and your own country, to your noble father, mother, and friends? Your soul should now be ravished in admiration of that Providence that has so unexpectedly delivered you from the most unhappy condition that a lady could be in.'

She lifted up her eyes at these words, and wiping the falling tears away said, 'Father, till I saw Ardelisa I found my conscience undisturbed, I submitted to the fatal necessity of my circumstances; and Christianity forbidding me to finish life by my own hand, I thought I had done all that was required. But that noble lady's heroic conduct has convinced me I did not what I ought. She never would have permitted a lustful Turk to possess her, but by his death would have preserved her honor, or resisting to death not have survived it. I am no longer friends with myself and long to hide my face in a convent where tears shall wash away the stains of his embraces. Nay, Father, to you I confess I even loved him, saw him with a wife's eyes, and thought myself obliged to do so.'

The priest answered, 'Madam, you are deceived. In Ardelisa, who was married to another, it would have been a horrid crime to suffer another man for to possess her, but as you were single, a virgin, and made his by the chance of war, it was no sin in you to yield to him, and it would have been wilful murder to have killed him, or but conspired his death. Nay, a sin not to have been faithful to his bed; whilst he is living you ought not to marry. You might have been a means of his conversion; you ought to pray for him and consider he acted according to his knowledge and education.' Violetta thanked him and seemed much revived.

CHAPTER XIII

They had now sailed six days when the seventh night it grew dark and tempestuous; the wind changed and about midnight a storm arose so dreadful the pilot could no longer steer the ship so that she drove they knew not whither. At break of day they found themselves amongst the Aegean Isles. The ship had lost all her masts; they had but thirteen hands aboard, when the carpenter going down into the hold came back with a face that expressed the terrors of his mind. He cried, 'Hoist out the boats quickly, there is five foot water in the hold.' At these words a death-like paleness spread over every face; the captain, ladies, priest, Nannetta, Joseph, and five sailors entered the first boat, taking with them their gold, jewels, some trunks of clothes, biscuit, a vessel of wine, and some quilts, bedding, and salt meat—what they could possibly put in without endangering the boat's sinking—and then they made away for the island which was nearest, on which they landed safely but had the misfortune to see the other boat sink, which the greedy sailors had too deeply loaded. The ship floated a little while and then disappeared, being swallowed up by the merciless waves. And now being on shore, they were desirous to know where they were, which they soon discovered to be on the island Delos, which lies in the Archipelago, the largest of the Cyclades once famous for the Temple of Apollo but now entirely abandoned by the Turks and desolate of all inhabitants. Here they must remain till some discovery could be made of a better place to remove to, which they proposed to do by means of their boat, in which next to Providence they placed all their hopes. They hasted to bring all ashore, the tempest continuing, and drew the boat on land. And now necessity taught them what to do in a place where there was neither house nor market. Going up a little way from the shore, they found two or three ruinous huts, which they entered as joyfully as if they had been palaces. In one of these the two ladies went with Nannetta, the captain ordering a quilt and some coverlids, the best they had saved, to be put into it, as likewise Ardelisa's trunk in which was the clothes and treasure belonging to the ladies. Into another hut the priest, Joseph, and he entered; there he placed the wine, biscuit, and meat, knowing he must now husband that lest they should want before they could be supplied with more.

And now having ordered all things the best that was possible in so unhappy a place and circumstance, the captain and priest went to the ladies, whom they found much dejected and out of order. They said all they could to comfort them, desiring them to eat something. Joseph brought them meat and wine, and the sailors gathered leaves and sticks and made fires in the huts, being handy and used to shift. The captain ordered them also some meat and wine, which they ate as cheerfully as if nothing had happened. And now the good father, seeing the ladies sad addressed himself thus to Ardelisa: 'Madam, ever since I have had the honor to know you, I have observed something so noble and Christian in all your deportment that I believed you incapable of fear or ingratitude to God, who this day has given you a signal deliverance from death. It is not many hours ago since we expected to be swallowed up in the deep and thought death stared us in the face, but now the divine power has brought us to firm land and to a place where if we are alone and have no inhabitants to comfort or relieve us, we have no enemies to fear, no inhuman Turks to murder or enslave us. We may sleep here in security. And as for food, Providence that provides for the wild beasts and birds will doubtless provide for us; in us who have had such uncommon and extraordinary proofs of his favor it would be an unpardonable sin to distrust him now. Summon up then your faith and reason to aid you, and be not cast down.' These words seemed as cordials to them all; they ate thankfully what was set before them, and the captain, priest, and boy returning to their hut, the sailors to theirs, they slept as sweetly as if they had lain in palaces on beds of down.

CHAPTER XIV

The next morning the sky being cleared up and the winds ceased, the cheerful sun began to shine. The captain, priest, and sailors walked out of their huts to view the shore and country. They saw many sea birds upon it, and plenty of ruins, with some goats and swine, which they supposed cast there by some shipwreck, but so wild that they fled away as soon as anybody came in sight of them. At last the captain thought it best to send three of the sailors out in the boat to discover if any place could be found near that more convenient to remove to or buy provisions at till some Christian ship arrived to take them in, which it was probable would not be long, because this island affords plenty of good water and is safe for Christians to air goods on or mend their vessels. The boat was accordingly got out and the sailors entered it, the captain charging them not to venture far from that island. But they were either taken or drowned, for they never returned again with the boat. For some days they lived on what provisions they had brought with them, and the two sailors and Joseph walking daily up and down the island, which is many miles in circumference, gathered up plenty of eggs, which the sea fowl laid there, and now and then some small fishes, which they catched in some little brooks which are in the island.

But now the biscuit was spent and bread wanting; they began to despair of the boat's return, which they had every day expected till now. The ladies, unused to such Hardships fell both sick. The good Father searched every where for herbs medicinal to relieve them; but, alas! so many things were wanting that they were ineffectual. How could cordials and restoratives be had when neither wine or spirits could be made? The captain, whose concern for Violetta equaled the passion he had for her, denied himself what was requisite to support his own life, for fear of her wanting. Whilst the poor ladies, whom sickness and want had rendered unable to walk, were watched by Nannetta, who was almost as feeble as they. The priest, captain, and sailors did nothing but wander about in search of food. They had brought two muskets and some powder ashore with them, but that being spent the guns were useless. They now contrived pitfalls and snares, which they made with twigs plucked from small trees and bushes, which were very plenty by the seaside, and with these they had pretty good success, catching sea fowls and sometimes rabbits. These they brought home, dressed, and divided, giving first to the ladies. But, alas! what could this do to sustain the lives of eight persons? Water was all they had to drink.

One evening the boy catched a young goat and, unable to carry it, tied a string about its neck and led it home. The dam with another twin kid followed, hearing it bleat. This young goat being brought to the hut belonging to the captain and tied there drew the other two to follow her in, and so they were taken. One of the young ones they immediately killed and feasted upon. The dam they preserved for her milk and the other kid as a treasure when they could get no other food. With the milk of this goat the ladies' lives were in a manner wholly preserved, the boy feeding her and the kid with what he could get of greens, of which there was no want, and now they all grew so weak for want of food that they were scarce able so much as to seek for it. Silence seemed almost to reign amongst them, every one being unwilling to speak his despair to his friend. Their hollow eyes were continually directed to the sea, from whence they only hoped relief. Nothing but the arrival of some Christian ship could save them from perishing.

141

The priest on this occasion showed himself more than man; he encouraged everybody else and seemed cheerful himself, and though he ate less than they yet seemed always satisfied. Though his meager face and leanness showed his decay, yet his tongue uttered no complaint. 'Come, my children,' says he, 'Mortality is subject to misfortunes, the way to heaven is difficult but the end glorious; there we shall want nothing. The Almighty's ears are always open to our complaints; trust him, in his own time he will deliver us or take us to eternal rest.' With these and such like discourses he comforted them daily.

CHAPTER XV

One night as they were retired to rest (for indeed sleep they could not, or at least but little, want of food having made them almost strangers to those sweet slumbers which are produced by good meat or wholesome nourishment) they heard a mighty storm. The winds blew as if nature were in convulsions, and the elements at strife. Then guns went off, by which they guessed some ship was near and in distress. So soon as the day break, the boy and sailors ventured out to see what they could discover, and there saw the dismal remains of a shipwreck upon the shore by the carcasses of several drowned men. Huge coffers floated on the waters and some lay upon the shore. The seamen and boy got what they were able and found some casks of salt beef, biscuit, rum, and bales of India goods, which showed it was some East India ship that was lost. They hoped to find some of the sailors, but none were saved alive on that place. By those that lay dead they guessed them Venetians.

By this time Father Francis and the captain came to them and gave them their assistance, and now getting home to their huts what they had got a new life seemed to appear in them. Thus the ruin of others procured their preservation, as is frequent in this world. And one of the vessels of rum being broached and each taking a dram with a biscuit, they resolved to return to work and search all the shore, the sea now ebbing, to see if they could get more, especially food, for treasure was to them useless. That gold that causes so much mischief in the world, for which men sell their souls and change their faiths, was here less valuable than a crust of bread. They succeeded so well that in five hours they had five barrels of beef and pork, seven of biscuit, three of rum, one of brandy, five of wine, and many rich goods and chests of clothes. Thus Providence to preserve them caused the winds and seas to bring them food and raiment. They likewise gathered up many pieces of the ship, planks, ropes, broken masts, sail cloth, etc., and now they began to think of making a habitation for all the family to dwell together, and nothing but a boat was wanting to make them happy. They in a few days accomplished their design of a house, for they made a large tent with the sail cloth on poles, with partitions so that it reached from one hut to the other. Here the ladies could be brought and seated to take a little air and to eat. They had likewise saved some barrels of powder and shot, which was of great use to them, for the men soon got strength enough to walk again about the island and shot wild hogs and fowl frequently. Thus they lived for two months.

CHAPTER XVI

One evening Joseph returned from shooting and told them [that] at the farther end of the island he saw a ship lie at an anchor at some distance from a creek, into which he saw a boat put. The men came ashore and about six of them left the boat and walked up the land towards a brook, as he supposed, for water. And on the ship's stern he could discern a red cross and thence concluded they were Christians. This news made them long for the next morning, when the captain, priest, and boy set out by day break and went to the place, which they reached in three hours time, so much had hope strengthened them; and there they found the shore full of seamen and a tent set up, in which they supposed the captain and passengers were. The priest went up to the first man he found near enough to speak to and asked him, 'Whence they were?' The man answered, 'From Venice.' 'What is your captain's name?' said the Father; 'Don Manuel,' answered the seaman, 'and the ship is a man of war called the St. Mark.' 'Now, friend,' said the priest, 'where are you bound?' 'Home, Sir,' he replied. 'Pray bring me and my friend to the captain,' said the priest, 'we are Christians cast on this island and beg to speak to him.' 'Speak and welcome, gentlemen,' said the man, 'my captain's a noble Venetian and will treat you generously, a worthier man never sailed the seas.'

They followed him to the tent and were received with such humanity as surprised them; but discoursing the captain to whom they related part of their misfortunes, they discovered it was Violetta's father they were talking with. Then the French captain, looking on the good father, said to the captain, 'Sir, did you not lose a daughter in the last dreadful war with the Turks? a lady the most lovely of her sex called Violetta.' 'Yes,' answered Don Manuel, 'I did, but why do you mention that?' 'She's here, my Lord,' said he, 'and in my care.'

Then the good Father and he related all the manner of her escape. What joy and satisfaction this news was to Don Manuel the mind can much better conceive than words express. They dined with him and after a noble treat he agreed to go along with them, ordering the ship to be brought round. In walking with them, he told them that as he was at sea with his ship with three other men of war in company going to meet some Venetian merchant ships that they expected from the East Indies, which they were ordered to convoy home, the storm happened, which had shipwrecked one of those ships, as he was since informed. This tempest parted the men of war and drove him out to sea, so that he was in great want of fresh water, for which reason he put in here.

They entertained him with Ardelisa's whole history, and so they passed the time till they reached their tarpaulin palace, into which being entered they found the two ladies. But when Violetta saw herself embraced by her father joy so overcame her that she fainted in his arms and recovering was congratulated by the whole company. And now the ladies and servants seemed so revived that all sorrow was forgotten. Supper was brought in and nothing spared of the provisions that yet remained, which before they used to divide with care for fear of wanting. As they were at supper, the first lieutenant of the ship was brought in to inform Don Manuel that the ship was come to an anchor near that place. Soon after him came several young gentlemen to compliment their commander on account of Violetta. This company passed some hours very agreeably admiring the strange accidents that had befallen them and particularly their meeting in this place. Don Manuel and those belonging to him returned to the ship and next morning, returning to shore, passed the day with his daughter and friends, bringing rich wines and sweetmeats to regale them. The seamen hasted to water the ship and get all things on board belonging to Ardelisa and her family, which they performed in five days; and then the ladies, [the] French captain, Father Francis, Nannetta, Joseph, and the two sailors went aboard the Venetian ship, leaving the desolate island and their huts with many things which they thought not worth taking away, which might nevertheless be of great use to any others who should have the same occasion for them. Ardelisa desired the goat and the kid might be brought aboard, which she loved much because its milk had preserved hers and Violetta's life, and therefore she resolved to carry it to France with her. So it was brought in the boat, being grown so tame it would follow Joseph like a dog.

They set sail for Venice the 2nd of February, 1711/12, having lived on the island from the 29th of August to that time, which was five months and four days; and they arrived safe at Venice in fourteen days, where the ladies were conducted to Don Manuel's house accompanied by the French captain, the priest, and their servants. And there Donna Catherina received her daughter with the greatest transports imaginable, weeping for joy, the young lady doing the same—a sight so moving it touched all the company. Here Ardelisa and the rest were entertained magnificently and not only invited but even constrained to continue till a French ship arrived to carry them to France.

CHAPTER XVII

Ardelisa was treated by all Don Manuel's relations and showed all that was worthy observation in that noble city, whose situation alone renders it a wonder. The French captain, Monsieur de Feuillade, was the only person who was not here diverted. He thought only of the approaching separation that was to be made between him and Violetta, to whom he had given a thousand testimonies of his passion but never made any plain declaration of love, which he was withheld from doing by these considerations. First, he was not the eldest son of that noble family to which he belonged, being second brother to the Count de Feuillade, who now enjoyed the title and estate. He had indeed great expectations from the Marquis de Rochmount his uncle who was his god-father and had no heir and was very ancient. But then he reflected that Violetta was a lady of the nicest virtue and would, perhaps, scruple to marry whilst the infidel who had been happy in the enjoying of her lived. These thoughts had till now kept him silent; but his passion was too great to suffer him to part from her without declaring his love. He resolved therefore to take the first opportunity to reveal it to her, which was difficult by reason of the abundance of company that visited at Don Manuel's and frequent diversions to which the ladies were invited abroad.

One morning he rose very early and went into the gardens to walk, being melancholy. After some time he entered a banqueting house where he sat down and was in a profound meditation, when he heard a rustling behind the quickset hedges, and lifting up his eyes saw Violetta alone, very pensive. She passed by and went up a small mount upon which there stood a summer house which for prospect and the painting it was embellished withal equaled if not excelled any in Venice. Into this she entered and sat down; he imme-diately followed her thither and there threw himself upon his knees before her, saying, 'Charming, divine Violetta! see here a man who adores you, who has loved you from the first moment he saw you; and yet through respect continued silent and would not importune you whilst you were unfortunate. You are now returned home and secured from all future mischiefs, and I the most unhappy of all men must e'er long leave you. The thoughts of this sep-aration are insupportable. Tell me, divine creature! may I hope that you are not wholly insensible of my services? and that you will sometimes remember me with compassion? I am going to my native country, to a place where my friends and fortune are, but I would much rather stay here and die at your feet and could wish I had not one moment survived our deliverance from the desolate island, since it is the means of depriving me of your sight. Oh! speak! Is your soul insensible to love? May I not hope?'

Violetta, much disordered, seemed to ruminate before she spoke; and at length replied, 'Sir, I am neither insensible nor ungrateful; your affection has been so easy to be discovered in all the kind and generous things you did for me in my distress that it would be base in me not to acknowledge that I believe your passion sincere and noble. And the grateful sense I have of it is such that I will not dissemble with you. Were not my circumstances what they are, I would sooner consent to be yours than any man's living.'

At these words he kissed her hand with the greatest transport, saying, 'Madam, proceed no farther, let this charming sentence live for ever in my thoughts; no circumstance remains to bar me from being happy. Do you but bid me live, I shall surmount all obstacles. Your noble father will find noth-ing in my birth or fortune to render me unworthy such an honor. You are

145

not pre-engaged; the villain who possessed that lovely person had no title to it but lawless force. He neither was a Christian nor a husband; he used you as his slave and doubtless would, when ever his brutish lust inclined him to a change have bestowed you on some favorite slave to use or poison you.'

Violetta answered, with a flood of tears, 'Yet, while this villain lives honor forbids me to be yours. 'Tis true he forced me to his bed, but 'twas the custom of his nation and what he thought no crime; yet he was tender of me, and whilst he lives my modesty cannot permit me to receive another in my bed.' 'But if he's dead, Madam,' the lover cried, 'then will you give consent to make me blessed, for doubtless he is long so, the Turkish emperors never failing to send the bowstring to the man with whom they are once displeased. 'Twill not be many days before some vessel will arrive from Turkey, and then you'll be informed of all that's happened since we left it. Till then permit me to declare myself to your father and to hope.'

Violetta rising to put an end to the discourse answered only, 'Importune me no farther.' He said no more but taking her hand conducted her to the house and returned to the summer house where for some moments he reflected with much pleasure on what had passed between them. By this time Don Manuel rose and came into the garden with Father Francis, who was the favorite of the whole family. The captain joined them and after some other discourse thinking it a lucky opportunity discovered to Don Manuel in a manner the most respectful and gallant that was possible the passion he had for Violetta, in which the good priest seconded him, giving him and his family (whom he perfectly knew) such a character that Don Manuel received the offer very obligingly, telling the captain if his daughter was consenting he should not contradict her inclinations. After this Monsieur la Feuillade took the freedom of a lover often to dance, walk, and accompany Violetta abroad; and all her relations treated him as a person they esteemed Don Manuel's son.

CHAPTER XVIII

It was not long before a Venetian ship arrived, the captain of which brought an account of many extraordinary events that had happened at Constantinople since their departure. He said, 'That three days after Osmin's palace was burned, he having received the news of it fell sick and refused to eat, continuing silent. He fasted three days, and the fourth was found dead in his chains as he lay on the floor. His body,' said he, 'I saw dragged by the Sultan's order about the streets, which his servants afterwards were suffered to take and bury. Some days after the Grand Vizier returning from the army and being received coldly by the Sultan grew incensed against him; and fearing Osmin's fate formed a conspiracy and deposed the Sultan, setting up Mahomet, his younger brother, on the throne.' Then he told them that Monsieur Joyeuxe and his family were returned to France.

The news of Osmin's death gave Monsieur la Feuillade much satisfaction, but Violetta would not be prevailed upon to marry him soon. At length she promised if he would consent to let her retire for six months into a convent after that she would comply with his desires. These were hard terms, but he was forced to yield to them on condition he might visit her there. She however yielded to stay at her father's till Ardelisa went away, and the lover vowed the six months should begin from the day she received the news of Osmin's death.

As for Ardelisa, though entertained and diverted so highly, she thought each day a year till she saw her dear Lord again; and according to her wish a French ship arrived. Which news being brought to her, Monsieur la Feuillade and the priest went aboard and there seeing the captain knew him to be Monsieur de Fountain, Monsieur Feuillade's cousin, who was as much or more surprised at the sight of them. He embraced them, saying 'Heavens! did I ever think to see either of you again? Father Francis! what angel has preserved you alive till this joyful day? You, cousin, are thought dead. Your ship was reported to be cast away. I have good news to tell you; your uncle the marquis is dead and has left you all his estate and title. You are now Marquis of Rochmount.'

They went into the great cabin where they drank a bottle of wine with the captain and then took him ashore, telling him they would bring him to a lady at the sight of whom he would be yet much more surprised. They soon arrived at Don Manuel's, where they found Ardelisa waiting their return with impatience, but when she saw Captain de Fountain she was overjoyed, knowing he came from the place where her lord (if living) was. He thought himself in a dream; never was a more agreeable meeting of friends. When he assured her the Lord Longueville was in health, Ardelisa shed tears of joy. But he told her withal that he was retired into a convent of Franciscan friars, where notwithstanding his friends' entreaties he was determined to stay the rest of his life if no news of her being yet alive arrived by a messenger whom he had sent to Turkey on purpose to get a particular account of that unfortunate accident 'in which your father, you, and all the family were supposed to be murdered.'

Here Ardelisa gave him an account of all that had happened to her since that time, as likewise that the Consul had sent him letters long since of her escaping in that dreadful night. Monsieur Fountain answered, 'They questionless are come to his hands by this time, but it is six months since I have been in Picardy.' Then Father Francis looking on Violetta, who spoke not all this while, said, 'Madam, we have news for you too, which will not be disagreeable; Monsieur de Feuillade is this day able to make you Marchioness of Rochmount.' So Monsieur de Fountain informed her that the title and estates of the old marquis his uncle was given to him. Upon which Violetta looking gravely on her lover said, 'My lord, Violetta is not a match for a marquis; you will doubtless repent of a love so ill placed.' 'Madam,' said he, 'were it possible for me to be angry with you, it would be now. No, had I the empire of the world, I should dedicate myself and that to your service and would refuse it if you were not to share it with me.' Ardelisa smiled, saying 'What you refuse the Marquis, you must grant to me; deny me not the pleasure of seeing you married before I leave Venice. The friendship is such between us that methinks you should not let me go to France alone; let us continue to share one another's fate and end our lives together. France is a country charming as your own.' Violetta replied, 'Charming Ardelisa! to whom I owe my deliverance from a life worse than death, heaven knows how dear I prize your friendship and your conversation. But can I leave my parents? Did not duty forbid me to consent, my heart is so much yours I should not be able to part with you.'

At these words Don Manuel entered the room, to whom Father Francis told all the news. The ship stayed here two months to unload and take in goods; at the end of which time Captain de Fountain gave Ardelisa notice to prepare for her departure to France, and then she so pressed Violetta to marry that she yielded. And in fine Don Manuel and his lady consented that she should accompany her lord to France, where they promised to give them a visit the next spring.

Don Manuel gave her a noble fortune in jewels and bills and was extremely satisfied with his son-in-law, who was now possessed of a lady whose temper and person was such as made her a portion of herself,[12] and whose fortune, being Don Manuel's only child, was so great as might have deserved as noble a husband if she had wanted part of the excellencies she possessed. This wedding was splendid as their quality, and when they went aboard the ship for France they were accompanied by all Don Manuel's relations, by whom an entertainment was provided suiting the magnificence of his temper.

We will omit the tender expressions of Donna Catherina at parting with her daughter, with all the acknowledgments Ardelisa made for the noble entertainment she had received, as likewise the good priest who was much esteemed by all. They all took leave of one another, and the ship set sail with a fair wind and arrived safe at Calais, July 1, 1712.

With what transport did Ardelisa see her native land again! The good father prostrating himself upon the shore gave thanks to God for his and their safety. And now they consulted how to go to their homes. Ardelisa resolved that her arrival should not be made public presently, having a desire first to make a trial of her lord's affection. So they determined to go first to the Marquis' seat, which was about five miles short of the Count de Beauclair's, Ardelisa's cousin, in whose hands the Count de Vinevil had intrusted his estate. They therefore hiring a post-chaise for the ladies and horses for themselves, Nannetta and Joseph took the road for Rochmount, where they soon arrived with all the treasure, as jewels, etc. the ladies had saved and Violetta's

---

[12] *portion of herself*: a portion (or dowry) in her self.

father and mother had given her, taking the goat with them. They found the old steward and servants in the house, the Count de Feuillade, the Marquis' elder brother, having delayed to take possession or alter any thing till he was satisfied his brother was dead, to whom he was left successor in the title and fortune. But when the servants saw their young lord enter the gate they received him with such joy as cannot be expressed. He thanked them with much tenderness and showing Violetta said, 'Here I have brought you a lady who you will find yourselves happy in serving.' All this while Ardelisa kept her hood over her face, Violetta saying, 'Sister, you are not well, you shall have a bed got ready for you immediately.' The servants flew to get all in order; the Marquis conducted his lady and Ardelisa to a noble chamber where he left Nannetta to undress them, being much tired with the journey; and leaving order for supper went in a coach with Father Francis to the Count his brother.

CHAPTER XIX

The news of the Marquis' arrival spread so fast that returning home accompanied with his brother he found the court hall and parlors full of relations, friends, and tenants, and having caressed them all, he took only his brother upstairs to Violetta. Entering the room, the Count knew Ardelisa. It is easy to imagine how entertaining this conversation must be; she gave him the reason why she would be private for that night, which he was so well pleased with that he agreed to take Father Francis home with him in the coach that night and to go along with him to the convent to the Lord Longueville the next morning as she desired. He much admired Violetta, his new sister. The Marquis was obliged to return to the company below, and in some time most of the visitors took leave, good manners obliging them to withdraw because it was near night and the Marquis come off a journey. Some of his nearest relations stayed supper, and so importuned him for a sight of his lady that he was forced to bring her down to table.

This opportunity Ardelisa took to send Nannetta for Father Francis, who entering the chamber she spoke to after this manner: 'Father, the great confidence I place in you makes me desire the favor of you to go to my dear lord. After you have given him an account of my deliverance, of which perhaps the letters have already informed him, proceed to relate to him all that has happened to me since, to the time of my being taken into Don Manuel's ship, and there finish, telling him that I there fell sick and died, requesting you to go to him if ever you saw France again. And here say all that's moving, as my dying message to him; and well observe his looks and words. And if you find his passion is decayed, cease to importune him farther.' And here she wept. 'I would not break his peace,' said she, 'or force him to the world again to be looked coldly on and loved for duty only. I'll sooner enter a convent and die silent and unknown.'

149

'Madam,' said he, 'your doubts are criminal. But you would I suppose render him more sensible of his good fortune by first giving him a glimpse of the most unhappy state fate could reduce him to. I'll to oblige you try his constancy and doubt not to bring him with me to you.' He returned to the company, who soon took leave, and then the happy Marquis with his lady wishing Ardelisa good repose retired to an apartment, where the rich furniture surprised and convinced her by what little she had already seen that France was the most noble country in the world. Here they returned heaven thanks, and now freed from all anxious thoughts, being arrived where nothing was wanting to make them happy, they committed themselves to sleep. But Ardelisa could not rest; she talked with Nannetta all the night.

CHAPTER XX

Next morning the Count de Feuillade, with whom the good father went as was agreed, called him and hasted to the convent, where they found the Lord Longueville much altered, to whom the Count spoke after this manner, 'My dear friend, you will wonder doubtless at this early visit, but I bring a person with me who has news of consequence to impart to you. He has been in Turkey.' At these words the Lord Longueville fixed his eyes upon him: 'Father Francis,' said he, 'my God! what do I see? Is my dear Ardelisa safe and alive? No news but that can comfort me.' 'That I am Father Francis, my lord,' he replied, 'is certain, and I wish I could give you news suiting your wishes of your lady. All that relates to her I shall acquaint you with.' Here they sat down, and he rehearsed all her adventures and his own, in which the Lord Longueville did not once interrupt him with one question. But when he told the manner of her dying in her voyage to Venice, he turned pale. The good father hasted to a conclusion and finished in these words: 'The last words, my lord, she spoke were relating to you, which I omit because they were so tender I cannot repeat them with dry eyes and therefore would doubtless wound your soul. Now you must resolve to submit to Providence and be content.' 'Yes,' answered he, 'I am; my God, I submit.'

Here the drops ran from his swollen eyes, and he could say no more. At length he pursued his discourse saying, 'Father and friend! I thank you both and beg you'll witness how resigned I bear the greatest loss that e'er mortality sustained. Be witness, heaven! how dear I loved her, and since she can be mine no more on earth, this day I'll quit the world. Tomorrow's sun shall see me in the humble habit of a friar, these walks shall bound my wishes, and I will know no pleasure but the hopes of seeing her again. Farewell world and sensual joys, in death I place my hope.' Here he crossed his arms, a death-like paleness overspread his face, and he fainted.

The Count and Father, much surprised, called for help, at which the Prior and some friars came and fetching wine and spirits brought him back to life. Then they, repenting the trial they had made, looked confusedly upon one another. At length the priest said, 'Pardon me, heaven! and you, my Lord! this sin. You are imposed upon, fair Ardelisa lives. At her request I made this trial of your constancy. Come with me, I will bring you to her.' At these words he lifted up his eyes, 'Ah! do not flatter me,' he cried, ''tis cruel.' 'By all that's good,' replied the Count, ''tis true, she lives.'

Then they brought him to the coach and told him as they went along all that had passed in her abode at Venice and return to France. And being come to the Marquis', who was just up, they were received with the greatest demonstrations of friendship. He immediately sent to know if Ardelisa was stirring; Nannetta took the message and said her ladyship was not dressed. 'The Lord Longueville is below,' said the servant. E'er the words were spoken, he came to the door, conducted by Joseph who had seen him enter that hall, and throwing himself at his feet told him his lady was there. He entered the chamber and seeing Ardelisa on the bed side caught her in his arms so suddenly that she scarce knew him. Excess of joy did for some time lock up their tongues, so that they continued silent. But at length they both recovered and broke forth in words so tender and so passionate that none but lovers can conceive. The servants all withdrew, and now God had rewarded their long sufferings by making them happy in one another. A universal joy appeared in all this family, and the Count de Beauclair being sent for saw this happy couple and honorably restored his uncle's, the Lord de Vinevil's estate, to Ardelisa. Thus these two lords and ladies lived in perpetual felicity and friendship, and Father Francis with much entreaty consented to be chaplain to Lord Longueville. Nannetta and Joseph married and were nobly provided for.

The next spring the Marquis and his lady had a visit from Don Manuel and Donna Catherina, whom they entertained as became their quality and affection. The same year Violetta blessed her lord with a son and Ardelisa hers with a daughter, who bear their names.

Thus Divine Providence, whom they confided in, tried their faith and virtue with many afflictions and various misfortunes. And in the end rewarded them according to their merit, making them most happy and fortunate.

THE

British RECLUSE:

OR, THE

SECRET HISTORY

OF

CLEOMIRA,

Suppos'd DEAD.

A NOVEL.

Women are govern'd by a Stubborn Fate;
Their Love's Insuperable, as their Hate!
No Merit their Aversion can remove,
Nor ill Requital can efface their Love. Waller.

By Mrs. *ELIZA HAYWOOD,*

Author of LOVE *in* EXCESS; *or, the*
FATAL ENQUIRY.

The SECOND EDITION.

LONDON: Printed for D. Brown, Jun. at the *Black-Swan*, with-out *Temple-Bar*; W. Chetwood, and J. Woodman, in *Russel-Street Covent-Garden*; and S. Chapman, in *Palmall.* MDCCXXII.

Price 1s. 6d.

Eliza Haywood
(1693–1756)

LITTLE is known of Eliza Haywood's early life, but her career as actress, playwright, novelist, journalist, poet, translator, writer of conduct books, and even publisher was visible and controversial enough to assure that traces of the historical woman survive. By 1719, she was no longer in the marriage she described as 'unfortunate'. In letters written in 1729 or 1730, she mentions her husband's and her father's premature deaths; either before or after her husband's death, she had acted in Smock-Alley, Dublin, in 1715. One of these letters mentions two children, 'the eldest of whom is not more than 7 years of Age'.[1] The best modern detective work surmises that the elder was the child of Richard Savage, the writer and friend of Samuel Johnson, and the younger of William Hatchett, with whom she lived for at least twenty years. She died on 25 February 1756 and was buried on 3 March in the St Margaret's parish churchyard, Westminster.

By the end of her life, she had published over eighty works, including at least sixty prose fictions. So influential was she that Sir Walter Scott used her in his equivalent of Nathaniel Hawthorne's more familiar competitive complaint about a 'damned mob of scribbling women': Scott accused her of spawning 'the whole Jemmy and Jenny Jessamy tribe'. The general resistance to the novel and, later, her Tory politics contributed to making her a satiric target, but, as is so often true, these arrows testify to her importance in the history of the novel. Pope made her the prize to be awarded in a competition between booksellers known to publish a large number of novels and punned on her children and her two scandalous chronicles as 'babes of love' (*Dunciad Variorum* [1728], ll. 2.148–82 and 149 n.); Fielding, however, cast her as 'The Muse' in his *Eurydice Hiss'd*. In the first half of the eighteenth century, only Daniel Defoe's *Robinson Crusoe* (1719) and Jonathan Swift's *Gulliver's Travels* matched the sales of her *Love in Excess* (1719). Her 1720 translation of Edme Bursault's *Ten Letters from a Young Lady of Quality* attracted 309 subscribers. Her career intersects with Henry Fielding's at significant moments. She was part of his company at his theatre in the Haymarket, and her *Opera of Operas*;

[1] For biographical help I am grateful to Catherine Ingrassia, who shared her original research, and to the now-standard source, Christine Blouch's 'Eliza Haywood and the Romance of Obscurity', *Studies in English Literature*, 31 (1991), 535–52.

or Tom Thumb the Great (1733, with William Hatchett) is a sequel with a happy ending to his *Tragedy of Tragedies*. Hatchett's *The Fall of Mortimer* (1731) was the second target of pre-Licensing Act censorship after John Gay's *Polly*; Haywood acted in his *Rival Father* (1730) and some of Fielding's most politically provocative plays, including *The Historical Register of 1736* and *Eurydice Hiss'd* (1737). In fact, the night before Walpole brought the Licensing Act before the House of Commons and closed the Haymarket, these plays were performed for her benefit night. Her *Dramatic Historiographer* (1735) went into at least seven editions before 1756. Her political fiction, *The Adventures of Eovaii* (1736), joins some of Fielding's work in attacking Robert Walpole. Many of her other 1730 publications were probably anonymous political writings. *The Fortunate Foundlings* (1744) and *The History of Miss Betsy Thoughtless* (1751) share innovative narrative strategies with Fielding's *The History of Tom Jones, A Foundling* (1749).

She, Penelope Aubin, and Daniel Defoe dominated prose fiction in the decade of the 1720s, and she may have done more than the other two to set the course of the English novel. *Fantomina* (1725) and *The British Recluse* (1722) are representative compositions from this amazing decade in which she published about forty prose fictions, a number of translations, two political 'scandalous memoirs', *Poems on Several Occasions* (1724), and two collections of her works, both with previously unpublished material. Both of the anthologized fictions contain the explicitly erotic writing that earned Haywood the title, 'Great Arbitress of Passion' or, less flattering, 'purveyor of "the luscious style" '. Both, however, also demonstrate Haywood's creative strengths and her serious treatment of the sex-gender and the class systems.

These fictions, as many of her other stories do, explore the part imagination, hopes, and wishes play in deluding human beings. As she does in the *The British Recluse*, Haywood often announces one of her intentions to be showing 'what Miseries may attend a Woman, who has no other Foundation for belief in what her Lover says to her, than the good Opinion her Passion has made her conceive of him'. Almost as often, she illustrates that men are as vulnerable as Beauplaisir in *Fantomina* to their notions of what women are like and to the illusions desire creates.

P.R.B.

The British Recluse; or, The Secret History of Cleomira, Supposed Dead

> Women are govern'd by a Stubborn Fate;
> Their Love's Insuperable, as their Hate!
> No Merit their Aversion can remove,
> Nor ill Riquital can efface their love.
>
> Waller.[1]

[1] Spoken by Almintor in Edmund Waller, *The Maid's Tragedy*, *The Maid's Tragedy altered with some other pieces* (London, 1630), 37.

Of all the *Foibles* Youth and Inexperience is liable to fall into, there is none, I think, of more dangerous Consequence, than too easily giving Credit to what we hear; it is always the Source of a thousand Inadvertencies, and often leads the way to a numerous Train of destructive Passions. If we could bring ourselves to depend on nothing but what we had Proof for, what a world of Discontent should we avoid! *Hope* and *Fear* would then be buried in *Certainty*, and *Love* and *Resentment* never be at Enmity with *Reason*. Whereas, by relying on Appearances (and perhaps, such too, as are formed only by our own Wishes and Apprehensions) we, for a seeming *Good*, embrace a real *Evil*, and run into Mistakes, which, without the Interposition of a peculiar Providence, must be fatal to our Interest and Peace of Mind in whatever Affair we suffer our Belief to be imposed on.

LOVE! as it is one of the first Passions for which the Soul finds Room, so it is also the most easily deceived. The good Opinion, which it naturally inspires, of the darling Object, makes it almost an Impossibility to suspect his Honour and Sincerity, and the Pleasure which arises from a Self-assurance of the Truth of what we so eagerly desire is too great for a young Heart, unaccustomed to such Struggles, to repel.

But, the following little History (which I can affirm for Truth, having it from the Mouths of those chiefly concerned in it) is a sad Example of what Miseries may attend a Woman, who has no other Foundation for Belief in what her Lover says to her than the good Opinion her Passion has made her conceive of him.

BELINDA, a young Lady of a considerable Fortune in *Warwickshire*,[2] being obliged by some Business to come to *London*, which she had never seen before, was recommended, by some of her Country Acquaintance, to a House where she might board. The Pleasantness of the Situation and the good Company she found in it gave her at once the Charms both of the Town and Country; but being naturally of a reserved Temper, and having something in her Mind which seemed to engross her Thoughts, she grew not presently acquainted with any Body. And tho' she observed, that at every Meal, a Plate of whatever came to table was carried away before any other Person was helped, yet she never had the Curiosity to ask to whom it was sent; till one Day, some Gentlemen happening to dine there, who formerly had been Boarders, they began to enquire, of the Gentlewoman of the House, how the RECLUSE did, ——if she continued her Solitary Course of Life,——and, if she had yet been able to find out the Cause of her Retirement. To which the Landlady replied that she was still in the same Mind in which they left her——and that to discover the Mystery of her concealing herself, she believed an utter Impossibility. Indeed, (said one of the Gentlemen) to *know* the Certainty of such an Affair may be a little difficult, but I think it no hard Matter to form a very probable *Conjecture*. In my Opinion, no Motive, but *ill requited Love*,

---

[2] *Warwickshire*: a beautiful, historically interesting county in central England which includes the towns of Coventry and Warwick.

could induce a Lady (so young and beautiful, as you describe this to be) to such an obstinate and peevish Resignation of all the Pleasures of Life. I rather think (answered a young Lady who happened to be there) 'tis the Effects of Grief for the Death of some near and dear Relation, a Parent perhaps, or——How Madam (interrupted the other Gentleman hastily) produce me but one Example, since the Fall of *Adam* of such a Constancy in Grief, and I shall willingly acquiesce to the Sentiments of so fine a Lady; but as I am positive you cannot, give me leave to say it is not only impracticable but also unnatural. Nor can I agree any more with my Friend's Notion of the Matter than with yours: All kinds of Passion, every Body knows, wear off with Time; and *Love*, of all others, as 'tis the gentlest and is subsisted only by *Delight*, of course must die when Delight is at an End. How then, can it be possible that a Woman, who has for a whole Twelvemonth lived in a retirement, where she neither has seen any Body nor been seen, if it were so that Love was the Occasion, should not by this be weary both of the *Cause* and the *Effect?* No, no, (continued he laughing) I rather think, my Landlady, to divert her self and amuse us, has formed this Story of a beautiful young Creature, whom, if the Truth were known, I dare swear is some withered Hag, past the Use of Pleasures, and keeps her self in private, lest her Countenance should terrify. Very well (answered the good old Gentlewoman) you may be as merry as you please with Age; but, Sir, I fancy if you could have persuaded me to have contrived some means for you to have come to the Sight of this Hag, as you call her, she has Eyes, which would have convinced you that there is a Power in *Love* beyond what now you seem to imagine of that Passion.

All dinner, and some time after, was past in this sort of Conversation; which, tho' *Belinda* had but a small Share in, yet it failed not to excite her Curiosity to a Desire of knowing as much as she could of this Adventure: And, as soon as the company were gone and she had an Opportunity of entertaining the Landlady alone, she took an Occasion to enquire what sort of Woman the RECLUSE, as they called her, really was,——how long she had been there, and by what manner introduced. I shall make no Scruple (said she) of informing you as far as I am able; but the Account I can give is so small that it will only serve to increase your Desire of knowing more: About a Year past, being told a Lady in a Chair asked to speak with me, I went to the Door, but not knowing her, looked a little surprised, fancying she might be mistaken; I believe she guessed what my Thoughts were, and before I had time to disclose them, Madam! (said she) I have something to communicate to you, which I am not willing any Person should be witness to; and, if you are at Leisure, should take it as a Favour if you would give me an Opportunity of discoursing you. I then immediately desired her to come into the Parlor; and the Door being shut, I am, (resumed she) an utter Stranger to you, and indeed design to continue so to all the World; it was but by an Accident I heard of the Accommodation you have for Boarders and gladly would become one, if you approve of it on the conditions I shall propose. They must be very strange ones (answered I) that could make me refuse the Company of a Lady such as you appear to be; there are too many Charms in that Countenance not to give me an Ambition of a nearer Acquaintance. I beg therefore that you will put me out of the Pain of believing there is a possibility that anything could oblige me to deny myself that Honour. She returned this little Compliment, only with a Bow, but which had something in it of more graceful and obliging than any Words could be; and, after a Pause, the conditions I mean (said she) are only these. *First*, That you never will endeavour to know more of me, than I am willing to reveal;——That you will suffer no one to enter the Apartment ordered for me but the Servant who shall bring me in my Meat (for I will never dine at Table) and give that Attendance which is necessary. And *Lastly*, That you will be satisfied to accept of a Quarter's Payment, of whatever we shall agree on, always beforehand, for your Security in taking a Person so altogether unknown to you into your House. I will give you (continued she, perceiving I looked amazed) time to consider on what I have said and in a Day or two will wait on you for an Answer; as she spoke these Words, she went hastily into her Chair, leaving me in as great a Consternation at her Behaviour as ever I remember myself to have been in at anything in my whole Life. *Belinda* could not here forbear interrupting her by asking a thousand Questions as to her Dress, her Beauty, and whether she observed anything of that Melancholy in her Countenance the first time, which she had since discovered. To all which the Landlady replied that the Surprise she was in at that time hindered her from taking much Notice, either of her Garb or Person; but that, since her being in the House, she was always dressed rich, but extremely careless, and would often go with only her Hair and a Nightgown[3] for many days together. But in spite (said she) of the little Care she seems to take of herself, Heaven never formed a Creature more exactly lovely; nor do I think it possible for the nicest Eye to discover the least Defect, either in her Face or Shape. What is she (resumed *Belinda*) as to her Wit and conversation? I have already told you (answered the other) that she refuses to let us know her Perfections that way by never stirring from her Apartment, nor permitting any of us to come into it; but if we may form a Judgment of her Genius by the Entertainment which alone she seems to take Delight in, that of reading the best Authors, we must believe it to be very Elegant; she has an admirable Collection of Books; and my Maid, who waits on her, tells me she never goes in without finding her engaged in some one of them. Then you ventured (said *Belinda*) to take her without any further Knowledge? I considered (replied she) that there could be no great Hazard in it; and, besides, there was something so inexpressibly engaging in her Mien and manner of Address that I believe it almost an Impossibility she should be refused anything. This Account gave *Belinda* the greatest Desire imaginable to

---

[3] *Nightgown*: a long, loose gown designed for informal or at-home dress. The gown was an overgarment that women wore fastened at the neck only, at the waist with a sash, or with decorative buttons and loops from neckline to hem.

be acquainted with her and never left soliciting the *Landlady* to use her Interest to procure it. The old Gentlewoman, who was extremely good-humoured, promised to do her Endeavour but said withal that she was afraid it was a Work she should not be able to accomplish. You must tell her (said *Belinda*) and perhaps with more Truth than you imagine that you have a Person in your House, who justly may be termed one of the most unfortunate on Earth,——that I am charmed with her manner of Life——that I could like nothing so much as to partake such a Retirement——and that if she would permit me, sometimes, to mingle my Tears with hers, I would be satisfied with the Opportunity of indulging my Grief, without any farther Intrusion on her Secrets, than she shall give leave. This (answered the *Landlady*) if anything will do——and as you have so ingeniously contrived the Plot, it must be entirely owing to my want of Ability in carrying it on if it should miscarry; and (continued she) I go about it with the more Courage because that reserved and indeed too grave Look (for so young and fine a Lady) which you always wear, will, if she consents to see you, give some Credit to my Words. You need not indeed (resumed *Belinda* with a deep sigh) be under any Apprehensions that my Behaviour will be in the least contradictory to whatever you shall tell her of my disposition to indulge a Melancholy, which I have but too much Reason for. You may talk after what manner you please (said the other) but I am too well acquainted with your Circumstances not to know that you can have no *real* Causes for that Pensiveness, which, to deal freely with you, very much obscures the Lustre of your Charms. I know not indeed (continued she, with a Smile) what *Imaginary* ones your Fancy may suggest. Young People, too often, take Pleasure, as it were, in finding out something to afflict themselves with.——I am afraid you have seen some Gentleman too lovely for your Repose; and, perhaps, he may be (for Love is a blind Deity) of a Quality *above* your *Hopes*, or of a Degree *below* your *Discretion* to make choice of——or, 'tis possible, may have proved ungrateful——or, may be already married——or engaged——or else——She would, doubtless, have run on with all the Circumstances that can make a young Woman in Love unhappy, if *Belinda* (a little too nearly touched,[4] putting on a more than ordinary Severity in her Countenance) had not interrupted her by saying, Madam! whatever the Occasion of my Melancholy may be, I am so much of the RECLUSE's Mind, as to resolve to keep it Secret. Pardon me, (resumed the Landlady, perceiving she was nettled) my Words were meant no otherwise than to divert; and to make what Reparation I can for the Inadvertency of them, will confess that if a Person of *your* Age is too apt to seek occasions of tormenting herself, one of *mine* is liable to as great a Fault, that of talking too much of Affairs which are not any way her Business. Some Company happening to come in, broke off the Conversation. *Belinda* retired to her Chamber, and the Landlady remained with her Head full of contrivance by what means she should bring about the Performance of her Promise.

---

[4] *touched*: personally affected.

The next Day an Opportunity offered very lucky for her Purpose; the RECLUSE sent for her to pay her some Money; and as soon as that Affair was dispatched, she began to labour the success of the other and was so fortunate in her Negotiation that as much averse as she found the RECLUSE at first, the Assurances she gave her that *Belinda's* Desire of her Society sprung only from a belief that there was a Sympathy in their Afflictions at last prevailed on her to receive a Visit from her. Having obtained this Grant, the good old Gentlewoman, eager to acquit herself of the Promise she had made, entreated that *Belinda* might have leave to wait on her that Night; to which the RECLUSE, having permitted her coming at all, easily consented.

The meeting of these two Ladies was something particular[5] for Persons of the same Sex; each found, at first sight, so much to admire in the other that it kept both from speaking for some Moments. The RECLUSE considered *Belinda*, as indeed she is, one of the most lovely Persons on Earth; and *Belinda* found the RECLUSE so far beyond the *Landlady's* Description, something so Majestic, and withal so sweet and attractive in her Air——such a Mixture of the most forceful Fire and most enchanting Softness in her Eyes that she became wholly lost in speechless Wonder; till the RECLUSE (who, tho' as young as *Belinda*, was Mistress of a much greater Presence of Mind) broke Silence in these Words.

If, Madam (said she, with a Voice and Accent no less charming than her Person) you are enough in Love with Misery to wish to be Partaker of it with me, I heartily can bid you welcome to this Scene of woe: but if your Griefs are of a Nature that will admit Relief, the Society of a Wretch like me will be far from adding to your Consolation. To *forget* the Misfortunes I lament (replied *Belinda*) would be, perhaps, a greater Ill than any I yet have known——'tis my Desire always to *remember* them, and nothing sure can so well enable me to do it with Patience, as the Knowledge that so many excellent Qualities, as you appear to me Mistress of, cannot be exempted from Calamities. Alas! (resumed the RECLUSE, bursting into Tears) 'tis the little Knowledge you have of me inclines you to so favourable an Opinion. Believe me Madam (continued she, weeping still more) were you acquainted with the History of this Wretch you see before you, you would allow that as none like me has ever *suffered*, so also none ever has like me *deserved* to suffer. I believe, Madam! (answered *Belinda*) one of the greatest Impossibilities you can attempt is that of persuading me, or indeed anybody that sees you, to that Opinion. These little Civilities being over, they fell into a Conversation suitable to that Melancholy these Misfortunes had involved them in, and they agreed so perfectly in their Sentiments concerning the Instability of all humane Happiness——the little Confidence there was to be put in the Protestations of Friendship——and that the only way to attain true Content was in an absolute Retirement from the World and a Disregard of everything in it; that

---

[5] *particular*: unusually strong specific attraction.

when they parted (as *Belinda* thought it improper to make her first Visit very long) it was with a mutual Satisfaction, and each began to conceive for the other a real Tenderness which has ever since remained unshaken.

The next Day (being desired to do so by the RECLUSE) *Belinda* made her a second Visit, and, after some Discourse like what had passed the Evening before, the conversation turned, perhaps undesignedly by either of them, on *Love*; but when once entered, neither seemed to grow weary of the Subject, and both spoke in so feeling a manner that if a third Person had been witness of what they said, he need not have been very quick of Apprehension to discover what was the Source of both these Ladies' Troubles. They sat together till past Midnight; and when *Belinda* took her Leave, it was not without making an Appointment to pass the next Evening as they had done this.

As soon as *Belinda* was alone, she began to run over in her Mind all the Particulars of the Conversation she had with the RECLUSE and was now *confirmed* in what she before *imagined*, that *Love* had been the sole Cause of her Retirement: She would have given almost one of her Eyes to have been let into the Secret of the whole Affair but durst not attempt to ask it, for fear of disobliging her, if the RECLUSE, who was little behind her in Curiosity, had not, at the next Visit, purposely given her an Opportunity.

I know not, Madam! (said she, soon after they were together) whether there be a possibility for you to imagine from what Cause the Miseries you see me in have proceeded, but I am half positive that I can more than guess the Origin of that Melancholy which induces you to support the Society of a Wretch like me!——I cannot doubt, Madam (replied *Belinda*, blushing, yet pleased she had so favourable an Opportunity of speaking her Mind without Offence) your Penetration in a much greater Matter, since I, who have but little Discernment and less Experience, have been bold enough in my Imagination to assure myself that whatever the *Effects* may be, the *Cause* of both our Sorrows is the same. I am so much of your Mind (resumed the other) that I am willing to put it to the Trial. Here (continued she, taking Pens and Paper) do you write, and I will do the same, and by reading what each other have set down, both will avoid the Confusion of speaking first. Agreed! (said *Belinda* and immediately did as the RECLUSE desired) on Exchange of the Papers, *Belinda* read in that which the RECLUSE had writ; *Undone by* Love *and the Ingratitude of faithless Man.* And the RECLUSE found in that which the other had writ these Words; *For ever lost to Peace by* Love *and my own fond Belief.* As I expected! cried they out both together; and after a little pause, Not all the Ills (rejoined the RECLUSE) which Fortune watches to oppress us with are half so ruinous, so destructive as this one Passion! Nothing, indeed, (replied *Belinda* weeping) is to our Sex so fatal. Oh Love! (continued she) Thou gilded Poison, which kills by slow Degrees, and makes each Moment of our Life a Death! Why, Oh why do we suffer our fond Hearts to harbour thee?——Why are we not like Man (resumed the RECLUSE, bearing her company in Tears) inconstant, changing, and hunting after Pleasure in every Shape?——Or, if our Sex, more pure, and more refined, disdains a Happiness so gross, why have we not Strength of Reason too, to enable us to *scorn* what is no longer *worthy* our *Esteem?* In these, and the like Exclamations, they passed some Time, and had, doubtless, given a greater Loose to the over-boiling Passions of their souls, if their mutual curiosity to know each other's Adventures had not obliged them to leave off.

The RECLUSE would fain have persuaded *Belinda* to relate her Story first; but that Lady excused herself in Terms so obliging and full of Respect that the other could not press her any farther, and only said, I should hardly be prevailed on to a Recital of those Misfortunes which, indeed, have fallen on me but too justly, till by knowing yours I should have hope to find Excuse: But, as I am confident no woes were ever like mine, I have good-nature enough to acquaint you with 'em first, to the end that the Knowledge of mine may make your own seem less and enable you with more Ease to the Relation of them. *Belinda* answered her only with a Bow and a little shaking of her Head at once to thank her for her civility and show that she thought it impossible for any Affliction to exceed that which she endured: And the RECLUSE, after having paid a Tribute of Sighs, which the Remembrance of her Misfortunes always exacted from her, began to satisfy her Companion's Impatience in these Words.

THE STORY OF CLEOMIRA[6]

To make you perfectly comprehend the Truth of my Affairs (said she) I must acquaint you of what condition my *Parents* were: Though their Names I shall beg leave to conceal, lest by declaring to any one that so deservedly unhappy a Creature is their Child, I should disturb the sacred Quiet of their Ashes. She could not speak this without bursting into a Torrent of Tears, which, for some Moments, hindered her from proceeding: But as soon as she had a little repelled the Violence of her Grief, You must know (continued she) that my Father was a younger Branch of a Family which boasts a Place among the Prime of the *Nobility*; and, my Mother was descended from Ancestors whose noble Actions merited titles, though they wore none but that of being the Best and most Ancient of the Gentry. They had both been from their Infancy accustomed to a Court and had Spirits far above their Circumstances, which made them unable to endure the Thoughts either of a Retirement or appearing in Public with an Equipage any way inferior to what those of the same Rank maintained. Thus was I, who was their only Child, bred up in all the Pomp and Pride of Quality and great Part of what should have been reserved for my Fortune spent in my Education and lavished on those unnecessary Ornaments and Expenses, which all young Girls, who are fond of making a Show, affect. I was not much above thirteen when my Father died: His Loss

---

6 This kind of division is common in the French romances; Haywood often used their conventions.

was so real a Grief to my Mother that for a long Time she remained inconsolable, nor did her former Gaiety ever return. Instead of entertaining any
Thoughts of a second Marriage, she transplanted all the Tenderness she had
born my Father on me; and the consideration how improbable it was for her
to match me according to my Birth, or the Expectations I had been bred to,
(my Father being able to leave me no more than three thousand Pounds)
every Day increased her Affliction: Nor were these Reflections unaccompanied
with Fears that my Youth and some Attractions which her Love made her
fancy she saw about me might draw on Temptations to the Disadvantage of
my Reputation; she therefore resolved on the sudden to quit the Court, as a
Place too dangerous for a young Woman to continue in who had not a fortune sufficient to entitle her to the honourable Affections of the *Great* and too
much Pride to listen to the solicitations of the *inferior* Sort who frequented it.
That the less Notice might be taken of the Change of her Humour, she pretended an Indisposition and that the *London* Air did not agree with her, and
in a short Time took a House about six Miles distant from it. This was like
present Death to me, but all I could say was of no Effect; the more pressing I
appeared to *stay*, the more she thought it needful I should *go*; and the
passionate Fondness I expressed for the Town Diversions and Disdain of a
Country Life, confirmed her that it was absolutely necessary at once to prevent the Dangers she imagined threatened me and repel the Growth of that
Ambition which she found had already taken too deep a Root in my youthful Heart. In fine, we went: and this so sudden and disagreeable an Alteration
in my Manner of Living gave me a Shock which I know not how to express.
My Mother, entirely throwing off the *fine Lady* began to practice the mere
Country Gentlewoman, and used her utmost endeavour to make me do so too.
She was continually telling me that my Fortune, joined with all she could be
able to do for me, could entitle me to no greater Hopes.——That it was time
for me to learn to play the good Housewife[7] and forget that there ever were
such Things as Balls, Plays, Masquerades, or Assemblies.[8] All this, which was
really the Effect of her *Prudence*, I looked upon as *Whimsy*; and the Restraint
she laid me under of not visiting or being visited by any Persons, whom she
could have the least Apprehension of, I considered as an Affront to my
Understanding. I am obliged (said she, my dear *Belinda*) to enter into these
Particulars, because this sudden Change from all the Liberties in the World,
to the most strict Confinement, is all the Excuse I can make for my ill
Conduct——But why (continued she, after a Pause) should I allege that for
my Vindication, which Time, perhaps, and consideration might have made
easy to me if a more fatal Enemy to my *Repose*, as well as my *Interest*, my

---

[7] *Housewife*: the word implies frugality as well as domestic skill.

[8] *Masquerades, or Assemblies*: at masquerades men and women in costume mingled more freely
than at other kinds of parties and took advantage of being, or pretending to be, unrecognized.
Public masquerades became the rage in the 1720s. Count Heidegger's at the Haymarket often
attracted 1000 ticket purchasers. Assemblies were fashionable gatherings attended by both sexes
for conversation, news, and cards.

Honour, and my *Virtue*, had not made it more hateful to me. Here was her Speech, a second Time, interrupted by her tempestuous Grief; and *Belinda* was forced to make Use of all the Arguments she was Mistress of to persuade her to Moderation.

At last, getting leave to resume her Discourse, One Day (said she) one fatal Day——would to God it had been the last of my *Life*, as it was of my *Repose*, two Ladies came to visit my Mother, and speaking of a magnificent Ball that Night at Court, told her they were come on purpose to entreat her to permit me to accompany them. By the Account I have given, you may judge how little Probability there was she should consent; but whether she was really overcome by their *Reasons* or only yielded to their *Persuasions*, being Persons she very much esteemed, I know not; but when I least expected it, she ordered me to make myself ready to wait on them. Never was any Prisoner, who long had languished in a Dungeon, more rejoiced to see the open Air than I to find myself once more in Court, where everybody welcomed me, every body caressed me, and, indeed, I believe some of them with a good deal of sincerity: For not being of a Quality *great* enough to create *Envy*, nor so *mean* as to beget *Contempt*, and tolerably well humoured; I am sensible there were many whose kind Wishes I heartily possessed. I had my Admirers too; at least, there were several young Sparks, and those not of the lowest Rank, who took Pleasure in making me believe so. Not that my Heart was any way affected with what they said, though I had Vanity enough to encourage it: *Love* was a Passion I had so little Notion of that I considered it no more than as a Fiction and only dressed up by the Poets in such Variety of Shapes to make the Amusement more entertaining: But this, alas! was the Unlucky Hour in which I was to be convinced of the real Being of that Power I so slightly had regarded and soon learned to pity, by my *own*, those Pains which, with an unregarding Ear, I often had heard *others* mourn.

About the middle of the Ball, as I was dancing with a young Nobleman, who had done me the Honour to take me out,[9] I saw, on a sudden, the Eyes of the whole Company turned towards the Door; but, being too busily engaged in what I was about, had not time to consider what the meaning might be, till having ended my Dance, and it being my Turn to take a Partner, a Lady of my Acquaintance whispered me and said, There's the fine young Lord——(I will not call him by any other Name than that of *Lysander*.[10]) He is lately (continued my Friend) come from his Travels and but this Moment entered; it will be an envied Gallantry if you lead him out. While she was speaking, I directed my Eyes where I perceived she looked and saw a Form which appeared more than *Man* and nothing inferior to those Ideas we conceive of *Angels*; his Air! his Shape! his Face! were more than Human—— Myriads of lightning Glories darted from his Eyes as he cast them round the

---

[9] *take me out*: had asked her to dance and taken her out on the dance floor.

[10] *Lysander*: the name has considerable literary resonance; in William Shakespeare's *Midsummer Night's Dream*, Lysander was an Athenian in love with Hermia.

Room yet tempered with such a streaming Sweetness! Such a descending
Softness as seemed to *entreat* the Admiration he *commanded*! A thousand
Times have I attempted since to *speak* what 'twas I felt at this first fatal
Interview, but *Words* could never do Justice to the Wonders of his *Charms* or
half describe the *Effect* they wrought on me: Oh! had his *Soul* been worthy
of that lovely, that transporting *Outside*, I should have been too blest, been
happy to as superlative a Degree, as now I am *curst* and wretched. But not to
tire you with unavailing *Wishes* or as fruitless *Exclamations*, I Loved——was
plunged in a wild Sea of Passion before I had time to *know* or stem the Danger.
I had so many disordered Motions in my *Heart* that I am amazed my *Feet*
kept any just Measure with the Music; or that so little used as I had ever
been to disguise my Thoughts my *Eyes* did not betray the Confusion of my
Soul and make visible to the whole Company what I was not yet acquainted
with myself: But whether the great Concourse of much finer Ladies who were
there hindered me from being much regarded or those Changes which I am
very sure appeared in my Countenance were only taken for the Effects of
Bashfulness in dancing with a Person who was altogether a Stranger, I cannot tell, but I escaped that Raillery, which I must have expected to have met
with if any body had been sensible of the true State of my Condition. When I
had done Dancing, I mingled with those Ladies who came with me and some
others of my Acquaintance: *Lysander* soon joined us and entered into a
Conversation which showed his Wit was, if possible, superior to his Beauty:
He was perfectly well bred, obliging and gallant and had something of I know
not what peculiarly Graceful and Enchanting in his voice and Manner of
Address; and what added to his other Engagements, at least *endeared* 'em to
my (already doting) Heart was that, though he said nothing in particular to
me at that Time, yet I could easily discern he aimed at pleasing only me. But
he behaved himself not in so general a Manner the whole Night. A little after,
perceiving I was separated a good Distance from the Persons I had Been with,
he came up to me, and making a low Bow, Madam (said he) how fortunate
am I, who after having been in many Courts, where I have seen Ladies who
justly may be called Beautiful, and since my return Home have met with
nothing that could bring me into good Humour with my Native country, have
now the Blessing of beholding a Face, which not only sums up all the different Loveliness of *other* Charmers but has also an immensely Divine Treasure
of its *own!*——*Others* may move the Heart by slow Degrees and with some
one Perfection captivate the Sense, but *you* have Graces which strike the very
Soul and at first sight subdue each Faculty. Blush not, fair Excellence! (continued he, finding I was silent, as indeed I had no Power to speak) I tell you
but the Sense of all Mankind——but what Millions of Tongues are full of and
what your happy Glass, as often as you look in it, informs you. If, my Lord
(replied I, recollecting myself as well as I was able) there were a Possibility of
being unacquainted with my own Defects, so good-natured a Compliment
might give me Graces which before I wanted; But as I have the Misfortune of

knowing myself but too well, all the Advantage I can gain by it, is the Honour of being in the company of a Person whose wit can find something to praise in those the least Praise-worthy. Oh most Angelic (resumed he, tenderly pressing my unresisting Hand) most adorable of your Sex! rob not the brightest Temple of the deity, your divine Self of your just Due.——If (but that's impossible) you can distrust the Force of your too potent Charms, the Effects they have on *me* will quickly tell you what they are——Could those inspiring eyes but look into my Soul, they would perceive their Power——Pardon this Declaration: a vulgar Passion, and for a vulgar Object, may wait on the dull Formalities of Decorum, but what I feel for *you* bursts out and blazes too fierce to be concealed——It is not to be expressed——it is not to be imagined how he looked while he was speaking these Words, and much less in what Manner I behaved at hearing them: Surprise, and Joy, and Hope, and Fear, and Shame, at once assaulted me and hurried my wild Spirits with such Vehemence that had I answered at all, it must have been something strangely Incoherent; but, happily for me, some Company came that instant to the Place where we were standing and delivered me from the greatest Perplexity I could be in. I did not, however, recover myself the whole Time of my being there, yet so much was I infatuated, so lost to all Thought of Reason or Discretion that whenever he approached me, I had not Courage to avoid him as I might easily have done without being taken Notice of. 'Tis sure he took all Opportunities of Entertaining me in the Manner he had begun, and without doubt, as he has since owned to me, he saw enough in my Eyes to make him know the Pleasure I took in hearing him speak far exceeded my confusion at what he said.

It was almost Morning when the Ball broke up, and there being no Possibility of my going Home till next Day, I past that Time at the Ladies House who brought me out: But though the Fatigue and Hurry of the Night would at another Season have made me glad of Rest, I had *now* enough to keep me waking. *Lysander's* Charms, his Beauty, his Wit, the Declaration he had made me, and the Manner in which I had received it give me sufficient Matter of Reflection: I could not think I had listened to any Protestations of *Love* from a Man I had never seen before without an inexpressible Shock to my Modesty; but these considerations soon gave Place to others even more destructive to my Peace: *Lysander* was too lovely, and appeared too deserving, for me to repent, for any long Time, the Complaisance I had showed him, and my greatest Trouble was the Fear that I should never see him more. I resolved to say nothing to my Mother of what had passed, believing with Reason enough, that she would not only condemn me for Mismanagement but also take such Measures as should for ever deprive me of the Sight of him: *Love* taught me a cunning which before I was a Stranger to; and though I burned with Desire to be talking something of my adored *Lysander* and vent some Part of the Overflowings of my ravished Soul, yet I so well dissembled that at my Return Home I never mentioned the least Syllable which could give Suspicion; and contented myself, as well as I was able, with the Belief that *Lysander* (who, I found by his calling me by my Name, had enquired who I was) would find some means to send to me: Nor did that Hope deceive me. The very next Day, happening to be at a Window, I perceived a Fellow walking backwards and forwards before our House; it presently came into my Head that there was a Probability he might be a Messenger from *Lysander*. I observed his Motions a good while, and finding he still lurked about with his Eyes continually fixed on our Door, I made a pretence to go down; and standing there a little, the Man drew nearer, but with a Circumspection which confirmed me my Conjectures were true: Nobody being within hearing, I called to him and asked him if he wanted anything. Madam (answered he softly, and pulling a Letter out of his Pocket) by the Description which was given me, I believe *this* is designed to you. It is, it is (cried I, as soon as I saw the Superscription) and immediately ran in, too much transported to say any more. I got into an Arbor in the Garden to peruse the dear Contents, which I very well remember, and are too deeply engraven in my Mind ever to be forgotten.

To the Divine CLEOMIRA.

If the most adorable Cleomira *wanted any Proof of the dominion of her Charms, besides the just Title they have to reign over the Souls of all Mankind, this had come to convince her of a Truth, which Yesterday she seemed so cruelly to doubt. But you are too Divine to be ignorant of your attributes, and, if there is any thing in you, which is not of a Piece with Heaven, it is that you are not sufficiently stored with Mercy to look favourably on a Man who has no other Merit than his Zeal. It is with an inconceivable Terror I look back on that Declaration, which the Force of the most violent Passion that ever was, obliged me to make, in so unpolite and unprepared a Manner; and tremble when I consider how much Reason you have to condemn the Presumption of this. But, if as many Years of humble faithful Services as Fate has allotted for my Life, may purchase a Pardon for the Sin of my Temerity, I devote them entirely to you— —Henceforward rule my every Word and Action— —I had almost said my every Wish, but Oh! that is not in your Power, vast as it is! for should you command me to cease burning with impatient Desires to obtain the Blessing of pleasing you, I freely own, I could not— —nay, I would not, in that, obey you— —in spite, even of your self I must for ever Love— —for ever Worship You! Permit me then to owe to your Bounty, what else my own Obstinacy will give me, the title of the*

Most excellent Cleomira's
truest, and everlasting Votary,
LYSANDER.

There was a *Postscript* (continued the RECLUSE) in which he pressed very strenuously for an Answer, the Words of which I do not very well remember; and indeed 'twas needless to have troubled you with this, or many others of the like Nature; but as there are some of his Letters, which in the Course of my Story I shall be obliged to repeat, I thought it proper to let you see the mighty Difference 'twixt *Hoping* and *Possessing*; to what an elevated Height the wings of Fancy soar, while in Pursuit; and how low, how faint, and drooping is their Flight when there is nothing farther to be obtained. I will not pretend to tell you what my Transports were while I was reading; if, as you confess, you really know the Power of Love, *your own* Heart will make you comprehend what 'twas *mine* felt much more than any Words could do. I was almost distracted for fear the Messenger should be gone, and I have no Opportunity to send an Answer; but he was better instructed by his Master; and when I opened the door, he presently started out from behind a great Tree that grew before the House. I made a Sign to him that he should stay and went to my Chamber to write: I dared not allow time for Thought, lest any Interruption should happen, and only following the Dictates of my inconsiderate and transported Passion, returned an Answer in these Words.

To the Noble LYSANDER.

If Cleomira *were half so worthy Adoration as* Lysander *truly is, she might, without any Difficulty, be brought to believe all you say to her: but, as I am sensible I have no other Graces than those your Fancy is pleased to bestow on me, you cannot blame me, if I am a little Diffident of the Continuance of a Passion so weakly grounded——I shall not, however, desire you to desist giving me any farther Testimonies of it; because, as you say, while you are possessed of it, entreaties of that kind would be altogether unavailing. I think myself extremely obliged to you for the Caution with which your Letter was delivered, and if you favour me with any more, hope you will make Use of the same, which will be of the greatest Consequence to the Peace of*

CLEOMIRA.

Notwithstanding the Violence of my Passion, there were some Intervals in which I endured severe Upbraidings from my Modesty for engaging thus precipitately in a Love-Affair; but they lasted not long, and at every Return grew weaker than before: *Lysander's* Idea would suffer nothing but itself to have any Prevalence in my Soul, and the Glory, methought, of appearing amiable in his Eyes was more Happiness than all the World besides could give.

The next Morning, almost the first Person I saw was the Messenger again, walking as he had done the Day before; I made no doubt but he had another *Billet* for me, and the first Moment I had an Opportunity went down to receive it: I was not deceived: for as soon as I had opened the Door, he slipped a Paper into my Hand and retired to his Covert quick as Lightning. The Words of this were;

To my Adored CLEOMIRA.

How much was I mistaken while I believed it impossible there was a Charm more touching than your Wit and Beauty; your Goodness ravishes beyond Both!——the Brightness of your Eyes inflame the Heart——the Harmony of your Voice enchants the Ear——but this divine Sweetness of your Nature diffuses Heaven, and gives Raptures which Angels *only, and the happier* Man *whom* Cleomira *favours, can be blessed with!——Say, with what Words, thou wondrous Abstract of Perfection! Thou loveliest——wisest——Best of all created Beings! Shall I repay a Condescension so unhoped——unmerited? To be permitted to adore you, is Ecstasy too great to bear in Silence!——Oh give my impetuous Transports leave to vent themselves,——let me beneath your Feet declare the mighty Sense I have of so unvalued an Obligation——let, on that happy Earth you tread on, my humble Body avow the lower Prostration of my devoted Soul, and never rise till by some Arguments forcible as my Passion, I have convinced you with how much Truth, Purity, and everlasting Zeal, I am your Slave. I have not been so sparing of my Enquiries, as not to know it will be almost impossible to obtain the Blessing I entreat at your House; but if you can think of any other where with Convenience I may be favoured, let the same unequaled Excellence of Disposition, which has already done such Miracles for me, incline you to let me know it by the Bearer: As also if you will feast my longing Eyes with a transient View from your Window, as I pass by tomorrow Morning on Horseback. Tho' your Idea has never been absent from my Soul since the first Moment I beheld you, yet my impatient Sense reproaches me that I have lived these two long Days, without endeavouring at least a greater Proportion of Felicity, and testifying by all the ways I am able, how much I am the never-too-much deified* Cleomira's

Eternally devoted and most
passionate LYSANDER.

Anybody but *me* would have been too much alarmed at the reading these Lines to have returned any Answer, unless it were such a one as should have entirely taken away those Hopes my former complaisance had inspired. The Boldness of desiring me to appoint a Meeting was so great, as all the fine things he said to me could not atone for, and was sufficient to have taught me how dangerous it was to make any condescensions of this kind to a Man I had so little Knowledge of. To *another*, I say, this might have been a timely Warning; but alas! I was so blinded with my Passion that I could think of nothing but which way I should gratify it, and without any Struggles from that Bashfulness which till now had never forsook me, writ him a reply in this Manner.

To the worthy LYSANDER.

The Gratitude you express for that, perhaps, too great compliance you have found in me, is infinitely obliging: for I would much rather you should impute it to any thing, than to that Vanity, which too often influences a Woman of my Age, to encourage Addresses her Heart is no way affected with, and, tho' it may appear too free a Declaration, I am so little acquainted with disguising the Truth, that I cannot forbear telling you, it is to your Merits alone you are indebted for the Liberty of a Correspondence, which you are pleased to think agreeable. Your Information, that it is impossible for me to receive the Honour you would do me at our House, has not deceived you, and I must also let you know I am too strictly confined to

promise it at any other. I must therefore leave it entirely to Fortune, to procure me
any farther Pleasure in your Conversation than what your Letters afford, but in
the mean time shall not fail being at the Window that overlooks the Road, in the
Hope of seeing a Person, whose Regard shall always be most valuable to

CLEOMIRA.

When I had sent this away, I feigned myself a little indisposed to avoid the
necessity of Talking, for Speech was now become a Pain, since I dare not
employ it in the Praise of my adored Lysander. I passed the whole Day, and
good part of the Night, in contemplating the Happiness I should enjoy next
Morning: and it could be called scarce Dawn when I got up and took my Post
at the appointed Window, whence I believe it would have been impossible for
anything to have removed me. My Mother was no sooner out of Bed than she
enquired after my Health; her Tenderness making her doubt the Disorder I
complained of was increased, because I had not been in her Chamber, as it
was my Custom every Morning, to entreat her Blessing: and being told where
I was, came in to me, not a little surprised to find me in a Room, which, by
reason of the great Dust of the Highway, was very seldom made use of and
the least Pleasant of any in the House. She did not fail to ask the Cause of my
being there; and I told her, that not being very well, I hoped some Benefit
from the air, which I thought blew fresher on that side of the House than on
the other. She could have no Suspicion of the Truth, and this Excuse passed
well enough. Breakfast being ready, she sent a Servant to call me, but I not
being prevailed on to come, she ordered it should be brought where I was.
This vexed me to the Heart, for I was not willing that any body, much less
that she should be a Witness of this Interview, tho' at such a distance, with
Lysander. I knew she had discerning Eyes, and feared she might discover more
than I wished she should, in one, or both of our Faces. I refused to drink Tea,
scarce spoke, or if I did, it was so peevishly and unmannerly that I am
amazed she did not leave me in a Rage to indulge my ill Humour; but she
taking my Behaviour for the Effect of Vapours,[11] continued to sooth me by a
thousand endearing Expressions, which were wholly lost upon me: I had no
eyes, no Ears, no Heart open for any thing but *Lysander*. At length he came,
and with a Mien and Air so soft, so sweet, so graceful that Painters might
have copied an *Adonis*[12] from him fit indeed to charm the queen of Beauty.
He was dressed in a strait Jocky-Coat[13] of green Velvet, richly embroidered at
the Seams with Silver; the Buttons were *Brillians*, neatly set in the Fashion of
Roses; his Hair, which is black as Jet, was tied with a green Ribbon, but not
so straightly but that a thousand little Ringlets strayed over his lovely cheeks
and wantoned in the Air; a crimson Feather in his Hat set off, to vast
Advantage, the dazzling Whiteness of his Skin! In fine, he was all over

[11] *Vapours*: nervous disorder exhibited in depression, moodiness, light-headedness, hysteria.
[12] *Adonis*: beautiful youth loved by Venus and Proserpina.
[13] *Jocky-Coat*: great coat with large brass buttons, affected by aristocrats as it was originally
a coat worn by horse dealers.

Charms——all over glorious, and I believe it impossible for the most Insensible to have beheld him without adoring him——what then became of me!——Oh God! how fruitless would any Endeavours be to represent what 'twas I felt!——Transplanted——Ravished——I wonder the violent Emotions of my *soul* did not bear my *Body* out of the Window.——O would it had been so that Love and Life might then have had an End and escaped the Woes which both have since endured. The great Trampling which the Horses made (for he had four Servants in rich Liveries[14] and gallantly mounted attending him) obliged my Mother to rise from her Chair to see what it was that occasioned it. She came to the Window the Moment that *Lysander* was making me a profound Reverence: I know not how I returned it, but doubtless with a Confusion suitable to what I felt within, and which was but too visible to my Mother's Observation; for after he was passed by, and my Eyes were pursuing him as far as I was able, she roused me from the enchanting Dream I had been in by pulling me by the Sleeve from the Window, and looking earnestly in my Face, as tho' she would penetrate into my Soul, bad me tell her who that Gentleman was. I know not, Madam! (answered I, with a Voice which sufficiently discovered the Insincerity of my Words.) I am afraid, (said she, changing her Countenance to more Severity than ever I had seen her wear) you know him but too well: acquaint me therefore this Moment with the Truth, where, when, and how often you have seen him. I could not immediately gather Courage to make any Reply to this Command; and, when I assured her, as I truly might, that I had never seen him but at the *Ball*; she was so far from giving Credit to what I said that she flew into the greatest Passion I had ever seen her in; and after she had a little vented it in some Exclamations on the follies of Love, and disobedience to Parents,[15] left me alone to meditate on her Words.

This was a dreadful Alloy to the Pleasure I had lately enjoyed: I perceived the Secret I had taken so much Pains, and fancied myself so artful in concealing, was by my own Inadvertency discovered.——I could not reflect on the Indignation of a Mother, who, bating[16] the Restraint she laid me under, I had reason to think a most Affectionate one, without a concern very near *remorse*, for doing any thing to occasion it; but when I reflected on the Injustice she did me (for so my *Love* taught me to consider it) in condemning my Admiration of a Person so every way deserving as *Lysander* appeared to be; I regretted nothing but the Power she had over me, lest she should exert it yet more and deprive me of any future means of seeing him. I had been happy never to have been more deceived than I was in my Conjecture that she would take all possible Precaution to prevent my having any conversation with a Person whom she so justly believed dangerous.

---

[14] *Liveries*: distinctive suit and badge worn by servants to identify them with their employers.

[15] *disobedience to Parents*: the eighteenth century took the fifth Commandment, 'Honour thy Father and thy Mother that thy days may be long upon the Land which the Lord thy God giveth thee' (Exod. 20: 12) very seriously, and it is the subject of many novels.

[16] *bating*: leaving out, not taking into account.

I had not past many Hours in contemplating the Misfortunes I fancied myself in before an old Woman (formerly my Governess) and now a sort of Overseer in the Family[17] came into the Room and took upon her to reprove me in Terms I could not well support; on my giving her some tart Replies, she told me that she had Orders from my Mother to confine me to my Chamber, till I had learned the Lesson of Humiliation. I was forced to obey and indeed was well enough contented to be anywhere to avoid the hearing of such Sermons. All that I thought an Affliction was, that 'twould be impossible for me to *receive* or *answer* any Letters from Lysander; and it was only on this Account that I passed three Days of my Confinement in mortal Inquietudes: On the fourth, I saw the *Mercury* to my *Jove*,[18] mounted on a little Heap of Rubbish that the Gardener had thrown out and peeping over the Wall: the poor Fellow, as I since understood, had been every one of those Days watching about the House, but not being able to get a Sight of me, either at the Door or Windows, he at last came round that way. The Appearance of this Man made me almost mad, till casting in my Mind, if there were not a Possibility of giving him Notice of my Condition, Invention furnished me with this. I opened the Window, and thrusting myself out as far I could made a Sign to him that he should tarry a little where he was; then taking a Piece of Paper, writ in it these Words:

I *Know who you come from, and therefore guess your Business.——Let your Lord know I am in the strictest Confinement imaginable on his Account——I fear it will be impossible for me to continue the Happiness of a Correspondence with him——It will be to no Purpose for you to stay, or return any more on the Design you are sent on, but if you are taken Notice of, may occasion worse Usage, if possible, than what I now endure.*

CLEOMIRA.

I pulled a Lead out of the Sleeve of my Gown[19] and Wrapping it up in this Paper to give it Weight made a shift to hurl it to the Place where he could reach it. He took a Letter out of his Pocket and held up to shew me, making several Motions by which I understood he was charged to give it me; but by shaking my Head and putting my Handkerchief to my Eyes, I testified the Impossibility of his Attempts and Part of the concern I was in: I say but Part; for after he was gone, and I began to reflect that, indeed, I never should be able to see *Lysander* more, no Tongue can express the Emotions of my Soul: For many Days I did nothing but weep, and that in so violent a manner that the Servants whom my Mother sent in to wait on me apprehended I should fall into Fits. This, when it was told her, gave so considerable an Alarm to her Tenderness that it half dissipated her Anger; and, when I least expected it, she ordered I should come down into the Parlour, and receiving me with her

[17] *Overseer*: a head servant who directs other servants and may keep accounts.

[18] *Mercury*: messenger to Jove, the supreme Roman deity, lord of heaven and of light.

[19] *Lead*: pieces of lead were used as weights to make sleeves hang in desired, flattering positions.

usual Affability, You have suffered enough (said she) for the Imprudence of contracting an Acquaintance without my Approbation; but as I shall forget it, at least so far as never to reproach you with it, so I would have you remember it enough to make you avoid for the future any Faults of the like Nature. And, to convince me that there is nothing farther between you and this Gentleman than what you would have me believe, you must resume that Cheerfulness which is becoming your Youth and the little Cause you yet have met with to be otherwise. My Heart was too full to suffer me to make any other Reply to these Words than a low Curtsy; but when I had gathered Courage enough to speak, I endeavoured to assure her that my Melancholy proceeded from no other Cause than being on a sudden deprived of all those Diversions I had ever before accustomed to: But that, since it was her Pleasure, I would use my utmost Efforts to make it easy to me. She seemed satisfied with what I said, and, perhaps, believing she had been a little too severe, from that Time took me abroad with her wherever she went; she carried me to visit several Relations and a great many Acquaintance whose Society I formerly took Delight in: But, alas! this *now* could afford no comfort to my bleeding Heart; it rather *increased* than *diminished* the Anguish of my secret Discontent, and since I could not see Lysander, I could have been better pleased to have seen no body. There was no Possibility of conveying a Letter to him, I knew not where to direct, or if I had, notwithstanding the Privileges my Mother now allowed me, she scarce ever trusted me out of her Sight. Thus for two Months did I languish out my Nights in fruitless Wishes and my Days in the most tormenting (of all) Employments, that of being obliged to wear a seeming Gaiety when all my Soul was full of Horror and Distraction. In this Time a new Family came into the Neighbourhood, they soon made an Acquaintance with ours, and my Mother was so well pleased with the good Breeding and Gravity of the Master and Mistress of it that she entered into an Intimacy with them much sooner than was her Custom to do with anybody. They visited frequently at our House, and my Mother always made me accompany her to return them, though much against my Inclination, for, as I have already told you, my own Thoughts, unquiet as they were, gave me more Satisfaction than any company's but *Lysander* could bestow. Both the Man and the Woman seemed wonderfully charmed with me, took all Occasions of complimenting me, and Mrs. *Marvir* (for that was the Name they were called by) would often endeavour to engage me in particular Conversations, which I, as carefully as I could without being rude, avoided: Till one Day, she began a little kind of Raillery on my affecting a Demureness in my Behaviour, which, she said, she was sure was not in my Nature: My Mother, who was willing to take all Opportunities of persuading me to Cheerfulness, joined with her in this Assertion, and between 'em both I was pretty much put to it (so inwardly perplexed as I was) to make any Defence, which, by the Awkwardness of it, would not discover that I had, indeed, something at my Heart which clouded the Gaiety of my Looks. I am afraid (said Mrs. *Marvir* to my Mother) that your Daughter is in Love: I warrant if we should search her Chamber, we should find a Number of amorous Books and Epistles of the same Nature. I never had that Curiosity (replied my Mother) but I hope she would receive none of the *latter* without my Knowledge, and I have taken Care to instill such Principles in her Mind as will not let her be over fond of the other. Will you give me leave to hunt? (resumed she laughing.) Yes, with all my Heart (answered I, glad to put an End to this Discourse.) I waited on her up Stairs, where after she had a little looked about her and praised the Pleasantness of the Chamber, having a full Prospect of the Garden, I told you (said she) that I should find something here more tender than you would have the World be sensible of. I dare swear (continued she, taking a Letter from my Toilet and giving it to me) the Contents of this may justly be called Amorous. I had no sooner cast my Eyes on the Direction than I knew the Hand to be *Lysander's*: The Consternation I was in may be more easily imagined than expressed: I had not Power to break the Seal but continued looking sometimes on her, sometimes on the Table, and sometimes on the Letter, as wondering by what means it had been conveyed there. Cease your Surprise (resumed she) it was no other who laid the Letter on your Toilet than she who took it off and delivered it to your Hand and she who you need make no Scruple to confide in, since your *Lysander*, your adoring, dying *Lysander*, has thought me worthy of the Trust of bearing you his Soul, his Vows, and everlasting Faith. I will make some Excuse (continued she) for leaving you above that you may have Time both to read this and return an Answer, which I have engaged to bring him. I could not get leave from my Astonishment to make any reply to what she said, but when she was gone had my Senses enough about me to lock the Door and then fed my impatient and transported Wishes with these Lines.

To my Soul's only Treasure, the adorable

CLEOMIRA.

How easily might be spared the Stings——the Scorpions——the never-dying Fires, and all the fancied Tortures which Priests invent to ride the frighted World, if any of those Soul-enslavers knew what it was to love like me! Absence from Cleomira is a Hell which all their laboured Policy wants Skill to paint——Within any burning Breast ten thousand real Furies rage, and tear me with Variety of Anguish——Mad with Desire, and winged with daring Hopes, sometimes I could tear down the envious Walls, and baffle all Impediments which hold you from me—— —Sometimes, despairing, chilled with deadly Horror, I fancy you regardless[20] *of my Woe, and easy under this Restraint——One Moment imagine I see a favoured rival bask in your Smiles! gaze on your Eyes in happy tranquil Transport! and kiss that Hand, which but to touch I would forego my Life——The next, distracted, think I behold you dragged by a cruel Mother to some detested Choice your Soul abhors, then soften into more than Female Tenderness, and weep for you and for*

---

[20] *regardless*: unaware or giving no regard to.

myself.——Oh CLEOMIRA! *All the Names of Misery! of Woe! of Anguish insupport-*
able, are poor to what, indeed, my Soul endures for you——My Passion, and my
Pains, are, like your Charms, unutterable! *and only can be felt——This Age of*
Absence has been spent in nothing but Contrivances to shorten it, till these good
People, whose Fidelity you may rely on, were so fortunate to get into your
Acquaintance——O then, thou dearest! brightest! loveliest of thy Sex! indulge the
fond Design, and let them not be less regarded by you, now you know they are the
Instruments by which you must receive the Testimonies of a Passion too sublime to
be inspired by any but your divine Self, and which can be felt, in so high a Degree,
by none but

Your eternally devoted

LYSANDER.

I need not tell you the Raptures of my overjoyed Soul at reading this Letter;
my Answer to it will sufficiently inform you that I had no consideration but
of the Ecstasy it produced.

To the most excellent LYSANDER.

You paint the Woes of Love in so extravagant a Manner, that one had need be
more than ordinarily sensible of that Passion, to be able to give any Credit to a
Description so far beyond what is commonly conceived of it. I am afraid Lysander
is too well acquainted with his Perfections not to know the Effects they must pro-
duce, and but feigns to feel what he alone is capable of inspiring: Were I really pos-
sessed of as many Charms as your all-powerful Wit would dress me up in, you have
a thousand Opportunities of diverting your Thoughts; Business——Variety of
Objects——and gay Conversation, make your Hours slide away in vastly different
Entertainments—while I, of much the softer Sex, and consequently susceptible of a
deeper Impression, have nothing to do but to indulge a Passion, which in the begin-
ning seems delectable——The Dawn, *indeed, promises ten thousand future Joys—*
—what the Meridian *will be, is wholly in your Faith and Honour to be*
proved——But, I have so implicit a Dependance on both, that I will make no
Scruple to confess the Transport of hearing from you again, is more than
Recompense for all those Inquietudes you have so perfectly represented in yours, and
which I hope will be no more the portion of

Your CLEOMIRA.

When I had finished this I went down to the Company and soon found an
Opportunity, unperceived, to slip it into Mrs. *Marvir's* Hand. Scarce a Day
passed after this without my receiving a Letter, either through hers or her
Husband's means. I will not trouble you with the Repetition of them, being
of no great Consequence to my Story and would draw it into a Length too
tedious for your Patience: By *those* you have heard, you may guess the
Purport of the *rest*, so shall only tell you that every one of his grew more
pressing for an Engagement of my Affection and mine still more complying. I
passed my Time *contentedly* enough, though not so *happily* as I wished. The
continual Assurance he gave me of his Passion and the Hopes that through

these Peoples means I should soon enjoy the Blessing of his Presence were Cordials sufficient to keep a Love less ardent than mine alive. And, indeed, I had no great Exercise for my Patience: *Lysander* was too eager, and his Agents too industrious, to permit *me* to grow cool in my Desires or imagine *him* to be so.

One Evening, my Mother and I, being invited to sup at *Marvir's* House, while he engaged her in a serious Discourse, his Wife took me into the Garden: The Transports of my beating Heart informed me to what End I was brought there, before she had time to tell me that *Lysander* waited my Approach in the Arbor. But, when I came near enough to see him, no Confusion sure was ever equal to mine!——The Reflection that this was but the third Time I had *seen* him——but the *second* in which I had an Opportunity to speak to him——the Condescension of my Letters——and that which I now gave of meeting him, came all at once into my Head, and I was ready to sink with Shame. But never did any Votary approach the Image of the Saint he worshipped with more Humility and awful Reverence than *Lysander* me! He fell at my Feet,——embraced my Knees, and kissed my Hands with such a tender Transport——such an enchanting Mixture of Delight and Fear, as one would think no false Love could feign and was impossible to behold unmoved: My Spirits were in too violent an Agitation to suffer me to raise him from the Posture he was in, till gaining Confidence to do it himself and interpreting my Disorders in his Favour, he took me in his Arms, all blushing——trembling, and incapable of Defence, and laying his Head upon my panting Bosom seemed to breath out all his Soul in fervent Tenderness. He held me thus some Moments before I knew what I was doing; and when, at last, I struggled to get free, it was so faintly that he might easily perceive the Liberties he had taken were not unpardonable: I looked for Mrs. *Marvir*, designing to upbraid *her* for the Boldness her Guest had been guilty of; but she was gone, and the Reproaches I made him were such as did not discourage him from a Repetition of his Crime. In short, all the Time of our being together (which I believe was above an Hour) was past in nothing but offending and forgiving: I found by myself that Love is a Passion that disdains Restraint and thought it unjust to be angry at almost any thing the Force of it might Influence him to commit. To go about to tell you what he said——in what Manner he looked——and with what Graces everything he did and spoke were accompanied would be to wrong him; for no Words, no Accents, no Motions but his own can give you any just Idea of his Perfections.——Never was any so formed to *Charm* and to *Betray*——never was such foul Deceit, Hypocrisy, and Villainy couched in such seeming Sweetness, Softness, and Sincerity.——Heaven! with what a counterfeited Vehemence has he exclaimed against the Inconstancy of his Sex!——With what an appearance of Sanctity and Truth has he invoked the Saints and Angels to be a Witness of his Vows! when, lavish of them, he has a thousand——thousand times protested that *Cleomira* should ever be more dear to

175

him than Life! Oh record 'em, all ye blessed Spirits! and in the last great Day, when I alone can hope for Justice, bring 'em in dreadful Testimony against him and force his black, his leprous Soul to own Conviction!

Here the Remembrances of some Passages made this unhappy Lady wholly unable to prosecute her Discourse; and all that *Belinda* could say to mitigate the Rage of Temper she was raised to proved of no Effect till a Shower of new returning Tears in part allayed the Tempest: When she was a little come to herself, After this (resumed she) I had many Opportunities, by Mrs. *Marvir's* Contrivance, of indulging my fond Wishes in *Lysander's* Presence, and so zealous was he in making me believe the Passion he pretended was sincere that in those Days, when there was no other way to see me, he would come disguised and walk before the House till I had taken Notice of him, then by some Motion discover who he was and tell me by his Eyes a thousand tender Things nor stir from the Place till by my withdrawing myself he knew it was improper he should stay any longer. I cannot but say, fierce as my Passion was before, this uncommon Assiduity of his made a vast Addition to it, and I thought it the greatest Hardship in the World that I could not have the Freedom of conversing with him without all this Difficulty on both sides. Mrs. *Marvir*, who kept continual Watch over my Humour, took this Advantage of my Discontent and whenever we were alone endeavoured to heighten it; she was always representing the Injustice my Mother did me in debarring me from all those Liberties young Ladies in this Kingdom are permitted to enjoy and made use of all her Cunning to convince me that those Restrictions were laid upon me only to wean me by degrees from the Pleasures of the World that I might be the more willing to accept of a Husband, who, she told me, my Mother had provided for me. By what I can guess from her Discourse (said she) you are to be married to a Country Gentleman and that in so short time as will amaze you. She spoke this in such a Manner as gave me no suspicion of the Truth; and reflecting how much my Mother had laboured to persuade me into a good Opinion of a Country Life, was assured in my Mind that she had really somebody in View to whom she designed to sacrifice me: and 'tis impossible to represent the Perplexity this Belief involved me in. If any such thing happen, Madam (said I) how should I avoid it? I know not (answered this wicked Woman, having brought me to the Point she aimed at) unless by choosing a Guardian, you entirely divest your Mother of the Power of disposing of you. She said no more at this time, because my Mother happened to come into the Room; but whenever they had an Opportunity, it was with such like Speeches both she and her Husband entertained me; till at last, the Fears of what they had infused into my Imagination—the Hopes of enjoying my beloved Liberty and my infinitely more beloved *Lysander's* Company uncontrolled made me resolve to do as they advised. I could think of no Person so proper for me to make Choice of for a Guardian as *Marvir* himself. It was not very difficult to persuade him to it, (it being the only thing he wanted) tho' at first he seemed averse. Every thing being concluded on, one Morning, before my Mother was out of Bed, I left her House and went to *Marvir's*, whence immediately I took Coach with him for *London*; and by electing him according to Law, put it out of her Power to oblige me to return. Her Behaviour, on the first Knowledge of what I had done, was all Distraction; she fell into Fits, raved, came to *Marvir's* House, and without any Regard to that Decorum she was used so strictly to observe, loudly exclaimed against their Treachery and my Ingratitude and Disobedience: I had not Assurance to appear before her, and they (having gained their End) could endure the Brunt of her Upbraidings: In a few Days we removed to *London*, and I was out of the Fear of meeting her: But her Tenderness soon getting the better of her Indignation, she sent a Letter to me full of Persuasions in the most endearing of Terms to return to her again. I had the Courage to write to her, tho' I had not to see her, and returned an Answer of Excuses for the Measures I had taken but told her it was wholly owing to that unreasonable Restraint she had laid me under—that I abandoned her only in Pursuit of that innocent Liberty, which all Persons of my Age were desirous of enjoying and that I never would make Use of it to the Disadvantage of my Reputation or the Dishonour of my Family, and that in all material Affairs of Life, tho' I had chose a *Guardian*, I would do nothing without consulting *Her*. This was far from being any Satisfaction to her; she writ me several Letters, sometimes entreating, sometimes commanding and threatening and engaged all those Relations, who were near enough to Interest themselves in my Behaviour, to come and talk to me. But the People I was with took care I should be seen by none of them, alleging, as a proof of their Love to me, that they would not have me teazed with any Solicitations of that Nature. I was very well satisfied with their Proceedings, I saw *Lysander* every Day, and while I listened to his Vows, should not have been pleased with an Interruption of any kind. That Ardent, yet Respectful Passion which appeared in all his Words and Actions, was to me a Heaven, which nothing else could give. I had not, for some time, any Reason to suspect he had the least dishonourable Thought; for tho' the little Power I had of disguising my Sentiments had made me guilty of many imprudent Actions and emboldened him to the taking greater Freedoms than otherwise he would have dared to have attempted, yet he offered nothing which justly could be called offensive to Virtue; till one Night——Oh ever be accurst that Night—that Hour—that damned undoing Minute when all good Angels slept and left to Fiends the Fate of *Cleomira*! I had undressed and thrown myself on the Bed restless and uneasy that *Lysander* had not been to visit me that Day, for it was now become an inconsolable Affliction to me to pass four and twenty Hours without seeing him; I was so buried in Thought that I heard not the Tread of any body coming into my Chamber, 'till I saw a Man stand close by me: It was about ten o'clock, at that time of the Year when there is scarce any Darkness, and, willing to indulge Contemplation, I had not called for Candles and could not presently discern who was there, but not suspecting it any other than Mr.

Marvir (who might be come to call me to Supper) without removing from the Posture I was in, asked carelessly what he wanted. He must be a very ill Judge of Happiness (answered he) that could form a Wish beyond the Treasure which this Bed contains. These Words, and the Accent of his Voice, always dear and charming to my Ears, soon told me it was *Lysander* and obliged me to endeavour to rise; but he had thrown himself down by me while he was speaking, and seizing both my Hands, and gently forcing them to circle his Waist, joined his Lips to mine with too strenuous a Pressure to suffer me to reproach the liberties he took—What could I do, surprised in this unguarded Moment?—full of Desires and tender Languishments before, his glowing Touch now dissolved my very Soul and melted every Thought to soft Compliance—in short, I *suffered*—or, rather let me say I could *not resist* his proceeding from one Freedom to another, till there was nothing left for him to ask or me to grant. The guilty Transport past, a thousand Apprehensions all at once invaded me, Remorse and Shame supplied the Place of Ecstasy— Tears filled my Eyes——cold Tremblings seized my Limbs—and my Breast heaved no more with Joy but Horror.—Too sure Presages of that future Woe, which this black Hour brought forth.—It was not in the lovely Undoer's Power, dear as he was, to make me satisfied with what I had done, and the whole time he stayed with me, which was best part of the Night, I uttered nothing but Reproaches: the next Day, and many following ones, I entertained him in no other Manner; and it was some Weeks before all his Wit, his Tenderness and seeming Truth could make me hope I had not done a Deed I should, all my Life, have Occasion to repent. But what is it a Woman may not in time be persuaded to by the Man she loves! He behaved himself in such a Manner, so kind, so soft, so ravishingly tender, respectful and engaging—made so many solemn Protestations of eternal Faith and imprecated such unheard-of Curses on his Falsehood, if ever he should give me Cause to tax him with it, that one would think indeed the most hardened Villain could not thus have dared to dress his Perjuries in such a Form of Sanctity!—How could I then, who *loved* him, *disbelieve* him?——No, it was not in Nature——it was not in Reason that, after what he had sworn, I could be doubtful of his Sincerity or Honour; and I must have considered him as monstrously unworthy of my Love before I could think there was a Possibility he should ever cease to Love me. Thus, was I, at last, raised to the highest Pinnacle of humane Felicity! an Assurance of the real and everlasting Tenderness of the Man who took up all my Wishes: but when I thought myself most happy——most secure, I was on a sudden thrown from all my Height of Transport to the lowest State of Misery and Despair. Ever since my being at *Marvir's* House, I had not passed one Day without seeing *Lysander*; and the first Absence, which was about a Week, filled me with most terrible Suspicions: I did not fail to acquaint him with them by Letters, which he answered with the same Fondness he had accustomed me to, and made Excuses for not visiting me in that time, which seemed plausible enough:

When next I saw him, nothing seemed more endearing—nothing more Ardent than he seemed to be, yet he pretended some Business and stayed not with me so long as he was wont. After he was gone, happening to cast my Eyes on the Ground, I saw a Paper lying, which I, imagining it might be dropped by him, hastily took up; part of it had been torn off, and what remained was so blotted that I could scarce read it; I discovered, however, that it was a most passionate Declaration of Love to some Woman, but who, I was altogether a Stranger, for there was no Name—You may believe (my dear *Belinda*) this was enough to give a Heart so truly tender as mine a most terrible Alarm! I laid it up carefully, designing to show it him when he should come next Day, as he had promised he would; but alas! I expected him many succeeding ones, in vain! 'till growing quite out of Patience, I writ to him according to the Dictates of my Jealousy and Discontent: This indeed engaged a Visit from him; and after he had again made some slight Pretenses for his Absence, began to *rally* me with so much Artifice for the Imagination I had formed of his being in Love in another Place that I was weak enough, on his swearing it was so, to believe the Letter I had found was only a foul copy of one he intended to send to me in that time when he had not an Opportunity of seeing me; and was pretty well satisfied as to his Constancy: But tho' I assured him, my whole Dependance on the Truth of what he said hung on the proof of his visiting me as usual, and he seemed willing I should judge his Truth by that Testimony, yet I saw him not again in another Week. Now the Mist my good Opinion of him had cast before my Eyes began to wear off, and *Reason*, unobserved by *Passion*, showed me how truly wretched I had made myself—but what did it avail? My Fame, my Virtue, and my Peace of Mind were lost, no more to be retrieved: Penetration was but the Mirror which showed me my Deformity but could direct me to no Means which could restore those Beauties, which Guilt and Shame had utterly defaced. From seeing me every Day, he had already fallen to once a Week; soon he came but once a Fortnight; afterwards a Month, and that too was to be accounted a Favour.—Soft as I am by *Nature* and made more so by *Love*, this Usage turned me all to Indignation; I raved, upbraided, threatened, said I know not what, and sometimes was resolved to revenge my Injuries by his Death: but, alas! he grew not less lovely for his being less faithful; and whatever I determined against him in his *Absence*, was in his *Presence* all dissolved. 'Tis true, he never came without renewing his former Protestations of eternal Faith and coined each Time some new-invented Oath to assure me he was still the same. He *seemed* to mourn the Necessity of being so often absent with a Tenderness equal to that I *truly* felt but as perfect a Master as he was in the Art of feigning, I was too well acquainted with the Force of *Love* not to know that where it is sincere no Obstacles would be able to impede the Gratification of it: and one Day, when he had been telling me a tedious Tale of Business and Hurry of Affairs and I know not what, which had prevented his coming, I could not restrain the Violence of my just Resentment; Ungrateful Man!

(said I) when watchful for my Ruin, no Business had the Power to hold you; all Day and every Day each flying Minute was Witness of your Vows——but now,——now, when I have given up all my Soul——am lost to all the World but you, I may alone, unpitied, mourn my Fate and curse the Fondness that betrayed me to your Scorn.——He would not suffer me to go on long in this Strain, but taking me in his Arms and tenderly embracing me, Unjust and cruel Charmer! (interrupted he) if I could be capable of the coldness, the Perfidy you reproach me with, I could not sure have courage to appear before you.——Nor could *you*, if you really believed me Guilty, with that dear, that Angel Look behold me.——No, 'tis the height of Passion only makes you talk thus, as such I take it; and tho' I grieve to see you rend your gentle Breast with causeless Agonies, yet I consider it with a kind of Transport, since it assures me I am indeed more valuable to you than any Merit but my Truth can give me Title to. Oh the Dissembler! with what an Air of Tenderness did he utter these and a thousand of the like Expressions and with what inexpressible Endearments were they accompanied?—Enraged and Stormy as I was before, my soul, now all becalmed again, *Believed*—and was again *Deceived.*—In this Manner did I continue for a considerable Time, sometimes hoping—sometimes despairing—but never certain or confirmed of any thing——all Horror in his Absence—all Ecstasy in his Presence——the Business he pretended, which was Attendance at Court, where he daily expected Preferment, was feasible enough; but then I thought it impossible that no Hour, no Moment in a Week, or in so *many* Weeks, could not be spared—in fine, my Brain was in a perpetual Whirl—Reflection, tossed in wild Uncertainty, became disjointed quite; and tho' I was always *Musing*, yet I was often without the Power of *Thinking*——all my Days were spent in doubtful Expectation and my *Nights* in Tears and heart-rending Agonies too terrible for Description—and if sometimes Nature over-wearied sunk into a Slumber, it could not be called Rest; for even then, my ever-wakeful Fancy hurried my Spirits with confused Ideas in tormenting Dreams—*Lysander's* Image was never from my Sight, and always he appeared unkind and far unlike the Dear—the Soul-enslaving Lover he had been and still would feign. To add to my Affliction, I was with Child, and every Motion of the unborn Innocent increased at once my Tenderness and Grief——'Tis not in Thought to form any just Notion of what I felt——All Passions but Hatred took their turn to persecute me; and sure, had not Heaven reserved me for an Example of its Power in lengthening Woe to a degree beyond what could be imagined, I could not have survived the Torments of an Hour. On his first declining to visit me, I writ often to him; but of late had desisted from giving him that Trouble because he had told me, his Father, whose Hands they might possibly fall into, would have Curiosity enough to open them: Whether this was Reality or whether he said so only to spare himself the pain of Counterfeiting a Tenderness any oftener than he was obliged to in my Presence, I know not, but I had that implicit Obedience to his Will in everything that I very

180

seldom put it to the Venture. But, one Day, after silently enduring an Absence of five Weeks, I was no longer able to restrain the impatient Struggles of my Soul and sent him these Lines.

To my too dear LYSANDER.

Pardon me, if, convulsed and torn with Pangs too dreadful for Expression, the Anguish of my Soul, in spite of me, breaks forth into Complainings—Am I forever to live this Life of curst Uncertainty?——Is there a Necessity your Actions must always contradict your Words?——Oh! be once sincere, and tell me which I must believe——There was a Time when with a thousand Vows you swore, that Absence was the severest Trial a Lover could go through——yet now you bear it—bear it with Ease—with Unconcern!—and can I then still hope you Love?—O Heav'n! it is not, cannot be—by your own Arguments you stand convicted, and I endeavour to deceive myself in vain——Heart-rending thought!—I long have held you True——believed your Oaths with such a Faith as what we pay to the divine Mysteries of Salvation; and 'tis difficult—'tis wondrous to think you can be false!——What then must be the Proof? Madness!—Confusion!—Everlasting Woe!—Horror with-*out a Name!—Save—save me from it! Dissemble yet a little longer; my* Fears *will quickly send me to my* Grave, *let not* Despair *weigh down my sinking* Soul *as well as* Body——. *If I no longer have the Power to please you, let the Remembrance of those happy Moments in which I* had, *engage, at least, your Gratitude——If not your* Love, *bless me with your* Friendship—Pity *me; if, no more; for, my* Lysander, *sure I merit that——The Thoughts of you anticipate my earliest Prayers, and still continue for my Evening Theme—How often, when all have slept, and nothing but the Stars and silent Moon were conscious of my Watchings, have I poured out the Anguish of my bleeding Heart, and to those dumb and unavailing Witnesses vented the wild Extravagance of my Passion, rather than wound your Ears with the unwelcome Tale! 'Tis harder to* accuse you *than to* die—*Yet, while I have Breath, 'twill all be spent in Wailings, if you are still cruel enough to suf-fer me to linger in a Condition which justly gives me the Title of*

The most Injured,
and most Miserable,
CLEOMIRA.

At the Return of my Messenger, I received an Answer which you will scarce believe could be writ by the same Hand or dictated by the same Heart from which those you have already heard proceeded.

To the lovely CLEOMIRA.

Your Sexes Souls are of such narrow Space, that the least Passion swells them even to bursting: I would have the Woman I admire endeavour to enlarge her Genius, and find room for other Views than Love——Not but I think myself infinitely obliged to yours, *and shall never cease the Professions of* mine.——*I will see you in a few Days, and, if possible, convince you that I am*

Your most Faithful
LYSANDER.

One would think I needed no other Proof than the Style and the Shortness of this *Billet* to inform me that I was indeed as wretched as I could be; but spite of Reason, I must join in his Barbarity and be my own Tormentor—my Soul, too curious, would search deeper still though sure to find what would but more distract me: The Fellow whom I employed to carry my Letter told me that not finding *Lysander* at home, he was directed to the Place where he was and delivered it to him in the Presence of a young Lady, whom he was leading to a Chariot, and that as soon as he had writ the Answer they went out together. This was enough to give my already *justly* suspecting Heart a jealous Curiosity and I immediately dispatched him again to find out, if possible, who the Lady was. He was so successful in his Enquiry that he brought me Word that her Name was *Melissa* and that *Lysander* was frequently with her——That they had been seen together at the Play, at the Ring,[21] in the Mall,[22] and several other public Places: If I was before alarmed, what now became of me at this Information? I had formerly had an Acquaintance with this Woman and knew her Temper to be the most intriguing[23] upon Earth; and though from a very mean *Fortune*, and worse *Character*, a Gentleman of a good Estate had raised her to an envied State of Grandeur, she had neither Gratitude nor Conduct sufficient to prevent her from *coquetting* with every Man that thought her worth taking Notice of: Nay, she was so notoriously Imprudent, I may say *Shameless*, that she *sought* all Opportunities of dishonouring her Husband and could not hear of a Man famed for any Perfection without desiring to engage him; she would write to the most absolute Strangers, and her being often repulsed by those whose Discretion made them despise her did not discourage her from attempting others: This is (*Belinda*) the true Character of this vile Woman; and the Reflection that a Creature so every way undeserving should rob me of his Heart rouzed that little Pride, which all Women have some share of, to a *Disdain*, which, not able to overcome my more superior *Softness*, gave me Disorders which cannot be expressed. Since I am to be abandoned (said I to myself) I ought to be pleased that he has abandoned me for a Creature whom none will envy him the Possession of——One, who is not of a Humour to regard any one farther than the Reputation of being admired by him—One, to whom *all* Men are alike and, as charming as he is, will not fail to sacrifice him to the next that makes his Addresses to her. And yet, who knows (cried I again) but this unfaithful— this inconstant Creature may engage him longer than I, with all my Truth and Tenderness, could do—She has *Arts* to which *my Innocence* is a Stranger, and will, no doubt, make use of them all to secure a Conquest so much to the Advantage of her Glory. In this manner did I torment myself; and though I thought nothing could add to what I felt before, yet now I found that to be neglected for *another* was a Sting more terrible than the Neglect itself. Once I

[21] *Ring*: circular course in Hyde Park for driving and walking.
[22] *Mall*: fashionable walk in St James's Park, a place to see and be seen.
[23] *intriguing*: scheming, plotting.

believed that the *Death* of *Lysander* would be the extremest of all Woes, but now I wished him dead rather than in the Possession of a *Rival*.

When next I saw my Traitor, I uttered all that my Rage and Jealousy suggested; but, with his usual Artifice, he appeared unmoved: And when I upbraided him with the Leisure he had to wait on *others*, when he had none for *me*, he swore that being an intimate Acquaintance of her Husband's and meeting them by Accident at a Place where he had Business was desired by him to conduct her where she was going, which Piece of Gallantry, he said, he could not handsomely refuse: To give the more Credit to this, he seemed to dislike her Person—ridiculed her Humour——and laughed so heartily at my being capable of any Uneasiness on her Account that I was half persuaded to believe him. I had not, however, so entire a Dependance on his Truth, but that I employed (unknown to *Marvir's* People, who I found were his Creatures) the same Man, who had brought me the first Intelligence, to watch him wherever he went, resolving to be satisfied one way or other. Alas! I fancied that if I could be once thoroughly assured of his Perfidiousness, I should be able to tear him from my Soul, at least extirpate all the Tenderness I had for him; but, how little did I know myself? When by the Diligence of my Spy, I found out that he visited her often——was with her even at those very Times when he pretended the utmost Regret that he could not be with me—Nay, discovered that they had private Meetings, and by all Circumstances was convinced, not only that she was a Rival infinitely more beloved than I, but also that she was in Possession of all those Joys, which to obtain I had forfeited my Innocence, my Honour, and my Peace of Mind for ever,—in spite, I say, of all these Proofs—these stabbing Proofs of his Ingratitude, I could not—did not love him less: I reproached him, indeed, and endeavoured to make him think my Resentment had extinguished my Tenderness; but he still denied each particular of my Accusation and, at last, seemed angry that I distrusted his Sincerity: Till I, mean-spirited Wretch! was forced to appear satisfied with what he said, least by persisting to *allege* what, I found, he was determined never to *confess*, I should provoke him never to see me more: And when I consulted my fond doting Heart, found I could better bear to share him with another than have no Interest in him at all: But what I suffered in such a Submission may perhaps be guessed, but never described. It was now my Woes fell thick upon me, my Pregnancy began now to discover itself to all who saw me; and *Marvir* and his Wife, who had all this Time counterfeited an Ignorance of what had passed between me and *Lysander*, seemed prodigiously uneasy at it, pretended a Concern for the Reputation of their House, used me in a Manner which I little expected from them of all the World, and told me plainly that I must not continue with them any longer: But if I would go into the Country till I was delivered of my Burden, they would enquire for a Place where I might be in private. I complained to *Lysander* of their Unkindness, but received very little Consolation from him: He only told me he was sorry they should behave otherwise to me

than I had Reason to expect but that he believed they *meant* well and that
he could not help joining with them in the Opinion it was best for me to go
into the country. My Concern for leaving a Place which contained all I
valued in the World and the cool Tranquility with which he advised me to
banish myself from him were new Stabs to my already bleeding Heart; but I
had now been a good while accustomed to receive Wounds of that nature,
and my Spirits were too much depressed with a continual Weight of Sorrow
to be able to exert themselves to resent almost any Usage. Besides, what could
I do? helpless as I was! I had no Friend to whom I durst make Application
and must be obliged, in the Condition I was, to do whatever those in whose
Power I had put myself would have me. They were so eager for my Departure
that a Place was soon found for me to go to: And in a few Days I took Leave
of that Town and that Person, for whose sake I had renounced every Thing
that ought to have been dear to me. *Lysander* had indeed the Complaisance
to accompany me a few Miles on Horseback, and perceiving me ready to die
with Grief, made a thousand Promises of coming down to visit me in a short
Time; tho' I had no Reason, from his late Behaviour, to hope he would do as
he said, yet this seeming Kindness a little revived me, and I went through my
Journey with more Fortitude than I imagined I could. As soon as I arrived at
the Place destined for my Abode, I writ to him, reminding him of the Promise
he had made, and conjuring him, by every tender Plea I could invent, to make
it good; but I received no Answer. Always willing to excuse him as far as I
was able, I fancied my Letter had by some accident miscarried and sent
another but to as little Purpose as before—Then I grew wild with Grief and
was ready in some ungovernable Sallies of Passion to lay violent Hands on
my own Life—I resolved, at last, if possible, to *extort* an Answer from him
and prevailed on a Countryman, for a good Gratification,[24] to ride to Town
on purpose to deliver a Letter into his own Hands and charged him not to
return without some Token he had seen him. The Contents of what I writ
were these.

To my Inhumane and Unrelenting Charmer.

Is it then possible that Lysander, *the protesting* Lysander, *can from all Angel
change to a very* Fiend? *For only they delight in the Perdition they occasion—Have
you with your Love thrown off all* Pity *too and* Complaisance, *that you vouchsafe
not to condole, at least, the Ruins you have made?—Oh most Ingrateful! Cruel!
Barbarous of all that ever was called Man!—What have I done that can deserve
such Usage?——Is it because I have forsook the Ties of Duty, Interest, Honour,—
given up my Innocence,—my Peace, and everlasting Hopes, that you despise me?—
Monster! For whom have I done this?—Can you reflect it was for you, and your
whole Soul not melt in Tenderness, and soft Compassion?—Yes, yes, you can!—
Wretch that I am!—I have cast away all that could make me truly Valuable, and
now am justly subjected to your Scorn—But though I live unworthy of your Love,*

---

[24] *Gratification:* tip, gratuity.

my Death *must surely give you some* Concern—*at least the* Manner *of it, when you shall know it was for you I died—That my last Breath formed nothing but your* Name,—*and in the extremest Agonies of my departing Soul, lamented more your Cruelty than all that dreadful Separation could inflict—Oh do not, therefore, trifle with a Passion, which if the Strength of Reason in your Sex keeps you from being too deeply touched with, is too impetuous for the Weakness of mine to resist; and who can tell how far the Torrent may transport me—History is not without Millions of Examples of Women who have dared to die, when Life became a Burden; and sure, if any ever could justify Self-murder, the wretched* Cleomira *may—None ever* loved—*none ever* despaired *like me, or had so* just *a Cause for both——The Means of Death are always easy to be obtained, and I am this Moment hurried to that Rage of Temper, that I know not how long I shall be able to refrain the Use of it—O then be quick! and save my Soul the Guilt of* Murder, *and your own the Pangs of never-ending* Remorse, *which, when too late to remedy, you'll feel—Yes, forgotten and abandoned as I am, when I am dead, my* Ghost *will be before you ever, haunt all your Dreams—poison your Pleasures, and distract Reflection— Then, though I want a Voice, my Wrongs will speak, and rouze your sleeping Conscience to Remembrance of your* Vows—*Your broken damning Vows!—— Heaven! That Heaven whose* Blessing *you have* renounced, *whose* Curses *you have* imprecated, *if ever you proved* false, *will then exert the Power of swiftest Vengeance, and Penitence be vain to wash away your Guilt, or call me back to Life—For me, I have nought to fear; I feel already all the Pains of* Hell, *nor can another* World *torment me worse than this has done—Horror and Madness overtake me——I know not what I say, and to my other Crimes am ready to add* Blasphemy——*could curse Heaven,*[25] *and Earth, and Man——wish to behold the World in Flames!——the Universe dissolved——For all, all are Foes to wretched* Cleomira!—*Oh ease me—pity me—write to me—see me! If not for mine, yet for the Sake of the Dear yet unborn—the tender Pledge of our once mutual Love— Think how the frighted Innocent starts at its Mother's Anguish, and is a sad Partaker of all the Sufferings you inflict on me——I will, if possible, support the galling Load of Life till the return of my Messenger, but in your Answer is the Fate of*

The undone

CLEOMIRA.

All the Horror and Distraction which I endeavoured to represent in this Letter was infinitely short of what I truly felt. I had so little Hope of Comfort from him it was sent to that all the time of the Fellow's being gone I had one continued Agony with the Apprehension that at his Return I should be more ascertained of *Lysander's* Cruelty; and had his Stay been long, I believe it would have been impossible for me to have supported it with Life: But the poor Man's Speed out-run my Expectations, eager as they were, and though

---

[25] *curse Heaven*: reference to the third Commandment, 'Thou shalt not take the name of the Lord thy God in vain', Exod. 20: 7.

it was near fifty Miles to *London*, he dispatched his Business and came back in two Days; as soon as he saw me, he put a Testimony of his Success in the Business I employed him in, and trembling between Hope and Fear, I found in it these Words.

To the unkind CLEOMIRA.

The Discovery you make of your causeless Uneasiness gives me an infinite Concern: I had writ to you before, but that I waited to hear first from you, which, by all that is sacred, I never have done till now: And if you have sent, as your Messenger informs me you have, your Letters have miscarried. Be assured that I am still the same I ever was, and if any Part of that Rapidity which in the Days of courtship I professed, be now abated, it is sufficiently made up by an Increase of Tenderness—I beg, for the sake of the dear Infant you mention, and for mine who suffer with you in the Knowledge of your Griefs, that you will entirely banish them, as Enemies as well to Reason as to Happiness. I hope the hurry of my Affairs will shortly have an End, and I shall enjoy the boundless Pleasure of seeing you again; till then, I hope you will be satisfied with this Assurance, joined to the innumerable others I have given you, that I am

Yours for ever,

LYSANDER.

You will certainly believe I was not in my Senses when I shall tell you that these few, and indeed but ill-dissembled Lines of Kindness, drove from my Bosom all the Anxiety that had possessed it: I thought of nothing now but Joy and Rapture; and in spite of all the Reasons *Lysander* had given me, accused myself of Injustice for writing to him in the manner I did; and to make Reparation for the Reproaches of my last, dictated another according to the Transport I now was in—I ought to blush at the Memory of so shameful a Weakness, but as I have promised you a faithful Relation of my Story, will omit nothing that may give you a just Notion of my Folly or his Perfidiousness and Ingratitude. The Lines I writ were these.

To my adored LYSANDER.

To make you able to conceive the Ecstasy with which I read your dear obliging Letter, I must be able to inspire you with that Sublimity of Passion, which Charms like your own have on the Power of doing. But think! Lysander! think what a Soul must feel raised from the lowest Hell of Misery to the highest Heaven of Felicity!— —Oh! If I may Credit those endearing Lines, I have all that Fate can give!—If, did I say? I must——I will——Lysander is all Honour, and he a thousand Times has sworn himself my everlasting Votary——How have I wronged you then? Divinest of your Sex!—But you must pardon me—I love—am absent—am unworthy—and in such a Circumstance, Patience were a Virtue out of Season———O therefore, let it not be too long before you bless me with your Presence, lest I again relapse!— again be wretched—Haste to my Arms, while Hopes are quick within me,—while vigorous Transport sparkles in my Eyes, and my Soul glows with pleasing Expectation—Let not the Fervor of my Joy abate, till in your Arms I have nothing left to wish, and, I indeed, can say thou art all mine, as I am thine! My for ever dear Lysander!

Thine in the most passionate
and tender Manner,

CLEOMIRA.

After this, I lived for some Time in more Tranquility than I had known for many Months: And, though it was past my doubt that he had intrigued with *Melissa*, yet believing it but a transient Amour, of which he was now grown weary, found it no Difficulty to pardon him: And this renewing of his Tenderness to me, made me assure myself it would be in the Power of no Woman, hereafter, to engage him so far as to render him forgetful of what he owed to me: But, alas! this Peace of Mind was not of any long Continuance; eight or nine Days being elapsed without my receiving any Letter from him; I still thought he was coming, and the Hopes of *seeing* him made full amends for the not *hearing* from him; but after that, my Fears again returned, and I grew restless as before. I constantly walked out every Evening into a Field that overlooked the Road, my Expectations of meeting him not having quite forsook me. One of the Times that I was thus employed, I encountered a Person whose *Sight* gave me as much *Surprise* as the *News* she brought me did *Affliction*. It was my Nurse, an honest faithful Creature, who hearing I had left *London*, enquired at *Marvir's* House where I was gone; but receiving no Satisfaction from them, by diligently asking among the Neighbours, heard by one, who by some Accident had learned it, that I was at ****; and so, by describing me to the Stage-Coachman, discovered what Part of the Country I was carried to and had travelled down on purpose to acquaint me that my Mother lay at the point of Death—That it was believed her Grief for my Behaviour had been the Cause of her Illness——That all she seemed to lament was the Misfortunes she feared would fall upon me——and wished for nothing but to see me before she died. This sad Account, given me by the poor Woman in the most moving Circumstances, struck me to the very Soul——I now began to consider *whom* it was I had abandoned and *for* whom! And the more I reflected on *Lysander's* Ingratitude, the more Ungrateful did I appear myself!—To be the Occasion of a *Parent's* Death——a Parent who had always most tenderly loved me and from whom I never had been absent (till the time of my utterly forsaking her) two Days together in my Life filled me with so just a Horror that I know not if it would have been even in *Lysander's* Power to have consoled me. How gladly would I now have returned to her and implored her Pardon for my Errors——endeavoured to give her Comfort and never leave her more; but, alas! the Condition I was in deterred me from the Execution of these pious Wishes; I could entertain no Thoughts of appearing before her till I was delivered of that Witness of my Shame, nor could the poor Woman persuade me to it; she rightly judged that to see me, as I then was, would rather be an *Increase* of her Affliction than any *Mitigation* of it, and told me she would return without saying she had seen me, since there was no Excuse to be made for my not coming to *London* but that which had better remain untold. The Concern which I perceived in the Countenance of this faithful Creature and the mannerly Freedom which she took in expressing her Grief for the Misfortunes I had brought on myself and Family obliged me to give her the whole History of my Affairs since the fatal Choice I made of *Marvir* for my Guardian, and withal conjured her to make all possible Enquiry into *Lysander's* Character and Behaviour, and to give me a faithful Account of what she could discover. But it seems she had never learned to write, and I was unwilling the Secret should be trusted to any other Hand, therefore desired she would treasure it up in her Memory till I came to Town, which I resolved to do as soon as I was brought to Bed. I did not think it proper to carry her to the House where I was, but giving her something to refresh herself in her Journey back, took my leave of her, who parted from me with Tears in her Eyes and all the Marks of an undissembled Grief. The more I ruminated on the sad Relation she had made me, the deeper Impression it made in my Soul; and that, joined to *Lysander's* Unkindness, who in spite of his Promise neither came nor sent to me, threw me into a Condition which is not to be conceived. The Horrors of my *Mind* had such an Influence over my Body that it was impossible I should be able to bring a living Child into the World; my Youth, however, and the natural goodness of my Constitution brought me through that dangerous State in which those who find most Ease have little reason to be assured of Life—— I was safely delivered of a Boy, but alas! the Grief-killed infant never saw the Light, and I knew nothing what it was to be a Mother but the Pains. It was certainly only my Impatience to be gone from a Place where I could hear nothing of *Lysander*, which made me willing to use any means proper for the Recovery of my Strength: but the Hopes of seeing him and knowing from his own Mouth my Doom invigorated my drooping Spirits and enabled me to endure Life rather than die in the terrible Uncertainty I then was in. I found I was in a little more than a Month's time in a Condition to travel and was too eager to delay a Moment. I would not go to *Marvir's* House; I was assured I should hear nothing there but what they were ordered by *Lysander* to tell me; and the late Unkindness they had showed me, made me resolve never to live with them again: but as soon as I got to *London*, went directly to my Nurse's where I had the mournful Account of my dear Mother's Death, told in so tender and moving a Manner, that I too was ready to expire at hearing it. When the first hurry of my Grief for so great and irretrievable a Loss was over, I began to question her about *Lysander*: She told me she had neglected nothing that might be conducive to my Peace but that all she had been able to learn concerning him was that he had lately an intrigue with *Melissa*; that by their ill Conduct it had been discovered to her Husband, who, as a just Reward for her Infidelity, entirely cast her off; that she was now reduced to the same wretched Circumstances this injured Gentleman had took her from; that *Lysander* had little Regard to the Miseries he had contributed to bring her to, and she was become one of the most exposed and unpitied Women in the World. I confess, I was ungenerous enough to find some little Consolation in the Knowledge of my Rival's Misfortunes; not but, as much Reason as I had to hate her, for being the first Occasion of estranging the Affection of *Lysander* from me, I should have highly discommended him for his Neglect of her in her Affliction had it fallen on her only through her Love to him; but as I knew her Inclination to be so amorous (to give it no worse a Name) that it had influenced her to commit *numerous* Faults of the like Nature, and even without the least Temptation, I looked on her as unworthy Commiseration.—But to leave her to all the Miseries which attend a common Prostitution, I resolved to know how I now stood in *Lysander's* Opinion; I writ to him, acquainting him that I was come to Town and desiring to see him. When I had done that, I began to consider my Affairs as to my Money. I thought it unsafe to be lodged any longer in *Marvir's* Hands and employed one to bring him to an Account; but that Villain had made such Bills and managed everything so much to his own Advantage that of my three thousand Pounds I found I had not much more than fifteen hundred remaining. The Person who I had engaged in this Business knew very well what my Father left me and persuaded me to have recourse to Law. But the other knew himself secure enough as to that Point; and when it was hinted to him, he writ me a Letter to tell me that if I insisted to bring him to any public Account for the Money he had laid out, he could easily prove it had been expended only for my Use and bid me consider that in the Condition I had been there was Occasion for more than a trifling Sum to bribe those to Secrecy, who were obliged to be entrusted with the Knowledge of it. This was enough to let me see, if I attempted any thing against him, he would expose me in the most shameful Manner he could; I was glad, therefore, to accept what little I could get, without daring to molest him for the rest. But I will not (my dear *Belinda*) detain your Attention with any Particulars of this, which (in Comparison with my others) I looked on as a trifling Vexation. Above a Week was past since I sent to *Lysander*, and he had not yet answered my Letter: I was very well assured he had received it; and tho' I had little Hopes of the Continuance of his *Affection*, I expected from his *Complaisance* some sort of an Excuse for the Inhumanity he had been guilty of; my *Amazement* at this unlooked-for Slight was almost equal to my *Grief*: I now indeed felt more Resentment than I had ever been capable of before. Neither to come to me nor write after so long an Absence, and all I had suffered on his Account, could make me consider him no otherwise than as the vilest and most justly to be abhorred of all his Sex. And since I had no other way to revenge, resolved to use my Pen to him in such a Manner as should let him know I was no less insensible of his Indignities than I had been of his Love; but before I did so, an Accident happened to give me a fresh Theme for my Reproaches. Going thro' the *Strand*[26] one Day in a Chair, it was suddenly stopped by a Footman, who told me his Lady desired to speak with me and entreated I would come into her Chariot: Neither the Livery nor the Wearer of it were Strangers to me, and I knew he belonged to a Lady, who when I frequented the Court was one of my greatest Intimates, and I immediately discharged my Chair and did as he desired. Nothing could receive me with greater Demonstrations of Kindness than *Semanthe*, (for so I shall call her) and after she had gently upbraided me with breach of Friendship, for not letting her know where I had been all the time of my absconding, began to ask me a thousand Questions about my Affairs: But mine was a Story very improper to be related to her, who, tho' I knew she had a great deal of Good-nature, was not of a Temper to have approved my Proceedings; and therefore I turned the Discourse, as soon as I could, into an enquiry after her Affairs, which she very ingenuously informed me of, little suspecting the Effect of what she told me. I am (said she) very near changing my Condition; but the Person who has prevailed on me to do it is so truly deserving that without a Blush I may confess that the sooner I yield to his Desires, the sooner I make myself the happiest of my Sex. Ah Madam! (cried I interrupting her) take Care how you depend on the Sincerity of Mankind; it requires more Experience than you or I are Mistresses of, to form any just Judgment of their Deserts.[27] It is no wonder that you talk so (replied she) since I have not yet told you the Name of my Charmer; but when I have, I doubt not but you will acknowledge, as all the World who know him do, that every Perfection that Heaven can adorn a Mortal with are centered in my Admired—Oh God! who was it but my *Lysander* that she named!——Lightning could not have blasted me more than this one Word, and I believe the most artful of all my Sex could not in such a Circumstance have dissembled her Confusion; but the Shock was too mighty for my Weakness to sustain, and wholly deprived of Speech, I fell against the side of the Chariot, senseless, and in all Appearance dead, and came not to myself till I was brought to *Semanthe's* Lodgings: The first thing I saw when I opened my Eyes was her, busily employed in helping her Maids to use Means for my Recovery. The Sight of her and the Remembrance of what she had told me threw me again into Convulsions, which lasted for some Time; and when, at last, I had gathered Power to speak, it was in such a fashion, so wild and so confused that the Standers-by believed I was taken with a sudden fit of Frenzy. I desired a Chair might be called to carry me Home; and making some sort of an Apology, I know not what, for the Trouble I had given, took leave of my happy Rival. My poor Nurse (for I had been at her House ever since I

---

[26] *the Strand*: the street that links Westminster to the law courts in the Old City (the one square mile of London that was within the Roman walls and is still the heart of the business and banking district). Originally, it was a bridle path along the river, as its name signifies.

[27] *Deserts*: worthiness, merit.

came to Town) was terribly alarmed at the Condition she beheld me in, and, when I had repeated the Occasion of it, joined with me in the most bitter Curses we could both invent on the Perfidiousness of Mankind: I remained for some time in mortal Agonies, unable to determine on any thing: Sometimes I was for returning to *Semanthe*, to acquaint her with *Lysander's* Engagements to me and implore her to forbear any farther Invasion on a Right[28] I had so dearly purchased——Sometimes I was for going to *Lysander's* House, and by publicly reproaching him with his Vows, deter him from the Breach of them—but Modesty rejected both these Resolutions as soon as formed; and by my Nurse's Persuasion (who feared that proceeding to any Violence would be altogether unavailing, and only serve to expose me more) I contented myself with uttering the Fury I was possessed of in a Letter; which though incoherent and distracted as my Mind, I believe you will not think it too severe for the Occasion.

To the Inconstant, Ungenerous, and Perfidious LYSANDER.

I have so long been accustomed to Indignities from you, that Had I not in Possession your Letters, those Witnesses of your well dissembled Tenderness, I should believe I had been enchanted with some delightful Dream, and that there never was any such thing in Reality, as that Lysander *could take the Pains to make me believe he loved me, since for no other Cause, than returning the Passion he pretended, he now can use me with a Brutality as unexampled as my own Meanness of Spirit, which has hitherto suffered me to sit down tamely with my Wrongs, and not endeavour, at least, a suitable Revenge—Poisons and Daggers are the Upbraidings you should receive from me.—Yet I, fond Wretch! have still subjected my very Will to yours, wrung my own Hands, while you have wrung my Heart——And when a thousand times, with more than Devil-like Cruelty, you've conjured up all that was raging in me, with my own Tears I have appeased that Tempest, which only Blood—your dearest Blood should have had Power to quell.—Not one Particular of your Baseness is unknown to me——Cold——cold Betrayer!—Dark designing Villain! Your Neglect, your Absence, your Silence all sprung but from one Cause, that cursed Mutability of Temper, which damns half your Sex, as fond Belief and Tenderness does ours——I was not Ignorant of your Intrigue with Melissa, even from the Beginning, to the guilty Rapture which concluded it—Yet I was patient, and but to Heaven accused you of Perfidiousness—Fool that I was, I hoped my Truth, my Constancy, and Softness, in Time, might make a Convert of you——But now, now that I find you are for ever lost; that Marriage is about to give another that Title, which alone is due to me, by your own Vows, and by all those Sufferings I have bought it with—Now, I grow, indeed, like you, a very Fiend! and methinks could smile at Mischief—Yes, if you can—if you dare attempt to make* Semanthe *yours; may the* Priest, *about to join you, be struck Speechless—May Earthquakes shake the Ground—The Temple's Roof unclose—Thunder and darting*

[28] *Right*: before the 1754 Hardwicke Marriage Act, Lysander's promises were actionable as a contract. Lawrence Stone notes that they were 'far more successful than actions of seduction', *Road to Divorce* (Oxford: Oxford University Press, 1990), 86.

Lightnings proclaim Heaven's just Abhorrence of your Mockery of the sacred Ceremony, and mark the Bridegroom *for a vile Prophaner!—But, Oh! should all the Curses which my Injuries deserve, and jealous Fury can invent, fall on you— should Judgments terrify, or even Pity for me, dissuade you from her Arms, what would it avail?—Could it afford one grain of Comfort to my tormented Soul?— No.—Since you're* mine *no more, no matter whose—Your* Heart *is lost, for ever lost to* me; *and when compared with that, your* Body *is a Trifle.—Go on then— pursue the Dictates of your changing Nature, be proud of Perjury, and wanton in Deceit. A Time will come, when Remorse will be sufficiently my Avenger.—For me, I shall not long endure the pain of Thought; Madness, or Death, will ease me of Reflection; but while I have Life or Sense to know how very wretched you have made me, be kind enough, at least, to feign Compassion for the Woes you give: And lay the blame of your* Inconstancy *on* Fate—*the unavoidable Impulse of your Nature—or anything which may make me think you pity me; for since, in spite of all you have done, I still must Love you; I would fain imagine you possessed of some one good Quality, to justify my passion—Oh God! I can no more—Farewel, dear, cruel Destroyer of the Soul, and Ruin of the Everlasting Peace of*

The most wretched

CLEOMIRA.

In about four or five Days after I sent, I received an Answer, which I think proper to repeat that you may see there is nothing of Rude or Base impossible for a *Man* to do when once a Woman, by forfeiting her Honour, has put it in his Power to use her as he pleases.

To CLEOMIRA.

I received your Letter with some Surprise, but with none of that Tenderness you seem to aim at inspiring, or what really has possessed my Soul at reading some of your former ones; nor can you blame my Change of Humour, since your own Extravagance has been the Cause: Believe me Cleomira! *whatever in our Days of Courtship we profess, the Excess of any Passion is ridiculous to a Man of Sense; and* Love, *of all others, more excites our* Mirth, *than our Pity—That foolish Fondness, with which your Sex so much abounds, is before Enjoyment charming, because it gives us an Assurance of obtaining all we ask; but afterwards 'tis cloying, tiresome, and in time grows odious——Had your Passion, at least the Show of it, been less Violent, mine might have had a longer Continuance; and as there is nothing more unnatural, than that a Woman should expect a Man can be in Love with her always, the best way to retain his Complaisance is, not to take notice of his Alteration, or oblige him, by a troublesome Importunity, to explain himself in the Manner I now am forced to do to you: I confess indeed, that I am going to be married to a Lady, whose Discretion will, I hope, prevent any of those Discontents and Jealousies, which first made my Amour with you grow uneasy: That I once loved you, I shall ever acknowledge, and desire you would be as just in assuring your self, that your own Mismanagement was the Cause I could do so no longer. The little Storms of Fury which appear in your Letter, are too frequently met with in Stories, to be wondered at, and are of as little Consequence to move me, to either Fear, or Pity, as your proclaiming the Occasion would be to the Disadvantage of my Reputation; but if you can resolve to confine your Passion within the Bounds of Prudence, though you lose a* Lover, *you shall always find a* Friend *in*

LYSANDER.

I am very apt, indeed, to believe that *Lysander* in this spoke the Sense of all his Sex; and one would think that such an *Eclaircissement*[29] was enough to have cured me of all Passions but Disdain and Hate—Nothing sure was ever so insulting, so impudent, so barbarous; yet was my Soul, and all its Faculties, so truly his, that though at the first Reading I resolved not to think of him but with Detestation, I relapsed immediately, and instead of wishing I had never seen him, found a secret Pleasure, even in the midst of Agony, in the Reflection that he had loved me once: And, if at any time a start of just Resentment rouzed itself within me, when I would give it vent in *Curses*, a Power superior to Rage arrested the flying Breath, and changed it into *Blessings.* I still loved him with such an Adoration that I could not bring myself to think that anything he could do was wrong and began *indeed* to lay the blame of my Misfortune on my own want of Merit to engage the Continuance of his Affection rather than on any Vice in him; and it was with all the Difficulty in the World I forbore writing to him again, to tell him so.— Was ever any Infatuation—was ever any Madness equal to mine!—Oh God! the bare Remembrance of it makes me condemn myself and acknowledge that a Creature so meanly Souled[30] deserved no better Fate.

The poor RECLUSE for some Moments was able to proceed no farther; a thousand mingled Passions now struggled in her labouring Breast with too much Vehemence to be suppressed, and throwing herself down on the couch she sat on, began again to pour out the Anguish of her Soul in a Torrent of Tears. Though *Belinda* could not forbear sympathizing with her, yet finding that her Griefs were indeed past Remedy, thought nothing she could say would any way avail to her Consolation and only bore her Company in this Dumb Scene[31] of Sorrow: But the RECLUSE had too much Complaisance and Good-nature to be able to endure the Influence she perceived her Afflictions had over the tender Disposition of the other and composing herself as well as she could, continued her Discourse in this Manner.

If (said she) I could have found Words of Force sufficient to have vented any of those various Passions which tormented me, my afflicted Soul, per-haps, might have received some little Intervals of Ease; but there were none to express a Condition such as mine!—To *love* to the highest degree of Tenderness what I ought to have *abhorred*—To *adore* what I knew deserved my utmost *Scorn*—To have buried *Hope* and [have] *wild Desire* survive—To have Shame, Remorse, and all the Vultures of conscious Guilt gnaw on my

---

[29] *Eclaircissement*: clarification.
[30] *meanly souled*: endowed with a mean or ignoble soul.
[31] *Dumb Scene*: i.e. wordless.

aching Thought—To wish for Madness and yet Sense remain was Misery! was Horror, sure, without a Name! A thousand Times in a Day I was about to put an End to Life and all its weight of Anguish: Nor was it Reason or Religion but merely the Consideration that Death would take from me all Power of hearing what became of *Lysander* that preserved me.

Thus did I live, if such a State can be called Life, till the Day of *Lysander's* Marriage; but when I heard that, imagine you behold a Wretch in the most raging Fit of Lunacy, and it may give you some Idea, though but a faint one, of what I then appeared! I tore my Clothes, my Face, my Hair, threw myself on the Floor, beat my Breast, made the House ring with echoing Shrieks and Lamentations, and was scarce restrained by my Nurse from running in this manner to the Church where the Ceremony was performed; and it was but when I had no longer Strength to rage that partly by Force and partly by Persuasion, she got me into Bed: The Violence of my Agitations threw me into a Fever; but though I would take nothing but what I was compelled to and committed Extravagancies in this Illness enough to have killed twenty of much a stronger Constitution than myself, yet I could not die: In spite of the Malignity of the Distemper, in spite even of *myself*, I recovered. But not all the bodily Indisposition I had endured had been able to weaken the Passions of my Soul; I still loved and still despaired—My Thoughts were always with *Lysander* and pursued him everywhere even to the bridal Bed, that Grave where all my Hopes were buried. My Nurse's House happening, unluckily, to stand in a Street pretty near that in which *Lysander* lived, as soon as I had Strength to walk about my Chamber, I had the Mortification from my Window to behold him and *Semanthe*, now his Wife, pass by in their Chariot almost every Day: You may believe this Sight gave no small Addition to the Horrors of my Despair; but I will not pretend to repeat what it was I felt whenever these grating Objects met my Eyes; it shall suffice to say 'twas more than I could bear, and I resolved to rid myself of what I *then* endured without any apprehensions of what Futurity might give. Death was my determined Care, but in what manner I should apply it was now my only Study; and, after a long Debate in my Mind, *Poison* was the Means I fixed on as being not only the most decent but also the most private Way I could perform this Deed of Desperation; for I was unwilling the World should be sensible of what I had done and when I was no more, preserve my Shame still flagrant with those scurrilous Ditties,[32] which Actions of the Kind I was about to do are always Themes for. I took Care to conceal my Intentions from my Nurse and that she might be the less watchful over me, began to counterfeit a Cheerfulness, which Heaven knows was far distant from my Heart. The poor Woman was overjoyed to find me, as she thought, so much more easy than I had been, and I went out one Day, unsuspected, to procure the fatal Drugs: I had recourse to an Apothecary who had been used to make up Medicines

---

[32] *Ditties*: street ballads, often rapidly composed about crimes and other sensational news events and sold as cheap broadsheets.

194

for our Family, and because I knew how scrupulous People of that Profession are obliged to be, I told him I had a little favourite Dog which by some Accident was run mad, and having made Use of a thousand Experiments for a Cure for him in vain and not enduring to have him destroyed any other way, I would have something to give him to put an End to his Misery in the most gentle manner I could; something of a sleeping Potion, I said, which by degrees should seize upon the Seats of Life and give a sure but easy Death. The Man looked on me with a good deal of Surprise, and, as I thought, more Penetration than I desired he should have; but, after a little Pause, went about mixing the Composition: I was very well pleased to think I had so artfully deceived him and came home with the Physic,[33] which I designed should make a perfect Cure of all my Miseries. As I was going to drink it, I began to think I could not leave the world in Peace without a Farewell to my unjust but still too dear *Lysander*, and taking up some Paper, writ to him these Lines.

To the dear Ruiner of my Soul and Body.

As my Passion for you was built on a more lasting Foundation than that of yours to me, so not all your Cruelty can have Power to shake it: I must be yours, though you cease to desire I should be so; and since I cannot hope, *nay, now you are another's,* dare not wish *any future Testimonies of my Affection should be pleasing, I take the only means to rid you of the Trouble: A Draught of Poison stands before me, and the Moment I conclude this Letter, I take my Journey to that World whence there is no Return—What will be my Portion there I know not, but am sure of this, that if departed Souls have any Intelligence of what's acted here, your Pity for my Fate will mitigate the sharpest Torments. A tender Sigh sometimes, not even my Rival would deny; and perhaps, a Time may come, when you shall own I merited much more: I do not, however, wish you should be touched too deeply with Remorse—You are too dear to me, for me to desire to give you Pain—Remember me, if you can, with some little Softness—Make not my Sufferings the Subject of your Ridicule, nor seem pleased if you hear others do so; and whenever my want of Beauty, Wit, or another Charm, rises as an Evidence against me, let my exalted Tenderness still balance that Deficiency; and reflect, that as I have lived, so now I die, my dear, dear* Lysander!

Only yours,

CLEOMIRA.

I kept my Word, indeed; for as soon as I had sealed this up, I drank the Ingredients I had brought home with me—I drank it without the least Alarm or any of those Apprehensions which so terrify the Minds of most People at the Approach of Death so much had Despair hardened my Heart and stupefied my Reason. In above an Hour, either the Draught *itself*, or the Force of *my Imagination* that it must be so, operated so strongly through my Veins that I grew exceedingly sick; and fearing the Effects would come before I had

---

[33] *Physic*: medicine, potion.

settled those Affairs I had in my Head, I called hastily for my good old Nurse. It was almost Midnight, and she was in Bed, and believing I had been so too, was not a little frighted when she came into my Chamber and found me dressed as I had been all Day and with something in my Countenance, as she said, of a Horror impossible to be expressed. I sent for you (said I) to take my everlasting Leave—to thank you for the faithful Services I have received from you and to make what Recompense my lessened Circumstances have left me Power to do. The poor Creature stared in my Face all the time I was speaking, but the Astonishment she was in made her either incapable of Understanding me or took away the Power of answering: Be not surprized (resumed I) I tell you this Night—I know not but this *Hour* is the last of my Life—Therefore, while I have Voice to utter the Meanings of my Soul, I charge you be attentive and perform my last Requests. She certainly thought my Griefs had turned my Brain, and hastily interrupting me as I spoke these Words, For Heavens sake, Madam, (said she) give not way to the Suggestions of your Melancholy; you are now, God be praised, pretty well recovered from an Illness in which we had just Reason to despair of you——You are now, as it were, risen from the Grave, and the signal Deliverance shows that you are destined for happier Days than those you yet have seen——Ah! do not then (continued she, with Tears in her Eyes) endeavour to disappoint the Designs of your all-wise Preserver, by indulging Grief to prey upon your Senses for the Loss of an unworthy Person, who at your return of Reason you must scorn. I could not suffer her to proceed in this Manner, but cutting her off from what she was going to say, No more (cried I); if by an ill-timed and unmannerly Zeal you would not forfeit all that good Opinion your Fidelity and Obedience has hitherto inspired—once more I tell you that I cannot—will not live—Death is already busy at my Heart, and, if I make not haste, may rob me of the only Wish I now can form and you of the Glory of serving to the last a Mistress, who if she had the Power would more express her Gratitude——Therefore, in few Words, by all that Truth and Honesty which I believe you possessed of, I conjure you to deliver a Letter you will find on the Table into *Lysander's* Hands the Moment I expire—to tell him that his Inconstancy was my Death and to relate the Manner of it in the most moving Terms you can invent. This is all I have to ask or to command——as to my Funeral order it as you please, but let me not be laid too near my Parents, lest my guilty Ashes should disturb the sacred Repose of theirs—All that remains of my broken Fortune after I am laid in Earth is yours. Though I spoke this with all the Solemnity imaginable it was to little Purpose; she still took it for the Effects of my Melancholy and began to resume her Dissuasions from letting such sad Thoughts get the better of my Reason; and I was forced to tell her what I had done before I could make her believe I was in any Danger of Death. But never did Amazement and real Grief appear more lively than in the Face of this poor Wretch at what I told her: At first she was entirely mute, and when she had Power to speak, her Words were nothing but

Exclamations: Then, on a sudden, thinking they were fruitless, was running for a Physician, for a Divine, and raising the whole Town for my Preservation; nor could any thing I should have said have prevented her, if my Strength had not prevailed to force her into a Chair, and holding her there obliged her to hear me tell her that the Poison I had taken was not of a Nature to be expelled, or if it were had now lain too long in me to be deprived of its Operation. Nay (said I) put the Case that what I have done should, by any means that I should be compelled to use, be rendered fruitless—not all the World should force me to live another Day——If I cannot die the way I choose, still I will *some* way——if not by Poison; there are Knives or Cords—My Garters may be my Executioners—Or if denied these Instruments, you cannot hinder me from strangling myself with my own Hands or dashing out my Brains against the Wall——To those *resolved*, Death always is at Call. I spoke these Words with a real Design to do as I said, and if she had got Liberty to have brought any Persons in to restrain me, I had certainly that Moment taken some unfailing Method to prevent anything they could have done to save me: But with these and the like Speeches, at last I persuaded her to content herself with *lamenting* my Desperation without endeavouring to do any thing to *remove* it. And having convinced her of my Obstinacy to die, to spare the Infamy of Self-murder, she promised me to keep the Deed concealed and give out I died of an Apoplexy:[34] But I thought I should never have prevailed on her to carry the Letter to *Lysander*, her Abhorrence to him as the Author of all my Misfortunes and now of my Death was so great that she assured me the Task of dying with me would be far less severe than the beholding such a Monster; but my Tears and repeated Entreaties at last overcame all her Scruples, and I engaged an Oath from her (for I would not in that Case trust her Promise) that she would in the Morning see him and say all that I required. In a very little Time after I had brought her into the disposition I desired, I found a prodigious Heaviness, like that indeed of Death, seize on my Spirits; and making no doubt but that the fatal Moment was at hand, with my Nurse's Assistance (though, poor Soul, she was in too great an Agony to be able to afford me much) I got myself undressed and put to Bed, where I had not lain long before I lost all Sense of every Thing—*Lysander's* Charms—his Cruelty—my Ruin and Despair were now no more remembered—Oh! if one were sure to enjoy that Tranquility in a *real* Death that I did in my *imaginary* one, none would survive their Happiness. At my return to Thought, that is, when I was loosed from the Bands of Sleep, for it was no more which had bound down my Sense, I was in a Consternation impossible to be expressed—I looked on myself, then round the Room, and I believe it would have been pleasant enough, if anybody had been Witness of it, to have observed the Oddness of my Behaviour at my first waking: I remembered very well what had passed before I went to Bed, and

---

[34] *Apoplexy*: stroke or other sudden attack that destroys the senses and ability to move.

could not reconcile so seeming a Contradiction as that I should be still in a world I believed I had taken such effectual Measures to be freed from. As I was in this Dilemma, my Nurse came into the Chamber, not with her Eyes overflowed with Tears and wringing her Hands as she had done the Night before, but with all the Marks of a most perfect Satisfaction, and kneeling down by the Bedside, testified her Joy in most fervent Thanksgivings to that Divine Power which had so graciously been pleased to disappoint the unnatural Purpose of my Heart. I could not forbear interrupting her Ejaculations by some wild sort of Enquiries how I came to be still living, which she presently satisfied me in these Words. When I had left you (said she) in all Appearance dead, I began to consider of the Promise you had obliged me to make, and it being near Morning, got myself ready to go with your Letter, resolving to take no Notice of your Death to my Family till my Return: After I had discharged that unwelcome Errand, I found a Man waiting at home to speak with me, and he told me the chief of it was to enquire if a Lady who lodged here was well and then named *you*: I was too much confounded at the Question to be able to answer him without trembling and faultering in my Speech, though, as well as I could, I said I hoped you were—that I left you so last Night: I wish (resumed he, taking me aside) she may continue so. Then, Madam, he told me he was the Apothecary from whom you had demanded Poison, but suspecting you designed it for some other Use than what you pretended and fearing if he should deny, you might procure it from some other, he had deceived you with an *Opiate*,[35] which could be no way prejudicial to the Health of the Person that took it, though it would hold the Senses in a much deeper and longer Sleep than what was Natural——He said also that he had caused you to be watched home to the End that he might relate the Truth to those about you if anything of what he imagined should happen. I was so impatient to know what *Lysander* had said, since I found she had been with him, that I could not give myself much Time to reflect on what she told me concerning the Apothecary, but I found her willing to evade repeating the Manner of his Behaviour and guessed by *that* he was inhuman to the last.— What, (said I) was he not shocked to hear I died for him?——If I could believe that after so fatal a Proof of Love he could persist in his Barbarity, I should rejoice my Purpose was defeated and would live to scorn him——If you are in earnest (interrupted she) and can, indeed, continue in a Resolution so truly Noble, I will inform you of all. Which after my assuring her I would do, she went on in this manner. I gave your Letter to him (said she) and after looking it carelessly over——Your Mistress sure is Mad (cried he, with an Air of Contempt) I long have thought her so, and the Romantic Stuff she has writ me here confirms it. Indeed, Madam, (continued the good Creature) I had scarce Power to refrain flying in his Face; but though my Hands forbore any Indignities, I gave my Tongue free Scope; and when I had told him—nay

---

[35] *Opiate*: sedative containing opium.

swore, as well I might, for firmly I believed it, that you were really dead, I called him every Name I could invent of Base, Perfidious and Deceitful; but he seemed as little to regard the Fury I was in as the News I brought him, and only saying——If she be dead the Letter requires no Answer, therefore be gone and cease your Clamour; but not finding I was very hasty to do as he bid me, for, methought it was some little Satisfaction to upbraid this Monster, he called one of his Servants to turn me out of Doors and walked from me as unconcerned as though I had brought him an Account of the most indifferent Affair that could have happened. I was too well satisfied in the Integrity of this good old Woman to doubt the Truth of what she said, and it was now that I began to feel that Resentment which by a thousand Barbarities he had long before deserved. And, after some little Struggles between departing Tenderness and growing Hate—'Tis done (said I) *Reason*, at last, has gained a Conquest over all that *Softness* which has hitherto betrayed me to Contempt—Now I will live, and *Love* alone shall die!—Nurse brought so many and well-grounded Arguments to strengthen me in this Resolution and expressed her Meaning in a Manner so much beyond what could be expected from her that I have often thought she was that Moment inspired by Heaven to assist my Weakness. In short, I gave the Thoughts of *Death* entirely over: I could not endure, however, to appear publicly in the World again, and as *Lysander* believed me dead, I was willing every Body else should do so too; I ordered a *Will* to be drawn according to Law, in which I made Nurse my *Heir* and sole *Executrix*, and she has performed every Thing I desired with such Exactness and Fidelity that not a Relation or Acquaintance has the least Notion of my being living: It was she who heard of the Convenience of this House for boarding in, but I would not let her come to make any Agreement for me, because she might chance to be known and consequently the Person she recommended guessed at. Since the Time of my being here she manages my little Fortune, receives the Income of it when due, and gives me an Account of it every Quarter, which is all the Business I have to do in this uneasy World. Thus, Madam, have I given you a faithful Account of the Causes which induced me to this Retirement; and I believe, you will own that they are such as merit no less than my whole Life's Contrition. For, as Mr. *Waller* very elegantly expresses it,

> Our Passions gone, and Reason in her Throne,
> Amazed we see the Mischiefs we have done![36]

Though *Belinda* had conceived the highest Esteem and Friendship imaginable for this *fair Unfortunate* and was willing to offer everything in her Power for her Consolation, yet she could not disapprove the Justice of her Lamentations or the Resolution she had taken of concealing herself. So much of the Night was taken up in the RECLUSE's History that *Belinda* was obliged to

[36] Adapted from lines spoken by the King in Edmund Waller, *The Maid's Tragedy, The Maid's Tragedy altered with some other pieces* (London, 1630), 41.

defer hers until the next Day; but the other engaged her to come into her Chamber early in the Morning, and as soon as Breakfast was over, demanded the Performance of her Promise, which she readily complied with, and struggling with some Sighs, which her aching Heart sent forth, on recollecting the Passages she was about to utter, began her Relation in this Manner.

THE STORY OF BELINDA.

I cannot (said she) boast either of a Family or any natural or acquired Endowments, which could entitle me to those Hopes the lovely and accomplished *Cleomira* might reasonably depend on: My Father was, indeed, a Gentleman, and if his Estate was not the greatest, yet it was superior to most Commons,[37] who had taken no other Measures to enlarge their Possessions than what was consistent with *Honesty* and that tranquil State of Life, which, I believe, he would not have forsook to have been Master of both *Indies*:[38] And though my Education was only such as the Country affords, yet, had I followed those Precepts which my Infancy was taught, it had been sufficient to have restrained me from doing anything which could draw on me the Contempt of the World. I had the Misfortune to lose both my Parents within a Year of one another; but my Father (who was the longest Survivor) had, a little before his Death, provided me a Husband, a Gentleman who long had loved me, and who was, indeed, deserving of a much better Match: his Person was extremely graceful and well turned, his Behaviour affable to all and complaisant as far as *Sincerity* would permit, his Solidity of Judgment and sound Reasoning surprized those of twice his Years, and though he had a peculiar Sweetness of Disposition which made it impossible for him to be an *Enemy* to any one, yet was it tempered with a due Regard to that Principle of honour which forbids any *Friendship* with the vicious Part of Mankind or for any private End or Interest to pretend it: *Virtue* and *Wit*, though in Rags, never failed to excite his highest Praises and most zealous Esteem and *Folly* and *Baseness*, though adorned with Grandeur, his Contempt and open Detestation. It was impossible for a Heart so entirely unprepossessed as mine *then* was to make any Objection to a Person such as I have described, especially when recommended by a Father, who I knew tenderly loved me and was most watchful for my Happiness; but as I had no *Repugnance*, so also I had no extraordinary *Satisfaction* in the Thoughts of this Match: I felt no Hopes, no Fears, no Wishes, no Impatience, nor knew what it was to be *uneasy* or *transported*. When I saw *Worthly* (for that was the Name of this excellent Man) I was well enough pleased, indeed, but when I saw him not I was the same; in fine, every thing was indifferent to me, and had this Insensibility continued I had lived one of the most contented Women in the World. Every Thing being con-

[37] *Commons*: commoners, neither nobility nor gentry.
[38] *both Indies*: the East Indies (India, adjacent regions in Asia, and Indonesia) and the West Indies (the Antilles, islands between North and South America).

cluded on, a Day was fixed for the Celebration of our Marriage; but on the sudden Death of my Father, which happened about a Week before, for Decency's sake, it was put off to a longer Time; nor could *Worthly* (ardent Lover as all his *Actions* spoke him) say any Thing to the contrary. He constantly visited me every Day, and I looking on him as a Man ordained by Heaven and him who had the Disposal of me for my Husband, allowed him all the Freedom of Conversation imaginable. The Alteration which the Death of my Father had made in our Family gave him an Opportunity of proving his Love and Generosity in a manner which justly rendered him very dear to my *Esteem* (oh would to Heaven it had to my *Affection* too) but I have since found there is an Infinity of Distance between Love and Friendship. My Father, little suspecting he was so near his End, had made no *Will*, and being possessed of scarce any *personal* Estate, and the *real*[39] descending to my Brother, then a Student in the University, it was generally feared among our Relations that myself and younger Sister would be entirely Portionless: This Discourse soon reached *Worthly's* Ears, and he came to me one Day with a more than ordinary Satisfaction in his Countenance to tell me that nothing could have happened more lucky for his Wishes than this means of testifying to me and the whole World that it was my *Love* alone he was ambitious of and that he was so far from desiring my Brother should make good anything of what my Father had promised that he would not be deprived of the Glory of proving himself not altogether unworthy my Regard by marrying me without a Fortune to receive with me the Treasure of an Empire. I must have been void both of Gratitude and Common Sense if I had not acknowledged this Behaviour to have been generous above the Rank of ordinary Lovers, especially when I considered it could be none of those idle Compliments which Men are often full of when they think we have no Occasion to make Use of their Service: I knew *Worthly's* Temper too well to suspect the Sincerity of what he said and knew also that he was too well acquainted with my Brother's Character to expect anything from him. He was when he left our House extremely Wild and Thoughtless, wholly addicted to his Pleasures and seemed so little inclinable to any solid Reflections for the good of his Family, or himself, indeed, that it was the universal Discourse of the Country that he would make but an ill Use of his Patrimony: But he disappointed the Belief of every Body; and when he came from the University, (as he did soon after my Father's Death, to take Possession, he being more than of Age,) he made it appear that Learning is the best Polisher of the *Principles*, as well as *Manners*, of those who apply themselves seriously to it. He settled the Affairs of the Family in a fashion beyond what could have been hoped; and having heard of my intended Marriage with *Worthly* and what my Father designed to give me, said he would be far from contradicting the Will of so good a Parent though not compelled to it by any form of Law; and sending for a Scrivener,[40]

[39] *real*: property, as opposed to stocks, bonds, and annuities.
[40] *Scrivener*: professional copyist and notary.

not only made me Mistress of the Fortune which had been promised but bound himself to give my Sister the same whenever she should Marry or come of Age; and because there was no ready Money left, he made over the Estate to pay it, reserving only to himself a Competency to maintain him at the University, whither he soon went back and designs to continue for some Years. My Brother's Generosity did not, however, lessen my Obligations to *Worthly*; my Esteem for him increased daily, and he had, indeed, so many excellent Qualities that it was impossible but the more one knew him, the more one should find to admire: In fine, all that I knew of Love was his, nor had I the least Notion there was any thing farther in that Passion than what he had inspired me with.——Happy had I been never to have been unde-ceived, but my ill Fate decreed it otherwise, and sad Experience soon informed me that the Effects of *Love* are not *Tranquility* and *Ease*.

Not having been at any public Place (except Church) since the Death of my Father, *Worthly* would needs persuade[41] me to go in his Coach to see a famous Horse-race, which was to be run a few Miles distant from the Place where we lived: There was a prodigious Concourse of People, and great part of them of the best Fashion in the Country round about; the Sight gave us a great deal of Diversion; and when it was over, *Worthly* conducted myself and Sister (for I took her with me) to a House, where there was a noble Collation[42] prepared for our Entertainment; and in this, as in every thing else, he testi-fied the Pride he took in obliging me: As we were returning Home, the Coachman having drank too plentifully, drove in such a furious Manner (in spite of his Master's often calling to him to take Care) that we were over-turned; none of us were hurt, but this Accident was the occasion of a Misfortune much worse than any thing that could have happened by the Fall. A Gentleman who was riding the same Way and saw all that passed came up to us, and alighting from his Horse, made us several Compliments on the Occasion, and, perceiving the Condition our Coachman was in, entreated *Worthly* to accept of a Servant he had with him, who he said had often drove a Coach and understood it very well: The Fright that my sister and I were in made *Worthly* gladly accept of the Offer; and immediately the young Man, by his Master's Command, changed Seats with the Coachman: All the time of our little Journey, the obliging Stranger rode by the Coach side, and enter-tained us with a world of Gallantry; for, besides the Charms of his Person, which nothing sure could ever equalize, his manner of Address had some-thing in it so inexpressibly engaging that had *Cleomira* seen him, *Lysander* would have appeared less lovely. The RECLUSE could not forbear shaking her Head, and sighing at these Words; as believing it impossible for any Man to be possessed of Graces, which could obscure those of her *Lysander*; but she would not interrupt the other by entering into an Argument, which 'twas

[41] *would needs persuade*: colloquial, combining the sense that he needed to persuade her and that he thought it would be good for her and was determined.
[42] *Collation*: table of refreshments.

202

probable they should not easily agree upon, and *Belinda* went on thus. *Worthly* (continued she) was infinitely charmed with his Conversation, and gave me to understand, when we came near Home, that I could do no less, in return to the Civilities he had shewed us, than invite him in: My Complaisance for him was sufficient to have made me yield to his Desire in a much greater Matter; but, alas! I granted this with a Pleasure, which at that Time I knew not the meaning of nor once imagined that from the Wit and Beauty of this lovely Unknown I had drawn in an Infection at my Eyes and Ears, which mixing with my whole Mass of Blood, was to poison all the Quiet of my future Days: I cannot tell you what 'twas I felt, while in his Presence, but it was a Mixture of Delight and Pain, a kind of racking Joy and pleasing Anguish. He stayed not very long at our House, *Worthly* was impatient to have him at his own that he might, in a Fashion which he would not take the Freedom to use in ours, requite the Civilities we had received from him on the Road; and it was not till I was left alone and had Leisure for Reflection, that I found myself unhappy enough to feel for this Stranger, what *Worthly's* constant Assiduity and my Knowledge of his many Virtues never could inspire. I suffered many Conflicts on the first Discovery that it really was *Love*, which so suddenly, and without Reason, had taken Possession of my Soul: My just Sense of the Obligations I had to *Worthly* and my Engagements to him (from which I could not without both Ingratitude and Dishonour recede) and my wild Passion for a Man, who, perhaps, might never regard me with any thing more than an Indifference—a Man who 'twas likely might be already married or prepossessed with a more deserving Object——a Man whose Temper, Principles, and Circumstances were altogether unknown to me filled me at once with Shame, Remorse, Confusion, and Despair. My mind in this Disorder, 'twould be needless to say it was impossible for Sleep to enter my Eyes; I passed the Night in a manner vastly different from all I had ever known before; nor did the Day bring any more Tranquility. In the Afternoon, *Worthly*, according to Custom, came to visit me; but, alas! his Presence was now no longer welcome, nor could all his good Qualities have rendered him supportable had not his whole Discourse been of the too lovely Stranger. He told me that he had been informed by himself of all his Circumstances; that he was a Baronet, his Name Sir *Thomas Courtal*; that having made the Tour of *Europe*, he thought his Travels would not be complete unless he could be able to give as good an Account of the Kingdom he was born in, as of others; and to that End was proceeding in his Progress, through every County in which there was anything rare or valuable to be seen. He added to this Relation so many Encomiums on the graces of his Person, the charms of his Wit, and the seeming sweetness of his Disposition that had I not been already too much prepossessed in his Favour, what he said was enough to have made me so. Presuming on my Interest with you, (said this unsuspecting Lover) I have engaged that you shall give me leave to bring him to wait on you sometimes, while this part of the country is happy in his Presence, which I hope (continued he looking tenderly on me) will be long enough to see me blest in the Title of your Husband. O God! with what Emotions did my Bosom swell, when he pronounced these Words! a thousand times I was about to lay open all the weakness of my Soul and warn him of so dangerous a Guest, but Shame as often deprived me of the Power.——Yes, I protest, it gave me a Concern I cannot well express to see this generous, this undesigning Man thus lay a Snare for the Destruction of his own Hopes: Yet, how could I avoid it without making a Confession too shocking for my Modesty or his Passion to be able to sustain? In fine, I having said nothing to oppose it, he brought him the next Day to visit me, and they became so intimate in a little time that he scarce ever came without him. O what a Trial was this for a Heart so inexperienced as mine! How did I struggle to repel my daily-increasing Wishes? and how strenuously did I endeavour to outbalance *Courtal's* enchanting Graces by the solid Perfections of the other? But all in vain; the towering Flame grew higher by my Attempts to quell it, and a little time convinced me that Almighty Love despises all Control. *Worthly's* continual Solicitations for the Celebration of our Marriage rendered him more disagreeable, and the Trouble he put me to in finding Excuses to delay it made the Sight of him intolerable: He had too much Penetration not to discover there was an Alteration in my Behaviour; but having never received Testimonies of anything more than my Esteem, imagined it proceeded only from the little Inclination he had always found in me to change my Condition and redoubled his Pressures in such a manner as made me stand in need of much more Artifice than I was Mistress of to put him off without letting him into the Secret of my Reason for it. To heighten my Aversion and strengthen my Obstinacy in refusing him, I had of late observed in the charming *Courtal's* Eyes a certain Languishment they were not used to wear; I often heard him sigh, observed him to look pale and tremble when on any Occasion he touched my Hand, Symptoms which I now began to know were infallible Tokens of a Tenderness far beyond that which springs from bare Esteem. And while I flattered my fond Wishes with a Belief that I was secretly beloved by him, I began insensibly to hate the other, whom I looked upon as the only Bar 'twixt me and all the Joys this World could give. Though *Worthly* was one of the most obsequious Lovers that ever was, yet he was too eager to brook a Delay for which he could assign no Reason; and finding me still more and more averse to any Discourse of Marriage, he solicited all my Relations and Acquaintance to speak to me and learn the Cause, if possible, why I should now refuse what (if my Father's Death had not deferred) had been granted with my free Consent many Months before. I suffered a vast deal of Persecution from all those People he had engaged in his interest, and I know not what the unanswerable Arguments they pleaded in his Favour might not at last have persuaded me to if he had not (Oh ill-directed and unlucky Choice!) employed even his adored Rival too in this Affair. I was one Day in my Chamber musing and full of unsettled Resolutions when I was told that *Courtal* was below; his very Name alarmed me, but when I came down and found he was alone, it is impossible to guess at my Surprise: he easily perceived it in my Countenance and approaching me with the most humble and submissive Air, A Guest, Madam! (said he) of so little Merit as the unhappy *Courtal* would have small reason to hope a Welcome *here*, if his Presumption were not authorized by him, who, blessed with the Divine *Belinda's* Love, knows the way to obtain Pardon for himself and me:—From *Worthly*, Madam! (continued he, perceiving I was silent) the fortunate *Worthly*, I am sent to tell you how much he languishes under the Impossibility of waiting on you this Evening and to assure you (if you can doubt it) that though unlucky Affairs detain him from your Presence, his Soul and all his Wishes are with you. Though I was prodigiously confounded to find that *Worthly* had engaged him to this visit, yet I was much more so at his manner of telling it me, but after I had desired him to sit, Any Friend of *Worthly's* (answered I) shall always find Welcome from *Belinda*: But I think so much is owing to the vast Merits of Sir *Thomas Courtal* that there can be no need of any second Name to introduce him anywhere. I designed these Words no other than a Compliment, but the Confusion with which I spoke them, gave him too much Reason to believe I had a farther Meaning; and looking on me with Eyes which seemed to read my Soul—Oh God! (said he) what sweet Enchantment do those Words contain! The powerful Spells disclose an opening Heaven to my ravished View! and wrapped with Joys immortal, make me forget the Hell of Misery I am doomed to.—Then, after a little Pause, and venting two or three Sighs, which seemed so vehement as though at each his Heart were rent asunder, Pardon, Madam (resumed he) the Violence of a sudden Transport, which some delusive Hopes that Moment fired me with and made me neglect the Business which alone has given me the Boldness of waiting on you. I felt, all the time he was speaking, Emotions, which I know not how to account for; I have already told you that I had discovered, or fancied that I had discovered, by some Looks and Words, which seemed to be unguarded that he loved me; and tho' I desired nothing so passionately as to be assured he did so, yet I dreaded the Eclaircissement and began to tremble with Fear that he should say something which I was altogether unprepared to answer: I have often reflected since how silly my inward perturbations made me seem: *Courtal* must certainly guess from what Source the Disorders he perceived in my Countenance proceeded or believe me to be extremely wanting in Conversation; and I was so ambitious of appearing amiable in his Eyes that I know not if I would not have chose he should be sensible of the Truth rather than impute my Behaviour to any natural Defect: But whatever his Thoughts were, he eased my Confusion by immediately falling into a Discourse of *Worthly*. He gave him Praises which, though not more than he deserved were more than I was willing to hear, at least from the Mouth that spoke them and then began to tell me how ill the Impatience of his Love made him brook my delaying to give him a Happiness, which he had so much Cause to hope would long since have been completed and that he begged I would assign some Period to his Sufferings that he the better might be enabled to endure them. If before I was alarmed at the Apprehension of *Courtal's* entertaining me in another Manner, I was now ten times more so that he did not.—It stung me to the Soul to find that when he had so favourable an Opportunity to discover his Sentiments, he should employ it in a Theme, which (if he had those Inclinations that I had flattered myself I had inspired) must be so disagreeable to his own Desires! My Fears now turned to Indignation! I raged to think my Wishes had deceived me! and half despised him for his Insensibility! I wonder (said I, with an Air which I believe had a good deal of Contempt in it) that *Worthly* should take the Measures he does—does he think to tease me into Compliance?—and can he imagine that anything he can say, or the Persons he employs, will influence so far as to make me grant what is not consistent with my Inclinations? ——I am not disposed to Marry——at least as yet; and if I never should be so, he ought not to expect I should do a Violence to my *own* Humour to pleasure *His*. These, and the like ridiculous Expressions, which my Vanity, or my Love, or both, drew from me, were sufficient to let *Courtal* see how little real Tenderness I had for his Rival and doubtless encouraged him to make the Declaration he presently did. Ah Madam! (said he) you are but little sensible what the burning Impatience of a Lover's Wishes make him suffer—what strong Convulsions—what Soul-rending Pangs invade the Breast which throbs with doubtful Expectation!—For my part—could I, like *Worthly*, *Hope*——as all who know you must like him *adore*, I should be less enduring far!——Those lovely Eyes should never have leave to close or view another Object but myself—nor Night nor Day would I be absent.—I'd follow wheresoever you went——and with imploring, dying Looks—with softening Tears—with Groans and all the natural Eloquence of moving Passion hang on your Feet and grasp those happy Garments, till Coldness, Coyness, and Reserve was melted down——and your whole Soul was Tenderness and Pity. You might be mistaken (replied I, briskly) for if I did not *love*, such a Behaviour would make me *hate*. True, Madam (resumed he, holding down his Head and sighing) I know from the Unloved, all Proofs would be unwelcome, and it is that Knowledge has deterred me from discovering what I feel—Else had my Eyes and Tongue, before now, disclosed my Soul and told *Belinda* she engrossed it all.—But, hopeless—meritless—I have in Secret borne the festering Wound nor dare implore my fair Physician's Aid, lest instead of *Balm*, she should apply a *Corrosive*.——Even this, perhaps (continued he, taking one of my Hands, and eagerly kissing it) you would think too great a Recompense for the eternal Loss of my Repose. Though this Declaration would have prodigiously disordered me before, yet being made at a Time when I had just given over either the Hopes or the Fears of hearing any such thing, it confounded me much more; I knew not what to say nor how to look; I could not *repel* and was unwilling to *encourage*: But at last, thinking it best to take the middle Course, I affected to turn his Behaviour into Merriment, and with as much Gaiety as I could put on, I dare swear (said I) there is no Danger of your losing your Repose for any Woman in the World.——You have too much *Wisdom* to be much in *Love*, and most of your Sex have too much *Wit* and too little *Good-nature* not to despise the Effects of that Passion wherever you perceive them.—How Madam, (interrupted he) such Words coming from a Mouth like *yours* carry a Severity in them more cruel than anything I could apprehend from so angelic a Composition—while you tell me I have *Wisdom* and that I know not *Love*, you give the greatest Proof you can that you think me an *Idiot*; for to adore *Belinda* is sure the highest *Wisdom*, and to be insensible of her Charms is the last degree of *Folly* and *Stupidity*.——Ah would to Heaven! (continued he sighing) it were as much in my Power to influence you to Compassion for my Sufferings as it is to convince you of the Reality of them. I never doubted your Gallantry (answered I, scarce able to retain any part of that Humour I had assumed) but if I had, you give me now a sufficient Testimony of it in so artfully turning the Discourse we were upon, which indeed was too serious to be pleasing, into a *Raillery* much more entertaining.——He would not suffer me to proceed, but falling on his Knees before me and looking up in my Face with a Tenderness unutterable, Oh hold (cried he) lovely Insulter! give not to the most Almighty Truth a breaking—— bleeding Heart, never yet sent forth, so injurious an Epithet.——By Heaven!——by all that Man adores——by all we are taught to hope, to fear, or wish, you are dearer to my Soul than Health, than Grandeur, Knowledge, Light, Life, or my eternal Peace—than everything that Language gives a Name to.——But I may spare these Protestations (rejoined he, after a little Pause) too well do those enchanting Eyes trace their own Power—even now they penetrate, they pierce my Breast, and read much more, oh infinitely more, than I can say.——He would have gone on, but the Tread of somebody coming down Stairs obliged him to break off and relieved me from a Perplexity I know not how I should have got through: It was my Sister who came into the Room, just as he had risen from the Posture he was in; but the Confusion that she perceived in both our Faces made her (as she since told me) guess what sort of Conversation he had entertained me with; and, believing it would be little agreeable to me that he should have an Opportunity to renew it, never left us while he stayed. He could not, indeed, after she came in, express his Sentiments any farther by *Words*; but *Looks*, which I already too well understood, explained his Meaning and certainly, though at that time I knew it not, met with a Return too kind from mine. Just as he was taking his Leave, he got the Liberty to say softly——Oh Divine *Belinda*! remember me!——Pardon and Pity me.——Alas! it was I had only need of *Pity*, for never did any Creature pass a Night in greater Inquietudes than I did the succeeding one.—My Engagements to *Worthly* and the Impossibility of breaking them without rendering myself odious to all who knew me——my already furious Passion for *Courtal* and the little Assurance I had of the

Sincerity of his—my Ingratitude for the *one* and Weakness for the *other* shocked all that was noble and generous in me and made me incapable of Ease: I had *all* to *fear*, *nothing* to *hope*, nor could I form an Aim, which if obtained could give me perfect Happiness. If I should marry *Worthly* (said I to myself) how wretched must I be! Condemned to loathed Embraces and the detested Task of forced Civility——by painful Duty restrained from even the Wish of better Fortune; yet *Inclination* still at War with *Virtue*, guilty and innocent at once and miserable in both—or, should I indulge my Passion in the too charming *Courtal's* dear Society, could I expect Content! even in his Arms, my breach of Promise and Ingratitude to *Worthly*, his Despair, and the just Censures of the reproaching World would embitter all my Pleasures, turn the dear purchased Blessing to a Curse, and make my fancied Heaven a real Hell. In this manner would the different Agitations which tormented me make me argue with myself: Honour, Reputation, Gratitude were on *Worthly's* Side, but what are *these* when once opposed by LOVE! *Courtal's* bewitching Charms silenced, at last, all other Considerations, and *Passion* had entirely vanquished *Reason* if my Doubts of his Sincerity had not interposed: I could not be assured he loved me because he told me so, or if he did, how long his Passion might continue. I had heard and read too much of Men's Inconstancy, their Flatteries, their thousand Arts to lure weak Woman to Belief and Ruin not to tremble when I thought there was a Possibility he might not be exempted from those little Basenesses of his Sex.——These Meditations were the troublesome Companions of my Pillow, nor could my domestic Affairs, my Sister's agreeable Prattle, nor all the Amusements which the *Day* brought with it have power to drive them from my Thoughts: My *Body* restless as my *Mind*, displeased at everything, uneasy everywhere, I wandered up and down from Room to Room, till I heard *Worthly* was come to visit me. I was little prepared and less desirous to have seen him, but in the hurry of Temper had forgot to give Orders for my being denied. I received him in such a manner as let him plainly see he could not do me a greater Displeasure than in staying with me; he could not forbear taking notice of the more than ordinary Coldness and indeed Peevishness of my Behaviour; and gave me some Hints, though with all the Respect in the World, that a Passion so truly ardent and unblamable as his had ever been might have expected a more favourable Return.—There was too much Justice in his Complaints for me to be able to answer them and therefore endeavoured to quell them by telling him that, as there was nobody to whom I was obliged to be account- able for my Actions, to find fault with what I did was not the way to engage me to a Change. Madam! (said he) I never yet have been presumptuous enough to find fault with anything you think fit to do but now begin to cease the Hope of ever persuading you to anything in my Favour—I well see that in losing your Father, I lost my only Friend,—had he lived, your *Obedience* to him would have given me a Blessing, which I now despair of obtaining from your *Love*. He looked full in my Face as he spoke these Words, and offered to take me by the Hand, which in drawing back with a Reserve which came pretty near to Rudeness—I find (resumed he) my Presence is unwelcome— I will therefore trouble you no farther at this Time. May Heaven inspire you with more grateful Sentiments or give me a Heart able to support your Cruelty.——He had Power to utter no more, but turning hastily away, went out of the Room in such Disorder that it a little moved me; but these good-natured Emotions lasted not long and what entirely chased them from my Soul was a Letter I immediately after received from *Courtal*, the Words of which were these.

If to adore without a possibility of Hope be a Sin, it is a Sin only against our own Happiness, a Sin which all Mankind, who see you, must be guilty of, and which Heaven who gave you such Resistless Beauties must inspire you to forgive.— —Yes, you are too Angelic to condemn us for Faults, which are not in our Power to avoid.——'Tis my presuming Tongue, not Heart, that has offended; I need not entreat your Pardon for loving you, but for declaring that I do so, there is, I fear, a dreadful Cause,—I ought, indeed, to have died in Silence. I know not but your Soul, in spite of your Yesterday's Efforts to conceal it, is wholly taken up with a more deserving Object, and the Impertinence of my ill-timed Passion may have disturbed those soft Ideas which mutual Tenderness affords.——Tell me, Divine Belinda! if I have been so criminal, Death shall be at once the Punisher of my Rashness, and Cure of my Misery; but if your Breast has any room for Pity, Oh! give me leave to try at least to inspire it: None ever had a Plea more just, none would be more truly grateful than

Your eternally devoted

COURTAL.

You may judge with what Transports I read this Letter by those yourself has felt at receiving anything of this kind from the charming *Lysander*: And I thought I had a prodigious Command of my Temper that I forbore giving any greater Demonstrations of my Joy than what the following Lines contained.

'Tis impossible either to read or hear you without allowing you to be the most accomplished, most gallant, and witty of your Sex; but whether to be able to retain those Graces, be consistent with a Love so ardent as you would persuade me yours is, can only be judged by those versed in the Town manner of addressing. I have often heard say, by those more skilled than myself, that the greatest Symptoms of a true Passion is to be deprived of Utterance, and Incoherence in Expressions; and as I have not Vanity enough to imagine there is anything in me capable of engaging you to the Reality, am unwilling to be made the Property of an Amusement only. However, with that Sincerity, which we in the Country prefer to all things, I assure you that my Heart is utterly unprepossessed with any Idea of Mr. Worthly, farther than his good Qualities inspire in all who know him; and all my softer Wishes are at Liberty to extend themselves wherever they shall find an Object deserving, by his Constancy, the Regard of

BELINDA.

209

I passed the ensuing Night in infinitely more Tranquility than I had that before: *Love* banished all the remains of Gratitude which has so much disturbed me. I gave a loose to all the Tenderness it inspired, and in return, it flattered my fond Wishes with a near Prospect of inexpressible Delight: To heighten my Felicity, early in the Morning the assiduous *Courtal* sent me a second *Billet*, in which I found these Lines.

With what Words, Oh most Divine Belinda! *shall I express the Rapture of my overjoyed Heart, at reading your dear, obliging Letter! Even the Distrust you seem to have of my Sincerity, is capable of giving me no Pain, while you vouchsafe to assure me there is no greater Impediment to my Hopes:* This *my faithful Services will soon remove; but had a Person of more Merit taken up your Soul, I must for ever have despaired.—Permit me then to begin the pleasing Task of proving what I am, this Afternoon, and by giving me an early leave to breath out my Soul in Vows of everlasting Truth before you, convince me (of what is indeed too vast a Blessing to be easily believed) that you will not be displeased to find the most tender, and most* faithful, *as well as the most* passionate *of all Lovers is*

Your adoring

COURTAL.

The seeming Sincerity of these few Lines subdued my easy Faith, and I resolved no longer to distrust my Happiness. Oh! he is all Angel (cried I in a Rapture) divinely charming in *Soul* as well as *Body*; I must——I will—— believe him! and in this hurry of unruly Joy, writ him an Answer in these Words.

'Twould be an over-acted Modesty, and might justly be taken for Stupidity, *to feign an Insensibility of your Attractions: the proudest of my Sex would glory in the conquest of a Heart like yours, and I confess without a Blush to find myself that happy envied Woman would gratify an Ambition, which unknowing you there could not be a ground for. The favour of your Visits however, I know not, as yet, how to receive:* Worthly, *how small a part soever he had in my Heart, has met with Encouragement from my Father, and in obedience to his Commands, from me, and Prudence forbids too sudden a turn in an Affair of so much Consequence; but if I find you in the little Wood behind our House, about five this Evening, you shall know more of the Sentiments of*

BELINDA.

You will, doubtless, wonder that a Maid so little accustomed to Conversation should not start at the very Thought of an Assignation such as this; but whether it were that the Inexperience of the World and the Baseness of Mankind kept me from *imagining* the Danger or the Violence of my Passion from *regarding* it, I must leave to the Charity of your Opinion. But, I confess, I felt not the least Regret for what I had writ and had no Uneasiness but what sprung from my Impatience for the appointed Hour; at last it came, and while I told the Clock, my Soul exulted with a Pleasure which till then I never knew. I believe I need not tell you I found *Courtal* in the Wood ready to receive me;

210

you will easily imagine that the most trifling Inclination will, before Enjoyment, wing the Assiduity of that ungoverned and inconstant Sex; but I wish there were a Possibility of informing you in what manner he accosted me, for there was something in it so much beyond Imagination charming and engaging that it in Part would justify my Behaviour toward him—All his Gestures were so humble and beseeching yet withal so graceful——All his Looks were accompanied with such a piercing Softness—All his Words expressed so real a Tenderness, so perfect a Sincerity, and so pure a Zeal that even you, too sadly skilled in the vile Arts of false deceiving Man, must have believed and trusted him. I walked with him, heedless of the swift passing Hours, till Day was almost spent, and it was not till the want of Light deprived me of the Pleasure of gazing on him that I considered how long I had been with him and that we were wandered, insensibly, perhaps, to *either* of us, at least to *me* I am sure it was so, a great Distance from the House and into the thickest and most obscure Part of the *Wood*. But it was in vain that I reminded him how convenient it was that I should return; he was too pressing, I too transported to be able to refuse him so small a Favour as my Company a few Moments longer. Never was a Night more delectable, more aiding to a Lover's Wishes! The arching Trees formed a Canopy over our Heads, while through the gently shaking Boughs soft Breezes played in lulling Murmurings and fanned us with delicious Gales; a thousand Nightingales sung amourous Ditties, and the billing Doves cooed out their tender Transports—everything was soothing—everything inspiring! the very Soul of Love seemed to inform the Place and reign throughout the whole. A little tired with walking, my too dear Companion had prevailed on me to rest myself on a fine grassy Bank, which was at the Foot of a great Tree: he took the licensed Freedom to place himself by me; and, methought, we sat with all the Sweets of Nature blooming round us, like the first happy Pair while blest with Innocence, they knew not Shame nor Fear. But he, alas! had other Notions, and aiming only at my Ruin, believed he could not choose a fitter Season and perhaps never should have so favourable an Opportunity as this: He now began to mingle Kisses and Embraces with his Vows; my Hands were the first Victims of his fiery Pressures then my Lips, my Neck, my Breast; and perceiving that, quite lost in Ecstasy, I but faintly resisted what he did far greater Boldnesses ensued——My Soul dissolved, its Faculties overpowered—and Reason, Pride, and Shame, and Fear, and every Foe to soft Desire charmed to Forgetfulness my trembling Limbs refused to oppose the lovely Tyrant's Will! And, if my faultering Tongue entreated him to desist or my weak Hands attempted to repulse the encroaching Liberty of his, it served but, as he said, the more to inflame his Wishes and raise his Passion to a higher Pitch of Fury. Oh! I had been inevitably lost had not Heaven sent me a Deliverance, even in the Moment I was about to be made the most wretched of its Creatures. *Worthly*, born for my Preservation! *Worthly*, doomed to do me all manner of good Offices, though to my own Destruction, had been to enquire for me and not finding me at home, happened to come into the *Wood*, not mistrusting I was there, but to indulge that Melancholy my late Carriage had inspired: Chance had led him to that Part where we were, and hearing my Voice, he kept himself concealed and was Witness to all the latter Part of our Conversation: He heard enough, Heaven knows, to make him scorn and hate me; yet, generous to the last, when I was on the very Brink of Ruin, he rushed forth and saved me. Rise, Villain! (said he) and prepare for a different Encounter——you shall not live to wrong another in the Manner you have done me; nor shall that Woman, ungrateful as she is, fall a Sacrifice to your base Desires. The Surprise that *Courtal* was in at these Words, and the Knowledge who it was that spoke them, did not hinder him from putting himself in a Posture to receive him; he had his Sword out almost as soon as the other. But what was my Confusion—my Distraction, to find myself thus exposed, and to the Man from whom of all the World I most desired my Weakness should be concealed! I had certainly run between their Swords and received those Wounds each designed for the other, but Shame and Horror struck me motionless; and without the Power even of endeavouring to prevent it, must have been Witness to some fatal Consequence of which myself was the Cause, if my Sister, being told by some body that saw me where I was and wondering at my Stay, had not at that Instant come with some of the Servants in search of me. The enraged Rivals, on the first Appearance of the Lights she brought with her, sheathed their Swords, but she saw enough in all our Faces to inform her that something extraordinary had happened: But it was in vain for her to enquire; we all were speechless with our several Agitations, till *Worthly*, turning to *Courtal*, We are prevented now (said he) but I shall take a Time more proper to reward your Villainy: And giving him a furious Look, flung hastily away without staying for his Answer. *Courtal* was either less disturbed or had infinitely more Command of his Temper than any of us on this Occasion, and seeming to take no Notice of his Rival's Words, gave me his Hand in order to conduct me home; but I could not now endure he should look on me, or touch me; and leaning on my Sister with one Hand, and with the other holding a Handkerchief before my Face, to hide as much as possible my Disorders, made what haste I could from that unlucky Place. He did not leave us, however, till we got quite to our Door, and as we went made Use of all his Rhetoric to persuade me to think no other wise of what had happened, than as a Matter of no Consequence. It was wholly improper I should answer him as I *would*, therefore forbore answering at all: Nor was it to any Purpose that my Sister begged me to make her a Relation of this Adventure after we came home, and only telling her, that I was not in a talking Humour and bidding her trouble me no farther, I shut myself into my Chamber, and there gave a loose to all the distracted Emotions of my Soul——Oh! what did I not endure this cruel Night, and what, indeed, must I for ever endure in the Reflection on the dreadful Consequence! *Belinda* could not come to this Part of her Story without falling into Agonies, much like those which had so often interrupted the RECLUSE in the Course of hers; and it was now that Lady's turn to comfort, which she did with such Success that the other was soon able to resume her Discourse in this manner.

The Shame and Confusion that I was in (said she) at what had happened was not all that tormented me; I had *Fears*, which were, if possible, more alarming even than my *Remorse*: I knew very well the Violence of *Worthly's* Passion for me—I saw the just Rage my Behaviour had put him in and remembered what he said to *Courtal* at parting and could not hope this Adventure would end without Blood: After a thousand Inventions how to prevent the Mischief I with so much Reason dreaded, I resolved, at last, to try my Power once more with *Worthly* and composed my Thoughts as well as I could to form a Letter to him, in which I confessed that I had been ungrateful to his Affection and by my Folly and ill Conduct had now rendered myself utterly unworthy the Continuance of it but conjured him by the memory of that Tenderness he once had for me not to publish my Weakness to the World by making any Noise of this Affair. I writ also to *Courtal* and entreated him by all the Passion he professed for me, and by those Assurances my late Condescension had given him of mine to avoid all Occasions of meeting *Worthly*, and if he should receive any Letter or Message, like what his last Words imported, to lay aside his *Honour* in favour of his *Love* and the Consideration how much my Reputation must suffer in a Quarrel of that Nature. I expressed these Requests to both of them in the most moving Terms I was capable of, and what Effect I might have wrought I know not; for though I went not to Bed all Night, it was so late the next Day before I had finished that just as I was sealing up the last, I was interrupted by my Sister's knocking violently at my Chamber Door and calling to me to open it, in a Tone and with a Disorder which told something more than ordinary was the Cause before I gave her Entrance; but when I had—Oh Sister! (said she) *Worthly* is killed—murdered by *Sir Thomas Courtal*, and his Servants say it was on your Account they fought.——Oh God! what chilling Horrors seized my whole Frame when she pronounced these Words? If she spoke anything more, I was incapable of hearing it, for I fell immediately into a Swoon in which I lay so long that, as they since told me, neither she nor the Maids that she called to my Assistance believed I should ever recover: But my Miseries were not to have so short a Date, and I again returned to Sense—to all the Racks of Thought and cursed Remembrance. As soon as my Agonies would give me leave to speak and to enquire, I received the Confirmation of the dismal Story: They told me that the Body of *Worthly*, covered with Wounds and all besmeared with Blood, was just brought by our House in order to be carried home, his Seat not being above a Bow-shot distant from ours, and that a Servant who was Witness to his dying Words and seemed acquainted with the whole Affair waited to speak with me. As much as I dreaded to hear what the Fellow had to say to me, yet I ordered he should come up, and when he did, desired him to give me an Account of all he knew concerning this unhappy Accident, which he presently did in these Words. Early this Morning (said he) my Master called me up, and giving me a Letter, commanded me to carry it to the Inn where Sir *Thomas Courtal* lay: I found him in Bed, but he immediately rose and gave me an Answer in writing: At my Return my Master was dressed, and as soon as he had read what I brought, prepared himself to go out and seeing me about to follow him, as was my Duty, he forbid me with a Peevishness which he was not used to express himself with: This Charge, and the Agitations I had observed both in his Countenance and that of Sir *Thomas's*, while he was reading the Letter, gave me some Suspicion of the Truth: I acquainted one of my Fellows with my Conjecture, and we both thought it our Duty to seek him; but in resolving what to do we had wasted so much Time that at our Entrance into a Field (not far from hence, and which we thought, if anything of what we imagined were true, would be as likely a Place as any for the Scene of Action) we met Sir *Thomas*, who seemed to be in a prodigious Hurry: I asked if he had seen my Master, and he answered that he had not; but we did not put so much Confidence in what he said but that we went on in the way we perceived he came from and soon found my poor Master breathing out his last. When we came near him, *Harry* (said he to me, with a Voice scarce intelligible) I am killed—Tell *Belinda* that I die for her—and warn her to take Care of——He was able to bring forth no more, for at that Instant Death closed his Lips forever. Here the poor Fellow ended his sad Account and was just going out of the Room half blinded with his Tears when I called him back to ask what was become of *Courtal*: You may be sure, Madam, (answered he) that I would leave nothing undone for the Revenge of my dear Master's Blood, and as soon as the Body was carried home, took Persons with me to search for him at the Inn; but he was too speedy for my Diligence and with both his Servants had taken Horse, and, I fear, is gone beyond the reach of those sent in Pursuit of him, for we could get no Intelligence which Road he took. Though I had all the real Concern imaginable and Grief for Worthly's Death, and the Cause of it, yet, I confess, I could not hear that *Courtal* was out of Danger without a secret Joy, which was but too guilty: I dissembled it, however, and dismissed the Fellow with a Belief that all the Sorrow I had been in sprung only from the Loss of his Master; all our Family were of that Opinion, and I had the Opportunity of veiling my other Troubles under that Cover, which was both just and laudable. I had, indeed, so much Anxiety of Mind with everything together that I was not able to stay in a Place where all I saw or heard would but more put me in Remembrance of my Misfortunes; and I will not tell you, but the Impossibility of ever seeing *Courtal* there again was the chief Reason of making it odious to me. I therefore ordered the Coach to be got ready and the same Day went to a Relation's House about eight Miles farther in the Country, desiring my Sister, if any Letter should come, to send it to me there, for I imagined *Courtal* would write to me as soon as he thought himself out of Danger. I gave her so strict a

Charge to take Care of it that joined to some other little Remarks she had made on my late Carriage made her not far from guessing the Truth of my Sentiments, and she took the Liberty of reproaching me with Ingratitude and Inconstancy: I gave myself but little concern to persuade her that I did not deserve to be taxed with those Vices, but redoubling my Desires that she would send any Letter that should be directed to me, took my Leave. What I did soon after will convince you that nothing, indeed, was able to abate that wild Passion that *Courtal* had inspired me with: For having waited at my Cousin's House about nine or ten Days and hearing nothing from home, I grew so uneasy that I resolved to be gone from thence. I remembered to have heard *Courtal* say he had Business in *London*, which would oblige him to defer the Progress he intended to make through the Counties until next Year, and fancied he might be gone directly thither. I did not doubt, but if he were, I should be able to find him out; and when once this Belief had settled itself in me, I delayed not a Moment, but borrowing Horses and a Servant of my Cousin, went straight to *Warwick* and from thence took the Stage for *London*. It was that Kinswoman who directed me to this House, having formerly been a Boarder here herself; and assuring me, that if any Packet came from our House she would send it immediately after me, made me pretty well satisfied in my Mind that no Mistake would prevent the Blessing of hearing from him and knowing where to find him in case I should miss him in *London*.

The Fatigue of my Journey did not hinder me from sending, as soon as I came here, to all public Places to enquire for him, but no such Person was to be found; and what amazed me most was, that a Man of that Fashion and so noted as I imagined him to be, should be utterly unknown to every Body: I did not in the least doubt but that if I had not the good Fortune of meeting with him here I should be able to get a perfect Account of his Character and Circumstances; but, alas! the Name of *Courtal* was as little known as the *Arabian* Dialect, and I might have spent my whole Life in a fruitless Inquisition had I not believed my want of Intelligence was in great Measure owing to the Carelessness of those I employed and resolved to be my own Spy in an Affair of so much Consequence to my Peace: I had no sooner determined on this, than an Opportunity offered as lucky as I could have wished. One of the Boarders here happened to have a young Lady a Relation of hers come to visit her; there being a very good Tragedy acted that Night, they agreed to go to see it, and having talked of it before me, asked if I would accompany them thither: Though I had very little Relish for that or any other Diversion as my Affairs were, yet I was extremely pleased with the Proposal, believing no Place more probable to give me a Sight of him, whose Presence was all my Wishes aimed at. Neither of them were dressed for the Boxes, and I had an inexpressible Satisfaction in my Mind to think that if I should be so fortunate to meet *Courtal* there I should have the Opportunity to observe his Manner of Behaviour unseen by him: In short, we all went in a *Dishabillee*[43] to the

---

[43] *Dishabillee*: dressed in a style intended to appear careless or informal.

Gallery[44] and chose to sit in the very Corner of it, where without being much taken Notice of ourselves, we might see with Ease all the Persons that came into the House. The Ladies that came with me, knowing me to be a Stranger, were so complaisant as to give me an Account what and who most of the Company of any Note were as they came into their Places; but I had little Ears for their Discourse, my Soul was all collected in my Eyes, and busily employed in search of him, whom the hope of seeing only had engaged my being there: Long I had looked in vain, until the House being pretty full, and I beginning to despair of being so happy, at last I saw him enter: His Charms were too peculiar, and my Thoughts too full of them, not to make me know him the Moment he set his Foot into the Box—Good God! how lovely did he appear that Night! how graceful! those Perfections which in the Country, where a *Bon Mien*[45] is a Prodigy, one might think shown to Advantage were no less distinguishable among a Crowd of *Beaux*! Surrounded by those, who by their very *Air* one might perceive made it their Study to attract, he shone with a superior Brightness and with an unaffected manly Majesty asserted the Dignity of his Charms and seemed to scorn each trifling Emulator. As I was contemplating on his unmatched Beauties, I heard one of my Companions say to the other, Cousin! do you see who is yonder? Yes, (replied she that was spoke to) I find that Villain, to his other Vices, has that of being ashamed of nothing. How unconcerned he looks (resumed the former) and yet, I believe, this is the first Time of his appearing since his late base Action. They had a good deal more of this kind of Discourse between themselves, which I but little regarded, not knowing of whom they were talking, nor the least imagining that anything of what they said was any Concern of mine, till some Ladies coming into the Box over against us, I saw *Courtal* quit his own, and stepping hastily into that in which they were, seemed to entertain them with a world of Gaiety and with a Familiarity which gave me a Taste of what (by the little I felt) I believe to be the most dreadful of all Passions, *Jealousy*! One of them, although I hated her for the Freedom I saw she used him with, I could not forbear thinking perfectly agreeable; but she that sat by her, though not the thousandth Part so engaging, appeared to have the greatest Share of *Courtal*'s Admiration: I perceived he looked on her with a beseeching Air and a Tenderness in his Deportment, which made me almost mad; while the other often pulled him by the Sleeve, patted his Hand, whispered to him, and seemed by a world of little Fondnesses to endeavour to oblige him to a more peculiar Regard. Judge what my Condition was at a Sight so unexpected, so fatal to my Hopes! I felt in one Moment all that Despair, and Rage, and Jealousy could inflict, and it was as much as I could do to restrain myself from giving some Proof of it, which would have made me ridiculous to the whole Assembly. Not being able to observe their Motions any longer with

---

[44] *Gallery*: inexpensive seats in a gallery above the boxes, which were elevated above the pit. Most theatres had several galleries, and servants and lower-class people sat in the upper gallery.
[45] *Bon Mien*: good face (colloquial, bad French).

Patience, I turned to her that sat next me and asked if she knew who those Ladies were. One of them (answered she) is the *Wife*, the other the *Mistress* of that Gentleman that just now placed himself behind them—The *Wife!* (interrupted I, in a much greater Surprise than can be easily comprehended) the *Wife!* did you say, Madam? Yes, (resumed she) that Lady in the Green and Silver Brocade[46] is his *Wife*, but tho' she is accounted one of the most celebrated Beauties in Town and is certainly a Woman of a very excellent Temper, had a vast Fortune, and has not been married much above a Year, yet she possesses but a small Share in her unworthy Husband's Affection: I dare swear, she has this Moment a Weight of Discontent upon her Heart, though her Prudence enables her to conceal any Marks of it in her Countenance and Behaviour: That Creature by her in the flowered Damask,[47] who has neither Beauty, good Shape, or anything to recommend her but a little flashy Wit and a vast deal of Assurance, she is obliged for her Domestic Peace to be civil to, although everybody knows her to be the most cruel Enemy she has and that her Husband passes most of his Hours and great Part of his Substance with her. All the Time she was speaking, although I listened attentively to what she uttered, I had my Eyes fixed on *Courtal*; I loved with too much Passion not to be assured it was he I saw before me;—I knew *I* could not be mistaken, but I imagined *her* to be infinitely so: What she told me was so inconsistent with the Idea I had formed of his Humour, or the Character I had heard of his Circumstances, that I could not believe one Tittle of what she said. Madam, you are prodigiously deceived (cried I, in a kind of Disdain) in the Persons you are talking of; that Gentleman was my particular Acquaintance in the Country, and I am confident has no Wife, or if he had, is not of a Principle so vile to use her in the manner you describe. I know not (said the other Lady) what he may have done to entitle him to your good Opinion, but am very certain there are too many here who know him to be a far worse Monster than my Cousin has represented him. I should be very much ashamed (rejoined I more warmly than before) to take the Part of a Man, who really could deserve those Severities some Reports may have exacted from you: But must ask your Pardon if I tell you that I cannot recede from what I have said, because I am confident if Sir *Thomas Courtal* were sensible of the Accusations he lies under, he would find it no difficult Matter to clear himself—Sir *Thomas Courtal* (cried they both out) for Heavens sake who are you talking of? The Man (answered I, more amazed at that Question than at what they had told me of him) whose Character you have been so free with—Bless me! (said one of them) I know him not; nor I (cried the other) I thought we had all this while been speaking of my *Lord*——

Here *Belinda* made a full Stop, as considering whether she should name him; and after about a Moment's Reflection—You will pardon me (said she to the RECLUSE) if I conceal the real Name of this ungrateful Man, for I

---

[46] *Brocade*: expensive, heavy fabric woven with a rich, raised design.
[47] *Damask*: rich patterned fabric, often made of silk; less expensive than brocade.

confess, in spite of the Deceit he has used me with and the Crimes he has been guilty of, I have still a Tenderness for him which makes me unwilling to expose him. And the RECLUSE, assuring her she would be far from desiring to know any more than she should think fit to reveal, gave her leave to proceed in her Discourse in this manner.

If before (continued she) I thought these Ladies were mistaken, I was now confirmed they were so when they named a Person altogether a Stranger to me. I knew (said I) you must at last acknowledge your Error that Gentleman to whom you give the Title of *Lord* is no more than a *Baronet*, his Name Sir *Thomas Courtal*, and I am sure, if he were sensible of it, would be very sorry to have any Resemblance to a Man so base. Good God! (said one of them) you will not go about to persuade us that he in the White trimmed with Gold is any other than the Person we have named. I am very certain it is not (answered I). As we were in this Dispute, a Woman came to us to know if we wanted any Fruit. Since (said the Lady) we are not able to convince you, let this Woman be the Judge; these sort of People are acquainted with everybody, and she can have no Interest in disguising the Truth. When she had spoke these Words she beckoned the woman, and making a Pretence of buying some Fruit, desired her to tell us who that Gentleman was; she immediately confirmed what my Companions had said and run on in a good deal of impertinent Chat about him: You see (resumed the Lady that boards here) how much your Eyes, or the great Likeness there may be between two Persons, has deceived you; but we have sufficient Reasons to know what he is, which when we come home I will acquaint you with. At that Instant the Curtain drew up, and the Attention I found they were willing to give to the Play prevented any further Discourse: But how I passed the Time of the Performance cannot be conceived without being possessed with Agitations such as mine. I had no Room to hope there was a Probability of so many Persons being mistaken, and his Behaviour to the Ladies that sat in the Box with him confirmed the Character I heard of him to be too true; but presently after I received a Demonstration which took from me all Possibility of doubting the Reality of my Misfortunes. When the Play was done, having no Servant there to provide us a Coach, we were obliged to wait at the Door for one to come to us, which it could not do immediately, being hindered by a Chariot which stood ready for its Owner's approach. I observed there were two or three Footmen belonging to it, and one of them, though now in a different and much richer Dress, I perfectly remembered to be the Man that officiated in the Place of poor *Worthly's* Coachman that fatal Day in which I first beheld the perjured *Courtal*, and since had been the Bearer of those *Billets* I received from him, I pulled my Hood as forward as I could to prevent his seeing my Face, and changing my Voice, asked him to whom that Chariot belonged; and he had no sooner told me (as I feared he would) the Name which had given me such Confusion than I perceived him coming, the Lord, or *Courtal*, or both, for both indeed were one: He conducted the Ladies he had been with into the

Chariot, and stepping hastily into a Chair which stood there, deprived me of the Opportunity of speaking and upbraiding him, as else I should have done in the distracted condition I then was without any regard how improper it was I should do so in such a Place and before the Company I had with me: After this we got into a Coach, and the Lady who came to visit her that lodges here, sat us down, it being in her way home. One would imagine that to find myself thus cruelly deceived had been sufficient to have made me forego all the Tenderness which had led me into such Misfortunes; and if I could not think of him with Hatred, to endeavour not to think of him at all: But in spite of the just Rage I was in, the Impatience, the jealous Curiosity of a Love still remained. I remembered that one of the Ladies told me they had particular Reasons to know who the Person was whom I affirmed to be Sir *Thomas Courtal* and had hardly Patience to stay until Supper was over for the Performance of the Promise she made me to acquaint me with them. I was beginning to stretch my Invention to form a Story to make her believe that it was wholly on the account of a Friend and not of any farther Consequence to me which had made me so Inquisitive; lest by giving her occasion to suspect the Truth, I should expose myself to the Ridicule of the whole Family: but I might have spared myself that Trouble. The Aversion she had to him kept her from regarding anything but the Pleasure it gave her to have an Opportunity of telling a Story so much to his Disadvantage; and I had little occasion for Entreaty to engage her to satisfy my Curiosity and make me sensible that the Man I had considered as so worthy Adoration that all I could do for him was rather a Merit than a Fault was indeed the most vile, and most perfidious of his Sex.

She illustrated the History she gave me with many Circumstances, which aggravated the foulness of the Fact; but so much time has been taken up in the recounting of my own Affairs that I will not detain your Attention in relating the Particulars of this and shall only, by giving you the Heads of what she told me, let you see that I am not the only Woman whom his Artifices have rendered miserable. The Sister of that Lady who came to visit her that lodges here, tho' for a very different Reason, is as unhappy as myself and suffers as much in the not loving him as I do for loving him too well. She is, it seems, one of the most agreeable Women in Town; her Accomplishments are such as cannot fail of attracting a great number of Admirers; but among the rest, there was a young Man of Quality, who professed the highest Esteem for her, and she thought herself no less happy in his Addresses than he did in her Acceptance of them. They long had loved each other with a most violent though pure Affection, but either through Disparity of Birth, or some other Reason, both thought convenient to keep their Amour a Secret. That Villain (for I shall henceforth call him by no other Name) being an intimate Friend of the Lovers was the only trusted Person. He conveyed Letters between them, and through his means they had frequent Opportunities of meeting. He continued faithful for some time, but *Miranda* was it seems too *charming* not to be capable of making an Impression on any Heart, much more on one so amorous as his; and he is too *Base* not to make use of any means, which might give him the gratification of his Wishes, and too *artful* to be at a Loss to find them: As by his Contrivance they had often *met*, so by his Contrivance they were at last entirely *parted*; both having a Confidence in his Sincerity yielded an implicit Faith to what he said, and he soon formed a Stratagem to make each appear to the other more worthy of *Hate* than *Love*; till, if they could not entertain a *real* Aversion, they feigned at least to do so; and keeping their Resentments still warm, by new Inventions, prevented either from endeavouring an Eclaircissement. The *Lover*, though he imagined he had bestowed his Heart on a Person altogether unworthy of the Present, was too truly touched with the Passion he had professed to be able to withdraw it; and finding it impossible to continue in the same Climate with her, without continuing to adore her and having too great a Spirit to avow it, after what he supposed he knew of her Ingratitude, resolved to put it out of his Power to do anything below the dignity of that Reason, which all People ought to make use of in an Affair of that kind, when they find themselves ill treated without a justifiable Cause by the Person who once has flattered them with a show of Tenderness. In short, to the Amazement of the whole Town and the great Grief of all his Friends and Acquaintance, (but he whose Arts had occasioned him to do it) he went to travel; and the Lady, though her very Soul went with him, believing herself injured by his Ingratitude and the Insinuations of his faithless Friend, scorned to make any trial of her Power to prevent him.

The beloved Rival once removed, this common Deceiver of them both— nay, of the whole World, thought there was no Obstacle remaining to his Wishes and doubted not the influence of his too often successful Charms. In a very few Days he declared himself her Lover and made no scruple to let her know he hoped she would reward his Passion. But, *this once*, he found his Designs frustrated; however she had disguised it, she still retained too great a Tenderness for her absent Lover to entertain the least Thought of putting any other in his Place; and besides, was a Woman of too much Honour and Discretion not to look on all Attempts made upon her Virtue with the utmost Contempt; and that this was so, there was no room to doubt, since she knew him to be married. The Lady, who gave me this Account, told me that nothing could be more enraged than she was at the Declaration he made her; that she rejected all his Offers and forbad him ever to visit her any more: But, as it is the Nature of that ungrateful Sex still to pursue what flies them, he redoubled his Efforts: denied the Liberty of speaking, he writ to her in the most moving and *seeming* sincere Strain that ever Heart dictated; but after the receipt of the first Letter, the known Character on the Superscription prevented her from reading what the next contained, and she immediately sent it back unopened. Yet still, undaunted he went on, and to make her sensible how capable he was to make even Contradictions join, and by the Effects of his too powerful Wit dress the foulest Vice in all the Beauties of the fairest Virtue, he sent long Epistles to argue down her Honour and to persuade her that to a Passion so sublime as his to be cruel only was a Crime. But whether it was owing to her good Sense or the Prepossession of *another* Idea, which made her insensible of *his* (I must say) unmatched Perfections, I know not; but as excellent a Logician as he is, all his Sophistry here proved Vain. And tho' she could not avoid receiving some of his Letters, because he either disguised his Hand, or got some other Person to direct them, yet they had no other Effect on her than what was very different from his Expectations; she hated him still more, shunned him as a Monster, and if, by chance, she saw him at any public Place, (as he took all Opportunities of being where she was) her very Countenance discovered the secret Disdainings of her Soul; and though wherever she turned he followed her with Eyes trembling with Tenderness! and all the Languishments of despairing Love! (Looks, Heaven knows, he is too well used to wear) a stern Severity only shone in hers! And if, to avoid being taken Notice of, she was obliged to answer the Civilities he paid her, Scorn lightened in her Glances! whenever she spoke, proud Indignation triumphed in her Accents! and haughty Detestation sparkled in her Air! Such a Deportment, had his Passion been of that kind which is worthy of the Name of *Love*, must have reduced him to a Condition justly meriting Compassion; but Love is a Flame too bright, too pure, to blaze in a Heart so full of Fraud and vile Hypocrisy. As Affairs were in this Posture between them, there came an Account that the Ship in which the poor, unfortunate, deluded Lover embarked was cast away and all on Board it lost, and at the very same time, his equally deceived Mistress received a Letter, which he had writ to her from a Seaport Town, where they happened to put in. That unhappy Gentleman, though he had been made to believe her infinitely undeserving of it, still retained the same Tenderness he had ever professed and had not the Power to forbear letting her know it, though he had the Power to leave her: In this Testimony of his continued Faith, there was some little Mixture of upbraidings, which made her no Stranger to the Cause of his Departure and that it was not *his* want of Love, and Truth, but the seeming Reasons he had to doubt of *hers* which had deprived her of her Lover. Had it been possible to have recalled him, with what a Transport must she have welcomed such an Eclaircissement; but, alas! he was now irrecoverably lost. She found his Faith, his Constancy, his Tenderness, but found at the same time she was past the possibility of receiving any Benefit of her Virtues; and if one rightly considers her Condition, I know not if it were not less Misery to have believed him *false* than know him *true* and know him lost for ever. I will not go about to make any Repetition of what I was told concerning the Surprise, Despair and Rage which seized the Heart of this unfortunate Lady at so unexpected a Catastrophe. 'Tis easy for you to imagine she must be transported with an uncommon Fury; but while she was venting the Anguish of her Soul in Curses on the hated Author of her Miseries, he was contriving means to gratify his Desires on her; and finding it in vain to prosecute his lawless Suit, by those ways he had began it in, he had the unbounded Impudence to resolve on others yet more impious! and seek by *Force* to obtain what he was now convinced Entreaties would forever fail to give him. Opportunity was all he wanted to perpetrate his Design, and none for a long time offering, he grew desperate enough to despise all Consideration; and knowing she very often went to Evening Prayers, he waited at the Church Door with a Hackney-Coach[48] and was about to seize and drag her violently into it. The Action was so sudden that though there were many People coming out at the same time, the Surprise it gave them would have prevented her receiving any Assistance if two Gentlemen that were passing by had not had presence enough of Mind to draw their Swords in her Defence just as he had so far compassed his Intent as to be getting into the Coach himself after having thrust her into it. He wanted not Courage to engage with them both, but a crowd of People immediately coming about them put a stop to any Mischief either to him or them. Had such a piece of Villainy been attempted by a meaner Man, he certainly had been secured; but his Quality made everybody unwilling to create to themselves so powerful an Enemy, and he had the Liberty of retreating, venting ten thousand Curses on his ill Fortune and the Gentlemen who had frustrated his Design; while *Miranda*, though half dead with the Fright, was safely conducted home by her Deliverers. Such an Attempt on a Lady so much distinguished as *Miranda* and made by such a Person must certainly occasion a great deal of Discourse in the World; and her Brother, who is a Colonel, would have been suspected to have but little Regard to the Honour of his Family if he had not resented it in the manner he did. The next Day he sent a Challenge to the intended Ravisher, which being answered as he expected it would they met in that Field, behind *Mountague-House*,[49] so famous for Duels; but, in spite of the Justness of his Cause, the Brother had the worst of it; and the other, leaving him wounded and as he thought Dead, made his Escape, nor dared appear in Town until he heard, contrary to everybody's Expectation, that his Antagonist was out of Danger; and that Night which showed him to me at the Playhouse was the first of his being seen since the time he fought.

Belinda had no sooner finished this little History than she observed an excessive Paleness in the Face of the RECLUSE; and before she could have time to ask if she were ill, saw her fall fainting on the Couch: but there was no occasion to call in anybody to her Assistance; her Spirits were not above a Moment absent; and at their return, Oh Madam! said she, (looking on *Belinda* with Eyes streaming with Tears) how strangely has Fortune brought together two Wretches fit only for the Society of each other! We are indeed too nearly allied in our Misfortunes and to one fatal Source over both our Woes! I might

---

[48] *Hackney-Coach*: coach available for hire to anyone, the equivalent of today's taxi cabs.

[49] *Mountague-House*: lavish home of the Duke of Montagu, which became the site of the British Museum on Great Russell Street. At this time, it adjoined Lamb's Conduit Fields.

from the very beginning of your Story have imagined it—might have known that such prodigious *Charms* and such prodigious *Villainy* were no where blended but in my perfidious but still dear *Lysander*!—Your *Courtal*!—my *Lysander* are the same, and both are found only in the Person of the too lovely, faithless, *Bellamy*. The Surprise that *Belinda* was in at these Words took from her for some time the Power of answering, nor could she for a long while bring out any more than—Good God! is it possible?—Although lost to all the World, resumed the RECLUSE, and wholly regardless of everything that passed, this last Action of the Inconstant *Bellamy*, in spite of me, reached my Ear. And I suppose it was in the time of his absconding that he went to *Warwick* and took on him that borrowed Name of *Courtal* to prevent his being apprehended if any Account of what he had done should be brought down. Yes, said *Belinda* (now a little recovered from her Amazement) that was certainly the Motive which induced him both to take that Journey and to disguise his true Quality. For by the Account which the Lady gave me, I found it was not many Days after the Accident that we had the ill Fortune to be overtaken by him on the Road.

These fair Companions in Affliction passed some time in bewailing their several Misfortunes, sometimes exclaiming against the *Vices*, sometimes praising *Beauties* of their common Betrayer, till the RECLUSE, being desirous to know if there was any thing more to be heard of her *Lysander*, entreated *Belinda* to finish the remaining part of her Story. Alas, Madam! replied that dejected Lady, I have nothing farther to relate unless I confess I am weak enough to retain still in my Soul a secret Tenderness for the unworthy Man; and that not the Knowledge of his unexampled Perfidy and Inhumanity to you, his base Design on *Miranda*, nor the Miseries he has brought on myself can bring me to consider him as I ought. Although I resolve never to see him more, I neither can forget nor remember him as a Woman governed by Reason would do. Has he then not seen you since you came to Town? (interrupted the RECLUSE somewhat hastily.) No, on my Honour (answered the other) he knows not of my being here, nor I dare swear thinks my Presence worth a Wish; but were I sure he did, nay were I convinced that, although false to all my Sex beside, to me he would be true; nay did his Life depend on my granting him one Interview, I protest, by all that I adore, I never would consent. No, Madam, (continued she with the most resolute Air) I owe much more than such a self-denial to the Memory of poor *Worthly*—to the Friendship I have already conceived for you—and to the Justice of Revenging, as far as is in my Power, the little Regard he has hitherto paid our Sex. The RECLUSE seemed perfectly pleased with this Assurance and omitted nothing to strengthen her in this Resolution.

There grew so entire a Friendship between these Ladies that they were scarce a Moment asunder. *Belinda* quitted her Chamber, being desired by the RECLUSE to take part of her Bed. Their common Misfortunes were a Theme not to be exhausted, and they still found something for which to condole each other. In this Melancholy Entertainment did they pass some Days, till *Belinda* received Letters from the Country, which brought an Account that *Worthly's* Wounds having been searched by an able Surgeon were found not Mortal; that his greatest Danger had been loss of Blood; that he was now perfectly recovered and with new *Life* had entertained new *Wishes*. *Belinda's* Sister had expressed so tender a Concern for his Misfortunes, and so high an Esteem for his Virtues, that he found it no Difficulty to transmit to her all the affection he had bourne her Sister. The Wedding day was appointed, and soon after *Belinda* received an Account that it was solemnized to the general Satisfaction of all Friends on both sides and the lasting Happiness of the married Pair. Although *Belinda* was far from envying her Sister that good Fortune, which she was incapable of possessing herself, yet the Cause which rendered her so made her unwilling to behold it; and, in a short time, both their Resolutions of abandoning the World continuing, the RECLUSE and she took a House about seventy Miles distant from *London*, where they still live in a perfect Tranquility, happy in the real Friendship of each other, despising the uncertain *Pleasures* and free from all the *Hurries* and *Disquiets* which attend the Gaieties of the Town. And where a solitary Life is the effect of *Choice*, it certainly yields more solid Comfort than all the public Diversions which those who are the greatest Pursuers of them can find.

FANTOMINA:

OR,

LOVE in a Maze.

BEING A

Secret History

OF AN

AMOUR

Between Two

PERSONS of Condition.

By Mrs. *ELIZA HAYWOOD*.

In Love the Victors from the Vanquish'd fly.
They fly that wound, and they pursue that dye.
WALLER.

LONDON:

Printed for D. BROWNE *jun.* at the *Black-Swan*
without *Temple-Bar,* and S. CHAPMAN, at
the *Angel* in *Pallmall.* M.DCC.XXV.

Fantomina: or, Love in a Maze

A Young Lady of distinguished Birth, Beauty, Wit, and Spirit happened to be
in a Box one Night at the Playhouse; where, though there were a great
Number of celebrated Toasts, she perceived several Gentlemen extremely
pleased themselves with entertaining a Woman who sat in a Corner of the
Pit,[1] and, by her Air and Manner of receiving them, might easily be known
to be one of those who come there for no other Purpose than to create
Acquaintance with as many as seem desirous of it. She could not help testifying her Contempt of Men, who, regardless either of the Play, or Circle,
threw away their Time in such a Manner to some Ladies that sat by her: But
they, either less surprized by being more accustomed to such Sights, than she
who had been bred for the most Part in the Country, or not of a Disposition
to consider any Thing very deeply, took but little Notice of it. She still thought
of it, however; and the longer she reflected on it, the greater was her Wonder,
that Men, some of whom she knew were accounted to have Wit, should have
Tastes so very depraved.—This excited a Curiosity in her to know in what
Manner these Creatures were addressed:—She was young, a Stranger to the
World, and consequently to the Dangers of it; and having no Body in Town
at that Time to whom she was obliged to be accountable for her Actions did
in every Thing as her Inclinations or Humours rendered most agreeable to
her: Therefore thought it not in the least a Fault to put in practice a little
Whim which came immediately into her Head, to dress herself as near as she
could in the Fashion of those Women who make sale of their Favours and
set herself in the Way of being accosted as such a one, having at that Time
no other Aim than the Gratification for an innocent Curiosity.——She no
sooner designed this Frolic than she put it in Execution; and muffling her
Hoods over her Face, went the next Night into the Gallery-Box, and practicing as much as she had observed at that Distance the Behavior of that
Woman was not long before she found her Disguise had answered the Ends
she wore it for:——A Crowd of Purchasers of all Degrees and Capacities were
in a Moment gathered about her, each endeavouring to out-bid the other, in
offering her a Price for her Embraces.——She listened to 'em all and was not
a little diverted in her Mind at the Disappointment she should give to so
many, each of which thought himself secure of gaining her.——She was told
by 'em all that she was the most lovely Woman in the World; and some
cried, *Gad, she is mighty like my fine Lady Such-a-one,*——naming her own
Name. She was naturally vain, and received no small Pleasure in hearing
herself praised, tho' in the Person of another, and a supposed Prostitute; but

---

[1] *Pit*: the aristocracy usually sat in the boxes; a mixed group including gentlemen, men who
considered themselves literary, students from the Inns of Court (law schools), and the professional
classes sat in the pit and ostentatiously passed judgement on the plays and even their fellow audience members.

she dispatched as soon as she could all that had hitherto attacked her, when she saw the accomplished *Beauplaisir* was making his Way through the Crowd as fast as he was able to reach the Bench she sat on. She had often seen him in the Drawing-Room, had talked with him; but then her quality and reputed Virtue kept him from using her with that Freedom she now expected he would do, and had discovered something in him, which had made her often think she should not be displeased, if he would abate some Part of his Reserve.——Now was the Time to have her Wishes answered:——He looked in her Face, and fancied as many others had done that she very much resembled that Lady whom she really was; but the vast Disparity there appeared between their Characters prevented him from entertaining even the most distant Thought that they could be the same.—He addressed her at first with the usual Salutations of her pretended Profession, as, *Are you engaged, Madam?—* *—Will you permit me to wait on you home after the Play?——By Heaven, you* *are a fine Girl!—How long have you used this House?*——And such like Questions; but perceiving she had a Turn of Wit and a genteel Manner in her Raillery beyond what is frequently to be found among those Wretches, who are for the most part Gentlewomen but by Necessity, few of 'em having had an Education suitable to what they affect to appear, he changed the Form of his Conversation, and showed her it was not because he understood no better that he had made use of Expressions so little polite.——In fine,[2] they were infinitely charmed with each other: He was transported to find so much Beauty and Wit in a Woman, who he doubted not but on very easy Terms he might enjoy; and she found a vast deal of Pleasure in conversing with him in this free and unrestrained Manner. They passed their Time all the Play with an equal Satisfaction; but when it was over, she found herself involved in a Difficulty which before never entered into her Head, but which she knew not well how to get over.——The Passion he professed for her was not of that humble Nature which can be content with distant Adorations:——He resolved not to part from her without the Gratifications of those Desires she had inspired; and presuming on the Liberties which her supposed Function allowed of told her she must either go with him to some convenient House of his procuring or permit him to wait on her to her own Lodgings.——Never had she been in such a *Dilemma*: Three or four Times did she open her Mouth to confess her real Quality; but the Influence of her ill Stars prevented it, by putting an Excuse into her Head, which did the Business as well, and at the same Time did not take from her the Power of seeing and entertaining him a second Time with the same Freedom she had done this.—She told him, she was under Obligations to a Man who maintained her, and whom she durst not disappoint, having promised to meet him that Night at a House hard by,——This Story so like what those Ladies sometimes tell, was not at all suspected by *Beauplaisir*; and assuring her he would be far from doing her a

---

[2] *In fine*: in short.

Prejudice, desired that in return for the Pain he should suffer in being deprived of her Company that Night, that she would order her Affairs so as not to render him unhappy the next. She gave a solemn Promise to be in the same Box on the Morrow Evening; and they took Leave of each other; he to the Tavern to drown the Remembrance of his Disappointment; she in a Hackney-Chair[3] hurried home to indulge Contemplation on the Frolic she had taken, designing nothing less[4] on her first Reflections, than to keep the Promise she had made him, and hugging herself with Joy that she had the good Luck to come off undiscovered.

But these Cogitations were but of a short Continuance, they vanished with the Hurry of her Spirits, and were succeeded by others vastly different and ruinous:—All the Charms of *Beauplaisir* came fresh into her Mind; she languished, she almost died for another Opportunity of conversing with him; and not all the Admonitions of her Discretion were effectual to oblige her to deny laying hold of that which offered itself the next Night.—She depended on the Strength of her Virtue, to bear her fate through Trials more dangerous than she apprehended this to be, and never having been addressed by him as Lady,——was resolved to receive his Devoirs[5] as a Town-Mistress, imagining a world of Satisfaction to herself in engaging him in the Character of such a one and in observing the Surprize he would be in to find himself refused by a Woman who he supposed granted her Favours without Exception.— Strange and unaccountable were the Whimsies she was possessed of,—wild and incoherent her Desires,—unfixed and undetermined her Resolutions, but in that of seeing *Beauplaisir* in the Manner she had lately done. As for her Proceedings with him, or how a second Time to escape him without discovering who she was, she could neither assure herself, nor whether or not in the last Extremity she would do so.—Bent, however, on meeting him whatever should be the Consequence, she went out some Hours before the Time of going to the Playhouse and took Lodgings in a House not very far from it, intending, that if he should insist on passing some Part of the Night with her, to carry him there, thinking she might with more Security to her Honour entertain him at a Place where she was Mistress, than at any of his own choosing.

The appointed Hour being arrived, she had the Satisfaction to find his Love in his Assiduity: he was there before her; and nothing could be more tender than the Manner in which he accosted her: But from the first Moment she came in to that of the Play being done, he continued to assure her no Consideration should prevail with him to part from her again, as she had done the Night before; and she rejoiced to think she had taken that Precaution of providing herself with a Lodging, to which she thought she

---

[3] *Hackney-Chair*: like the taxis of today, hackney coaches and chairs (little coaches carried on poles by two men) were for hire and common means of getting around London.

[4] *designing nothing less*: planning nothing but to keep the engagement to meet him.

[5] *Devoirs*: paying dutiful service, saying the polite, expected compliments.

might invite him without running any Risk, either of her Virtue or Reputation.—Having told him she would admit of his accompanying her home, he seemed perfectly satisfied; and leading her to the Place which was not above twenty Houses distant would have ordered a Collation to be brought after them. But she would not permit it, telling him she was not one of those who suffered themselves to be treated at their own Lodgings; and as soon she was come in, sent a Servant belonging to the House to provide a very handsome Supper and Wine, and every Thing was served to Table in a Manner which shewed the Director neither wanted Money nor was ignorant how it should be laid out.

This Proceeding, though it did not take from him the Opinion that she was what she appeared to be, yet it gave him Thoughts of her which he had not before.—He believed her a *Mistress*, but believed her to be one of a superior Rank, and began to imagine the Possession of her would be much more Expensive than at first he had expected: But not being of a Humour to grudge any Thing for his Pleasures, he gave himself no farther Trouble than what were occasioned by Fears of not having Money enough to reach her Price about him.

Supper being over, which was intermixed with a vast deal of amorous Conversation, he began to explain himself more than he had done; and both by his Words and Behaviour let her know, he would not be denied that Happiness the Freedoms she allowed had made him hope.—It was in vain; she would have retracted the Encouragement she had given:—In vain she endeavoured to delay, till the next Meeting the fulfilling of his wishes:—She had now gone too far to retreat:—*He* was bold;—he was resolute: *she* tearful,—confused, altogether unprepared to resist in such Encounters, and rendered more so by the extreme Liking she had to him.—Shocked, however, at the Apprehension of really losing her Honour, she struggled all she could, and was just going to reveal the whole Secret of her Name and Quality, when the Thoughts of the Liberty he had taken with her, and those he still continued to prosecute, prevented her, with representing the Danger of being exposed, and the whole Affair made a Theme for public Ridicule.—Thus much, indeed, she told him, that she was a Virgin, and had assumed this Manner of Behaviour only to engage him. But that he little regarded, or if he had, would have been far from obliging him to desist—nay, in the present burning Eagerness of Desire, 'tis probable, that had he been acquainted both with who and what she really was, the Knowledge of her Birth would not have influenced him with Respect sufficient to have curbed the wild Exuberance of his luxurious Wishes, or made him in that longing,—that impatient Moment, change the Form of his Addresses. In fine, she was undone; and he gained a Victory, so highly rapturous, that had he known over whom, scarce could he have triumphed more. Her Tears, however, and the Distraction she appeared in, after the ruinous Ecstasy was past, as it heightened his Wonder, so it abated his Satisfaction:—He could not Imagine for what Reason a Woman, who, if she intended not to be a *Mistress*, had counterfeited the Part of one and taken so much Pains to engage him should lament a Consequence which she could not but expect, and till the last Test, seemed inclinable to grant; and was both surprized and troubled at the Mystery.—He omitted nothing that he thought might make her easy; and still retaining an Opinion that the Hope of Interest had been the chief Motive which had led her to act in the Manner she had done, and believing that she might know so little of him as to suppose, now she had nothing left to give, he might not make that Recompense she expected for her Favours: To put her out of that Pain, he pulled out of his Pocket a Purse of Gold, entreating her to accept of that as an Earnest of what he intended to do for her; assuring her, with ten thousand Protestations, that he would spare nothing, which his whole Estate could purchase, to procure her Content and Happiness. This Treatment made her quite forget the Part she had assumed, and throwing it from her with an air of disdain, Is this a Reward (*said she*) for Condescensions, such as I have yielded to?—Can all the Wealth you are possessed of, make a Reparation for my Loss of Honour?—Oh! no, I am undone beyond the Power of Heaven itself to help me!—She uttered many more such Exclamations; which the amazed *Beauplaisir* heard without being able to reply to, till by Degrees sinking from that Rage of Temper, her Eyes resumed their softening Glances, and guessing at the Consternation he was in, No, my dear *Beauplaisir*, (*added she*) your Love alone can compensate for the Shame you have involved me in; be you sincere and constant, and I hereafter shall, perhaps, be satisfied with my Fate, and forgive myself the Folly that betrayed me to you.

Beauplaisir thought he could not have a better Opportunity than these Words gave him of enquiring who she was, and wherefore she had feigned her self to be of a Profession which he was now convinced she was not; and after he had made her a thousand Vows of an Affection, as inviolable and ardent as she could wish to find in him, entreated she would inform him by what Means his Happiness had been brought about, and also to whom he was indebted for the Bliss he had enjoyed.—Some Remains of yet unextinguished Modesty, and Sense of Shame made her blush exceedingly at this Demand; but recollecting herself in a little Time, she told him so much of the Truth, as to what related to the Frolic she had taken of satisfying her Curiosity in what Manner *Mistresses*, of the Sort she appeared to be, were treated by those who addressed them; but forbore discovering her true Name and Quality, for the Reasons she had done before, resolving, if he boasted of this Affair, he should not have it in his Power to touch her Character: She therefore said she was the Daughter of a Country Gentleman, who was come to Town to buy Clothes, and that she was called *Fantomina*. He had no Reason to distrust the Truth of this Story, and was therefore satisfied with it; but did not doubt by the Beginning of her Conduct, but that in the End she would be in Reality the Thing she so artfully had counterfeited; and had good Nature enough to pity the Misfortunes he imagined would be her lot:

But to tell her so or offer his Advice in that Point was not his Business, at least, as yet.

They parted not till towards Morning; and she obliged him to a willing Vow of visiting her the next Day at Three in the Afternoon. It was too late for her to go home that Night, therefore she contented herself with lying there. In the Morning she sent for the Woman of the House to come up to her; and easily perceiving, by her Manner, that she was a Woman who might be influenced by Gifts, made her a Present of a Couple of Broad Pieces,[6] and desired her, that if the Gentleman, who had been there the Night before, should ask any Questions concerning her, that he should be told, she was lately come out of the Country, had lodged there about a Fortnight, and that her Name was *Fantomina*. I shall (*also added she*) lie but seldom here; nor, indeed, ever come but in those Times when I expect to meet him: I would, therefore, have you order it so that he may think I am but just gone out, if he should happen by any Accident to call when I am not here; for I would not for the World have him imagine I do not constantly lodge here. The Landlady assured her she would do every Thing as she desired and gave her to understand she wanted not the Gift of Secrecy.

Every Thing being ordered at this Home for the Security of her Reputation, she repaired to the other, where she easily excused to an unsuspecting Aunt, with whom she boarded, her having been abroad all Night, saying, she went with a Gentleman and his lady in a Barge to a little Country Seat of theirs up the River, all of them designing to return the same Evening; but that one of the Bargemen happening to be taken ill on the sudden, and no other Waterman to be got that Night, they were obliged to tarry till Morning. Thus did this Lady's Wit and Vivacity assist her in all but where it was most needful.—She had Discernment to foresee and avoid all those ills which might attend the Loss of her *Reputation*, but was wholly blind to those of the Ruin of her *Virtue*; and having managed her Affairs so as to secure the *one*, grew perfectly easy with the Remembrance she had forfeited the *other*.——The more she reflected on the Merits of *Beauplaisir*, the more she excused herself for what she had done; and the Prospect of that continued Bliss she expected to share with him took from her all remorse for having engaged in an Affair which promised her so much Satisfaction and in which she found not the least Danger of Misfortune.—If he is really (*said she, to herself*) the faithful, the constant Lover he has sworn to be, how charming will be our Amour?—— And if he should be false, grow satiated, like other Men, I shall but, at the worst, have the private Vexation of knowing I have lost him;——the Intrigue being a Secret, my Disgrace will be so too:——I shall hear no Whispers as I pass,—She is Forsaken:—The odious word *Forsaken* will never wound my Ears; nor will my Wrongs excite either the Mirth or Pity of the talking World:—it will not be even in the Power of my Undoer himself to triumph

---

[6] *Broad Pieces*: the 'unite' or 20-shilling piece was so called because it was broader and thinner than the recently minted guinea coin, which was worth 21 shillings.

over me; and while he laughs at, and perhaps despises the fond, the yielding *Fantomina*, he will revere and esteem the virtuous, the reserved Lady.—In this Manner did she applaud her own Conduct and exult with the Imagination that she had more Prudence than all her Sex beside. And it must be confessed, indeed, that she preserved an Economy in the management of this Intrigue beyond what almost any Woman but herself ever did: In the first Place, by making no Person in the World a Confidant in it; and in the next, in concealing from *Beauplaisir* himself the Knowledge who she was; for though she met him three or four Days in a Week, at that Lodging she had taken for that Purpose, yet as much as he employed her Time and Thoughts, she was never missed from any Assembly she had been accustomed to frequent.—The Business of her Love had engrossed her till Six in the Evening, and before Seven she has been dressed in a different Habit, and in another Place.— — Slippers, and a Night-Gown loosely flowing, has been the Garb in which he has left the languishing *Fantomina*;—Laced, and adorned with all the Blaze of Jewels, has he, in less than an Hour after, beheld at the Royal Chapel, the Palace Gardens, Drawing-Room, Opera, or Play, the Haughty Awe-Inspiring Lady—A thousand Times has he stood amazed at the prodigious Likeness between his little Mistress and this Court beauty; but was still as far from imagining they were the same, as he was the first Hour he had accosted her in the Playhouse, though it is not impossible, but that her Resemblance to this celebrated Lady, might keep his Inclination alive something longer than otherwise they would have been; and that it was to the Thoughts of this (as he supposed) unenjoyed Charmer, she owed in great measure the Vigour of his latter Caresses.

But he varied not so much from his Sex as to be able to prolong Desire, to any great Length after Possession: The rifled Charms of *Fantomina* soon lost their Poignancy, and grew tasteless and insipid; and when the Season of the Year inviting the Company to the *Bath*,[7] she offered to accompany him, he made an Excuse to go without her. She easily perceived his Coldness and the Reason why he pretended her going would be inconvenient and endured as much from the Discovery as any of her Sex could do: She dissembled it, however, before him, and took her Leave of him with the Show of no other Concern than his Absence occasioned: But this she did to take from him all Suspicion of her following him, as she intended, and had already laid a Scheme for.—From her first finding out that he designed to leave her behind, she plainly saw it was for no other Reason, than that being tired of her Conversation, he was willing to be at liberty to pursue new conquests; and wisely considering that Complaints, Tears, Swoonings, and all the Extravagancies which Women make use of in such Cases have little Prevalence over a Heart inclined to rove and only serve to render those who practice them more contemptible by robbing them of that Beauty which alone can bring

---

[7] *Bath*: a fashionable vacation and bathing spot with hot springs in south-west England.

back the fugitive Lover, she resolved to take another Course; and remembering the Height of Transport she enjoyed when the agreeable *Beauplaisir*
kneeled at her Feet, imploring her first Favours, she longed to prove the same
again. Not but a Woman of her Beauty and Accomplishments might have
beheld a Thousand in that Condition *Beauplaisir* had been; but with her Sex's
Modesty, she had not also thrown off another Virtue equally valuable, tho'
generally unfortunate, *Constancy*: She loved *Beauplaisir*; it was only he whose
Solicitations could give her Pleasure; and had she seen the whole Species
despairing, dying for her sake, it might, perhaps, have been a Satisfaction to
her Pride, but none to her more tender Inclination.—Her design was once
more to engage him, to hear him sigh, to see him languish, to feel the strenuous Pressures of his eager Arms, to be compelled, to be sweetly forced to
what she wished with equal Ardour was what she wanted and what she
had formed a Stratagem to obtain, in which she promised herself Success.

  She no sooner heard he had left the Town than making a Pretence to her
aunt that she was going to visit a Relation in the Country went towards *Bath*,
attended but by two Servants, who she found Reasons to quarrel with on the
Road and discharged: Clothing herself in a Habit she had brought with her,
she forsook the Coach and went into a Wagon in which Equipage she
arrived at *Bath*. The Dress she was in, was a round eared Cap, a short Red
Petticoat and a little Jacket of Grey Stuff;[8] all the rest of her Accoutrements
were answerable to these and joined with a broad Country Dialect, a rude
unpolished Air, which she, having been bred in these Parts, knew very well
how to imitate, with her Hair and Eye-brows blackened, made it impossible
for her to be known or taken for any other than what she seemed. Thus disguised did she offer herself to Service in the House where *Beauplaisir* lodged,
having made it her Business to find out immediately where he was.
Notwithstanding this Metamorphosis she was still extremely pretty; and the
Mistress of the House happening at that Time to want a Maid, was very glad
of the Opportunity of taking her. She was presently received into the Family;
and had a Post in it, (such as she would have chose, had she been left at her
Liberty,) that of making the Gentlemen's Beds, getting them their Breakfasts,
and waiting on them in their Chambers. Fortune in this Exploit was extremely
on her side; there were no others of the Male-Sex in the House, than an old
Gentleman, who had lost the Use of his Limbs with the Rheumatism and had
come thither for the Benefit of the Waters, and her beloved *Beauplaisir*; so that
she was in no Apprehensions of any Amorous Violence, but where she wished

---

  [8] Her clothes could be 'read' by her contemporaries. The cap was shaped to curve around the
face to the ears or below and had a frilled or laced-edged border; sometimes it had the fullness
of bonnets; although women of all classes wore caps, this style was usually associated with the
country and often worn under a hat by women working outdoors. Some women tied the skirt
up on both sides to display their decorative or embroidered petticoats, which, when short,
revealed their ankles and some leg. Jackets were close fitting, buttoned tightly at the waist, and
deep cut, which emphasized the woman's shape and also revealed the front of her dress or cleav-
age. Stuff was a fashionable wool fabric.

to find it. Nor were her Designs disappointed: He was fired with the first Sight of her; and tho' he did not presently take any farther Notice of her than giving her two or three hearty Kisses, yet she, who now understood that Language but too well, easily saw they were the Prelude to more substantial joys.—Coming the next Morning to bring his Chocolate as he had ordered, he caught her by the pretty Leg, which the Shortness of her Petticoat did not in the least oppose: then pulling her gently to him, asked her, how long she had been at Service?——How many Sweethearts she had? If she had ever been in Love? and many other such Questions, befitting one of the Degree she appeared to be: All which she answered with such seeming Innocence, as more enflamed the amorous Heart of him who talked to her. He compelled her to sit in his Lap; and gazing on her blushing Beauties, which, if possible, received Addition from her plain and rural Dress, he soon lost the Power of containing himself.——His wild Desires burst out in all his Words and Actions: he called her little Angel, Cherubim, swore he must enjoy her, though Death were to be the Consequence, devoured her Lips, her Breasts with greedy Kisses, held to his burning Bosom her half-yielding, half-reluctant Body, nor suffered her to get loose, till he had ravaged all and glutted each rapacious Sense with the Sweet Beauties of the pretty *Celia*, for that was the Name she bore in this second Expedition.——Generous as Liberality itself in all who gave him Joy this way, he gave her a handsome Sum of Gold, which she dare not now refuse for fear of creating some Mistrust and losing the Heart she so lately had regained; therefore taking it with an humble Curtsy, and a well counterfeited Show of surprize and Joy, cried O Law, Sir! what must I do for all this? He laughed at her Simplicity, and kissing her again, tho' less fervently than he had done before, bade her not be out of the Way when he came home at Night. She promised she would not and very obediently kept her Word.

His Stay at *Bath* exceeded not a Month; but in that Time his supposed Country Lass had persecuted him so much with her Fondness that in spite of the Eagerness with which he first enjoyed her, he was at last grown more weary of her than he had been of *Fantomina*; which she perceiving, would not be troublesome but quitting her Service remained privately in the Town till she heard he was on his Return; and in that Time provided herself of another Disguise to carry on a third Plot, which her inventing Brain had furnished her with, once more to renew his twice-decayed Ardours. The Dress she had ordered to be made was such as Widows wear in their first Mourning, which, together with the most afflicted and penitential Countenance that ever was seen, was no small Alteration to her who used to seem all Gaiety.——To add to this, her Hair, which she was accustomed to wear very loose, both when *Fantomina* and *Celia*, was now tied back so strait, and her Pinners[9] coming so very forward, that there was none of it to be seen.

---

[9] *Pinners*: a close fitting hat with a frill of linen and lace and long flaps on the sides that could be pinned down tightly; it was primarily a fashion of women of rank.

In fine, her Habit and her Air were so much changed, that she was not more difficult to be known in the rude Country Girl, than she was now in the sorrowful *Widow*. She knew that *Beauplaisir* came alone in his Chariot to the *Bath* and in the Time of her being Servant in the House where he lodged, heard nothing of any Body that was to accompany him to *London* and hoped he would return in the same Manner he had gone: She therefore hired Horses and a Man to attend her to an Inn about ten Miles on this side *Bath*, where having discharged them, she waited till the Chariot should come by; which when it did, and she saw that he was alone in it, she called to him that drove it to stop a Moment and going to the Door saluted the Master with these Words:

The Distressed and Wretched, Sir, (*said she,*) never fail to excite Compassion in a generous Mind; and I hope I am not deceived in my Opinion that yours is such:—You have the Appearance of a Gentleman, and cannot, when you hear my Story, refuse that Assistance which is in your Power to give to an unhappy Woman, who without it, may be rendered the most miserable of all created Beings.

It would not be very easy to represent the Surprize so odd an Address created in the Mind of him to whom it was made.——She had not the Appearance of one who wanted Charity; and what other Favour she required he could not conceive: But telling her, she might command any Thing in his Power gave her Encouragement to declare herself in this Manner: You may judge, (*resumed she,*) by the melancholy Garb I am in that I have lately lost all that ought to be valuable to Womankind; but it is impossible for you to guess the Greatness of my Misfortune, unless you had known my Husband, who was Master of every Perfection to endear him to a Wife's Affections.——But notwithstanding, I look on myself as the most unhappy of my Sex in out-living him. I must so far obey the Dictates of my Discretion as to take care of the little Fortune he left behind him, which being in the Hands of a Brother of his in *London*, will be all carried off to *Holland*, where he is going to settle; if I reach not the Town before he leaves it, I am undone for ever.——To which End I left *Bristol*, the Place where we lived, hoping to get a Place in the Stage at *Bath*, but they were all taken up before I came; and being, by a Hurt I got in a Fall, rendered incapable of travelling any long Journey on Horseback, I have no Way to go to London and must be inevitably ruined in the Loss of all I have on Earth without you have good Nature enough to admit me to take Part of your Chariot.

Here the feigned Widow ended her sorrowful Tale, which had been several Times interrupted by a Parenthesis of Sighs and Groans; and *Beauplaisir*, with a complaisant and tender Air, assured her of his Readiness to serve her in Things of much greater Consequence than what she desired of him; and told her, it would be an Impossibility of denying a Place in his Chariot to a Lady, who he could not behold without yielding one in his Heart. She answered the Compliments he made her but with Tears, which seemed to stream in such abundance from her Eyes, that she could not keep her Handkerchief from her Face one Moment. Being come into the Chariot, *Beauplaisir* said a thousand handsome Things to persuade her from giving way to so violent a Grief, which, he told her, would not only be destructive to her Beauty, but likewise her Health. But all his Endeavours for Consolement appeared ineffectual, and he began to think he should have but a dull Journey in the Company of one who seemed so obstinately devoted to the Memory of her dead Husband that there was no getting a word from her on any other Theme:—But bethinking himself of the celebrated Story of the *Ephesian* Matron,[10] it came into his Head to make Trial, she who seemed equally susceptible of *Sorrow* might not also be so too of love; and having began a Discourse on almost every other Topic and finding her still incapable of answering resolved to put it to the Proof, if this would have no more Effect to rouse her sleeping Spirits:——With a gay Air, therefore, though accompanied with the greatest Modesty and Respect, he turned the Conversation, as though without Design, on that Joy-giving Passion and soon discovered that was indeed the Subject she was best pleased to be entertained with; for on his giving her a Hint to begin upon, never any Tongue run more voluble than hers, on the prodigious Power it had to influence the Souls of those possessed of it, to Actions even the most distant from their Intentions, Principles, or Humours.——From that she passed to a Description of the Happiness of mutual Affection;—the unspeakable Ecstasy of those who meet with equal Ardency; and represented it in Colours so lively, and disclosed by the Gestures with which her Words were accompanied, and the Accent of her Voice so true a Feeling of what she said, that *Beauplaisir*, without being as stupid, as he was really the contrary, could not avoid perceiving there were Seeds of Fire, not yet extinguished, in this fair Widow's Soul, which wanted but the kindling Breath of tender Sighs to light into a Blaze.——He now thought himself as fortunate, as some Moments before he had the Reverse; and doubted not, but, that before they parted, he should find a Way to dry the Tears of this lovely Mourner to the Satisfaction of them both. He did not, however, offer, as he had done to *Fantomina* and *Celia*, to urge his Passion directly to her, but by a thousand little softening Artifices, which he well knew how to use, gave her leave to guess he was enamoured. When they came to the Inn where they were to lie he declared himself somewhat more freely and perceiving she did not resent it past Forgiveness, grew more encroaching still:——He now took the Liberty of kissing away her Tears and catching the Sighs as they issued from her Lips; telling her if Grief was Infectious, he was resolved to have his Share; protesting he would gladly

---

[10] *Ephesian Matron*: the matron was so famous for her fidelity to her husband that women from neighboring countries came to see her. When her husband died, she watched over the burial vault day and night, weeping inconsolably. A soldier guarding the nearby crosses of recently crucified criminals heard her, comforted her with words and food, then seduced her. While he stayed with her, one of the crucified bodies was taken for burial; in order to prevent the soldier's disgrace and punishment, the matron told him to replace the body with that of her former husband; Petronius, *The Satyricon*, 'Eumolpus', 111.

exchange Passions with her and be content to bear her Load of *Sorrow*, if she would as willingly ease the Burden of his *Love.*——She said little in answer to the strenuous pressures with which at last he ventured to enfold her, but not thinking it decent for the Character she had assumed to yield so suddenly and unable to deny both his and her own Inclinations, she counterfeited a fainting and fell motionless upon his Breast.——He had no great Notion that she was in a real Fit, and the Room they supped in happening to have a Bed in it, he took her in his Arms and laid her on it, believing, that whatever her Distemper was, that was the most proper Place to convey her to.——He laid himself down by her and endeavoured to bring her to herself; and she was too grateful to her kind Physician at her returning Sense, to remove from the Posture he had put her in, without his Leave.

It may, perhaps, seem strange that *Beauplaisir* should in such near Intimacies continue still deceived: I know there are Men who will swear it is an Impossibility and that no Disguise could hinder them from knowing a Woman they had once enjoyed. In answer to these Scruples, I can only say, that besides the Alteration which the change of Dress made in her, she was so admirably skilled in the Art of feigning, that she had the Power of putting on almost what Face she pleased, and knew so exactly how to form her Behaviour to the Character she represented that all the comedians at both Playhouses are infinitely short of her Performances: She could vary her very Glances, tune her Voice to Accents the most different imaginable from those in which she spoke when she appeared herself.——These Aids from Nature joined to the Wiles of Art, and the Distance between the Places where the Imagined *Fantomina* and *Celia* were might very well prevent his having any Thought that they were the same, or that the fair *Widow* was either of them: It never so much as entered his Head, and though he did fancy he observed in the Face of the latter, Features which were not altogether unknown to him, yet he could not recollect when or where he had known them;—and being told by her, that from her Birth, she had never removed from *Bristol*, a Place where he never was, he rejected the Belief of having seen her, and supposed his Mind had been deluded by an Idea of some other, whom she might have a Resemblance of.

They passed the Time of their Journey in as much Happiness as the most luxurious Gratification of wild Desires could make them; and when they came to the End of it, parted not without a mutual Promise of seeing each other often.——He told her to what Place she should direct a Letter to him; and she assured him she would send to let him know where to come to her, as soon as she was fixed in Lodgings.

She kept her Promise and charmed with the continuance of his eager Fondness went not home but into private Lodgings, whence she wrote to him to visit her the first Opportunity, and enquire for the Widow *Bloomer.*——She had no sooner dispatched this Billet, than she repaired to the House where she had lodged as *Fantomina*, charging the People if *Beauplaisir* should come there, not to let him know she had been out of Town. From thence she wrote to him, in a different Hand, a long Letter of Complaint, that he had been so cruel in not sending one Letter to her all the Time He had been absent, entreated to see him, and concluded with subscribing herself his unalterably Affectionate *Fantomina*. She received in one Day Answers to both these. The first contained these Lines:

To the Charming Mrs. *Bloomer*,

It would be impossible, my Angel! for me to express the thousandth Part of that Infinity of Transport, the sight of your dear Letter gave me.——Never was Women formed to charm like you: Never did any look like you,——write like you,——bless like you,——nor did ever Man adore as I do.——Since Yesterday we parted, I have seemed a Body without a Soul, and had you not by this inspiring Billet, given me new Life, I know not what by To-morrow I should have been.——I will be with you this Evening about Five:——O, 'tis an Age till then!——But the Cursed Formalities of Duty oblige me to Dine with my Lord—who never rises from Table till that Hour;—therefore Adieu till then sweet lovely Mistress of the Soul and all the Faculties of

Your most faithful,

BEAUPLAISIR.

The other was in this Manner:

To the Lovely *Fantomina*,

If you were half so sensible as you ought of your own Power of charming, you would be assured, that to be unfaithful or unkind to you, would be among the things that are in their very Natures Impossibilities.——It was my Misfortune, not my Fault, that you were not persecuted every Post with a Declaration of my unchanging Passion; but I had unluckily forgot the Name of the Woman at who's House you are, and knew not how to form a Direction that it might come safe to your Hands.——And, indeed, the Reflection how you might misconstrue my Silence, brought me to town some weeks sooner than I intended——If you knew how I have languished to renew those blessings I am permitted to enjoy in your Society, you would rather pity than condemn

Your ever faithful,

BEAUPLAISIR.

P.S. I fear I cannot see you till To-morrow; some Business has unluckily fallen out that will engross my Hours till then.——Once more, my Dear, Adieu.

Traitor! (*cried she*,) as soon as she had read them, 'tis thus our silly, fond, believing Sex are served when they put Faith in Man: So had I been deceived and cheated, had I like the rest believed, and sat down mourning in Absence, and vainly waiting recovered Tendernesses.——How do some Women (*continued she*) make their Life a Hell, burning in fruitless Expectations and dreaming out their Days in Hopes and Fears, then wake at last to all the Horror of Despair?——But I have outwitted even the most Subtle of the deceiving Kind, and while he thinks to fool me is himself the only beguiled Person.

She made herself, most certainly, extremely happy in the Reflection on the Success of her Stratagems; and while the Knowledge of his Inconstancy and Levity of Nature kept her from having that real Tenderness for him she would else have had, she found the Means of gratifying the Inclination she had for his agreeable Person in as full a Manner as she could wish. She had all the Sweets of Love but as yet had tasted none of the Gall and was in a State of Contentment, which might be envied by the more Delicate.

When the expected Hour arrived, she found that her Lover had lost no part of the Fervency with which he had parted from her; but when the next Day she received him as *Fantomina*, she perceived a prodigious Difference; which led her again into Reflections on the Unaccountableness of Men's Fancies, who still prefer the last Conquest, only because it is the last.——Here was an evident Proof of it; for there could not be a Difference in Merit, because they were the same Person; but the Widow *Bloomer* was a more new Acquaintance than *Fantomina*, and therefore esteemed more valuable. This, indeed, must be said of *Beauplaisir*, that he had a greater Share of good Nature than most of his Sex, who, for the most part, when they are weary of an Intrigue, break it entirely off, without any Regard to the Despair of the abandoned Nymph. Though he retained no more than a bare Pity and Complaisance for *Fantomina*, yet believing she loved him to an Excess, would not entirely forsake her, though the Continuance of his Visits was now become rather a Penance than a Pleasure.

The Widow *Bloomer* triumphed some Time longer over the Heart of this Inconstant, but at length her Sway was at an End, and she sunk in this Character, to the same Degree of Tastelessness as she had done before in that of *Fantomina* and *Celia*.——She presently perceived it, but bore it as she had always done; it being but what she expected, she had prepared herself for it, and had another Project in *embryo*, which she soon ripened into Action. She did not, indeed, complete it altogether so suddenly as she had done the others, by reason there must be Persons employed in it; and the Aversion she had to any *Confidants* in her Affairs and the Caution with which she had hitherto acted, and which she was still determined to continue, made it very difficult for her to find a Way without breaking through that Resolution to compass what she wished.——She got over the Difficulty at last, however, by proceeding in a Manner, if possible, more extraordinary than all her former Behaviour:——Muffling herself up in her Hood one Day, she went into the Park about the Hour when there are a great many necessitous Gentlemen, who think themselves above doing what they call little Things for a Maintenance, walking in the *Mall*,[11] to take a *Camelion* Treat,[12] and fill their Stomachs with Air instead of Meat. Two of those, who by their

---

[11] *Mall*: half-mile-long fashionable promenade in St James's Park.
[12] *Camelion Treat*: changeable, fleeting, built on air. Chameleons at that time were thought to live on air.

Physiognomy[13] she thought most proper for her Purpose, she beckoned to come to her; and taking them into a Walk more remote from Company, began to communicate the Business she had with them in these Words: I am sensible, Gentlemen, (*said she,*) that, through the Blindness of Fortune, and Partiality of the World, Merit frequently goes unrewarded, and that those of the best Pretensions meet with the least Encouragement:—I ask your Pardon, (*continued she,*) perceiving they seemed surprized, if I am mistaken in the Notion that you two may perhaps be of the Number of those who have Reason to complain of the Injustice of Fate; but if you are such as I take you for, have a Proposal to make you, which may be of some little Advantage to you. Neither of them made any immediate Answer but appeared buried in Consideration for some Moments. At length, we should, doubtless, Madam, (*said one of them,*) willingly come into any Measures to oblige you, provided they are such as may bring us into no Danger, either as to our Persons or Reputations. That which I require of you, (*resumed she,*) has nothing in it criminal: All that I desire is *Secrecy* in what you are intrusted, and to disguise yourselves in such a Manner as you cannot be known, if hereafter seen by the Person on whom you are to impose.—In fine, the Business is only an innocent Frolic, but if blazed abroad, might be taken for too great a Freedom in me:——Therefore, if you resolve to assist me, here are five Pieces to drink my Health and assure you that I have not discoursed you on an Affair I design not to proceed in; and when it is accomplished fifty more lie ready for your Acceptance. These Words, and, above all, the Money, which was a Sum which, 'tis probable, they had not seen of a long Time, made them immediately assent to all she desired and press for the Beginning of their Employment. But Things were not yet ripe for Execution; and she told them that the next Day they should be let into the Secret, charging them to meet her in the same Place at an Hour she appointed. 'Tis hard to say, which of these Parties went away best pleased; *they*, that Fortune had sent them so unexpected a Windfall; or *she*, that she had found Persons, who appeared so well qualified to serve her.

Indefatigable in the Pursuit of whatsoever her Humour was bent upon, she had no sooner left her new-engaged Emissaries, than she went in search of a House for the completing her Project.——She pitched on one very large and magnificently furnished, which she hired by the Week, giving them the Money beforehand, to prevent any Inquiries. The next Day she repaired to the Park, where she met the punctual Squires of low Degree; and ordering them to follow her to the House she had taken, told them they must condescend to appear like Servants and gave each of them a very rich Livery. Then writing a Letter to *Beauplaisir*, in a Character vastly different from either of those she had made use of as *Fantomina* or the fair Widow *Bloomer* ordered one of them to deliver it into his own Hands, to bring back an Answer, and to be

---

[13] *Physiognomy*: the pseudo-science of judging character by the bones and features of faces.

careful that he sifted out nothing of the Truth.——I do not fear, (*said she,*) that you should discover to him who I am, because that is a Secret of which you yourselves are ignorant; but I would have you be so careful in your Replies that he may not think the Concealment springs from any other Reasons than your great Integrity to your Trust.——Seem therefore to know my whole Affairs; and let your refusing to make him Partaker in the Secret appear to be only the Effect of your Zeal for my Interest and Reputation. Promises of entire Fidelity on the one side and Reward on the other being past, the Messenger made what haste he could to the House of *Beauplaisir*; and being there told where he might find him, performed exactly the Injunction that had been given him. But never Astonishment exceeding that which *Beauplaisir* left at the reading this Billet, in which he found these lines:

To the All-conquering BEAUPLAISIR.

I Imagine not that 'tis a new Thing to you, to be told, you are the greatest Charm in Nature to our Sex: I shall therefore, not to fill up my Letter with any impertinent Praises on your Wit or Person, only tell you, that I am infinite in Love with both, and if you have a Heart not too deeply engaged, should think myself the happiest of my sex in being capable of inspiring it with some Tenderness.——There is but one Thing in my Power to refuse you, which is the Knowledge of my Name, which believing the Sight of my Face will render no Secret, you must not take it ill that I conceal from you.——The Bearer of this is a Person I can trust; send by him your Answer; but endeavour not to dive into the Meaning of this Mystery, which will be impossible for you to unravel, and at the same Time very much disoblige me:——But that you may be in no Apprehensions of being imposed on by a Woman unworthy of your Regard, I will venture to assure you, the first and greatest Men in the Kingdom, would think themselves blest to have that Influence over me you have, though unknown to yourself acquired.——But I need not go about to raise your Curiosity, by giving you any Idea of what my Person is; if you think fit to be satisfied, resolve to visit me To-morrow about Three in the Afternoon; and though my Face is hid, you shall not want sufficient Demonstration, that she who takes these unusual Measures to commence a Friendship with you, is neither Old, nor Deformed. Till then I am,

Yours,

INCOGNITA.

He had scarce come to the conclusion before he asked the Person who brought it from what Place he came;——the Name of the Lady he served;——if she were a Wife, or Widow, and several other Questions directly opposite to the Directions of the Letter; but Silence would have availed him as much as did all those Testimonies of Curiosity: No *Italian Bravo*,[14] employed in Business of the like Nature, performed his Office with more Artifice; and the impatient Enquirer was convinced that nothing but doing as he was desired could give him any Light into the Character of the Woman who declared so

---

[14] *Italian Bravo*: daring villain, hired assassin.

violent a Passion for him; and little fearing any Consequence which could ensue from such an Encounter, resolved to rest satisfied till he was informed of every Thing from herself, not imagining this *Incognita* varied so much from the Generality of her Sex as to be able to refuse the Knowledge of any Thing to the Man she loved with that Transcendency of Passion she professed, and which his many successes with the Ladies gave him Encouragement enough to believe. He therefore took Pen and Paper, and answered her Letter in Terms tender enough for a Man who had never seen the Person to whom he wrote. The Words were as follows:

To the Obliging and Witty

INCOGNITA.

Though to tell me I am happy enough to be liked by a Woman, such, as by your Manner of Writing, I imagine you to be, is an Honour which I can never sufficiently acknowledge, yet I know not how I am able to content myself with admiring the Wonders of your Wit alone: I am certain, a Soul like yours must shine in your Eyes with a vivacity, which must bless all they look on.——I shall, however, endeavour to restrain myself in those Bounds you are pleased to set me, till by the Knowledge of my inviolable Fidelity, I may be thought worthy of gazing on that Heaven I am now but to enjoy in contemplation.——You need not doubt my glad Compliance with your obliging Summons: There is a Charm in your Lines, which gives too sweet an Idea of their lovely Author to be resisted.——I am all impatient for the blissful Moment, which is to throw me at your Feet, and give me an Opportunity of convincing you that I am,

Your everlasting Slave,

BEAUPLAISIR.

Nothing could be more pleased than she, to whom it was directed, at the Receipt of this Letter; but when she was told how inquisitive he had been concerning her Character and Circumstances, she could not forbear laughing heartily to think of the Tricks she had played him and applauding her own Strength of Genius and Force of Resolution, which by such unthought-of Ways could triumph over her Lover's Inconstancy, and render that very Temper, which to other Women is the greatest Curse, a Means to make herself more blessed.——Had he been faithful to me, (*said she, to herself,*) either as *Fantomina*, or *Celia*, or the Widow *Bloomer*, the most violent Passion, if it does not change its Object, in Time will wither: Possession naturally abates the Vigour of Desire, and I should have had, at best, but a cold, insipid, husband-like Lover in my Arms; but by these Arts of passing on him as a new Mistress whenever the Ardour, which alone makes Love a Blessing, begins to diminish, for the former one, I have him always raving, wild, impatient, longing, dying.——O that all neglected Wives, and fond abandoned Nymphs would take this Method!—Men would be caught in their own Snare, and have no Cause to scorn our easy, weeping, wailing Sex! Thus did she pride herself as if secure she never should have any Reason to repent the present

243

Gaiety of her Humour. The Hour drawing near in which he was to come, she dressed herself in as magnificent a Manner as if she were to be that Night at a Ball at Court, endeavouring to repair the want of those Beauties which the Vizard should conceal, by setting forth the others with the greatest Care and Exactness. Her fine Shape and Air and Neck appeared to great Advantage; and by that which was to be seen of her, one might believe the rest to be perfectly agreeable. *Beauplaisir* was prodigiously charmed as well with her Appearance, as with the Manner she entertained him: But though he was wild with Impatience for the Sight of a Face which belonged to so exquisite a Body, yet he would not immediately press for it, believing before he left her he should easily obtain that Satisfaction.——A noble Collation being over, he began to sue for the Performance of her Promise of granting every Thing he could ask, excepting the Sight of her Face, and Knowledge of her Name. It would have been a ridiculous Piece of Affection in her to have seemed coy in complying with what she herself had been the first in desiring: She yielded without even a Show of Reluctance: And if there be any true Felicity in an Amour such as theirs, both here enjoyed it to the full. But not in the Height of all their mutual Raptures could he prevail on her to satisfy his Curiosity with the Sight of her Face: she told him that she hoped he knew so much of her as might serve to convince him she was not unworthy of his tenderest Regard; and if he could not content himself with that which she was wishing to reveal, and which was the Conditions of their meeting, dear as he was to her, she would rather part with him for ever than consent to gratify an Inquisitiveness, which, in her Opinion, had no Business with his Love. It was in vain that he endeavoured to make her sensible of her Mistake; and that this Restraint was the greatest Enemy imaginable to the Happiness of them both: She was not to be persuaded, and he was obliged to desist his Solicitations, though determined in his Mind to compass what he so ardently desired, before he left the House. He then turned the Discourse wholly on the Violence of the Passion he had for her; and expressed the greatest Discontent in the World at the Apprehensions of being separated;—swore he could dwell for ever in her Arms, and with such an undeniable Earnestness pressed to be permitted to tarry with her the whole Night, that had she been less charmed with his renewed Eagerness of Desire, she scarce would have had the Power of refusing him; but in granting this Request, she was not without a Thought that he had another Reason for making it besides the Extremity of his Passion and had it immediately in her Head how to disappoint him.

The Hours of Repose being arrived, he begged she would retire to her Chambers; to which she consented, but obliged him to go to Bed first; which he did not much oppose, because he supposed she would not lie in her Mask,[15] and doubted not but the Morning's Dawn would bring the wished Discovery.——The two imagined Servants ushered him to his new Lodging;

[15] *Mask*: masks were worn not only to disguise identity but outdoors to protect the face from inclement weather.

where he lay some Moments in all the Perplexity imaginable at the Oddness of this Adventure. But he suffered not these Cogitations to be of any long continuance: She came, but came in the Dark; which being no more than he expected by the former Part of her Proceedings, he said nothing of; but as much Satisfaction as he found in her Embraces, nothing ever longed for the Approach of Day with more Impatience than he did. At last it came; but how great was his Disappointment, when by the Noises he heard in the Street, the Hurry of the Coaches, and the Cries of Penny-Merchants,[16] he was convinced it was Night no where but with him. He was still in the same Darkness as before; for she had taken care to blind the Windows in such a manner, that not the least Chink was left to let in Day.——He complained of her Behaviour in Terms that she would not have been able to resist yielding to if she had not been certain it would have been the Ruin of her Passion:—She, therefore, answered him only as she had done before; and getting out of the Bed from him, flew out of the Room with too much Swiftness for him to have overtaken her if he had attempted it. The Moment she left him, the two Attendants entered the Chamber, and plucking down the Implements which had screened him from the Knowledge of that which he so much desired to find out, restored his Eyes once more to Day:——They attended to assist him in Dressing, brought him Tea, and by their Obsequiousness, let him see there was but one Thing which the Mistress of them would not gladly oblige him in.——He was so much out of Humour, however, at the Disappointment of his curiosity, that he resolved never to make a second Visit.——Finding her in an outer Room, he made no Scruple of expressing the Sense he had of the little Trust she reposed in him, and at last plainly told her, he could not submit to receive Obligations from a Lady, who thought him incapable of keeping a Secret, which she made no Difficulty of letting her Servants into——He resented,—he once more entreated,—he said all that Man could do to prevail on her to unfold the Mystery; but all his Adjurations were fruitless; and he went out of the House determined never to re-enter it, till she should pay the Price of his Company with the Discovery of her Face and Circumstances.——She suffered him to go with this Resolution and doubted not but he would recede from it, when he reflected on the happy Moments they had passed together; but if he did not, she comforted herself with the Design of forming some other Stratagem, with which to impose on him a fourth Time.

She kept the House and her Gentlemen-Equipage for about a Fortnight, in which Time she continued to write to him as *Fantomina* and the Widow *Bloomer* and received the Visits he sometimes made to each; but his Behaviour to both was grown so cold, that she began to grow as weary of receiving his now insipid Caresses as he was of offering them: She was beginning to think in what Manner she should drop these two Characters, when

---

[16] *Penny-Merchants*: street hawkers with cheap wares.

the sudden Arrival of her Mother, who had been some Time in a foreign Country, obliged her to put an immediate Stop to the Course of her whimsical Adventures.——That Lady, who was severely virtuous, did not approve of many Things she had been told of the Conduct of her Daughter; and though it was not in the Power of any Person in the World to inform her of the Truth of what she had been guilty of, yet she heard enough to make her keep her afterwards in a Restraint, little agreeable to her Humour, and the Liberties to which she had been accustomed.

But this Confinement was not the greatest Part of the Trouble of this now afflicted Lady: She found the Consequences of her amorous Follies would be, without almost a Miracle, impossible to be concealed:——She was with Child; and though she would easily have found Means to have screened even this from the Knowledge of the World had she been at liberty to have acted with the same unquestionable Authority over herself as she did before the coming of her Mother, yet now all her Invention was at a Loss for a Stratagem to impose on a Woman of her Penetration:——By eating little, lacing prodigious strait, and the Advantage of a great Hoop-Petticoat,[17] however, her Bigness was not taken notice of, and, perhaps, she would not have been suspected till the Time of her going into the country, where her Mother designed to send her, and from whence she intended to make her escape to some Place where she might be delivered with Secrecy, if the Time of it had not happened much sooner than she expected.—A Ball being at Court, the good old Lady was willing she should partake of the Diversion of it as a Farewell to the Town.—It was there she was seized with those Pangs, which none in her condition are exempt from:——She could not conceal the sudden Rack which all at once invaded her; or had her Tongue been mute, her wildly rolling Eyes, the Distortion of her Features, and the Convulsions which shook her whole Frame, in spite of her, would have revealed she laboured under some terrible Shock of Nature.——Every Body was surprized, every Body was concerned, but few guessed at the Occasion.—Her Mother grieved beyond Expression, doubted not but she was struck with the Hand of Death; and ordered her to be carried Home in a Chair, while herself followed in another.——A Physician was immediately sent for: But he presently perceiving what was her Distemper, called the old Lady aside, and told her, it was not a Doctor of his Sex, but one of her own her Daughter stood in need of.—Never was Astonishment and Horror greater than that which seized the Soul of this afflicted Parent at these Words: She could not for a Time believe the Truth of what she heard; but he insisting on it, and conjuring her to send for a Midwife, she was at length convinced of it——All the Pity and Tenderness

---

[17] *Hoop-Petticoat*: moralists and humorists frequently attacked women's fashions as hiding, if not encouraging, immoral behaviour. By tightening her corsets with the laces and raising large hoop skirts slightly above the stomach, a woman could hide her pregnancy for many months. *Spectator* no. 2 for 2 Mar. 1711 has Will Honeycomb say that he can 'inform you . . . whose Frailty was covered by such a Sort of Petticoat'.

she had been for some Moment before possessed of, now vanished and were succeeded by an adequate Shame and Indignation:——She flew to the Bed where her Daughter was lying, and telling her what she had been informed of, and which she was now far from doubting, commanded her to reveal the Name of the Person whose insinuations had drawn her to this Dishonour. ——It was a great while before she could be brought to confess any Thing, and much longer before she could be prevailed on to name the Man whom she so fatally had loved; but the Rack of Nature growing more fierce, and the enraged old Lady protesting no Help should be afforded her while she persisted in her Obstinacy, she, with great Difficulty and Hesitation in her Speech, at last pronounced the Name of *Beauplaisir*. She had no sooner satisfied her weeping Mother than that sorrowful Lady sent Messengers at the same Time for a Midwife and for the Gentleman who had occasioned the other's being wanted.—He happened by Accident to be at home and immediately obeyed the Summons though prodigiously surprized what Business a Lady so much a Stranger to him could have to impart.——But how much greater was his Amazement, when taking him into her Closet, she there acquainted him with her Daughter's Misfortune, of the Discovery she had made, and how far he was concerned in it?—All the Idea one can form of wild Astonishments was mean to what he felt:——He assured her, that the young Lady her Daughter was a Person whom he had never, more than at a Distance, admired.—— That he had indeed, spoke to her in public Company, but that he never had a Thought which tended to her Dishonour.——His Denials, if possible, added to the Indignation she was before enflamed with:——She had no longer Patience; and carrying him into the Chamber, where she was just delivered of a fine Girl, cried out, I will not be imposed on: The Truth by one of you shall be revealed.——*Beauplaisir* being brought to the Bedside, was beginning to address himself to the Lady in it, to beg she would clear the Mistake her Mother was involved in; when she, covering herself with the Clothes and ready to die a second Time with the inward Agitations of her Soul shrieked out, Oh, I am undone!—I cannot live, and bear this Shame!——But the old Lady believing that now or never was the Time to dive into the Bottom of this Mystery, forcing her to rear her Head, told her, she should not hope to Escape the Scrutiny of a Parent she had dishonoured in such a Manner, and point-ing to *Beauplaisir*, Is this the Gentleman, (*said she*,) to whom you owe your Ruin? or have you deceived me by a fictitious Tale? Oh! no, (*resumed the trem-bling Creature*,) he is, indeed, the innocent Cause of my Undoing:—Promise me your Pardon (*continued she*,) and I will relate the Means. Here she ceased, expecting what she would reply, which, on hearing *Beauplaisir* cry out, What mean you, Madam? I your Undoing, who never harboured the least Design on you in my Life, she did in these Words, Though the Injury you have done your Family, (*said she*,) is of a Nature which cannot justly hope Forgiveness, yet be assured I shall much sooner excuse you when satisfied of the Truth than while I am kept in a Suspense, if possible, as vexatious as the Crime itself is to me. Encouraged by this she related the whole Truth. And 'tis difficult to determine, if *Beauplaisir* or the Lady were most surprized at what they heard; he, that he should have been blinded so often by her Artifices, or she, that so young a Creature should have the Skill to make use of them. Both sat for some time in a profound Revery; till at length she broke it first in these Words: Pardon, Sir, (*said she*,) the Trouble I have given you: I must confess it was with a Design to oblige you to repair the supposed Injury you had done this unfortunate Girl by marrying her, but now I know not what to say:——The Blame is wholly her's, and I have nothing to request further of you than that you will not divulge the distracted Folly she has been guilty of.——He answered her in Terms perfectly polite; but made no Offer of that which, perhaps, she expected, though could not, now informed of her Daughter's Proceedings, demand. He assured her, however, that if she would commit the new-born Lady to his Care, he would discharge it faithfully.[18] But neither of them would consent to that; and he took his Leave, full of Cogitations, more confused than ever he had known in his whole Life. He continued to visit there, to enquire after her Health every Day; but the old Lady perceiving there was nothing likely to ensue from these Civilities, but, perhaps, a Renewing of the Crime, she entreated him to refrain; and as soon as her Daughter was in a condition, sent her to a Monastery in *France*,[19] the Abbess of which had been her particular Friend. And thus ended an Intrigue, which, considering the Time it lasted, was as full of Variety as any, perhaps, that many Ages has produced.

FINIS

[18] *discharge it faithfully*: children belonged to their fathers, who were the custodial parents regardless of their legitimacy.

[19] *Monastery in France*: the monasteries were centres of learning, and fashionable women often stayed there. They received visitors, improved their educations (dancing, music, art, poetry, and languages flourished), and enjoyed the society of other cultured women.

THE

REFORM'D COQUET;

A

NOVEL.

By Mrs. *DAVYS*,
Author of *The Humours of* York.

Nil moror quàm Puerilitèr, modò
*Utiliter.**   Erafm.

LONDON;
Printed by H. WOODFALL, for the AUTHOR;
and fold by J. STEPHENS, at the *Bible* in
Butcher-Row, near St. *Clement's* Church.
M.DCC.XXIV.   (Price bound 3 *s*.)

* Erasmus, 'I die not so much beautifuly as usefully', unidentified.

Reproduced courtesy of The British Library (12604 aaa 5).

Mary Davys
(1674-1732)

MARY DAVYS was born in Dublin and married the headmaster of the free school of St. Patrick's Cathedral, Dublin. He died at age 29 in November 1698; Mary Davys was 24, and Jonathan Swift, who knew the couple well, records that two years later she 'went for mere want to England'. As she tells it, she sold her first fiction, *The Lady's Tale*, in 1700 for three guineas and moved to York shortly thereafter. She returned to London and later moved to Cambridge and opened a coffeehouse. Swift was a reluctant correspondent of hers but saw her as late as about five years before her death and helped convey her legacy to her sister. In Cambridge she became part of an intellectual circle of friends. These students, clergymen, and gentlemen encouraged her writing and, according to her account, helped her publish *The Reformed Coquet* by subscription, a profitable practice she continued with all of her subsequent writing. Davys died in Cambridge five years after the publication of *The Accomplished Rake*, her last original novel, and the year *The Cousins* (1725) was republished as *The False Friend*.

Her first prose fictions, *The Amours of Alcippus and Lucippe* (1704) and *The Fugitive* (1705) were conventionally episodic tales, but her subsequent revisions of them and the Irish material in *The Fugitive* (retitled *The Merry Wanderer*, 1725) give them unusual interest. Even these early works have the kind of gritty material and willingness to engage in charged topics that set her apart from most of her contemporaries; for example, she satirizes British prejudices and ideas of the Irish, includes material on the Irish rebellion, and has incidents of suicide and striking portraits of poverty and its results. In 1716, her play, *The Northern Heiress*, was performed three times at Lincoln's Inn Fields. It uses York material and has a good plot in which Isabella, the heiress, pretends to have lost her fortune in order to test her fiancé's love. *The Reformed Coquet* (1724) shows the influence of Restoration and eighteenth-century marriage comedies; it was immediately popular and went through seven editions by 1760. The next year, to take advantage of her success, Davys published *The Works of Mrs. Davys* in two volumes, which included revisions of her early pieces, a comedy tantalizingly entitled *The Self-Rival: A Comedy As it should have been Acted at the Theatre Royal in Drury-Lane*, and several new prose fictions. Her final novel, *The Accomplished Rake; or, Modern Fine Gentleman* (1727), can be related fruitfully to later novels by Fielding and Richardson; it includes a 'rake's progress',

251

resourceful women characters, and a rich, carefully constructed plot. Her novels began to receive new attention in the mid-twentieth century. *Familiar Letters Betwixt a Gentleman and A Lady* appeared in the Augustan Reprint Series in 1955 with an introduction by Robert Adams Day, which praised it for 'middle-class realism, its characterizations, its breezy humor,' and its plot (ii); William McBurney included *The Accomplished Rake* in *Four before Richardson* (1963).

The Reformed Coquet is a carefully written, well-plotted novel. In the Preface, Davys places herself firmly in the tradition of the novel, a word she uses, and astutely comments on what she has drawn from it and comic drama for the delight of the reader. She calls attention to her art and, using the better-known tradition of dramatic prologues, classifies curmudgeonly readers humorously and confronts a common complaint already being made about women and women writers: 'would the Poets, Printers, and Booksellers but speak truth of it, they would own themselves more obliged to that one Subject [love] for their Bread, than all the rest put together'. Within a clever *Bildungsroman* that explores marriage and relationships between the sexes, she touches upon other women's issues such as nursing infants, old age, and laws concerning engagement and marriage. Although one of her characters laments that 'Nature has denied us Strength to revenge our own Wrongs', the heroine demonstrates that her cleverness and wit aided by a good man can do just that. The novel is full of clever tricks and disguises deployed for a variety of purposes, weaves strategies from several genres together expertly, and delivers what Davys promises: 'an hour or two of agreeable Amusement'.

P.R.B.

The Reformed Coquet; or, The Memoirs of Amoranda

DEDICATION

To the Ladies of Great Britain

At a time when the Town is so full of Masquerades,[1] Operas, New Plays, Conjurers, Monsters, and feigned Devils;[2] how can I, Ladies, expect you to throw away an hour upon the less agreeable Amusements my *Coquet* can give you? But she who has assurance to write has certainly the vanity of expecting to be read: All Authors see a Beauty in their own Compositions, which perhaps nobody else can find; as Mothers think their own Offspring amiable,

---

[1] *Masquerades*: evening parties at which the revellers wear costumes and hide their own identities carefully while guessing those of others. They were reputed to be good places for illicit meetings. See n. 8, *The British Recluse*.

[2] Magicians, tricksters, and other street hustlers were sources of amusement and annoyance. *Monsters*: people with hunchbacks or other physical deformities, who congregated around Tower Bridge.

how deficient soever Nature has been to them. But whatever my Faults may be, my Design is good, and hope you *British* Ladies will accordingly encourage it.

If I have here touched a young Lady's Vanity and Levity, it was to show her how amiable she is without those Blots, which certainly stain the Mind, and stamp Deformity where the greatest Beauties would shine, were they banished. I believe everybody will join with my Opinion, that the *English* Ladies are the most accomplished Women in the World, that, generally speaking, their Behaviour is so exact, that even Envy itself cannot strike at their Conduct: but even you yourselves must own, there are some few among you of a different stamp, who change their Gold for Dross, and barter the highest Perfections for the lowest Weaknesses. Would but this latter sort endeavour as much to act like Angels, as they do to look like them, the Men, instead of Reproaches, would heap them with Praises, and their cold Indifference would be turned to Idolatry. But who can forsake a Fault, till they are convinced they are guilty? Vanity is a lurking subtle Thief that works itself insensibly into our Bosoms, and while we declare our dislike to it, know not 'tis so near us; everybody being (as a witty Gentleman has somewhere said) provided with a Racket to strike it from themselves.

The Heroine of the following Sheets will tell you the Advantages of a kind friendly Admonition, and when the little Lightnesses of her Mind were removed, she became worthy of imitation. One little word of Advice, Ladies, and I have done: When you grow weary of Flattery and begin to listen to matrimonial Addresses, choose a Man with fine Sense, as well as a fine Wig, and let him have some Merit as well as much Embroidery: This will make Coxcombs give ground, and Men of Sense will equally admire your Conduct with your Beauty. I am,

LADIES,

Your most Devoted,
And most Obedient
Humble Servant,
MA: DAVYS.

THE PREFACE

IDLENESS has so long been an Excuse for Writing, that I am almost ashamed to tell the World it was that, and that only, which produced the following Sheets. Few People are so inconsiderable in Life, but they may at some time do good; and though I must own my Purse is (by a thousand Misfortunes) grown wholly useless to everybody, my Pen is at the service of the Public, and if it can but make some impression upon the young unthinking Minds of some of my own Sex, I shall bless my Labour and reap an unspeakable Satisfaction: but as I have addressed them in another place, I shall say no more of them here.

I come now to the worthy Gentlemen of Cambridge, *from whom I have received so many Marks of Favour on a thousand Occasions, that my Gratitude is highly*

concerned how to make a due acknowledgment: and I own their civil, generous, good-natured Behaviour towards me, is the only thing I have now left worth boasting of. When I had written a Sheet or two of this Novel, I communicated my Design to a couple of young Gentlemen, whom I knew to be Men of Taste, and both my Friends; they approved of what I had done, advised me to proceed, then print it by Subscription:[3] into which Proposal many of the Gentlemen entered, among whom were a good number of both the grave and the young Clergy, who the World will easily believe had a greater view to Charity than Novelty; and it was not to the Book, but the Author, they subscribed. They knew her to be a Relict[4] of one of their Brotherhood, and one, who (unless Poverty be a Sin) never did anything to disgrace the Gown; and for those Reasons encouraged all her Undertakings.

But as this Book was written at Cambridge, I am a little apprehensive some may imagine the Gentlemen had a hand in it. It would be very hard, if their Humanity to me, should bring an imputation upon themselves so greatly below their Merit, which I can by no means consent to; and do therefore assure the World, I am not acquainted with one member of that worthy and learned Society of Men, whose Pens are not employed in things infinitely above anything I can pretend to be the Author of: So that I only am accountable for every Fault of my Book; and if it has any Beauties, I claim the Merit of them too. Though I cannot but say, I did once apply myself to a young Genius for a Preface, which he seemed to decline, and I soon considered the Brightness of his Pen would only eclipse the glimmering Light of my own; so called back my Request, and resolved to entertain my Readers with a Pattern, in the Preface, of the same Stuff the following Sheets are made of; which will, I hope, give them an hour or two of agreeable Amusement. And if they will but be as kind to me, as they have been to many before, they will over-look one little Improbability, because such are to be met with in most Novels, many Plays, and even in Travels themselves. There is a little Story in the beginning of the Book of the Courtship of a Boy, which the Reader may perhaps think very trifling; but as it is not two Pages long, I beg he will pass it by; and my Excuse for it, is, I could not so well show the early Coquetry of the Lady without it.

The Reformed Coquet; or, The Memoirs of Amoranda

The most avaricious Scribbler that ever took Pen in hand had doubtless a view to his Reputation, separate from his Interest. I confess myself a Lover of Money, and yet have the greatest Inclination to please my Readers; but how to do so is a very critical Point, and what more correct Pens than mine have missed of. If we divide Mankind into several Classes, we shall meet with as

---

[3] *Subscription*: friends and acquaintances and readers of advertisements were invited to 'subscribe' toward the publication of a book or poem; they would pay part of the money to the publisher or author and the rest upon publication. Daniel Defoe, Alexander Pope, and many other major authors of the period occasionally published by subscription.

[4] *Relict*: widow.

many different Tempers as Faces, only we have the Art of disguising one better than the other.

The Pedant despises the most elaborate Undertaking, unless it appears in the World with *Greek* and *Latin* Motto's;[5] a Man that would please him must pore an Age over musty Authors, till his Brains are as worm-eaten as the Books he reads, and his Conversation fit for nobody else: I have neither Inclination nor Learning enough to hope for his favour, so lay him aside.

The next I can never hope to please, is the Dogmatical Puppy, who, like a Hedgehog, is wrapped up in his own Opinions, and despises all who want Extravagancies to enter into them; but a Man must have a superior share of Pride, who can expect his single Opinion should bias the rest of the Creation: I leave him therefore to pine at his Disappointment, and call upon the busy part of our Species, who are so very intent upon getting Money, that they lose the pleasure of spending it. I confess, the *Royal-Exchange*,[6] *South-Sea* with a P—x,[7] *Exchange-Alley*,[8] and all Trade in general, are so foreign to my Understanding, that I leave them where I found them and cast an oblique Glance at the Philosopher, who I take to be a good clever Fellow in his way. But as I am again forced to betray my Ignorance, I know so little of him, that I leave him to his, *No Pleasure, no Pain*; and a thousand other Chimera's, while I face about to the Man of Gallantry. Love is a very common Topic, but 'tis withal a very copious one; and would the Poets, Printers and Booksellers but speak truth of it, they would own themselves more obliged to that one Subject for their Bread than all the rest put together. 'Tis there I fix, and the following Sheets are to be filled with the Tale of a fine young Lady.

A certain Knight who lives pretty deep in the Country, had a Father whose vicious Inclinations led him into a thousand Extravagancies; whoring and drinking took up a great part of his time, and the rest was spent in gaming,[9] which was his darling Diversion. We have had so many melancholy Instances of the sad Effects of the Vice, that I dare say the Reader will not be surprized if I tell him, this Gentleman in a little time died a Beggar by it, and left the young Baronet no more than his Honour to live upon. Some Years before the old Gentleman died, the young one married a Lady clandestinely, whose Fortune was then all their Support, and by whom he had one Daughter, now seven Years of Age, and for whom I will borrow the Name of *Amoranda*. Sir *John S——d*, her Father, had a younger Brother bred an *East-India*

---

5 *Motto's*: epigraphs.

6 *Royal-Exchange*: opened by Queen Elizabeth I in 1570, the Royal Exchange provided a meeting-place for merchants. It burned in the Great Fire of London in 1666, and was rebuilt with shops, covered walks, vaults, and an open courtyard.

7 *South Sea with a P—x*: the South Sea Company had allowed wild speculation, and the inevitable crash in 1719 was called the South Sea Bubble and ruined many investors. Davys pretends ignorance by including the curse that many of her contemporaries were attaching to the company as though it were part of its name.

8 *Exchange-Alley*: street between Lombard, the place many businessmen met, and Cornhill leading to the Royal Exchange.

9 *gaming*: gambling.

Merchant;[10] his Success abroad was so very great, that it qualified him for showing large Bounty at home; and as he thought nothing so despicable as Honour and Poverty joined, he was resolved to set his elder Brother above Contempt and make him shine like the Head of so ancient a Family: in order to which, he first redeemed all the Land his Father had mortgaged for Money to fling away, then re-purchased all he had sold, till at last he had settled the Knight in a quiet possession of that Estate, which had for so many Ages devolved from Father to Son; but, as he was exceeding fond of his young Niece, settled the whole upon her, in case her Father died without a Son, not Making the least reserve in favour of himself. When he had, with the highest Satisfaction, done a Deed of so much Goodness and Generosity, he left the Family he had just made happy, and went again in pursuit of his Merchandize; in the meantime, *Amoranda*, who was a little Angel for Beauty, was extremely admired, no less for that than for a sprightly Wit, which her younger Years promised. If we trace Human Nature through all the Stages of Life, we shall find those Dawnings of the Passions in Children, which riper Years bring to the highest perfection; and a Child, rightly considered, may give us a very great guess at his Temper, when he comes to be a Man. An Instance of this we have in the young Creature already named, who had, 'tis true, all the Beauties of her Sex, but then she had the Seeds of their Pride and Vanity too. *Amoranda* was no sooner told she was pretty than she believed it and listened with pleasure to those who said her Eyes were Diamonds, her Cheeks Roses, her Skin Alabaster, her Lips Coral, and her Hair *Cupid's* Nets, which were to ensnare and catch all Mankind.

This made an early impression upon the Mind of young *Amoranda*, and she now began to think as much in favour of herself as it was possible for others to do. Her Babies were thrown by with scorn, and the time that should have dressed them, was spent at the Looking-Glass dressing herself, admiring all those Graces with which she was now sure she was surrounded; her Father's Visitors were no longer to use her with their wonted freedom, but she told them with an Air of growing Pride, she expected to be called Madam as well as her Mamma, and she was not so much a Child as they would make her. Whilst she was in the midst of her grand Airs, a little Boy came in, who used to call her Wife, and running to her, got his little Arms about her Neck to kiss her, as he used to do. But *Amoranda*, who was now resolved to be a woman, thrust him from her with the utmost Contempt, and bid him see her no more. The poor Boy, not used to such Behaviour, stood staring at her, in great surprize at the occasion of all this; but being a Boy of some Spirit, though not capable of a real Passion, he said, Madam, you need not be so proud, I have got a prettier Miss than you for my Wife, and I love her better than I do you by half, and I will never come near you again. Saying thus, away he went to make his Complaints at home. When *Amoranda* saw him

---

[10] *East-India Merchant*: the East India Company had a monopoly on trade to the East Indies (India, surrounding countries in Asia, Indonesia); boys could be apprenticed in it.

gone and with a design to go to another, the whole Woman gathered in her Soul, and she fell into a violent Passion of Tears; the thoughts of having another preferred to her was intolerable, and seeing the Boy go off with Insults gave her a very sensible Mortification: Resentment flashed in her Eyes, and her Breast heaved with such Agonies, as the whole Sex feel when they meet with Contempt from a slighting Lover. Her Mother, who was as full of Mirth as she was of Grief upon this cutting occasion, said to her, Why, *Amoranda*, did you send away your Spouse if you are angry now he is gone? My Spouse! *cried the young Incensed*, I scorn the little unmannerly Brat, he shall never be my Spouse: What, tell me to my face he liked another better! But I know who the saucy Jackanapes[11] meant, and if ever she comes here again, I'll send her to him: I hate them both, and so I'll tell them; who can bear such an Affront? I shall never be easy till I am revenged of them. Here was Pride, Jealousy, and Revenge kindled in the Breast of a Child; and as Princes love the Treason, though they hate the Traitor, so Women like the Love, though they despise the Lover.

> Poor *Amoranda*, what will be thy Fate?
> So soon to like the Love, the Lover hate.

Her Behaviour, however, gave good diversion to her Father and Mother; and under that mistaken Notion of everything looking well in a Child, she was encouraged in many things, which she herself would probably have been ashamed of, had there been time given for Reason to play its part, and help to guard her Actions: Most Mothers are fond of seeing their Children Women before their time, but forget it makes themselves look old.

Vanity, which is most Women's Foible, might be overlooked or winked at, would it live alone; but alack! It loves a long Train of Attendants, and calls in Pride, Affectation, Ill-nature, and often Ill-manners too for its Companions. A Woman thus surrounded, should be avoided with the same care a Man would shun his evil Genius; 'tis marrying a Complication of the worst Diseases.

I remember when I was a Child, a Gentleman came to make love to a Sister I had, who was a good clever Girl both in Sense and Person; but as Women are never perfect, she had her Failings among the rest and mightily affected a scornful Toss with her Head, which was so disagreeable, after a few Visits, to her Lover, that he came no more. My Father, a little surprized at his going so abruptly off, and being loth to lose so advantageous a Match for his Daughter, went to enquire after his Reasons, which, when he heard, he told the Gentleman he thought them very trifling. No, Sir, *said he*, a Woman who will throw up her Head at me before Marriage, will (ten to one) break mine after it. I know, *continued he*, if a Woman be dishonourably attacked, her Scorn is needful, her Pride requisite; but a Man of equal or superior Fortune, who has no Views but hers and his own Happiness, ought to be received with

---

[11] *Jackanapes*: originally the name of a tame ape or monkey, but it had come to mean an impertinent, vain fop.

another Air; and if ever I marry, I will have at least a prospect of good Usage. Thus the foolish Girl lost a much better Husband than she got by thinking her Pride added to her Charms and gave new Graces to her Behaviour.

Amoranda was now in the ninth Year of her Age, six more I leap over, and take her again in her fifteenth; during which time her Father died and left her a finished Beauty and Coquet; I might here have said Fortune too, being sole Heiress to three thousand Pounds a Year: her Mother and Uncle were left her Guardians; but the former being a Lady of an infirm Constitution, the Grief of losing a tender good Husband made such considerable additions to her former weakness, that in less than half a Year she died too, and left poor *Amoranda* open to all the Temptations that Youth, Beauty, Fortune, and flashy Wit could expose her to. Her Uncle but just come from the *Indies*, and whose Business would not admit of his going into the Country, had once a mind to send for her up to Town, but he considered *London* a place of too many Temptations; and since she was willing to stay in the Country, he was resolved she would, but desired she would let him send down one to supply his place and take care of her in his stead. During this Interregnum, *Amoranda* was addressed by all the Country round, from the old Justice to the young Rake; and, I dare say, my Reader will believe she was a Toast in every House for ten Parishes round. The very Excrescencies of her Temper were now become Graces, and it was not possible for one single Fault to be joined to three thousand Pounds a Year; her Levee[12] was daily crowded with almost all sorts, and (she pleased to be admired) though she loved none, was complaisant to all. Among a considerable number of Admirers, Lord *Lofty* was one who had so great a value for his dear self, that he could hardly be persuaded any Woman had Merit enough to deserve the smallest of his Favours, much less the great one of being his Partner for life: however, he thought *Amoranda* a pretty Play-thing, a young unthinking Girl, left at present to her own Conduct, and if he could draw her in, to give him an hour's Diversion now and then, he should meet her with some Pleasure; if not (though he did not despair) he was her humble Servant, and had no farther design upon her. One day he came to see her so early in the Morning, that she was hardly up when he came; but sent down word, as soon as she could get herself into a dress fit to appear before his Lordship, she would wait upon him. While *Amoranda* was dressing, my Lord took a walk into the Garden, either to amuse himself with a variety of pleasing Objects, or to meditate afresh upon his present Undertaking. He walked with the utmost Pleasure among the Jessamine and Orange-Trees; at the end of the walk was a Seat, over which was a fine painted Roof representing the Rape of *Helen*[13] on which he gazed with some Admiration and could not forbear comparing *Amoranda* to her, nor thinking

---

[12] *Levee*: a morning assembly held by a person of distinction, often a reception of visitors held shortly after arising from bed

[13] *Rape of Helen*: the painting could be of Helen's abduction by Theseus and Polydeuces when she was a young girl or of her abduction by Paris after her marriage to Menelaus.

the whole Scene unlike his own design. After he had viewed this fine Piece, he happened to cast his Eye a little forward and saw a Paper lie upon the Ground, which he went and took up, finding it directed to *Amoranda* in a Woman's hand: he was not long persuading himself to open it, by which you will believe my Lord a Man of none of the strictest Honour; however, he read it and found it thus:

If the Advice of a Stranger can be of any import, I beg of you, good Madam, to take care of Lord Lofty, *who carries nothing but Ruin to our whole Sex: believe me, who have too fatally experienced him, his whole Design upon you is to make you miserable; and if you fall into his Snare after so fair a Warning, nobody but yourself deserves the blame.*

This Letter put my Lord into a very thoughtful posture, and he now began to fear his hopes of *Amoranda* were at an end; the Hand he knew, and acknowledged the Person who wrote it a much better Painter than him he had been so lately admiring, since she had drawn him so much to the life. My Lord was a Man of the best assurance in *England*, yet he began to fear his Courage would not hold out to face *Amoranda* any more, and was just resolving to leave the Garden and go home, when he saw her coming towards him; he shuffled the Letter into his Pocket, and with a Countenance half confounded, went to meet her. Good-morrow, my Lord, (*said* Amoranda, *with the gayest Air*;) how are we to construe those early Sallies of yours? not to Love, I suppose; because Mr. *Congreve* tells us, *A contemplative Lover can no more leave his Bed in a morning, than he can sleep in it.*[14]

Madam, *said my Lord,* (*who began to gather Courage from her Behaviour*) a contemplative Lover has some respite from his Pain, but a restless one has none; I hope you will believe I am one of this last sort, and am come to look for my Repose where I lost it. Fie! fie! my Lord, how you talk, *said* Amoranda, you're a Man of so much Gallantry, there's no dealing with you. Come, *said she*, take my Hand, and let us go to the Fish-Ponds, I have ordered the Tackling to be carried down before us, we will try if we can find any Sport this Morning. Madam, *said my Lord,* everything is Diversion in your Company, and if you can captivate your Fish as fast as you do those of your own Species, your Ponds will be in a little time quite ruined.

O! my Lord, *said* Amoranda, if I catch too many of either sort, I have a very good way of disposing of them.

After what manner, *said my Lord.* Why; *said she*, one I throw into the Water again, and the other may consume in his own Flames. Madam, *said my Lord,* he's a cruel Deity, who is pleased with nothing but the Life of his Worshippers.

N—ay, *said* Amoranda, so he is; I own I pity the poor Fellows sometimes: but you know, my Lord, we can't love everybody, they should e'en keep out of harm's way.

---

[14] Paraphrase of Bellmour's speech at the beginning of *The Old Batchelour* (I. i. 2–4): 'I thought a contemplative Lover could no more have parted with his Bed in a morning, than a' could have slept in't.'

By this time they were come to the Pond, and the Anglers fell to work; but before they had caught anything to speak of, a Footman came to tell his Lady, Mr. *Pert* was come to wait upon her. Fly, *said* Amoranda, and tell him I come. My Lord, *said she*, you will please to pardon me a moment, I'll go and try if I can engage Mr. *Pert* in our Diversion, and bring him with me. Without staying for my Lord's Answer, she ran towards the House, and left him with the Angle in his hand: he had now a little time to consider the Lady, but what to make of her, he knew not; he took the Letter out of his Pocket, and read it over again, then said to himself,—'Twas lost Labour in the Lady who wrote it, for *Amoranda* takes no notice of it, her Behaviour is open and free as ever, I shall certainly meet with a critical Minute, and then adieu to Gallantry on this side the Country. Before he had ended his Soliloquies, he saw the Lady coming back alone, and went to meet her; What, Madam, *said he*, are you without an Attendant? Yes, my Lord, *said* Amoranda, I could not persuade Mr. *Pert* to venture this way, he said the Sun always put out the Stars, and he should give but a glimmering Light where there was such a superiour Brightness.

Madam, *said my Lord*, I once thought Mr. *Pert* so full of himself, that he scorned Improvement; but I find your Ladyship's Conversation has made a considerable Alteration.

Pray, my Lord, have done, *said* Amoranda, for I freely own I am not proof against Flattery, there is something so inexpressibly pleasing in it——Lard! you Men——Come, let us catch some Fish, and divert the Subject. Hang the Fish, *said my Lord*. Aye, *said* Amoranda, for we shall never drown them: But how comes it, my Lord, *said she*, you are so indifferent to such a fine Diversion? Because, Madam, *said he*, I have a much finer in view; tis to affront the Heart I am so eager in pursuit of to give way to any other Diversion. Come, Madam, *said he*, let us leave this Drudgery to your Servants, and take a Walk in yonder pleasant Grove, where I may have an Opportunity of laying open to you a Heart ready to burst with Love. Here he took her Hand, and led her towards the Garden, where *Jenny*, *Amoranda's* Maid, met them, and told my Lord, a Servant was just come to tell his Lordship his Brother was newly alighted. Never any News was more unwelcome than this was to my Lord, who made himself now sure of *Amoranda's* Consent to anything he should request of her, and he thought a very few Minutes would have completed his Happiness. He stamped and cursed his Disappointment, and, with Vexation and madness in his Looks, took his leave for that time. He was no sooner gone than *Jenny* (who was all poor *Amoranda* had now to advise her) began to talk to her Lady about Lord *Lofty*. I am no less concerned than surprized, Madam, *said she*, to see you so free in this Gentleman's Company, after the Account you have had of his Temper in general, and his particular Behaviour to the poor Lady who wrote to you. I wish it were in my power, *said she*, to prevail with you to see him no more; I read his Designs in his Looks, and am satisfied his Intentions are dishonourable. At this, *Amoranda* burst out a laughing. The poor Lady that wrote to me, *said she*, in a *jeering Tone*, one of his Tenant's Daughters, I suppose, who he, for a Night's Lodging, promised Marriage, perhaps, and the Creature thinks, because he made a Fool of her, he has and must do so by all the Sex: no, no, *Jenny*, some People, when they are gauled themselves, would feign make other Folks smart too; but I love to disappoint their Spite, and will, for that reason, take no notice of it.

Madam, *said* Jenny, that letter looks as if it came from a finer hand than you seem to think it does; look it over once more, and—Aye, *said* Amoranda, *feeling in her Pocket*, but where is it? I had it last Night in the Orange-Walk, and have certainly dropped it there, let us go and look for it. No, Madam, *said* Jenny, we need not, if you dropped it there, my Lord has found it, for there he walked all the while you were dressing. That can never be, *said* Amoranda, he is a Man of too much Honour to open a Letter directed to me; I am sure, *said she*, had he found it, I should have had it again, therefore go and look for it. While *Jenny* was gone in quest of the Letter, *Amoranda* began to recollect herself, and remembered she saw my Lord at a distance putting a Paper into his Pocket, and, when she came nearer to him, looked confused; however, she had said so much already in vindication of his Honour, that she was resolved to conceal her own Thoughts, and *Jenny* returning without it, they both went in.

As soon as Dinner was over, *Amoranda's* Visitors began to flock about her, while she, pleased with a Crowd of Admirers, received them all with equal Complacency, and Singing, Dancing, Music and Flattery took up her whole time. Her Heart was like a great Inn, which finds room for all that come, and she could not but think it very foolish to be beloved by five hundred, and return it only to one; she found herself inclined to please them all, and took no small pains to do so: yet had she been brought to the Test, and forced to choose a Husband among them, her particular Inclinations were so very weak, that she would have been at the greatest loss where to fix, though her general Favours gave every Man hopes, because she artfully hid from one what she bestowed upon another. Among the rest, she had two Lovers, who would very fain have brought her to a Conclusion; I shall call one *Froth*, and the other *Callid*. The latter, though he had no cause to despair, grew weary of Expectation, and was resolved to have recourse to other measures: but *Froth* pushed his Fortune forward, and, from an inward Opinion of his own Merit, did not doubt but he should bring *Amoranda* to crown his Wishes, and in a few days bestow herself upon him for Life. One day *Amoranda* and *Froth* were set in a beautiful Summer-house in the Garden, which had Sashes to the Highway, and here they sat when *Froth* thus accosted her. Madam, *said he*, it is now six weeks since I first broke my Mind to you; and if I am six more in suspense it will break my Heart too. I am not unsensible of, or unthankful for the Favours you have shown me, I know I am the happy Man who stands fairest in your Esteem, and since your Eyes declare your heart is won, why do you retard my Joys? You're a very pretty Fellow, *said* Amoranda *laughing*, to make yourself so sure of a Body! how can you believe I shall be so silly, as to think of marrying while I have so fresh a Bloom upon my Cheeks? No, Mr. *Froth*, *said she*, it will be time enough for me to be a Wife when that dreadful thing Decay gets hold of me; but if it will be any satisfaction to you, I don't care if I tell you, I have not a less Value for you than for the rest of my Lovers. Madam, *said he*, my Ecstasy would have been more complete had you said a greater. Oh, *said she*, that's enough for once, but I don't bid you despair. As she spoke these words, she turned her Head, and saw *Callid* coming, and having a mind for a little variety of Courtship, desired *Froth* to go and pull a few Nectarines; which he readily did, laughing in his sleeve at poor *Callid*, who he was very sure would meet with a cold Reception. As soon as *Callid* had reached *Amoranda*, he began with a very submissive Air, and said, Madam, I am now so far from coming to repeat my presumptive Love, that I come in the highest Despair to resign it; I am too sensible how little I have deserved a return from you, and since my Estate is too small for you—Your Estate, *said* Amoranda, *interrupting him*, I wonder, Mr. *Callid*, you should name it; 'tis trifling indeed compared to your Merit: I would have you believe I have so good a taste, as to set the highest Value upon the richest Gem, and I am sorry my Behaviour has given you any despairing Thoughts. Madam, *said he*, I have no cause to complain of your Behaviour, but Hope is a most tiresome thing when it hangs too long upon our hands; but here comes one to whom I must give place.

Believe me, *said* Amoranda, you mistake, and I will comply so far with your satisfaction, as to say, you stand as fair in my Esteem as he does. By this time *Froth* came to them, and complaining of Heat, threw up the Sash. Some little time after a Gentleman rode by and threw in a Glove at the Window; *Amoranda*, at whose foot it fell, took it up, and found there was something in it, which she concealed, but was much surprized at the Action. As she was putting it into her Pocket, she saw Lord *Lofty* coming, and leaving *Froth* and *Callid* in the Summer-house, went to meet him. What an age, *said he*, have I been detained from my charming *Amoranda*? Oh! come down this Walk, and let me tell you how Absence has tortured me ever since I left you.

While my Lord and *Amoranda* were walking in the other part of the Garden, *Froth* and *Callid* began to compare Notes and talk of the weighty Affair in which they were both concerned. Mr. *Callid*, *said Froth*, you and I come here upon the same Errand, and in regard to our former Friendship I must tell you, *Amoranda* is partly disposed of, and for that reason I would advise you to desist; a Man's Discretion is greatly to be called in question, who, after so many repulses as doubtless you have met with, will still go on in a fruitless attempt. 'Tis true, we are both men of merit, but Love you know is blind, and if she finds just difference enough to turn the Scale to my advantage, I think you ought to drop your Amour and leave the Lady and I to our own happy Inclinations. Hum—*said Callid*, you are, I must own, a Man of a sanguine Complexion, but a little too much upon the Volatile; your Understanding evaporates, and you never had a solid Thought in your Life, otherwise you would tell yourself, this Woman has no more regard to you than to all Mankind in general. Perhaps she has given you some Cause to hope; why, she has done the same by me, and is this minute doing the same by yon Nobleman, and tomorrow, five hundred more shall meet with the same encouragement, if they attack her. No, *Froth*, said he, this way will never do; but if you will give into my Measures, we may find out one that will. You and I have been long Friends, and old Acquaintance, our Estates are sunk to a low ebb, though we have hitherto made that a Secret to the World; *Amoranda* is not the Prize we seek after, it is her Fortune we want, and part of it, at least, we will have, if you will close with my Design. Well, said Froth, I never sign blank Bonds, let me know what your Design is, and as I like it, I will comply with it; but why the Devil, said he, should I lose the Substance for the Shadow? I am sure she bid me not despair an hour ago, and who would desire more Encouragement?

I find, said Callid, you are running away with the old Bait that has caught so many Fools already; for my part, I nibbled at it too, but it smelt so stale, I did not like it: and if you'll be advised by a Friend, who can see as far into a Millstone as you can do, you'll shun the Trap as well as I. Come then, said Froth, let us hear this Scheme of yours. I know, said Callid, it will at the first hearing seem a little impracticable, but I don't doubt of convincing you in a small time of its Possibility. I have often heard *Amoranda* say she passed her whole Evenings in this Summer-house when the Weather is hot; now where would be the difficulty of whipping her out of this low Window into a Coach provided ready and carry her to a House which I have taken care of, keeping her with the utmost privacy, till she resolves to marry one of us, and the other shall share the Estate.

Aye, said Froth, if this were but as soon done as said, I should like the Contrivance well enough; but pray, said he, don't you think her Maid and she would make a damned noise when they were carried off? Yes, said the other, I believe they would, but we might easily prevent it, by a pretty little Gag for a minute or two, till we got them into the Coach. Well, said Froth, but when we have taken all these Pains, what if she will marry neither of us, and the Hue and Cry catch us, as to be sure it will soon be after us; then, instead of a fine Lady, with a fine Estate, we shall each of us get a fine Halter.[15] Thou art a cowardly Puppy, said Callid, and I am sorry I have laid myself so open to you; do you think I do my Business by halves? or that an Affair of such Consequence is to be neglected in any part? No, the Devil himself can't find her where I intend to carry her; and if she will not immediately comply to marry one of us, she will at least come to terms for her liberty: you know we cannot stay long in *England*, unless we have a mind to rot in a Jail, and if we can but screw out each of us a thousand Pound, we will away to the Czar,[16] and let the Law hang us when it can catch us.

15 *Halter*: hangman's noose. Kidnapping an heiress was a capital offence.
16 *Czar*: Peter I (1672–1725), Czar of Russia (1682–1725), had visited Great Britain in 1698

Why Faith, *said* Froth, I believe such a Project might be brought to bear, but how should we get the Money brought to us? She shall draw a Bill upon her Banker, *said Callid*, for as much as we can get out of her, then we'll ride post to *London* and receive it. And when, *said Froth*, are we to go about this Work? For methinks I would fain have it over; I have still a fancy *Amoranda* will be mine, and if she be willing to marry me, will you promise not to oppose it? Nay, *said* Callid, if she will marry either of us, I do not see why it may not be me as well as you; I will not make a Deed of Gift of the Lady neither, but if it comes to that, she shall e'en draw cuts for us, and the lucky Loon take her.

What an unhappy Creature is a beautiful young Girl left to her own Management, who is so fond of Adoration that Reason and Prudence are thrust out to make way for it; 'till she becomes a prey to every designing Rascal, and her own ridiculous Qualities are her greatest Enemies: Thus it might have fared with poor *Amoranda*, had not a lucky hit prevented it, which the Reader shall know by and by. While this Contrivance was carrying on in the Summer-House, my Lord was employed in another of a different kind: he thought his Quality sufficient to justify all his Actions and never feared a Conquest, wherever he vouchsafed an Attempt. Madam, *said he*, why are we to spend our time in this Garden, where so many Interruptions may break in upon our Privacies? I desire an Audience where none but Love may be admitted.

My Lord, *said* Amoranda, did you ever see a finer Goldfinch in your Life than that Cock in the Pear-Tree? That very Cock, my Lord, is Grand-sire to all my little warbling Company within doors, I remember him, and know him by a little uncommon Spot over his Eye: Oh 'tis a charming Bird, I have set a Trap-Cage for him a thousand times, but the dear Creature is so cunning— Well, everything loves Liberty, and so do I; don't you, my Lord? Yes, Madam, *said he*, I loved it, and always had it 'till I knew you; but I am so entangled now in your Charms, I never expect to disengage myself again.

Well, I'll swear, my Lord, *said* Amoranda, that's a pity; methinks a Man of your Gallantry should never marry. Marry! *Said my Lord in great Surprize*, no, I hope I shall never have so little love for any Lady as to marry her: Oons! The very Word has put me into a Sweat, the Marriage-Bed is to Love what a cold Bed is to Melon-Seed, it starves it to death infallibly. Aye, I believe it does, my Lord, *said* Amoranda; however, one thing I have often observed, when once a Woman's married, nobody cares for her but her Husband; and if your Lordship's Remarks be true, not he neither: so that, my Lord, I think we must live single in our own defence. But, my Lord, *said she*—what was I going to say—Oh pray give me a pinch of Snuff. But Madam, *said my Lord*, this is trifling with my Passion, I cannot live upon such Usage; either ease my

and had captured the British imagination. His possible responsibility for his son's death after torture in 1718 was much discussed in the British press. As he modernized Russia, he employed many British engineers, doctors, craftsmen, and workers.

Sufferings, or take my Life. I'll swear, my Lord, *said* Amoranda, you are a bewitching Man; what a Breach have I made in good Manners by your agreeable Conversation! I left poor Mr. *Froth* and Mr. *Callid* in the Summer-House two hours ago and had quite forgot they were there: sure the poor Toads[17] are not there still. Damn the Toads, *said Lord* Lofty, are they a Subject fit for your Thoughts? No, my Lord, *said she*, you see I forgot them, but pray let us go in, we shall have the Owls about our Ears, if we stay here any longer, 'tis just dark. Lord *Lofty* was strangely ruffled at this Behaviour; and though he still hoped for a pleasing end of his Amour, he plainly saw it would not be so easily attained as he at first vainly imagined: he therefore took his leave for that Night and hoped the next Interview would prove more favourable. *Amoranda* was very glad when she found herself alone, that she might have time to examine the Glove which came so oddly into the Summer-House Window. *Jenny, said she,* call for Candles, and come here. When she was set, and had got Lights, she took out the Glove; Oh *Jenny, said she,* what a sad afternoon has my Curiosity had, and how much have I longed to see what I have got here? She opened the top of it, and found a Letter: So, *said she,* here is some new Conquest, but the strangest way of letting me know it that ever was invented. She opened it, and found these Words;

THIS Letter, Madam, does not come to tell you I Love you, since that would only increase the surfeit you must have taken with so many hundred Declarations of that kind already; but if I tell you I am in pain for your Conduct, and spend some Hours in pitying your present Condition, it will, I dare say, be entirely new to you; since (though many have the same opinion of your Behaviour) none have Courage, or Honesty enough to tell you so. Consider, Madam, how unhappy that Woman is, who finds herself daily hedged in with self-ended Flatterers, who make it their business to keep up a Vanity in you, which may one day prove your Ruin. Is it possible for any Fop to tell you more than you know already? or does not your Looking-Glass display every one of your fine Features with much more exactness than the base, the fawning Rascal who pretends to die at your Feet? Spurn him from you, Amoranda, as you would the worst Infection, and believe me rather than him, when I tell you, you are neither Angel, nor Goddess, but a Woman, a fine Woman, and there are in this Nation ten thousand such. If this little Admonition meets with a favorable Reception, you will, upon the first reading of it, discard three Fourths of your daily Attendants, who like so many Locusts are striving to devour you.

Why *Jenny, said* Amoranda, did you ever hear anything so impudent in your Life? Oh Lud, I have not patience with the familiar Brute, I would give a thousand Pounds to know the Author; what shall I do to be revenged? Truly Madam, *said* Jenny, I must own if this be a Conquest, 'tis made upon a very insulting saucy Lover; and yet I believe he means well too.

---

[17] *Toads*: subservient lackeys; often 'toadeater', one who is willing to do anything to maintain a position.

Mean well, *said* Amoranda; what good meaning can he have who persuades me to banish the Bees and live in the Hive by myself? No Madam, *said* Jenny, your Ladyship mistakes him, 'tis the Wasps he would have you discard, who come to sting and steal from those who have a better Title to the Sweets of your Favours: but Madam, *continued she*, do you think you should know him again if you see him?

Not I, *said* Amoranda, I never saw his Face, he flung in the Glove before I knew anybody was near; and had he not ridden away in a Cloud of Dust, I should have thought it had been a Challenge to some of the Gentlemen in the Summer-House; but what vexes me most, *said she*, is his Pity; I always thought a Woman of Youth, Beauty, and such a Fortune as mine is, might raise Envy in many, but Pity in none.

Here the Housekeeper came in to speak with her Lady, and put a stop to their present Discourse, by making way for something of greater moment. Madam, *said she*, if your Ladyship be at leisure, I have a Secret of great Importance to communicate to you. Prithee then, *said* Amoranda, let us have it, perhaps it may put something else out of my head. Madam, *said she*, I went this Afternoon into my little Room over the Summer-house, where you know I dry my Winter-Herbs, and while I was turning them, your Ladyship came in with Mr. *Froth*, and *Callid* came to you. You may please to remember, Lord *Lofty* gave you an opportunity of leaving them, which you had no sooner done, than they began to lay a most dangerous Plot against you; —(so told her Lady what the Reader has heard already) but, *continued she*, as soon as they had laid their Scheme, Mr. *Callid* said he would go and provide a Coach, and two or three Villains (like himself) to assist. As soon as he was gone, Mr. *Froth* began to consider with himself what was best to do, stick to the first Design, or discover all to your Ladyship. Now, *said he*, have I a fair Opportunity of turning *Callid's* Knavery to my own advantage, by discovering all to *Amoranda*; so signal a Service can be attended with nothing less than her dear self, and then I have her without any Hazard or Partner. But then, *said he again*, as my Friend has well observed, the Devil can't fix a Woman of her levity; perhaps when I have ruined his Design by telling her the Danger she is in, my Reward may be a Curtsy, and I thank you Mr. *Froth*, and when it lies in my power I'll serve you again: there's an end of his hopes and my own too. No, *said he*, without I were sure of making Sport, I am resolved I will spoil none, and good Luck assist our Undertaking; while yonder Lord is so much at her Service, we need expect no Favours but what we force, so *Callid* I follow thee to provide for them. Saying thus, he went out of the Garden through the Back-Door. Oh the impudent Rogues! *said* Amoranda: Well, and when, *Brown*, (for that was the Housekeeper's Name) is this fine Project to be put in execution? Tomorrow-night, Madam, *said she*. What, *said* Amoranda, whether I am there or no? though I spend a good deal of time there, I am not always there. No, Madam, *said Brown*, I forgot to tell your Ladyship that part of the Contrivance; you are to be entertained with a Dance of Shepherds and Shepherdesses in the Highway by Moonlight, just at the Summer-house Window, and if you happen to have any Company 'tis to be put off till next Night under pretence of one of the Dancers being not well. Very fine, said *Amoranda*, well since the worthy Gentlemen have begun a Scheme, I'll throw in my Counter-Plot among them and see who will come best off.

Amoranda made her Housekeeper a Present of some Guineas[18] and dismissed her. As she went out, a Footman came in, and told his Lady, an old Gentleman was just alighted at the Gate who brought her a Letter but must deliver it into her own hand. An old Gentleman! *said* Amoranda; wait upon him in however. The Stranger entered, and gave the young Lady a Letter from her Uncle, in which, when she had opened it, she found the following words:

I have at last, my dearest Amoranda! *fixed upon such a Person as I think fit to entrust you with; he is one for whom I have the greatest Value, or, to sum up all in one word, he is my Friend, and as such I desire you'll use him; let him in my stead interest himself in all your Affairs. I have so good an Opinion of your Prudence, as to believe you will not often want his Advice; neither will he offer it, unless he finds it necessary: for though he is an old Man, he is neither impertinent, positive, or sour. You will, I hope, from my past Behaviour towards you, believe you are very dear to me; and I have no better way of showing it for the future, than by putting you into such hands as* Formator's, *which is the Name of the Bearer; and if you would oblige me, show it by your Esteem to him, which will confirm me*
Your most Affectionate Uncle,
E. TRAFFICK

When *Amoranda* had read her Letter, she looked a little earnestly at *Formator*, possibly not very well pleased with a Guardian of such an Age; but she considered she had a Father and Mother to please in the Person of her Uncle, and he such a one as made up the Loss of both to her: for which Reasons she resolved to use him as directed in that Letter, and said to him, with a Smile, I find, Sir, I am no longer my own Mistress, but am now to live under your Restrictions; I promise you I will always listen to your Advice and take it as often as I can; but I hope, Sir, you will remember I am gay and young, you grave and old, and that the Disparity in our Years may make as great a one in our Tempers: I'll therefore make a bargain with you, if you will bear with a little of my youthful Folly, I will bear with a great deal of your aged Sagacity, and we will be as agreeable to one another as 'tis possible for Age and Youth to be.

Madam, *said* Formator, I agree to all your Proposals and shall be very cautious how I presume to advise; and if I ever do so, it shall be when your own Reason must side with me, and I see already you have too much Sense to act against that, unless by Inadvertency. All young People, Madam, are fond of Pleasure and every Thought that opposes it is thrust out with disgrace;

[18] *Guineas*: 21 shillings.

but—O Lud! *said Amoranda*, I believe you are to be the Chaplain too, if you talk thus much longer, you'll argue me out of my Senses; I told you I could not come into your grave Measures of a sudden. Come, Sir, there's nothing in it, an innocent Cheerfulness is much more acceptable both to God and Man than a crabbed sour Temper that gives everybody the Gripes to look at it. Madam, said *Formator*, you quite mistake me: I am not of that disagreeable Temper you have described; I would have both Young and Old act with that very innocent Freedom you speak of: but what I inveigh against, is an immoderate Love of Pleasure, which generally follows the Young and too often leads them to Destruction.

Pray, Sir, *said* Amoranda, what is it you call Pleasure?

Madam, *said he*, I call everything Pleasure that pleases us, and I dare say you will own a great many things may and do please us, which are in themselves very faulty: as for example, suppose a fine young Lady of a superiour Beauty should spread her Purlieus[19] to catch all Mankind, I doubt not but it would give such a one exquisite Pleasure; but it is at the same time a great fault to give other People exquisite Pain, as the rest of the Sex must certainly feel, when they see one Monopolizer engross the whole Male World to herself. Nay, *said* Amoranda, there never was any such thing in nature, as one Woman engrossing the whole contrary Sex; believe me, Sir, you all love Variety too well for that, and your Affections, like your Money, circulates all the Nation over; so that it is only who can keep their Lovers longest we strive for, not who can keep them always, for that we none of us expect. But come *Formator, said she*, I must own you are come at a very critical Juncture, and since my Uncle has enjoined me to use you as I would him, after Supper I will give you an early Proof of my Duty to him and my Confidence in you.

Supper ended, *Amoranda* told *Formator* the whole Story of *Froth* and *Callid*, their base Designs as well as beggarly Circumstances. *Formator's* Cheeks glowed with Anger, and, in the highest Transport of Rage, cried out, How can such a Woman, such a lovely Woman as you are, subject yourself to such Company? Is it possible that fine Sense, which breaks from those lovely Lips with every word you speak, can find agreeable Returns from such Vermin? Can a Man mingle his Wine with Mud, then drink it with pleasure?

Pardon me, dear Madam, *continued he*, if my Zeal for so good an Uncle to you, and so good a Friend to me, hurries me a little too far; 'tis not possible for me to see anything so deservedly beloved by him run into the least Weakness; beside, you seem to have too true a Notion of our Sex to be so grossly imposed upon by them. Say no more, good *Formator, said* Amoranda. I now promise to be governed in a great measure by you; and since my Uncle has sent you to supply his Place, I will use you with deference, and bring myself to comply with your Desires as far as possible. This Promise gave the old Gentleman ten thousand Joys, which sat triumphant on his pleased

---

[19] *Purlieus*: range, territory for hunting.

Countenance; and *Amoranda* could not forbear being pleased herself to see how much he was so. But, Madam, *said* Formator, methinks I long to know how you intend to use those Villains. That, *said she*, you shall do presently. When the hour is come for the execution of their intended Project, I design to place two sturdy Footmen, dressed in mine and *Jenny's* Clothes, in the Summer-house; the hour they have appointed, will favour my design as well as theirs, for ten o'clock's the time, and the Moon to be our Light: so that they will not easily distinguish betwixt the Fellows and us, till their sense of feeling lets them into the secret; for the Footmen don't want Courage, and I hope my designed Injuries will give them resentment to it: I dare say they will give them love for love and pay them in their own coin. What do you think, *Formator, said she*, will not my Contrivance do better than theirs? I hope so, Madam, *said he*; but I have one earnest request to make to you, and as it is the first, I hope you will not deny me. No, *said* Amoranda, I am sure you will ask nothing I ought to refuse, and therefore I promise. Then, Madam, *said he*, give me leave to personate you in the Summer-house tomorrow night.

Alas! *said she*, what can your feeble Arm do with such robust Rascals? they will make no more of you than they would of me myself, and methinks I would not have them go off without a good drubbing. Fear not, Madam, *said* Formator, this Arm can still do wonders in so good a Cause; a Vindication of *Amoranda's* Honour fills my Veins with young Blood, that glows to revenge her Wrongs. Well, *said* Amoranda, I find I have the Remains of a brave Man to take my part; and since you have so great a mind to show your Prowess, pray do: if you happen to be worsted, we'll invert the Custom, and instead of your delivering the distressed Damsel, she shall come and rescue you. This made *Formator* very merry, in spite of all his Gravity: but it was now Bedtime, and he was conducted to his Chamber by the Servants, who were ordered to use him with great respect. The next morning *Jenny* came to her Lady's Bedside, and told her she had been in the Garden, and had found a silver Box; I fancy, by the bigness of it, 'tis Lord *Lofty's* Snuff-box, *said she*, but there is nothing in it but a Paper. Draw the Curtains, *said* Amoranda, and let me see it; *Jenny* gave her the Box, and when she had opened the Paper, she found it was a Contract betwixt Lord *Lofty* and a Lady, of whom she had often heard, but never saw her; and if Lord *Lofty* receded from his Promise of marrying the Lady, he should then forfeit Ten Thousand Pounds, as an Addition to her Fortune. This Contract nettled *Amoranda* to the very heart: How! *said she*, does my Lord come here to affront me with his Declarations against Marriage, and at the same time is going to engage himself so firmly to another? Base as he is, *said she*, am I a Person fit only to divert those Hours in which he cannot gain admittance to one he likes better? Give me my Clothes, *said she*, I'll be revenged of him or lose my Life in the Attempt.

Poor *Jenny*, who never saw her Lady angry in her life before, began to repent she had said anything of the Box and was now afraid her Lady loved Lord *Lofty*. Madam, *said she*, I would not have your Ladyship in such a passion, for by the Date of this Contract, one would believe my Lord never intended to give it the Lady at all; it has been signed and sealed above a month, if it was dated at the same time. *Jenny, said* Amoranda, *recovering herself and smiling*; I fancy by your Looks, you are afraid I have an inward private Inclination for the worthless Peer: but as thou hast always been a faithful, honest Servant, I will contribute so far towards thy ease as to assure thee he is upon the same foot with the rest of his Sex, and I know none upon the earth I have a superior value for; but I own I have so just a resentment against his Behaviour to me, that if the Lady this Paper was designed for, will accept of it, I will certainly make her a present of it tomorrow. But, Madam, *said* Jenny, maybe my Lord may come and enquire for it. If he comes today, *said* Amoranda, tell him I see no Company, and tomorrow I will put it out of his reach—if my mind does not alter, *Jenny*, as I believe it will; for upon second thoughts, 'tis a matter of very great consequence, and I would not contribute to a Man's continual Uneasiness neither; however, I am resolved to see no Company today, except *Callid* and *Froth*, so pray give orders accordingly below stairs.

Jenny was very glad to see her Lady recover her Temper so soon, and when she had obeyed her Commands, she returned to dress her, and then *Amoranda* went down to *Formator*; they paid each other the common Compliment of a Good-morrow, and then went to breakfast in *Amoranda's* Closet, for fear of a Visit from Lord *Lofty*, who came before they had well begun. But his Errand was different from what they expected, for he neither enquired for, nor had missed his Box: but when they told him *Amoranda* saw no Company that day; I know it, Child, *said he*, she told me yesterday she would see nobody but me; Where is she? then without staying for an Answer, he ran from Room to Room till he found her. *Amoranda* thought his ill-mannered Freedom proceeded from his Concern for his Box, and was once going to return it, in order to get rid of him, but a better Genius twitched her by the ear, and bid her keep it. Madam, *said he, with his wonted Assurance*, how will you answer this Behaviour to Good-nature? and what have I done to deserve Banishment?

My Lord, *said* Amoranda, I retire sometimes from Company to make it more acceptable to me when I come into it again; and this, I think, I may do as often as I please without a Breach in either Good-nature or Good-manners. True, Madam, *said my Lord*, but I would fain be acceptable always. *Amoranda* found by this Answer he had not missed his Box, or at least did not suspect she had it, and therefore told him, she was surprized to hear him say he would be always acceptable, after having declared so heartily against Matrimony. I fancy, my Lord, *said she*, you will find a Mistress a little given to Variety, and will hardly like you always as much as you may think you deserve. *Formator*, who coloured at this Discourse, began to take up the Cudgels. My Lord, *said he*, I am sent here by very good Authority, and have a Commission to enquire every Man's Business that comes into this House; I therefore desire to know, if, as the Lady says, you declare against Matrimony, what your designs are in coming here? Prithee, Child, *said my Lord to* Amoranda, what queer old Prig is this? Hark-ye, Friend, *said he to* Formator, your Business is now in the other World, and you would do well to go and prepare for it without envying us the Pleasures you are past yourself. My Lord, *said* Formator, I am still very capable of Pleasure and the greatest I can possibly have is to preserve the lovely Charge committed to my Care, which I will do to the utmost extremity of my power; and do here promise you, till you give a better account of your Intentions, you shall never see her more. *Amoranda* was not very well pleased with what *Formator* said; for though she was perfectly insensible of any Passion for my Lord and knew his dishonourable Designs, she could not think of losing a Lover of his Title and Figure without some Emotion: and said to *Formator*, with a little warmth, I think, Sir, you assume a Power too great for so short a time, and I should take it kindly if you would give me leave to dismiss my Visitors myself. This gave my Lord a new Supply of Hope, and he asked *Amoranda* leave to pull him by the Nose. No, my Lord, *said she*, whoever lays a finger upon him has seen his last of me. Madam, *said* Formator, if I have been so unhappy as to say anything to disoblige you, I do here in the humblest manner ask your pardon; but if I am not to take notice of such Behaviour as Lord *Lofty's* I have no business here, but may forthwith return to him that sent me: for your part, my Lord, you *dare* not pull me by the Nose. Saying thus, he left the Closet, but sent *Jenny* directly up to her Lady, with a charge to stay with her till my Lord was gone unless she commanded otherwise, and then he knew what he had to fear.

Amoranda, on the other hand, found she had vexed *Formator*, which she began to be sorry for, because she knew it would highly disoblige one of the best Uncles in the world, and therefore begged my Lord to leave her for that time. He told her he would do ten thousand Things to oblige her and desired but one in return of all. When I understand you, my Lord, *said she*, I shall know what Answer to make; in the meantime, I repeat the Request I have already made you, to leave me now. My Lord, with a little too much freedom, snatched her to his arms, took a Kiss, and vanished. As soon as he was gone, she went down to *Formator* and found him in the Parlor in a very thoughtful, melancholy Posture; Formator, *said she*, I am come to tell you, I am under some Concern for what has happened today: I have, to oblige you, sent my Lord away, and do here faithfully promise you, I will never come into his Company more, without your Approbation. I own I have the greatest Inclination in the world to please you, and as I believe you sincerely my Friend, as such I will always use you, and let this little early quarrel rivet our future Amity. *Formator* was so transported at her good-natured Condescension, that he could hardly forbear throwing himself at her Feet; but he considered Raptures were unsuitable to his Age, so contented himself with saying, Madam, of what use is our Reason, if we chain it up when we most want it? had yours had its liberty, it would have shown you the villainous

Designs of your *Noble* Lover, it would have told you how much he desires your Ruin, that all the Love he has for you is to satisfy his own bestial Desires, rob you of your Innocence and Honour, then leave you to the World to Finish the Misery he began by being pitied and despised as long as you live; 'Tis true, Madam, *continued he*, you have a Fortune that sets you above the World, but when I was a young Fellow, we used to value a Lady for Virtue, Modesty, and an innate Love to Honour. I confess, Madam, *said he*, those are unfashionable qualities, but they are still the chief Ornaments of your Sex, and ours never think a Woman complete without them.

Give me leave, Madam, *said he*, to go a little farther, and tell you how great your misfortune has been, in being left so long to the Choice of your own Company; your Good-nature and want of Experience, together with a greedy Desire of Flattery, which, (pardon me, Madam) is a Weakness attending the whole Sex, has encouraged such a heap of Vermin about you, as Providence would not suffer to live, were it not to give us a better taste for the brave, the just, the honourable and the honest Man. *Amoranda* was so touched with what *Formator* said, that the Tears stood in her Eyes, and she was just going to beg he would have done, when the Bell rung for Dinner, and put a stop to what remained; she was never so lectured in her Life before, however, she told herself in her own Breast that every Word he said was true. As soon as Dinner was over, my Friend *Froth* came in, with a design to sift *Amoranda's* Inclinations once more; and if he found her leaning to his Side, as much as he desired, then to discover all; if not, to stay till *Callid* came, and join with him in the Invitation to the Entertainment at night. *Formator*, who was told before he came in who he was, left *Amoranda* and him together, and having a fair Opportunity of trying his Fortune once more, he thus began: Madam, I have often looked with envious Eyes on the Favours you confer on Mr. *Callid*, but, Madam, as you cannot have us both, I wish you would (for the ease of one of us at least) declare in favour of him you like, and let the other travel. Mr. Froth, *said she*, your Friend and you are endowed with such equal Merit, 'tis hardly possible to say which I like best; beside, if I should declare in favour of you, Mr. *Callid* would not believe I was in earnest; and if I should say I like him best, you are too conscious of your own Worth to think I speak from my Heart. In short, everything we do, you construe to your own advantage: if we look easy and pleased in your Company, we are certainly in Love; if grave and reserved, 'tis to hide our Love; thus you all imagine we are fond of gaining a Conquest over a Heart, which when we have got it, is perhaps so very trifling that we dispose of it at last, as we do of our old Gowns, give it away to our Chamber-Maid. But, Madam, *said Froth*, if you please we will lay by general Comparisons and come to particulars betwixt *Callid* and myself; and if I, from undeniable Reasons, prove I deserve best from you, will you promise accordingly to reward me?

I faithfully promise, *said Amoranda*, to reward you both as you deserve: but here's Mr. *Callid* coming, I'll warrant he has as much to say for himself as you have. (*Mr.* Callid *came to them, and said to* Amoranda) I have provided a little Country Entertainment for you, Madam, if you will do me the honour to see it anon. You are always so very obliging, *said* Amoranda,—but you know, Mr. *Callid,* I never go far from home. No farther than your own Summer-House, Madam, said he; I have engaged a few of my Tenants to appear in a rural Dress and give you a Shepherds' Dance, they have been practicing this Fortnight, and I am in hopes they may prove perfect enough to give you some diversion; I have ordered them to be there exactly at Ten o'clock, by which time the Road will be quiet and the Moon up; and Madam, *said* Froth, a Dance of Shepherds and Shepherdesses, looks so *Natural* by Moonlight.—Yes, *said* Amoranda, so it does, and I promise myself already a great deal of Pleasure from the Hour you speak of; but I wish I had known in the Morning, I would have engaged Lord *Lofty* to come himself, and have brought some Ladies with him: no matter, *said she,* we'll have it to ourselves, and Gentlemen, I desire you will not sup before you come, for I shall take care of a small repast for you, and we will sup in the Summer-House, that we may be near our Diversion. Come then, *Froth, said* Callid, we will go and see them do it once more before they perform in the Lady's View, for nothing could be so great a Baulk to me, as to have anything wrong where she is to be a Spectator. As soon as they were gone, *Amoranda* called *Formator,* and bid him choose a Companion for the Exploit in hand, for she told him, she had promised the two Gentlemen a Supper in the Summer-House, and she would fain have them have a Belly-full.

Formator took the young Lady's advice, and went to choose a good sturdy Fellow to personate *Jenny,* while he did as much by *Amoranda;* and when the appointed time was come, they took their Places in the Summer-House, with each a good Crab-tree Cudgel by him, and after a little expectation, the two impudent Varlets came, asked for *Amoranda* with their wonted sauciness, and being told she was in the Garden, flew to their hoped-for Prize. *Callid* ran as he thought to *Amoranda,* and catching her in his Arms, cried, No Resistance, Madam, by *Jove* you must along with me. *Froth* did the same by the supposed *Jenny,* and just as they were a going to gag them and call their Associates, who waited in the Lane for the Sign, to their Assistance, the two Ladies began to handle their Cudgels, and laid about them with such dexterity, that the Ravishers were almost knocked on the head, before they could believe they were beaten; so great was their surprize, and so little did they expect to meet with such resistance: but when they found the blows come faster on, without regard to either Sex or Quality, they began to draw their Swords; *Formator* struck *Callid's* out of his hand, and the Foot-Man tripped up *Froth's* heels, before he could get his out of the Scabbard, which he would not have attempted to do, but that he thought his Antagonist a Woman. All this while the two Ladies laid on so unmercifully that they began to cry Quarter and beg for Mercy, when the Noise reached the House, and they saw *Amoranda,* with Lights before her, coming in a great surprize, to see what the matter was.

Callid, when he saw her and *Jenny*, could hardly believe his half beaten-out Eyes, but stood staring, first at the real Lady, and then at the feigned one; but when he found how Matters went, he cried, *Froth*, thou Villain, thou hast betrayed me. If I have, said *Froth*, I am ill rewarded for it, and believe I shall never stir either hand or foot again. Well, Gentlemen, *said* Amoranda, are the Shepherds come? When does the Dance begin? 'Tis over, Madam, said *Formator*, these Gentlemen have been cutting capers this half-hour to a sorrowful new Tune. Why what is the matter said she? I hope you have not hurt them.

Nothing, Madam, *said* Formator, but *Harry* and I took a frolic to sit here this Evening in Masquerade, and those two Beaus had a mind to ravish us, I think, for they were going to gag us. I am sorry, Sir, (said he to *Callid*,) that I was forced to exercise my Cudgel upon you. I hope you will excuse it; had I been in another dress, I would have used another Weapon. I think, *said* Amoranda, he did not stand upon so much Ceremony with *you*, for I see he has drawn his Sword, though he took you for a Woman. Yes, said *Callid*, ready to choke with rage, despair, and disappointment, I took him for you, on whom I would have had a glorious revenge, had it proved so. Oh Death and Fury, *said he*, what malicious Devil interposed? but it is some Satisfaction to tell you how I would have used you had Fortune been so kind as to have put you in my power; know then, proud Beauty, I would——I know already (*said* Amoranda, *interrupting him*) as much of your designs, as you can tell me; but Gentlemen, *said she*, if the *Czar* should not take you into his Service,[20] when you have received the Money from my Banker, pray let me know, and I'll make a better Provision for you. I have an Uncle going to the *Indies* who wants Slaves, and I believe at my request, he would take you into his Service: in the meantime, do me the favour to leave this Place, for I have had just as much of your Company as I can dispense with. I hope, Madam, *said* Froth, (*whose Tongue was the only Part about him, he could stir without Pain*) you have more Hospitality in you, than to turn us out of your House in this Condition; you had more need send for a Surgeon, to set our dislocated Joints in order, and wrap us up in Seer-Cloth,[21] I don't believe I shall live a Week. That, *said* Amoranda, would be a great pity, the world would have a sad loss of so worthy a Man; but I hear you have a Coach hard by, I shall order two of my Servants to load each of them with a Knave and convey you both to it. I hope you will own I have been as good as my Word, I promised you a Supper and *Dessert*, and believe you have had both. Upon which, she and her retinue went away, leaving the two battered Beaus in the Summer-House, till a couple of lusty Fellows came, to take them up and shoot the rubbish into the Coach. The Servants who carried them away, left them, and returned home; and as soon as they were gone, *Callid* accused *Froth* of treachery, and laid the

---

[20] *into his Service*: as an indentured servant. Men and women sold themselves for a set number of years (usually seven) to merchants and brokers for passage to the New World.

[21] *Seer-Cloth*: sere or thin cloth strips.

whole discovery to his charge. *Froth* declared his Innocence, and urged his own share of the Suffering as a proof he was so; but *Callid's* disappointment had soured his temper, as well as made him desperate, and he was resolved to be deaf to all *Froth* could say in his own Vindication: and though they were both so bruised they could hardly stand, he made the other draw, who was innocent in Fact, though not Intention; and though they lived like Scoundrels, they went off like Gentlemen, and the first Pass they made, took each other's Life.

This News soon reached *Amoranda's* ear, whose tender Heart felt a great deal of pity for the tragical Catastrophe. But *Formator* told her, he thought she ought rather to rejoice, if she had a true sense of a Fellow-Creature's Sufferings; for, *said he*, when once a Man has out-lived his Fortune and his Friends, his next Relief is the Grave. He had now pretty well cleared the House of the Caterpillars that infested it, and began to take the greatest delight in his Charge; his constant Care was to divert her from all the Follies of Life, and as she had a Soul capable of Improvement, and a flexible good Temper to be dealt with, he made no doubt but one day he should see her the most accomplished of her Sex: in order to which, he provided a choice Collection of Books for her, spent most of his time with her, diverted her with a thousand pleasant Stories, possibly of his own making, and every moment was lost to *Formator* that was not spent with *Amoranda*.

Lord *Lofty* had made two Visits during this time, but *Formator* would not admit him, and by *Amoranda's* Consent told him she was engaged; which nettled the Peer so much, that he wrote to her in the bitterness of his Soul, the following words:

MADAM,

IF *it were possible for me to unriddle a Woman's Behaviour, I should immediately try my Skill upon yours; but as I believe Men of deeper Penetration than I have been baffled, I must e'en (with the rest) leave you to your own wild Mazes: One day caressed, the next cashiered, a third received again, and a fourth quite banished. However, though this be a common Treatment from most of your Sex, I never had cause to mind it so much in you, till this old whimsical Fellow came, to give you ridiculous Advice, and your Adorers endless Torment: What the Devil have our Years to do with his? or why must his pernicious Counsel disturb our Pleasures? If you have that value for me still, which you once gave me reason to hope you had, you will meet me in the little Grove at the end of your own Garden, about nine o'clock, where I will acquaint you with some Secrets you never knew before: I have contrived a way to it without coming near the House, and your old* Argus[22] *will never suspect you, if you come alone to the Arms of*

Your Faithful Admirer,

LOFTY.

---

[22] *Argus*: the monster with a hundred eyes that out of jealousy Juno set to watch Io.

Before *Amoranda* had done reading this Letter, a Servant came and told her a Gentleman on horseback at the Gate desired to know if he might be admitted to her Presence for a Quarter of an hour; his Business was a little urgent, but it would be soon over. Poor *Amoranda* had been so lately in jeopardy, that she was now afraid of everybody, and dared do nothing without *Formator*, who went to know the Gentleman's Name; but when he came to the Gate, he saw a poor, thin, pale, meagre young Creature, hardly able to sit his Horse, who looked as if he wanted a Doctor more than a Mistress: when he had viewed him well, he was ashamed to ask him any questions, thinking he might as well be afraid of a Shadow as such a Skeleton as he was, and therefore desired him to alight, which, with the help of two Servants he had with him, he did. *Formator* conducted him in, and left him with *Amoranda*; when the Stranger was set, (for he was very ill able to stand) he first begged *Amoranda* to shut the Door, that none might be witness to his wretched Tale but herself, and then with a flood of Tears began thus:

It is the way of the Damned, Madam, to desire all Mankind should be in their own miserable State; but though I am as wretched as they, I am not so envious: and it is to prevent your Fate and receive your Pity that I am come at this time to you. Sir, *said* Amoranda, your Looks, without your Tale, call for Pity; and I entreat you to drink a Glass of something to comfort you, before you spend the few remaining Spirits you have left, in a Story which, I foresee, will give you pain in the repeating. Alas! Madam, *said he*, Food and I are become Strangers to each other; but 'tis all the pleasure I have to repeat my Wrongs, and my tortured Heart is never capable of a moment's ease but when I am complaining. *Amoranda* was in the utmost perplexity to find out what whining romantic Lover she had got and could not imagine where the Adventure would end or how her Fate came to be concerned in the matter; but the poor Afflicted soon let her into a Secret, which she began to be impatient to know. Madam, *said the Stranger*, I am now going to tell you a Story, which will melt you into the greatest pity; but before I proceed, entreat you will not be too severe upon my Conduct, or say, when I have done, I have reaped the Desert of my own Folly. *Amoranda* promised her best Attention, without any Reflection at all; and the Stranger thus began:

The first thing I am to inform you of, Madam, is my Sex, which is not what it appears to be; I am a Woman, a wretched, miserable, unhappy Woman: my Father was the eldest Son of an ancient Family, born to a very plentiful Estate, and when he died, left only one Son and myself; my Mother died soon after I was born, and my Father left me wholly to the care of my Brother, who was at Age when he died, and my Fortune, which was five thousand Pounds, was to be paid me when I married, or was at age, and to be kept in my Brother's hands till then. I was then about fourteen Years old, and my Brother, who was Father too, used me with all the Tenderness that could be expected from so near a Relation; and had he kept within the Bounds of Honour and loved me only as a Sister, I might have reckoned myself in the

276

number of the Happy. A whole Year past over with the greatest Innocence, and my Brother's Love seemed faultless and natural; but when I was turned of fifteen, in the height of my Bloom and Pride of Beauty, I was one day dressed to the most advantage for a Ball in the neighbourhood, when my Brother came in, and looking steadfastly at me, *Altemira, said he*, Oh *Altemira!* you are too lovely. Then snatching me to his Bosom, pressed me with a Warmth which a little surprized me. I broke loose from his Embraces and asked him what he meant; he seemed a little confounded and left the Room. I confess I was under some apprehension of an approaching Misfortune, but was loth to harbour any Thought to the disadvantage of so dear a Brother, and therefore imputed the Action rather to Chance than Design. He came to the Ball, but would neither dance nor speak, nay, nor so much as look at anything but me, which only I took notice of. When the Company broke up, he conveyed me home, and as we were going, he sighed, and said, I had made him very wretched. How, Brother, *said I, not willing to understand him*, by what Behaviour am I so wretched to make you so? Oh *Altemira! said he*, cease to talk, your Actions had been better, had they been worse; for who can see so much Perfection without Love, without Adoration? Oh *Altemira!* I must, I will enjoy you. It is not possible for me to tell you, Madam, how shocking this was to me, I could hardly keep from swooning in the Coach; but my Passion found vent at my Eyes, and with ten thousand Tears I begged him to recall his scattered Senses, to arm his Reason for his own Defence, to consider I was a Sister, nay, a Sister who was left wholly to his Care, and one who had none to fly to for redress of Injuries but him; and am I so entirely miserable as to find my Ruin where I seek a Sanctuary? *said I.* Oh! by the Ashes of our dead Father and Mother, by all the Ties of natural Affection, of Honour, Virtue, and everything we hold dear in this Life, if you have any regard to my Welfare or your own, stifle this guilty Flame, and let me quench it with my Tears.

I wish, *Altemira, said he*, I could quench it with my own; but 'tis grown too fierce to be extinguished; I have kept it under a great while, and with my utmost Care endeavoured to suppress it: but alas! my Attempts were vain, it was too powerful for me, and is now broken out with such violence that unless you stop its force I must consume to Ashes in the midst of it. My Heart at those words sunk, both with Horrour and Pity; I saw an only Brother, whom I dearly and tenderly loved, a black Criminal entangled in a guilty lawless Love, while I, who only had the power of relieving him, lay under an indispensable Duty of refusing to do so. As soon as we alighted out of the Coach, we went to our different Apartments; how my poor Brother spent his Night, I know not, but mine went on with a heavy Pace, I counted every dull Hour as it came, and bathed in Tears, lay thinking how to extricate myself from the miserable Condition I was in. I found my unfortunate Brother was too far gone to be brought to reason, and had often heard a desperate Disease must have a desperate Cure, I therefore resolved to end his pain, by absence, and go where he should never see me till I was satisfied he had got the better of his own Folly.

In order to this, I got up when the Clock struck four, and calling up my Maid, who lay in a Closet just by me, I made her pack up some Clothes for me and herself, and taking all my Mother's Jewels, which were now mine, and what ready Money I had, we went down unheard or observed by anybody and took the road to a Wood hard by: I well knew as soon as my Brother was up, he would, as usual, come to enquire after my health, and when he missed me, make strict enquiry after me; I therefore thought it most advisable to stay a day or two where we were, till the search was a little over, and then pursue my intended Journey. My Maid favoured my design, though she knew it not, by stepping into the Buttery before she came out, and filling her Pocket with something for her Breakfast, which we lived upon two days. In a thicket in the Wood we found a Shepherd's Hut, deserted by the owner, where we lay that night; and the next day towards evening, we ventured to a Farmer's House, where for a Guinea to the Man, who was newly come and knew neither of us, he undertook to carry us both where I directed him. When I was about Eleven years of Age, we had a Female Servant, who was Cook, and had lived in the Family many Years. She just then married away, and to her I went: she was exceedingly surprised to see me at such an early hour, (for we rid all night) and no better attended. Here, said I to the Man who brought us, there's your Hire and a crown to drink, make the best of your way home again. I now thought myself the happiest Creature upon earth, for I saw myself safe, and had one to whom I dared intrust my Secret, which I never did to my Maid *Kitty*, because I would not expose my Brother, and for which he owed me and paid me a Grudge. The Woman, to whose House we were come, was always called when she lived with my Father by the name of her Place, *Cook*; and so I shall call her for the future: She married a Gardener, who lived some time with Lord *Lofty*: I presume, Madam, said she, you know the Man, and so do I too well. It was, no doubt, decreed that I should never have rest, otherwise I should have missed his fatal acquaintance. Pray, Madam, *said* Amoranda, give me leave to interrupt you so long, as while I ask you whether you ever favoured me with a Letter in your Life? That Madam, *said* Altemira, you shall know presently. I had not been three days at *Cook's*, before my Lord came that way a hunting, and just at dinner-time, being very hungry, he popped in upon us, before we were aware of him. 'Tis possible you will not readily believe I ever had a Face worth looking at, while you see no remains of a good one; but—There I interrupt you again, *said* Amoranda; for though you have now, a livid,[23] pale Complexion, your Features are still fine, and a little quiet of mind would raise those fallen Cheeks to their usual plumpness. Be that as it will, *said* Altemira, Lord *Lofty* saw something in it, which he thought worth his notice, and he

---

[23] *livid*: pallid, bluish, leaden.

no sooner cast an eye upon me, than he vowed an everlasting Love: he took *Cook* aside, and found out who I was, but not the occasion which brought me there. He spent the remaining part of the day with us and most of the night before he could be persuaded to leave us; and next day he came again and said ten thousand things to win a foolish Heart, and I must own, I began to be too well pleased with every Word which fell from his bewitching Tongue; he soon perceived it, and as soon took the advantage of my Weakness. One day as we were alone, he began to take some Liberties which I was not very well pleased with, and said; My Lord, you abuse the freedom I have given you, I have hitherto believed your intentions honourable, you know best whether they are so or no; if they are not, be assured your Quality will stand for very little in my esteem, and till I am better satisfied in that point, your Lordship must excuse me if I see you no more. Saying thus, I left the room and went to my own, where I locked myself up, and came no more out while my Lord stayed, which was some hours. The next Morning before my Eyes were well opened to read it, a Letter came from him, filled with ten thousand protestations of his sincerity, and if I would but give him leave once more to throw himself at my feet, he would soon convince me of his reality. I have already owned his oily Tongue had made an impression on my Heart, and I took a secret pleasure in hoping all he said was true; I sent no answer back by the Messenger, which was giving a tacit Consent to another interview, and I saw him at my feet before I thought the Messenger could have returned. Oh! what an assiduous Creature is Man, before enjoyment, and what a careless, negligent Wretch after it. Dear *Altemira, said my Lord,* why do you use me with such contempt? what shall I do to convince you of the real value I have for you? is there one Oath left, which I have not sworn to confirm my Love to you? or can my actions display themselves with greater ardency than I have already shown? Yes my Lord, *said I,* there is one action yet remains, which must authorise all the rest; that once done, I am yours forever, but till then, you know what you have to trust to. I understand you, Madam, said the base deceiver, and I greatly approve your cautious Proceedings, you shall soon be satisfied in every point, and I will break through all my own measures to make you easy; tomorrow's Sun shall see us one. After this promise he stayed not long, but left me in the greatest, the highest tranquility I ever knew. When my Lord was gone, *Cook* came to me, and told me she was afraid there was some juggle betwixt my Lord and *Kitty*; for I have seen him whispering with her twice, *said she,* and beg you will have a care what you do and how you trust her; she is very sullen at something and has been out of humour ever since she came here.

I know it, *said I,* and the reason is because I have not let her into the Secret of leaving my Brother's House. I wish, *said Cook,* you would part with her, I do not like her, I can recommend one to you just now, who will, I am sure, be very just to you.

No, *said I,* I will first be convinced of her behaviour, I hate a strange face.

Well, Madam, *said* Cook, I wish you may not repent it. For my part, I was so full of satisfaction at the Promise my Lord had made me, that I could find room for no other thought, and went to Bed that night two hours sooner than usual, that I might indulge it without interruption. As soon as day appeared, my poor unwary Heart gave a fresh alarm to Love and Joy and when I heard the Family stirring, I got up and dressed me to the best advantage, expecting every hour to see my Lord attended by his Chaplain. At last I saw my Lord enter, but no Chaplain, he came to me and said, My *Altemira*, I am now come to remove all your doubts, take this, *said he*, (pulling out a Paper) and let it convince you how much I love. I opened the Paper, and found it a promise to marry me, with a Bond of ten thousand Pound if ever he receded from his Word. I own I was pleased with the Paper which he gave me in great form, as his Act and Deed, before *Cook* and her Husband, who were both Witnesses to it: But I could not find out the meaning of it, and said, My Lord if you design to marry me, what occasion is there for all this formality and stuff? I presume you are your own Master; what then retards your design? I'll tell you, my dearest *Altemira*, *said he*, when you and I are alone. Well, *said I*, let me go and lay by this Paper, and I'll wait upon you again: I went up to my Chamber, and locked it up in a Scrutore[24] which stood in the room, and of which I had the Key, and then returned to my Lord, whom I found all alone; Well my Lord, *said I*, with a much freer air than usual, now we are alone, pray let me hear this Secret.

Altemira, (said this base Impostor) I now look upon you with a Husband's Eyes, you are *in Foro Conscientiae*[25] my Wife, and as such I will entrust you with all I know: About nine Months ago, I saw a Lady whom I admired then, as I do you now, and after I had made my addresses to her some time, she consented to crown my wishes, and we were to be married in a Month's time; but before it was expired (with the true Spirit of inconstancy which reigns in most of your Sex) she jilted me and admitted another, to whom she is to be married next Week. Now, my Dear, *said he*, should I marry first, she will fling all her own Levity at my door, and say the Falsehood was mine; for which reason, since she is so near marriage, I will deny myself the pleasure of thy dear Arms a few days, rather than undergo the Scandal of doing an ill Action to a fine Woman. Here was a gloss set upon as base a design as ever Villain invented; and I, who looked upon all he said as from an Oracle, gave a pleasing ear to it. He stayed not late that Night, but came again early next day, for he lived within three little Miles of *Cook*'s House, and every time he came, grew more familiar with me: I must confess to you, good Madam, I loved this Ingrate to distraction, and after such a firm substantial proof of his as I had locked up, I thought myself exceedingly secure; my fear and caution which used to attend me constantly, now left me, and I had no other desires than to please my undoer! Three or four days after he had given me the above-

---

[24] *Scrutore*: an escritoire, a writing desk.
[25] *in Foro Conscientiae*: literally, 'within the jurisdiction of conscience'.

mentioned Paper, he came, and said, My *Altemira*, you have never seen my House, I desire you will go with me today and dine there; I hope I have given you too many demonstrations of my Love to leave you any room for fear. My Lord, *said I*, 'tis now my Interest to believe everything that's good of you, and I have no fear of anything, but a want of Power to please you always. After some other discourse I went up to dress, and you may be sure I left no charm behind me, which I could possibly take with me. *Cook* was not willing I should go, but durst not be known to persuade me from it, because my Lord was a good friend to her Husband; however I ventured to go, and met with all the civil treatment in the World. I now thought myself at home and was pleased to think how soon I should give my Brother an account of my good Fortune from thence: but alas! my doom was near, my eternal Destruction just at hand. When we were at dinner, a Letter came for my Lord, which he read, and gave it to me, it was an account of the Lady being married, whom he had some days before told me of. Now *Altemira*, *said he*, 'tis our turn, tomorrow you and I will join our hands. When dinner was over, he sent his Chaplain for a License, who accordingly brought one which he showed me; the afternoon we spent in different Diversions, and at Night when I would have gone to *Cook's*, my Lord said I should never leave the House till it was my own, and begged I would be satisfied to stay all Night: he told me I should have a room to myself and Maid, and in the Morning *Hymen* should crown our wishes. I own I was not long persuading to comply; but soon consented to my own undoing, for about One o'Clock, when all the House was gone to Bed, I heard a little knocking at my Chamber door; *Kitty*, immediately rose without saying anything to me and opened the Door, my Lord entered and came to my Bedside. *Kitty*, the treacherous *Kitty*, put on her Clothes and left the Room, as she had been instructed. My dearest *Altemira*, *said my Lord*, it is impossible for me to rest, while you are so near me; give me a Bridegroom's privilege and let me lie down by you. I found myself under some concern at his Proposal, but considered a few hours would give him a just title to all I had in my possession: I called every circumstance to my memory; the firm engagement I had under his hand; the Letter from *London* of the Lady's Marriage; the License and Preparations, which were made; and the Millions of Oaths and Vows which I had received from a perjured tongue of an eternal Love; all those, in conjunction with an unguarded hour, made me a prey to the basest of Men. In short, Madam, he gained his ends, and after some hours' Enjoyment, got up and left me. *Kitty*, when he went out, came in again, but I was so little apprehensive of my own Fate, that I said not much to her, but got up and re-assumed all my Charms. When we were at Breakfast, my Lord said with a sort of raillery: It shall never be said, Madam, that you come to me to be married; if you think fit, we'll confirm our Vows at *Cook's*, as you call her. With all my heart, my Lord, *said I*, she is Witness to our Contract, let her also see our Nuptials. When we had done, the Coach was ordered to the door, and Lord *Lofty* put me into it, and accompanied me to *Cook's*. Now, Madam, *said he*, I will leave you for an hour and then return with my Chaplain: In the meantime, *said he to Cook*, send for what Provisions you think fit for dinner to my House, and do you dress it well, and I will help to eat it. This was no sooner said than my Lord whipped into the Coach and drove away. As soon as he was gone, my Maid came to me and said, Madam, I have heard by chance my Mother is not well; I beg you will give me leave to go and see her: If she recovers, I will return; if not, you may be pleased to provide yourself of another, I shall give you an early account. *Kitty, said I*, it falls out unluckily for you, but who can help misfortune? I am not willing to part with you, and if you can return in a month's time, so long I will stay for you. The Jade thanked me and went away.

I was now left alone with honest *Cook*, then she asked me if I was married? I told her, No, but very near it. She shook her head, and said she hoped I had brought the same Treasure back with me which I took to my Lord's, for he was going this Morning to *London*. How do you know? *said I, in a distracted tone*. I went, *said she*, to enquire for you last night, when I found you came not back, but was not admitted to see you; and I then heard orders given for the best Horses to be gotten ready for *London* in the morning. Good Heaven! *said I*, can this be true? Is there no such thing as Justice in Man? No Faith in their Oaths and Vows? Oh *Cook! said I*, if you are still my Friend, as I hope you are, send there this minute to know the truth of what you tell me: But I fear, *continued I*, there is too much in it, both by his bringing me here again, and by *Kitty's* going away, that Wench has certainly sold me to him, and I am undone; for Oh! *said I*, all is gone. While *Cook* was preparing to send to my Lord's, a Footman came with a Letter for me; he just delivered it and went off, which I opened, and read, as follows:

MADAM,

An unlucky Accident has forced me away to London; *it is so very sudden, that I have not time to excuse my going. I hope, at my return, I shall find you where I leave you; and you shall find me*

Your most Obedient,

LOFTY.

As soon as I had read this Letter, my Spirits sunk, and I remained breathless in my Chair; when *Cook* came in to know what News, she saw the Paper dropped at my foot and guessed something of the Contents. I was conveyed to my Bed, where I lay for some days in a most miserable Condition; though in the midst of all my cruel Reflections, I found my Conscience cleared myself, and I was in hopes my Lord's Bond would in some measure justify my Actions to the World. With this little Satisfaction I got up, and went to the Scrutore to take out and look at all the hopes I had left; I fully designed, if he refused to marry me at his return, to sue his Bond, recover the ten thousand Pound, and choose a quiet Retirement from the World, where I might end my days in peace; but Oh! what Tongue can tell my Surprize, Confusion and Despair, when I missed the Paper which I had put into a silver Box, and both were gone together.

I called *Cook* with a feeble Voice, who came to me, to hear my new Complaints. Oh *Cook! said I*, my Misery is now complete, I have lost my Lord's Bond, and Promise of Marriage; it was in a silver Box in this Scrutore. A silver Box, *said Cook*; I saw *Kitty* put one in her Pocket the fatal Day you went to my Lord's and asked her what was in it: She said, her Lady's Patches:[26] You would trust that wicked Queen, *said she*, whom I always disliked, and now—Ay, *said I*, and now she has undone me for ever; may her Perfidy to me meet with a just Reward. Nature was so far spent in me by my previous Trouble, that I sunk under this new Addition, past all hope of ever rising more; I was some Weeks before I had the use of my Reason, but lay like a stupid Log, taking what Sustenance they gave me, because I knew not what I did. At last, by degrees I recovered my Senses, but was infinitely less happy, than where I had none, because I was then free from Reflection; my cruel Disquiet of Mind made so great an alteration in my Face, that when I came to look at it, I could not believe I was *Altemira*. After I had been in this condition four Months, I heard Lord *Lofty* was returned from *London*; I immediately wrote to him in the most supplicating Terms, but he would not vouchsafe me an Answer: I wrote again, and he sent it back unopened. I had once a mind to go to him, but I thought his Behaviour to myself would be of a piece with that to my Letters, and I should only expose myself to his Servants and pick up new matter for fresh Grief: but I soon found why I was used with so much Contempt and heard he made his Addresses to the rich, young, beauteous *Amoranda*. I own, Madam, your Person and Fortune has an infinite advantage over mine; but a Man, who is resolved to be a Libertine, has no true value for a Woman's good Qualities; the best she can show to please him is to give into all his brutal Pleasures: and as I was sure you would shun such a Lover, I own I did write a Line to let you into the Temper of the Man. But now, Madam, that I have told you my Wrongs, I hope I have engaged your Justice, Goodness, and Pity, and you will no longer encourage his Addresses, but look upon them with the same Contempt as from a married Man. Madam, *said* Amoranda, your Case I own is very deplorable, and what would give me a sensible Affliction, were it not in my power to do you some service; but I believe I can make you a very acceptable Present and will contrive a way of serving you beside. At those words, *Amoranda* left *Altemira*, and returned with the Box and Bond; This, Madam, *said she*, is, I presume, the Loss you have so much lamented, and I do assure you, Lord *Lofty* has not been at *London* since his Injuries to you but at a Seat he has just by this House, and there he is now: that Box which I have now given you, he accidentally dropped in my Garden, nor does he know I have it; and till I see

---

[26] *Patches*: small, adhesive beauty marks made of silk or court-plaster, often cut in decorative shapes (stars, hearts, flowers) pasted on the face to highlight the complexion, attract attention, or cover blemishes. Although worn primarily by women, fashionable young men wore them, too.

you as firmly his as he has promised you should be, I will never leave contriving.

The sight of Lord *Lofty's* Bond, gave poor *Altemira* a satisfaction not to be expressed; the Blood which had so long forsaken her Cheeks began to run again in its wonted Channels, and Joy diffused itself in every Feature of her Face: Is it possible, *said she*, that I am so happy as to recover this testimony of his Villainy? 'tis some little satisfaction for my lost honour that I have this small justification of myself. 'Tis a very great one to me, *said* Amoranda, that I can contribute towards it, and if I can but gain one Point I have in my head, I hope I shall see you perfectly easy; but I have an old Gentleman in the House who must be let into the Secret, or nothing can be done.

Madam, *said* Altemira, my Secrets are too well known to the World; engage who you please in the Scheme, but spare me the confusion of hearing it. Then, *said* Amoranda, I will leave you employed while I go to my Guardian, and desire you will write a Letter to Lord *Lofty*, to let him know you have recovered the Bond and Contract which your perfidious Servant returned to him, and that you expect all the satisfaction the Law can give you; then leave the rest to me. Here she left *Altemira*, and sent *Jenny* with Pen and Ink to her, while she told *Formator* the whole Story; he needed no Addition to Lord *Lofty's* Character, to confirm him 'twas a very bad one: however, his Indignation was ready to boil over, and he expressed himself as every Man of Honour would do upon such an occasion. *Formator, said* Amoranda, I have this poor Creature's Wrongs so much at heart, that I shall never rest till I recover her Quiet; but you must give me leave, because I have promised never to see Lord *Lofty* more unless I have your Consent for it, and without seeing him nothing can be done.

Madam, *said* Formator, I applaud your just and generous Design, and am so far from desiring to hinder it that I will be your Assistant to the utmost of my power. Then, *said* Amoranda, give me leave to send for my Lord this minute and do you abscond. *Formator* consented to her Proposal; and she wrote the following Lines to my Lord, and sent then by a Footman just then.

MY LORD,

I do not want Inclination to meet you where you desired at Nine; but my Argus, *as you have some time called him, is gone abroad for this Night, so that we may have an Interview within doors. You know the Hand so well, that this Paper needs no other Subscription, but that*

I am Yours.

As soon as she had dispatched this Letter, she went to see how *Altemira* went on with hers, and found she had just finished it. I am beforehand with you, *said* Amoranda, for I have written to my Lord since I saw you, and sent it. 'Tis an Invitation to a Man I now hate, and if I can but gain my ends upon him—Come, let me see what you have written. She took the Letter from her trembling hand, and read:

If Prayers and Tears could mollify an unrelenting obdurate Heart, yours had long ago been softened into Justice and Pity: but as they have failed me so often, I think it needless to try them any more. To tell you, my Lord, of Heaven and Conscience, would only serve to make you sport; but methinks you should have some little regard to your bleeding Honour, which lies stabbed and mangled in a thousand places by your own Barbarities.

However, my Lord, I am now to tell you, a fortunate hit has put you into my power, and the Contract you gave me and corrupted my Servant to steal from me is once more fallen into my hands. I dare say you will easily believe I intend to carry it as far as the Law will bear, but am still forced to wish you would do a voluntary piece of Justice to

Your Injured

ALTEMIRA.

This Letter was sealed and directed for Lord *Lofty*; and the Summons *Amoranda* had sent him soon brought him to receive her Commands. In the meantime, neither *Altemira* or *Formator* knew anything of her Design; but as she hoped it would be attended with good Success, she was resolved to have the Merit of it wholly to herself.

Altemira's Letter she gave to one of her Footmen, with an order to bring it in when she called for Tea; and to say (if any questions were asked) a Man on horseback enquired for my Lord, desired that it might be delivered to him, and rode away.

Amoranda desired *Formator* and *Altemira* to go up into the Room over the Summer-House, where *Brown* heard all *Callid's* and *Froth's* Contrivance, and where they might hear what she said to my Lord; for in the Summer-House she intended to entertain him. They were no sooner placed in their different Posts than they heard the Visiting-knock, and my Lord entered and enquired for *Amoranda*, whom he found in the Summer-House: he ran to her with eager transport, and finding her alone thought opportunity had joined itself to his Desires, and he had nothing to do but reap a Crop he never intended to make a title to. My dearest *Amoranda*, *said he*, how shall I return this favour? with what joy did I receive your obliging Letter, and with what delight am I come to die at your Feet? My Lord, *said* Amoranda, you seemed so very earnest in your Letter for an interview, I was resolved to give you an opportunity, and shall now be glad to hear what you have to say. To say, my Angel! *said he*, can any Man want, a Theme that has so glorious a Subject as *Amoranda?* Come to my arms, my lovely Charmer, and let me whisper out my very Soul upon thy lovely Bosom. Hold, my Lord, *said she*, before you run into those violent raptures, let me know your designs a little; I confess you have often rallied[27] a married State, but that I rather take to be a sort of a Compliance to a debauched, wicked age, than any real inclination of your own; come, my Lord confess you have a mind to marry. To tell you, Madam,

---

[27] *rallied*: made fun of.

I have a mind to marry, is, to tell you I have not a mind to love you; why should you desire to subject yourself to one whom you may forever make your Slave? The very thoughts of being bound to love would make me hate; and take it from me, as a very great truth, Every Man breathing, makes a better Lover than Husband. Pray, my Lord, *said she*, from whence do you prove your Assertion? I must own my experience and observations are but young, and yet I know several married People, who in all appearance love one another exceedingly well.

Yes, Madam, *said he*, in all appearance, I grant you; but appearances are often false. Why then, said *Amoranda*, by the same rule, we may believe the love of one of you to your Mistress as forced and empty as that of a married Man to his Wife; we have no way to know either, but by their words and actions, and those that think contrary to both, we look upon with so much contempt that we shun their Conversation and think it a fault to be seen in their Company.

What a pity 'tis, *said my Lord*, so many good things should be said upon so bad a Subject. I wonder, *said Amoranda*, your Lordship does not get the House of Lords to endeavour to repeal the Law of Marriage:[28] Why should you Lawgivers impose upon other People what you think improper to follow yourselves? Oh! Madam, *said the Peer*, there are politick reasons for what we do; but if you would ever oblige me in anything, let us have no more of Marriage. Why really, my Lord, *said Amoranda*, I am not yet at my last Prayers, so that I hope you will not think Despair has any hand in what I have said; and to divert the discourse, we will have a dish of Tea. Here she rung a Bell, and called for the Tea-table, which was immediately brought, and followed by a Servant with a Letter for Lord *Lofty*; who no sooner cast an eye upon the Superscription, than he knew the hand to be *Altemira*'s. The effects of a conscious Guilt immediately seized the whole Man, his tongue faultered, his cheeks glowed, his hand trembled, and his eyes darted a wild horror; when striving to recover himself, he put the Letter into his pocket, and with a forced smile, said, A Man had better have a Wife itself, than a troublesome Mistress. Nay, my Lord, said *Amoranda*, if that Letter be from a Mistress, I am sure you are impatient to read it, I will readily dispense with all Ceremony, and beg you will do so. Madam, *said he*, the foolish Girl from whom this comes, I own, I once had an intrigue with, but—I don't know how it was, she had a better knack at getting a Heart than keeping it; besides, she gave me such a consumed deal of trouble, that I was almost weary of her, before I had her: No, my Charmer, *said he*, *Amoranda*, and only *Amoranda* commands my heart; I own no Mistress but her, nor will I ever wear any other Fetters, than those she puts me on. Now do I most steadfastly believe, *said she*, that you have said as much, a thousand times, to the very Lady, whose Letter you

---

[28] *Law of Marriage*: Great Britain was the only Protestant nation in Europe with no provision for divorce of any kind.

have in your Pocket; Come my Lord, *said she,* either read it while I am by, or I will go away to give you an Opportunity.

Madam, *said he,* rather than lose one Minute of your Company, I will do Penance for three or four; but be assured, I intended to have returned it unopened, as I have done several from the same hand: but to oblige you, I'll read it. While he was doing so, *Amoranda* watched his Looks, and found a fresh alteration in his Face at every line he read; but when he came to that part which told him *Altemira* had recovered his Contract, he turned pale as Death, stamped, and cried—Zounds—Bless Me, *said Amoranda,* what's the matter my Lord? is the Lady not well? My Lord, after he had paused a while, said, he was mistaken in the Hand, that the Letter came from his Steward, with an account of a very considerable loss he had had.

Pugh! *said* Amoranda, is that all? you know, my Lord, there are Misfortunes in all Families, as Sir *Roger de Coverley*[29] says; come, come, drink a Dish of Tea and wash away Sorrow. My Lord sat very moody for some time, considering that since *Altemira* had recovered his Bond and Contract, she would, if only to revenge his Ill-usage of her, be very troublesome: and again, he thought if once the World should come to see them, everybody would say he was a Villain if he did not marry her. He therefore resolved to put a stop to her Expectations by marrying of *Amoranda,* and then she would be glad to come to his Terms, and for her own Credit smother the matter. This was just as *Amoranda* expected and hoped for; she wisely imagined that if my Lord once saw himself under a sort of necessity of marrying, he would be for choosing the least Evil (as he thought all Wives were) and rather marry a Woman he had not enjoyed with as fine an Estate as he could expect than take one with an inferior Fortune, and of whom he could expect no more that what he had had already. *Amoranda* saw the Struggles of his Soul in his looks, how unwilling he was to come to a Resolution so much against his Inclinations; but he had just promised her, he would wear no Fetters but what she put him on, and she was as firmly resolved to fit him with a Pair.

My Lord, *said* Amoranda, your Tea will be cold; I wish I were worthy to know what weighty Affair employs your Thoughts?

A weighty Affair indeed, Madam! *said he;* for I am now bringing myself to a resolution of doing what I have often thought no Woman upon Earth could have had the power of persuading me to: But your Charms have dissolved every design, and I now offer you a Heart for Life. My Lord, (said *Amoranda*) a Man of your Estate and Quality leaves a Woman no room for Objection; but if I should comply too soon, you'll think I am too cheaply won and value me accordingly. Madam, *said he,* I am one of those who hate trouble, and the less you give me, infinitely the more you'll engage me to you: Come, my *Amoranda, said he,* your old, crabbed Guardian is now from home, and there

---

[29] *Roger de Coverley:* the country squire created by Richard Steele as one of the points of view in the *Spectator;* he was developed in subsequent numbers of the periodical. He speaks this line in the 5 July 1711 *Spectator,* in which he is giving a tour of his family portrait gallery.

is no time like that present; I will send just now for my Chaplain, and we will do in half an hour what I hope we shall never repent of. But my Lord, *said she*, the Canonical Hour[30] is past, and you have no License. The Canonical Hours, Madam, *said he*, are betwixt eight and twelve, and not a farthing matter whether Morning or Night; and for a License, I'll step home myself and take care of one. My Lord just remembered he had one by him, which he had purchased to bamboozle poor *Altemira*, and since he was in such haste, 'twas no more than scratching out one name, and interlining another; whipped into his Coach, bid his Coachman be at home in half an hour, and told the Lady in another he would be back. *Amoranda*, called down her two Prisoners, who had been within hearing all this while, and leaving them in the Summer-House, she ran in, called for a Pen and Ink, and wrote thus to my Lord:

I am, my Lord, in such Confusion, I have hardly time to write to you: Formator *is just come home; I know he hates you and will certainly prevent our designs, till he has writ to my Uncle. I therefore desire you will, with your Chaplain, come, as you once proposed, into the Grove your own way; and when it is dark, I will come to you: I doubt not but your Chaplain has the Matrimony by heart; if not, pray let him con his lesson before he comes.*

Yours in great haste,

AMORANDA.

When she had sent this Letter whip and spur after my Lord, she returned to the Summer-House and desired *Altemira* to come in and dress her in the same Gown she had on; for though it was now past nine o'clock, it was light enough to distinguish colours. As soon as they had got ready, they went to the Grove, and *Amoranda* placed *Altemira* just where my Lord was to enter and bid her whisper, under pretence of *Formator's* being in the Garden, as well to disguise her Voice, as to pronounce her own Name without being fairly heard; and when you are married, (said *Amoranda*) tell my Lord you will go in and go to Supper, and as soon as you can conveniently, get to Bed, and send *Jenny* to conduct him to you. She here told them, she had written to retard his return till it was dark; and now *Altemira, said she*, I hope you are near that happiness you have so long wished for: I think I hear the Coach. *Formator* (who was all this while with them) and I, will place ourselves where we shall hear you if you speak never so low; but you shall see no more of us, till my Lord is in bed with you, and then we will come in and wish you Joy. As soon as *Amoranda* had done speaking, my Lord came and found *Altemira* ready, whom he took for *Amoranda*; the Chaplain soon did the work and made them one to the unspeakable joy of the Bride. She observed all *Amoranda's* Orders, and whispering, told him she would go in, and send *Jenny* for him, as soon as she had an opportunity. My Lord sent away his Coach and Chaplain and waited with the greatest impatience for *Jenny*, who came

---

[30] *Canonical Hour*: the time during which marriages can be legally performed in parish churches in England.

after some time, and conveyed him in the dark to *Altemira*. As soon as my Lord was gone out of the Grove, *Formator* and *Amoranda* came out too, who dared not stir till he was gone, for fear of being heard; when they thought he was in Bed, they went into the Chamber, with each of them a light in their hand, to wish the Bride and Bridegroom Joy. *Formator* went in first; and when my Lord saw him, he thought he was come to take away his Spouse, and cried out, Be gone, Sir, she's my Wife. Fear not, my Lord, (said *Amoranda*, behind) nobody shall disturb you, only we are come to wish you Joy. How, Madam, (said my Lord, when he saw and heard *Amoranda*) are you there? To whom have you disposed of me, your Chamber-Maid? No my Lord, *said Amoranda*, I scorn so base an action, but I have given you to one, who has the best right to you; come *Altemira, said she*, sit up and let's throw the Stocking: besides, you are both gone supperless to Bed, and I have a Sack-Posset coming up stairs.[31]

When my Lord had looked sufficiently round and saw how matters went, he found it was a folly to complain and was resolved to turn the Scale and show himself a Man of Honour at last; in order to which, he turned to *Altemira*, and said, Can you forgive the Injuries I have done you, Madam? My Lord, *said Amoranda*, I dare answer for *Altemira's* pardon; but who must answer for yours? Madam, *said my Lord*, I am at age and will answer for myself, and do upon honour declare, I am pleased with what you have done; there is certainly a secret pleasure in doing Justice, though we often evade it, and a secret horror in doing ill, though we often comply with the temptation. I own my design was to wrong this innocent Lady, but I had an inward remorse, for what I was about, and I would not part with the present quiet and satisfaction that fills my breast to be Lord of the whole Creation. How great a truth is it, *said Formator*, that Virtue knows its own reward; and who that knows the pleasure of a good Action would ever torment himself with doing an ill one? My Lord, *said he*, this happy turn of temper, has made you a Friend, which you may one day think worth your Notice: and now, Madam, (said he to *Amoranda*) let us leave the happy Pair, and *Altemira* to tell her Lord every Incident, that helped to bring her wretched Circumstances to such a joyful conclusion.

The next Morning, my Lord sent for his whole Equipage and carried his Lady home, as became his Wife. *Formator* and *Amoranda* accompanied them to the House, where my Lord had first decoyed his *Altemira*; and as they went by, called at *Cook's*, who was soon informed of all the good fortune that attended her young Lady, and told her she had a Letter for her from her Brother, which she gave her. *Amoranda* told her Ladyship, there was nobody in Company, but who knew the story of her Brother; and desired she would read it, which she did thus:

---

[31] *Sack-Posset*: on the wedding night, the bride threw her stocking, and, according to tradition, the guest who was hit would be the next to marry. Sack posset was a delicacy made of curdled milk, sack (a white wine from Spain or the Canary Islands), sugar, and spices.

If I burnt in an unlawful Flame for my dearest Sister, I have quenched it with my Blood, I no sooner missed you, than ten thousand torments seized my guilty Mind; I spent three days in search of you, but every Messenger returned without any News: I feared the worst, and fell into the highest Despair. What have I done! said I, ruined an only Sister, left to my Care, who is now, if alive, destitute and a wanderer, and all this by an unlawful Love! Those thoughts distracted me so, that I took up a Sword which lay by me, and struck it into by Breast; my Wound proved not mortal, and a few days brought me a healing Balsam, for I was told where you were: I was resolved to drive out one extreme by another, and see you no more, till I had tried my Success on a Creature, superiour in every Charm to her whole Sex; she listened to my Love, and I pursued it, till I made the Fair-one mine. And if Altemira will but forgive what is past, I may call myself the happiest Man in the World. You will, doubtless, be desirous to know my Choice; and to let you see I have not lessened my Family by it, know the Lady is Sister to Lord Lofty, who lives so near Cook, that you must have heard of him. I hope you will now return to the arms of your

> *Repenting Happy Brother.*

Here was a new occasion of Joy for Lady *Lofty*, and my Lord was very well satisfied: they went all together to his House and spent a few days with them, till Colonel *Charge'em* came from *London* to visit his Lordship; who no sooner saw *Amoranda*, than he began to attack, nor she him than she began to parley: which, when *Formator* saw (whose Eyes were always open to *Amoranda's* actions) he told her, if she pleased they would go home in the morning. She consented, because she thought it in vain to deny; otherways, she had no dislike to a Feather nor did she think a laced Coat a disagreeable Dress, and she could have dispensed with a little more of the Man of War's Company; but her trusty Guardian put a stop to all farther Commerce betwixt them, by ordering the Coach to be ready early in the Morning, so that they were almost half-way home before the Colonel was up, who very probably would have been for waiting upon the young Lady home. Lady *Lofty* and *Amoranda*, after a mutual promise of an everlasting Friendship, parted with much unwillingness, but with a design to see one another often. As they were going home, their way lay between two steep hills, where they met a couple of Men masked. *Amoranda* was exceedingly frighted, and said she was sure they should be robbed; but *Formator* bid her have a good heart and called to the Coachman to stop. He got out of the Coach, and taking a Pistol from one of the Footmen, stood at the Coach door on one side, while two of the Servants, by his order, did the same at the other, and waited till the two Masks came to them. But they soon found Money was not their Errand, it was the Lady they wanted, who had no other guard than *Formator*, her Coachman, and two Footmen. One of them rid up and shot the poor Coachman, who fell out of the Coach-Box, wounded, but not dead; the same resolute Rogue rode up to the two Footmen on one side of the Coach, while the other engaged

Formator, who hid his Pistol, till he had his Enemy pretty near him, and then let fly a brace of Bullets at him, which kindly saluted his brain, and down he dropped. The other, who had beat back the Footmen, seeing *Formator* an old Man, rode round to dispatch him, and then get into the Coach-Box and away with the Lady; but he found the old Man pretty tough, for before the Servants could come to him, who were both disarmed, he had closed in with the Rogue, wrenched an empty Pistol out of his hand, which he had discharged at one of the Servants, but missed him, and with it knocked him down: he was only stunned with the blow, but *Formator* stayed not for his recovery; he ordered the two Footmen to get the wounded Coachman into the Coach, and one of them to get into the Coach-Box, and drive home with all speed. *Amoranda*, when the Coachman was shot, fell into a swoon, and continued in it, till *Formator* got into the Coach; he laid her head in his bosom and chafed her temples, till he had recovered her. Her Reason no sooner returned, than she enquired after his safety: Do you live, *Formator*, said she, and have you no Wounds? No, my lovely Charge, *said he*, (transported beyond himself, that he had her safe) I have no Wounds, but what the fear of losing you gave me; the dreadful apprehension of such a misfortune, stabbed me in a thousand places. Well, *said she*, I am glad you are not hurt, but I wish we were at home.

That, Madam, *said he*, we shall be presently; we have not above three Miles to your own House. As soon as they got home, a Surgeon was sent for to dress the Coachman's Wounds, who was shot through the arm; and *Amoranda*, was some days before she recovered her Fright. Three Weeks were now past since they left Lord *Lofty's* in which time, *Formator* had by a daily application endeavoured to form *Amoranda's* mind to his own liking; he tried to bring her to a true taste of that Behaviour which makes every Woman agreeable to every Man of Sense. A Man, *said he*, of true Judgment and a good Understanding has the greatest contempt in the World for one of those Creatures we commonly call a Coquet: Levity and a light Carriage is so very despicable in a Woman that it is not possible for the rest of her qualities, though never so good, to atone for them; how much more does it raise a young Lady's Character, to have one Man of sense vindicate her Conduct, than to hear a thousand Coxcombs, cry,—Gad she's a fine Woman, she's a fine Woman of Fire and Spirit? The Commendations of such Men, Madam, *said he*, are like the compliment of a Dog just come out of the dirt, while he fawns upon you, he defiles your Clothes. Nature, when it formed you, showed its greatest skill, and sent you into the World so very complete, that even Envy itself cannot charge you with one single blemish; your beauteous Form is all Angelic, and your Understanding no way inferior to it; a Temper mild and easy, and a Fortune great enough to satisfy the avarice of the greatest Miser: and why, lovely *Amoranda*, must all these fine accomplishments be eclipsed, by that Foible of your Sex, Vanity? Why have you such a greedy thirst after that Praise, which every Man that has his eyes and ears, must give you of course? For Heaven's sake, dear Madam, *said he*, disguise at least the pleasure you take in it, and receive it with a modest, careless indifference: a Man who once sees a Woman pleased with flattery has gained more than half his point and can never despair of success, while he has so good, so powerful an advocate about the heart he aims at. *Formator, said Amoranda*, were you never flattered when you were a young Man? I fancy you don't know the pleasure of it, but I am resolved I will never think it a pleasure again, because you dislike it in me; for it must be a disagreeable quality, or you would never argue so strenuously against it. Nay, and there's another thing which will make me leave it, and that is——Hush, *said she*, I hear a Coach stop at the door, let's go and see who's come. She ran into the entry, and was most agreeably surprized to see two young Ladies alighting, one of whom was a particular Favorite, and had been her Companion when a Child; the other Lady was a perfect stranger, but she came with *Amoranda's* Friend, and for that reason was equally welcome: they came in a little before Supper, and *Amoranda* was exceedingly pleased she had got a Female Companion or two. When they were at Supper and saw *Formator* sit at Table, *Arentia*, (for that was the young Lady's name) asked if he was a Relation of *Amoranda's*. She said he was better than a Relation, he was a Friend, and one to whose Care her Uncle had committed her. As soon as supper was over, *Formator* left the Ladies to themselves, and he was no sooner gone, than *Arentia* asked how long he had been in the Family. *Amoranda* said, about six Months: he is, *said she*, a very good sort of an old Man, if he were not so very wise; but the truth is, we foolish Girls are not to be trusted with ourselves, and he has taught me to believe we are the worst Guardians we can possibly have. Madam, (said the strange Lady, whom we must call *Berintha*) if we young People give into all the whims of the old, we shall be so too before we have lived out half our days; I hope Madam, we shall not have much of his Company, for of all things I hate an old Man. Oh! *said* Amoranda, you will like him, and will find him a very agreeable Companion; for all his Age, *Formator* has a sprightliness in his Conversation, which men of younger Years might be proud of. This Encomium of *Amoranda's*, raised a blush in *Berintha's* Cheeks, which she took notice of, and laughing said, If you had not just now, Madam, declared your aversion to old Men, I should be half afraid you had mind to rob me of my Guardian. After some other discourse it grew late, and *Amoranda* asked the Ladies, if they would lie together, or have separate Beds? *Berintha* said she always lay alone, which accordingly she did. Next Morning, after Breakfast, *Amoranda* took them into the Garden, and there entertained them with the Story of *Froth* and *Callid's* contrivance, with everything else which she thought would divert them; but while they were in the midst of mirth and gaiety, *Formator* came into the dining-room and with discomposed looks, walked a few turns about it, saying to himself: From whence proceeds this strange uneasiness? why is my Heart and Spirits in such an agitation? I never was superstitious, and yet I cannot forbear thinking *Amoranda* in some new

Danger; there must be something in it, and heaven in pity to her gives me warning: then after a little pause—I'll take it, *said he*, and watch the lovely Charmer: I know not why, but methinks I tremble at the thoughts of those two Women, and fancy I see her more exposed to ruin now than when she was surrounded with Fools and Fops. Saying thus, he went into the Garden, and walked at a distance from the Ladies, but kept his eye upon them; he perceived the new-come *Berintha*, close to *Amoranda*, one hand locked in hers, and the other round her waist: This sight increased his doubts and raised his indignation. At dinner he watched her looks and found her eyes always upon *Amoranda*: The sight was death to him, his Soul was racked and tortured, and while he flung dissatisfied looks at *Berintha*, she darted hostile glances at him; his suspicions grew everyday stronger, yet, was he in such a state of uncertainty, that he thought it not convenient to say anything to *Amoranda*, till one Morning she came down before the two Ladies were stirring, and saw *Formator* walking in the Hall. She was glad of so good an opportunity, for she had for several days taken notice of an unusual melancholy in his Looks. *Formator, said she*, what is the matter with you? what new trouble has taken possession of your breast? I see a Cloud upon your brow and cannot be easy till I know the occasion of it. Madam, *said he*, the source of my trouble proceeds from the real concern I have for your Welfare, which I have so much at heart that the least appearance of Danger gives it a fresh alarm. I confess myself extremely uneasy, but fear you will think me a very whimsical old Fellow, if I tell you; I suspect *Berintha's* Sex, and cannot but fancy he is a Man.

I shall always, *said* Amoranda, acknowledge myself obliged to you for your great Care and Caution, but beg, my good *Formator*, that you will not carry it too far: What in the name of Wonder could put such a Thought into your Head?

Madam, *said he*, Observation puts a great many things into our heads; you may please to remember, first, she would lie alone. Pugh! *said* Amoranda, that's what I love myself, and so may ten thousand more. True, Madam, *said he*, and had my Reasons stopped there, that would have dropped of course; but why so many kind Glances? so many rapturous Embraces? such loving Squeezes by the hand, an eager Desire to please you? Eyes ready to run over with Pleasure at every word you speak? Are these the common Marks of Respect betwixt one lady and another?

Consider, Madam, you have Youth, Beauty, Sense, and Fortune enough to bring our Sex to you in as many Shapes as ever *Jove* himself assumed, and we are always soonest surprized when we are least apprehensive of Danger.

Formator, said she, everything you say pleases me, because I know it comes from an honest Heart; but you are too full of Fears, and your Zeal and Care for my Safety makes you look at things in a false light: I cannot give into your opinion for several Reasons; first, I think it highly improbable a Person of *Berintha's* Sense should undertake so ridiculous a Project; next, I can never believe *Arentia*, who must be privy to it, would be so base as to betray me.

No, no, *Formator, said she*, there can be nothing in it, and I beg you will lay by your Fears. Saying thus, she left him, and went away to the Ladies, who, she heard, were both up. *Berintha* met her with an Air of Gallantry, and led her a Minuet; then catching her in her Arms, kissed her with some eagerness. Hold, *Berintha, said* Amoranda, Kisses from our own Sex and other Women's Husbands are the most insipid things in nature; I had rather see you dance, I fancy you do it very well, but can't be so good a Judge while I dance with you myself: you will oblige me if you take a turn or two about the Room. This she proposed on purpose to mind her step, which she found somewhat masculine, and began to fear *Formator* was in the right. Good Heaven! *said she to herself*, can this be true? Is it possible *Arentia* can be so treacherous? Is there no Justice, no Honour, no Friendship to be depended on in this vile World? Methinks I could almost hate it, and everything in it, unless[32] honest *Formator*. While she was thus musing, *Berintha* ran to her, and taking her again in her Arms, said, My dear *Amoranda*, what are you thinking of? Her dear *Amoranda* began now to disrelish her Embraces, and breaking from her a little abruptly, said, Madam, I was thinking of Treachery, Falsehood, broken Friendship, and a thousand other things, which this bad World can furnish us with. This Answer made both the Ladies colour, and they looked at one another with the utmost confusion, which *Amoranda* took notice of, and applying herself to *Arentia*, said, Why, Madam, do you blush? Your Youth and Innocence are doubtless Strangers to all those black things I accidentally named. *Arentia*, willing to extricate herself from her Confusion, said it was a Vapour. O! *said* Amoranda, is that all? then here's my Bottle of Salts for you; and yours, Madam, *said she to* Berintha, is a Vapour too I presume: I'll call for another for you, since your Distemper is the same, your Cure ought to be so too. But come, Ladies, *said she (being resolved to try them a little farther)* I will divert your Spleen with a sight I have not yet shown you. She then led them up two pair of Stairs, where there was a large old-fashioned wrought Bed. This Bed, Ladies, *said she*, was the Work of my Grandmother, and I dare say you will believe there was no want of either Time or Stuff when it was made. No, *said* Arentia, they had doubtless plenty of both, or it had never got to such a size; I don't believe it wants much of the great Bed of *Ware*.[33] Methinks, *said* Amoranda, they should bring up this fashion again, now that Men and their Wives keep so great a distance, they might lie in such a one with so much Good-manners. I dare say, *continued she*, we three might lie in it, and never touch one another. What think you, Ladies, shall we try tonight? No, *said* Berintha, for my part, I never loved one Bedfellow, much less two; besides, I never sleep well in a strange Bed. The Proposal however took off some Apprehensions from the two Ladies, but confirmed the third in her Fears.

[32] *unless*: except.
[33] *Bed of Ware*: an oak, four-post bed that was 11 feet square and 8 feet high at the Saracon Inn in Ware, Hertfordshire. It is mentioned in William Shakespeare's *Twelfth Night* (III. ii. 40–6).

Madam, *said* Arentia, I ventured to promise my Friend here, before we came from home, a great deal of pleasure upon your fine River, here's a cool Day, and if it be consistent with your inclination, we'll take a turn upon the Water this afternoon, for tomorrow we must think of going home. *Amoranda* was not sorry to hear that, but told them she could not answer them of a sudden, for she knew they did not care to have *Formator's* Company and whether he would consent she should go without him, she knew not.

I confess to you, Madam, *said* Berintha, I had much rather want the pleasure of the Water than the Plague of the Man; but hope you will prevail with him to stay at home, and let us go without him. Come, Madam, said *Arentia*, 'tis our last request, gratify us in this small matter, and complete the favours we have already received. Well, Ladies, *said* Amoranda, if you will excuse the rudeness of leaving you a minute, I'll go and try my Guardian's good-nature. She conducted the Ladies down again and went to *Formator*. I am come, *said she*, to tell you something, which will, I dare say, be very grateful to your ears; my two Ladies talk of going home tomorrow, but they have a great mind to take a little recreation this afternoon in the Barge, and I desire your Opinion of the matter. Madam, *said he*, I am strangely surprized at your having an inclination to go abroad with a Person you are utterly a stranger to; you know the Water for some Miles runs by nothing on one side but Woods and Deserts, and has on the other but one small Town; suppose there should be a trap laid for you, and you should fall into it, what account can I give your Uncle, either of your Safety or my own Care? I am sure, *Formator*, *said she*, you do not think so indifferently of me, as to believe I have a mind to be trepanned, or that I would not carefully avoid all danger; but I cannot see how it is possible, for me to be in any at this time, because I shall have all my own Servants about me, and if a hundred baits were laid, they could not reach me, unless I were to land; which I faithfully promise you; I will not do: and supposing the very worst you fear, to be true, and *Berintha* should prove a Man, he is neither a Devil nor a Monster, to devour all before him, I wish you were to go with us yourself. No, Madam, *said he*, I perceive myself a perfect Bugbear to them both and would not make your Company uneasy: May Heaven have you always under its kind Protection; I shall be transported at Night, when I see you safe at home again. Fear not, *Formator*, *said she*, that Providence which knows my innocent Intentions, will I hope conduct me back again. Here she left *Formator*, and went to order the Barge to be got ready, and then returned to the Ladies. Well, *said she*, I have ordered all things for our long Voyage, and as soon as we have dined we will embark. Nay, said *Berintha*, let us take a bit of anything along with us and not stay for dinner, we shall not have half pleasure enough before Night else. *Amoranda*, willing to gratify them this once, sent fresh Orders to the Barge-Men, who were ready in half an hour, and when *Jenny*, by her Lady's Command, had laid in Wine and cold Viands, they sailed down the Water with a pleasant gale. The three Ladies were set at one end of the Barge, and *Amoranda's* Servants, six in number, at the other: she herself was set between *Berintha* and *Arentia*, when *Arentia* thus began. Madam, *said she*, Fortune did me an early piece of Service in making me your acquaintance when I was yet but a Child. I have ever since done my endeavour to keep up amity and a good understanding betwixt us, and it shall be wholly your fault if ever there be a breach in our Friendship; but Madam, our time is short, and there is a story ripe for your ear, which I must beg you will listen to, and hope you will contribute so much to your own happiness as to comply with the Proposals we are about to make to you; 'tis neither my Cousin's inclination nor mine to use force, but something must be resolved upon in a very short space: Nay, Madam, *continued she*, don't look surprized, what I say is fact, and so you'll find it. *Amoranda* gave a scornful smile at what *Arentia* said, and asked her, if she thought her a Woman of so little Courage, as to be bullied into any Compliance in the midst of her own Servants. No, Madam, *said Berintha, Arentia* has gone a little too far, give me leave to tell the ungrateful tale, for so I fear it will prove. Why, then, *said Amoranda*, do you tell it? a fault committed by a chance or mistake, ought to be forgiven; but a wilful one we cannot so easily overlook. The poor Lady began now, to wish she had taken *Formator's* advice, and had staid at home, for she saw nothing, either of her right hand or her left, but a resolute arrogance in both their Countenances; however they kept within the bounds of Civility, and *Arentia* once more began: Know, Madam, *said she*, I am not going to tell you anything, but what you might be very well pleased to hear, I have a near Relation, who is a Man of the greatest merit, a Man of fortune and honour; he had the misfortune, (as I fear I may call it) of seeing you once at the *Bath*,[34] and though it be more than a twelve-month since, he still struggles with a Passion that will master him, in spite of all Opposition; Oh! turn to your left shoulder, *Amoranda*, and behold the Wretch.

Amoranda, who guessed where it would end, looked very serene and unsurprized, saying, *Arentia*, if your Friend *Berintha* be a Man of Fortune and Honour, as you say he is, why has he used clandestine means to get into my Company? Do you think, Sir, *said she, turning to him*, I am so fond of my own Sex, that I can like nothing but what appears in Petticoats? Had you come like a Gentleman, as such I would have received you; but a disguised Lover is always conscious of some Demerit, and dares not trust to his right Form, till by a false appearance he tries the Lady: if he finds her weak and yielding, the day's his own, and he goes off in triumph; but if she has Courage to baffle the Fool, he sneaks away with his disappointment, and thinks nobody will know anything of the matter. *Biranthus*, for that was his true Name, was stung to the very Soul to hear *Amoranda* so smart upon him, but was yet resolved to disguise his Mind as well as his Body, and said, You are very severe, Madam, upon a Slave who dies for you; but if I have done foolishly in this Action, *Arentia* should answer for it, the Frolic was hers, and it was

---

[34] *Bath*: fashionable spa where natural warm-water springs have been used for bathing since Roman times.

designed for nothing else. But, Madam, *said he*, Time flies away, and every Minute is precious to a Man whose Life lies at stake; it is now time to know my Doom, shall I live or die? Believe me, Sir, *said* Amoranda, it is perfectly indifferent to me which you do; and if nothing will save your Life but my Ruin, you will not find me very ready to preserve it at so dear a Price. If, *said* Biranthus, you give me cause to accuse you of Ill-nature, you half justify my Design upon you. Pray, *said* Amoranda, what is your Design? To force a compliance with my Wishes, *said he*, if you refuse a voluntary one. How, *said* Amoranda, *with a scornful Laugh*, will you pretend to force, while I am in the midst of my own Servants?

Biranthus, now grown desperate, told her she was too merry and too secure; for know, Madam, *said he*, those Servants of whom you boast, are most of them my Creatures; the Slaves have sold that Duty to me, which they owed to you, and therefore Compliance will be your wisest Course. Nay then, *said* Amoranda, I am wretched indeed: Oh *Formator!—Formator*, *said* Biranthus, is not so near you now, as he was when you were attacked in your Coach some weeks ago; I owe the old Dog a Grudge for his Usage of me then, and would have paid him now, but I had tried the Strength of his Arm and found it too powerful for me, otherwise you had had his Company this once, in order to see him no more; but you have taken your leave of him, as it is. And are you, *said* Amoranda, one of the Villains that—(*here she fainted away*). *Biranthus* was glad of so good an opportunity of getting her ashore, and calling some of the Men to his assistance, they clapped Pistols to the Breasts of the two Barge-Men, who were all *Amoranda* had on her side, and made them row to Land, just at the side of a great thick Wood. *Biranthus* and one of the Men took *Amoranda* up betwixt them, and carried her into the Wood, which the Barge-Men seeing, prepared to follow and bring her back, but were prevented by the rest of the Rogues, two of which they knocked over-board with their Oars, and the other they tied neck and heels in the Barge, then went in search of their Lady: but *Biranthus* had carried her such intricate Ways and so far up in the Wood that the poor Barge-Men thought there had been Horses ready for them in the Wood, and they had carried her quite away: however they were resolved to stay till night, in hopes of her Return. In the meantime, the Devils that carried her off had conveyed her into the most unfrequented part of the Wood and laid her on the Grass to recover herself; but who can express the Rage, Despair, and Grief, which appeared in her lovely Eyes, when they opened to such a Scene of Sorrow, when she saw herself in the full power of a threatening Ravisher, her own Servants aiding and assisting him, in the midst of a wild Desert, where nothing but Air and Beasts could receive her Cries? Oh *Amoranda*, *said she*, wretched *Amoranda*! what sullen Star had power when thou were born? Why has Nature denied us Strength to revenge our own Wrongs? And why does Heaven abandon and forsake the Innocent? But Oh! it hears not my Complaints.——Oh *Formator!* did you but know my Distress, you would come to my Relief, and once more chastise this odious impudent Ravisher. Oh wretched me! what shall I do? *Arentia*, who had been a long time silent, and was confounded at her own Baseness, went to her, and said, Why *Amoranda*, do you think yourself wretched? It is in your own power to be very happy, if you will but hearken to your Friends, and be—Peace, Screech-Owl, *said* Amoranda, thy Advice carries Poison and Infection in it; the very Sound of thy Words raises Blisters on me, so venomous is the Air of thy Breath. Oh Madam! *said* Arentia, we shall find a way to humble your Pride; and since you are resolved to make your Friends your Enemies, take the Reward of your Folly. Saying thus, she went away, leaving *Biranthus* and her own Man with her, to execute their abominable Design against her. When she was gone, the hated *Biranthus* came to her, and said, Madam, if you will yet hear my Proposals, I am now in a humour to make you very good ones; but if you refuse them, you may expect the worst usage that can fall to your share, and I shall please myself, without any manner of regard to your Quality or Complaints. 'Tis true, my Estate is not a great one, but your's joined to it will make it so; and you shall find me in everything such a Husband—As I, *said she*, no doubt, shall soon have reason to wish hanged: no, base *Biranthus*, *said she*, if Providence had designed me a Prey for such a Villain, I should have fallen into your first Snare, but I was delivered from you then, and so I shall be again. Before I would consent to be a Wife to such a Monster, I would tear out the Tongue by the roots that was willing to pronounce my Doom. I would suffer these Arms to be extended on a Rack, till every Sinew, every Vein and Nerve should crack, rather than embrace, or so much as touch a Viper like thyself. Then hear, *said he*, and tremble at thy approaching Fate. This minute, by the help of thy own Servant, I will enjoy thee; and then, by the assistance of my Arm, he shall do so too. Thou lyest, false Traitor, *said she*, Heaven will never suffer such Wickedness. Just as she spoke these last words, they heard a dreadful Shriek at a little distance; the Voice they knew to be *Arentia*'s, and *Biranthus*, who had taken hold of *Amoranda*, let her go again, and run to find out his Partner in Iniquity, who he saw just expiring of a Sting from an Adder.[35] He then cried out as loud as she had done, when the other Rogue ran to him, and left *Amoranda* to shift for herself. She was no sooner rid of them, than she heard the sound of Horses pretty near her, and began to run towards them. Good Heaven, *said she*, has at last seen my Wrongs, heard my Complaints, and pities my Distress: The Horses were now within sight of her, and she saw a graceful, fine, well-shaped Man upon one of them, attended by two Servants; to whom she thus applied herself: Stranger, *said she*, for such you are to me, though not to Humanity, I hope; take a poor forsaken Wretch into your kind Protection and deliver her from the rude hands of a cruel Ravisher. The Stranger looking at her, said, I presume, Madam, you are some self-willed, head-strong Lady, who, resolved to follow your own Inventions, have

---

[35] *Adder*: a viper, or, more generally, any snake.

left the Care of a tender Father to ramble with you know not who. Oh Sir! *said she*, some part of your guess is true; but Father I have none. Nor Mother? *said the Stranger*; nor Guardian? Nor Mother, *said she*, but a Guardian, a good one too, I have; and were I but once again in his possession, I would never leave him while I live.

Well, Madam, *said the Gentleman*, I am sorry for you, but I am no Knight-Errant, nor do I ride in quest of Adventures; I wish you a good Deliverance and am your humble Servant. Saying thus, he and his Servants rode away. Poor *Amoranda* followed them as fast as she could, and still with Prayers and Tears implored their Pity; but they were soon out of sight, and the loathed *Biranthus* again appeared, coming in full search of her, and designing to drag her to *Arentia's* Corpse, there satisfy his beastly Appetite, and sacrifice her to her Ghost. He found the poor Forlorn half drowned in her own Tears, pulling off her Hair, and wringing her lovely Hands, calling, *Formator*, Oh *Formator!* where are you? *Biranthus* rudely seized her on one side, and her own Man on the other, and was dragging her along, when her shrill Cries filled the Air, and reached the ears of the Gentleman, who had just left her, and now returned again. Villain, *said he to* Amoranda's *Man*, unhand the two Ladies. Sir, *said* Biranthus, there is no harm designed against her; but the cause of this Lady's Cries proceeds from her Concern for the Death of her Sister, who is just now stung to death by an Adder.

Oh! gentle Stranger, *said* Amoranda, believe him not, this very Creature, who has now spoken to you, is a Man disguised, and is now going to murder me; O, as you hope for Happiness, either here or hereafter, leave me not. Sir, *said* Biranthus, her trouble has distracted her, do but ride forty Paces farther, and you shall see the poor Lady lie dead. Lead on then, *said the Stranger*. When they came to the Place where *Arentia* lay dead, the Gentleman looked at her and shook his head, saying, how does Vice, as well as Virtue reward itself! But Madam, *said he to Biranthus*, if those two Ladies were Sisters, what Relation are you to them? None, none, *said* Amoranda, I have already told you he is a Man, a Monster, a Villain and a Murderer; this very Man, Sir, *said she*, set upon my Coach about a Month ago, shot my Coach-Man, and would have carried me away then, but I had my Guardian with me, my Guardian Angel I may call him, and he preserved me that time: the Rogue when he thought he had me sure, confessed he was a Man, and therefore, for Heaven's dear sake take me from him, though you throw me into the River when you have done. No Madam, *said the Stranger*, you look as if you deserved a better Fate than that; here, *said he to his Servants*, light, and set this Lady behind me: but *Biranthus* stepped between, and pulling out a pocket Pistol, discharged it at the Stranger, but missed him; which exasperated his Men so much, that one of them ran him quite through the Body. When *Amoranda's* Man saw him fall, he ran away as fast as he could, but was soon overtaken and brought back. *Amoranda's* Good-nature, as well as Gratitude, put her upon making ten thousand acknowledgements to her kind deliverer and begged of him to finish the Obligation by conveying her safe to her Barge. Madam, *said he*, I will wait upon you wherever you please to command me, but how shall we find the way out of this Wood? Sir, *said one of his Men*, I know the way to the Water-side. Upon which, he and his Companion went before, with *Amoranda's* Man bound with a Saddle-girth, till they came to the Barge: as soon as the two Barge-Men saw their Lady come again, they set up a loud acclamation of joy, and she got in again with the Stranger, who gave his Horse to his Servants, and they rode by the Barge till it was just at home. When *Amoranda* was set down, at her first coming into the Barge, she asked the Barge-Men what that was that lay in a lump at the other end. That Madam, *said the Men*, is one of our Rogues, who we have tied neck and heels; and where, *said she*, are the other two? Why, Madam, *said they*, we could not persuade them to be quiet, but they would needs go and help to carry your Ladyship away, so we knocked them down with our Oars, and they fell plum into the Water, and we ne'er thought them worth diving for but e'en let them go down to the Bottom, they will serve to fatten the Salmon. Well, *said* Amoranda, take this other Rogue, and tie them back to back, but set his neck at liberty, that part will have enough of the Halter, when he comes to be hanged. As they were going home, the Stranger asked *Amoranda* how she came into the Wood and in such Company. She briefly told him the whole Story; and Sir, *said she*, if you will but land and go in with me, you shall receive ten thousand thanks from as good an old Man as you ever saw in your Life. Madam, *said the Stranger*, I have had your thanks, which is more than a double recompense for the small service I have done you; and after that, all other will be insipid. Pray Sir, *said* Amoranda, will you satisfy me in one point? You seem now to be a very good-natured Man, why were you so cruel to me, when I first made my application to you in the Wood? Madam, *said he*, there is a Mystery in that part of my Behaviour, which you may one day know, for I hope this will not be the last time I shall see you; however, to mend your opinion of me, I will tell you, I left you with a design to return and went no farther than behind some Trees, from whence I saw you all the time. By this time, they drew near home, and after some other discourse, perceived the House: When they were almost at the landing-stairs, the stranger desired *Amoranda*, to let her Men touch the shore, that he might again take Horse, his Servants being just by; but she pressed him very much to go in with her, which he modestly refused, but promised to do himself the Honour of seeing her in a little time. When the Barge-Men had landed him, he gave each of them five Guineas[36] for their Fidelity to their Lady, and standing on the shore till he saw the Lady land, with a graceful bow to her at parting he mounted his Horse; and she, to return his Compliment, stood and looked after him, as far as her eye could reach him: when he was quite out of sight, she went in, calling to *Formator*. But *Jenny* came to her Lady,

---

[36] *five Guineas*: over £100 each, enough to live a middle-class life in London for a year.

and told her he went to walk in the fields, just when she went upon the Water, and they had not seen him since: But Madam, *said Jenny*, where are the Ladies? Oh *Jenny, said* Amoranda, my Spirits are too much worn out with Fatigue and Fear to answer you any question; I must repose myself a little, and when *Formator* comes in let me know, for I have a long tale to tell that good old man; in the meantime bid the two Barge-Men, *Saunders* and *Robert*, take care of their Charge. Here she went to her Chamber, and with a grateful Heart thanked Heaven for her deliverance; but the Agent it had employed, run strangely in her head. From whence, *said she to herself*, could he come? he is a perfect stranger here-about, and how he came into that Wood, which is no road, and at such a needful time, I can't imagine: sure, Providence dropped him down for my safety, and he is again returned, for he is too God-like to be an Inhabitant of this World, something so very foreign, to what I have observed in the rest of his Sex, a *Je-ne-sçay-quoy*[37] in every word, every action he is master of.—But what did he mean when he said his Behaviour had a Mystery in it?—will he come again?—he said he would and tell me this mighty Secret; I wish he may keep his Word, methinks I long to see him again;—but then, *Formator?*—what of *Formator?* he will not find a fault where there is none: *Formator* is strict, but then he's just and will not take away merit where he sees there is a title to it.——I wonder what Love is, if ever I felt either its pleasure or its pain, 'tis now. Those Reflections and her wearied Spirits lulled her to sleep, and her disturbed Mind had an hour's Rest. When *Jenny* had laid her Lady down and observed something very extraordinary in her Looks, she made all the haste she could, to go to the Barge, for Information from thence; but as she was a going, she met *Saunders* and *Robert* at the back-door, dragging in two more of her Fellow-Servants, pinioned down with Cords. Mercy upon us, *said Jenny*, what's the matter?

Aye, *quoth Robert*, Mercy's a fine word, but an[38] there be any shown here, I think we deserve none ourselves. Why don't you tell me, *said Jenny*, what the matter is? Matter, *said Saunders*, aye, aye, if such Rogues must go unpunished, for my part I will never take five Guineas again for being honest. Why, what the Devil have they done, *said Jenny?* Done, *said Robert*, nay, nay, they have done, and had like to have undone; but the Man has his Mare again, and so there's nothing done to any purpose, thank Fortune. Pox take you both, *said Jenny*, if I don't fit you for this, may I always long in vain, as I do now; you couple of amphibious Rats, I'll make you tipple in the Element you are best used to, till you burst your ugly guts, before you shall ever wet your Whistles with anything under my Care. Say you so, Mrs. *Jane, said* Saunders, then you shall swim in a Dike of your own making, before you ever come into my Barge again: you think, forsooth, because the Butler's your Sweetheart, nobody must come within smell of the Ale-Cellar, without your leave; but

---

[37] *Je-ne-sçay-quoy*: 'I don't know what'; that indefinable something.   [38] *an*: and if.

I-cod[39] your flat Bottom shall grow to the Cricket in the Pantry, before it shall ever be set on a Cushion in my Barge again. You may go, *said* Jenny, and hang yourself in your Barge, 'tis as good there as any where else, you great Flounder-mouthed Sea-Calf. While they were in this warm discourse, *Formator* came in, and asked *Jenny* if the Ladies were yet returned? My Lady, Sir, *said* Jenny, is returned but nobody is come with her but the two Barge-Men and a couple of the Footmen with Ropes about them in the wrong place I suppose. Where, *said* Formator, is your Lady? Gone to bed, Sir, *said* Jenny, but ordered me to let her know when you came in; I hear her ring just now. *Amoranda*, was not long coming down when she heard *Formator* was come in, but meeting him with the greatest pleasure, said—Oh! *Formator*, I'm glad we are met again, I will always allow you a Man of deep Penetration and a discerning Judgment; come, *said she*, let us go and sit down in the Parlour, and I will tell you such a story—you little think what a fiery trial I have gone through since I saw you. When they were set, Madam, *said* Formator, I fear you have been frighted, you look very pale, and yet I think we have had no high Winds today; but where, *continued he*, are the Ladies? Ladies, *said* Amoranda, the Monsters, the Fiends, you should have said, but they have received the just reward of their Wickedness and are now no more. What, *said* Formator, are they drowned. No, *said she*, I'll tell you their Catastrophe; so she began, and told him the whole story, but when she came to that part, where the stranger was concerned, she blushed and sighed, saying, Oh *Formator*, had you seen the fine Man, how graceful, how charming, how handsome——Pugh, I think I'm mad, *said she*, I mean how genteel he was; I'll swear, Formator, *said she*, now I look at you again, I think the upper part of your Face like his, and there is some resemblance in your Voices too, but that you speak slower and have a little Lisp.

Madam, *said* Formator, I prophesy, I shall not be liked worse for having a resemblance to this fine man; but beg you will have a care, he is a stranger as well as *Biranthus* was, and for ought you know may be as great a Villain. Oh! 'tis impossible, *said* Amoranda; if he be bad, the whole Race of Mankind are so: No, *Formator*, Probity, Justice, Honour and good Sense sit triumphant on his fine Face.

Madam, *said* Formator, *smiling*, 'tis well if this Gentleman has not made a greater Conquest than that over your Ravisher; but how can you forgive his cruelty, in riding away from you when you were in such distress? I told him of it, *said she*, in the Barge, and he said it was a mysterious action, which I should know more of another time. What, then, *said* Formator, he intends to visit you, I find. He said he would, do you think he will keep his word, *Formator?* said she. No doubt of it, Madam, *said he*, a Man of so much Honour as you say he is, will never make a Forfeiture of it by breach of promise to a fine Lady. I remember, *Formator*, *said she*, you told me some time ago, that a

<hr>

[39] *I-cod*: Ecod or Egads are other forms; an oath, softened in order to avoid blasphemy, from 'By God.'

Woman's conduct vindicated by one single Man of sense was infinitely preferable to a thousand Elogiums, from as many Coxcombs. I have now brought myself to an utter Contempt for all that part of our Species and shall for the future, not only despise Flattery but abhor the mouth it comes from.

I own, *Formator*, the groundwork of this Reformation in me, came from those wholesome Lectures you have so often read to me; but the finishing stroke is given by my own inclination. I believe it, Madam, *said he*, by your own inclination for the Stranger, who (that he may prove worthy of you) I wish may deserve as well in the eye of the World, as he seems to do in your own. Well, *Formator*, *said she*, I find you think I am in Love, and for ought I know, so I am, for I'm sure I feel something in my heart that was never there before; but this I here promise you, I will never marry any Man who has not your approbation as well as mine. Why then, Madam, *said he*, in return for your good nature, be assured, I will bring my Opinion as near to yours as I can, and doubt not but they will meet at last. But Madam, *said he*, what must be done with the two Rogues yonder? I know not, *said she*, I think 'tis best to pay them their Wages and turn them off. Yes, *said* Formator, off a Ladder,[40] if you please; should we take no more notice than that of stealing our Heiresses every Rascal who has twenty Guineas to bribe a Footman may come when he pleases: No, Madam, they must swing for example. I own, *said* Amoranda, they deserve it, but I'm not willing to take their Lives, perhaps a little Clemency may reclaim them. Madam, *said he*, the Mercy you would show them, is highly becoming your Sex; but you forget 'tis doing the World as well as yourself a kindness to rid both of a Villain; I therefore beg leave to send them tomorrow Morning to the County Jail. Then do what you will, *said she*, I leave it wholly to you. Next day at dinner, *Amoranda* looked very grave, and *Formator* very gay: Madam, *said he*, I begin to fear you are really in Love; else, where are all those pleasant Airs? that Vivacity in your Eyes? the Smiles that used to sit upon that fine Mouth? and the sprightly diverting Conversation, so agreeable to all that heard it? I think, *said he*, we must send a Hue and Cry after your deliverer in order to recover your Charms.

I believe, *Formator*, *said she*, what I have lost, you have found, methinks you rally with a very gay air; I am glad to see you grow so cheerful: but why should you impute my Gravity rather to Love than to the late Fright and Disorder I have been in? Do you think a danger like mine is to be forgotten of a sudden? While they were in this discourse, a Servant came in with a Letter for his Lady, and said the Messenger stayed for an answer. *Formator*, *said* Amoranda, you shall give me leave to read it, which she did as follows.

MADAM,

THE Raptures I have been in ever since yesterday, at the thoughts of having served you, has deprived me of a whole Night's sleep: What pleasure can this World give us, like that of obliging a fine Woman, unless it be that of her returning it! but

---

[40] *off a Ladder*: hang them.

as that is a blessing I do not deserve, it is likewise what I dare not hope for, because my wishes are superior to any Service I have, or can do you. Believe me, Madam, I aim at nothing less than your lovely Person, and wish for nothing more. Oblige me with one Line, to encourage a visit; and if I can but make myself acceptable to you, Formator *and I will talk about the Estate.*

Yours, ALANTHUS.

While *Amoranda* read this Letter, *Formator* watched her Eyes, in which he saw a pleasing Surprize. When she had read it, with a quite different Look from that she had all Dinner-time, she said, I have seen this Hand before, but cannot recollect where: Here *Formator, said she,* I find you are to be a Party concerned, pray read it and tell me whether I shall answer it. When he had read it, he returned it, and said, I fear, Madam, my Advice will have but little force; however, since you condescend to ask it, 'tis but Good-manners to give it: and I think you ought to have a care how you converse with a Man for whom you seem to have a tender Concern already, till you know something of his Circumstances.

Nay, *Formator, said she,* that's the part you are to look after, you know I have nothing to do with that; but I think there can be no harm in one Visit, and it would be a poor return for saving my Life and Honour to deny him the satisfaction of a Line: but I will write but a little, and you shall see it when I have done. She went to her Closet, and wrote the following words:

I confess myself so greatly obliged by the generous Alanthus, *that it is not possible for the little Instrument in my hand to make a suitable acknowledgment for what I have received; but beg you will accept in part, of what it can do, and expect the greatest addition from a verbal Thanks, which is in the power of*

AMORANDA.

As soon as she had done, she brought it to *Formator,* and when he had read it, she sealed it up and called for the messenger, whom she had a mind to pump a little. Friend, *said she,* I have written a Line to your Master, but you must tell me how to direct it.

Madam, *said he,* it can never lose its way while I am its Convoy; I'll undertake to deliver it safe. How many Miles, *said she,* have you rid today? That, Madam, *said he,* I cannot readily tell; for I called at several places wide of the Road. Was your Master born on this side of the Country? *said she.* I am very unfortunate, *said the Fellow,* that I cannot answer any of your Ladyship's Questions directly; but really, Madam, he was born before I came to him. Maybe, *said Amoranda,* you don't know his Name neither. Yes, Madam, *said he,* mighty well, and so does your Ladyship doubtless, for my Master always writes his Name, when he sends a Billet to a fine Lady. I fancy, *said Amoranda,* your Master's a Papist, and you are his Chaplain in disguise, for you have all the Evasions of a Jesuit. No, Madam, *said he,* I have only Religion enough for one, I want the cunning part; but, Madam, *said he,* my Master will be impatient for my return, so beg your Ladyship will dismiss me. Here

304

then, *said she*, take that Letter for your Master, and there's something for yourself, and be gone as soon as you please.

Formator stood all this while at a Window, leering at them and laughing to hear the Dialogue betwixt them. Well, Madam, *said he*, I am sure you are pleased, your Looks are so much mended. Pugh! *said she*, I think I have the foolishest Eyes that ever were, they can't keep a secret; but they can tell you no more that I have done already, I have owned to you I do like this man, who calls himself *Alanthus*, much better than any I ever saw before and am fully determined to die as I am, if his Circumstances will not admit of a Union between us. But I am now going to be very happy in a Female Confidant to whom I can entrust all my Secrets. Not another *Arentia*, I hope, *said* Formator. No, no, *said she*, it is a grave Lady, the only Relation I have on my Mother's side: I expect her tomorrow; she will be a rare Companion for you, *Formator*, and I can assure you she is a Woman of good Sense and a pretty Fortune: I know not but we may have a Match between you, and while I am contriving for a Companion for myself, I am perhaps getting you a Mistress. No, Madam, *said* Formator, I have as many Mistresses as I intend to have, already; but if she comes tomorrow, I think I'll go and meet her. I'll assure you, *said* Amoranda, I intend her for my Companion and Bedfellow all this ensuing Winter. Yes, *said* Formator, if *Alanthus* does not take her place. Say no more of that, *said she*, but I desire you will not go out tomorrow, because I fancy *Alanthus* will come, and I would fain have you see him. Madam, *said he*, I shall not want an opportunity of seeing him; his first Visit will not be his last: *Amoranda* cannot make a half Conquest.

I'll swear, *said she*, you are very courtly, and I begin to take a little merit to myself upon your account; for they say a brisk Girl makes a young old Man: but I'll go and undress me and by that time Supper will be ready. While *Amoranda* was undressing, she pulled out the pleasing Letter; and while she was reading it over again, *Jenny*, with the prying Eyes of a Chamber-maid, looked at it, and said, I wonder, Madam, what delight you can take in that rude, unmannerly Letter. What do you mean, *said* Amoranda, you never saw it in your life before? Why, Madam, *said* Jenny, is it not that you had thrown in at the Summer-house Window in the Glove? I will swear it is the same hand. Ay, *said* Amoranda, and so will I too, now you put me in mind of it; I knew I had seen the hand before but could not remember where. No, *Jenny*, *said she*, that Letter which you call rude, I now see with other Eyes and have reason to believe it came from a Friend. Nay, Madam, *said* Jenny, you know best how you can bear an Affront; had any Fellow sent me such a one, I would have spit in his face the first time I saw him: Tell me I was no Angel! an impudent Blockhead. I find, *said* Amoranda, your Lovers must be very obsequious, *Jenny*; prithee what sort of a Husband would you have? Madam, *said she*, I would have one that could keep me as well as you do, one that would rise to work in a morning and let me lie a bed, keep me a Maid to do the business of the House, and a Nurse to bring up his Children; and then I believe I should make a pretty good Wife. That is to say, *Jenny, said* Amoranda, if you can get a Husband that will keep you in perfect Idleness, you will be so very good, as to be very quiet; but I find you intend to take less pains than I shall do, for if ever I have a Child, I will not think it a trouble to nurse it, 'tis a Work Nature requires of us. Aye, marry, Madam, *said* Jenny, if I had followed Nature, I should have had Children long ago for somebody to nurse; but I hear the Bell for Supper, will your Ladyship please to walk down?

When they had done Supper, *Amoranda* showed *Formator* the first Letter, and asked him if he did not think it was the same hand which came subscribed *Alanthus?* Yes, Madam, *said he*, I believe it is; and how will you excuse such Plain-dealing? O! *said* Amoranda, you have taught me to relish it, and I have no longer a taste for Flattery; I see 'tis nothing but Self-Interest in your Sex and a Weakness in ours to be pleased with it. Believe me, Madam, *said* Formator, you make my poor old Heart dance with Joy to see this happy Reformation in you; and I shall give a speedy account to your Uncle of the advantageous Change in your Behaviour: As for *Alanthus*, I find he has made a way to your good opinion of him; and if I find his Estate answers, as he seems to hint it will, I will further his Amour and try to make you happy in the Man you like.

Formator, said the pleased Amoranda, do not you think I ought to have more than a common regard for the Man who snatched me from the Jaws of Death and Ruin? But what, *said she*, can be the reason of his concealing himself?

Madam, *said* Formator, Man is a rational Creature, and you say *Alanthus* has good Sense, he doubtless has his Reasons for what he does; but when I see him, I will give you my opinion of him more at large. It now grew late, and *Amoranda* went to bed, but *Alanthus* (whom she expected to see the next day) had taken such possession of her Head and Heart that poor Sleep was quite banished. The Sun no sooner got up, than *Amoranda* did so too; and leaving a restless Bed, went into the Garden to try if variety of Objects would divert her Thoughts: after she had spent some time among the Birds and Flowers, she thought she heard the noise of Horses in the Highway, and somebody groan; she ran and called *Jenny*, who came, and they with the Gardener ran to the Summer-house, and having opened the Shutters, they saw a fine young Lady on a *Spanish* Gennet[41] in very rich Trappings, the Lady herself in a pale Wig with a laced Hat and Feather, a Habit of Brocade, faced with a silver Stuff, and attended by three Servants in rich Liveries, and her Woman, all well mounted; but just at the Summer-house Window, one of her Men fell down and broke his Leg. *Amoranda* had a just compassion for the unfortunate Man and saw his Lady's Journey retarded; but the late Attempts which had been made upon her, made her afraid to desire her to come in: however, Good-manners took place of her Fears, and she said,

---

[41] *Gennet*: a small horse bred in Spain. Readers would recognize class and gender markers.

Madam, if you will honour me so far as to ride into the Court and alight, my Servants shall get you a Surgeon. The Lady accepted of the Invitation, and *Amoranda* met her at the Gate; when she had conducted her in with that respect which she thought due to her Quality, she ordered her Coach to be got ready to carry the Servant to the next Market-Town, within three little Miles, and where there was a very good Surgeon. *Amoranda* then called for Breakfast, and while they were drinking Tea and eating Sweetmeats, she kept her eye so long upon the strange Lady, that she was almost ashamed, and thought she saw every Feature of *Alanthus* in her, only hers had a more effeminate Turn.

Madam, *said she*, if I may hope for the honour of being better acquainted with you, and that you have not resolved to make your Journey a secret, I should be very proud of knowing your Family, and where you travel this way. Madam, *said the young Lady*, I never thought anything so troublesome as a Secret, and for that reason never keep any: I can assure you, there is not one Circumstance of my Life worth knowing; but if it will oblige you to answer directly to the Questions you have asked, I will briefly tell you: My Father, who has been some years dead, was marquis of W——r; I left a tender Mother yesterday, to go in search of an only Brother, of whom I hope to hear at Lord B——s: he has been from us above this half year, and though he writes to us often, we know not where he is. Lord B——s is my Mother's Brother and lives so near you, I presume, I need not name the Town, but think it is not above twelve Miles from hence. And pray, Madam, *said* Amoranda, is not the young Marquis, your Brother, called *Alanthus*? Yes, *said the Lady*; do you know him, Madam? I believe, *said* Amoranda, I saw him once on horseback when I was from home one day; he is a fine Man, and I think your Ladyship like him. By this time the Servants returned, who had carried their Companion to the Surgeon; and the young Lady again took horse, after she had refused a great many Invitations from *Amoranda* to stay a day or two with her, but obliged herself to call as she returned and stay a week with her then.

As soon as she was gone, a thousand Thoughts crowded themselves into *Amoranda's* Breast, and as many pleasing Ideas danced in her Fancy; she well knew *Formator* would share her Joy, and therefore called for him to communicate the whole Affair to him; but was told he rode out in the morning before seven o'clock and said he should not return till night. She despaired of seeing *Alanthus* that day, thinking his Sister would wholly engross him; however, she was resolved to put on all her Charms both that day, and everyday till he came, and called *Jenny* to go up and dress her to the very best advantage. Dinner over, *Alanthus*, who had Love enough to leave all the world for *Amoranda*, came in a Chariot and two Horses, attended only by as many Footmen. She was resolved to take no notice she had seen his Sister or knew anything of his Quality but leave him wholly to himself, and let him make his own discovery when he thought fit. She received him however with a modest delight in her Countenance, and he approached her with Love and Transport. Madam, *said he*, if my faultering Tongue does not well express the Sentiments of my Heart, you are to impute it to that Concern which, I believe, most Men have about them, when they first tell a Lady they love. But *Amoranda, said he*, if you have well consulted your own Charms, you may save me this Confusion and believe I love you, though I never tell you so; for nothing but Age or Stupidity can resist them. *Alanthus, said she*, you come upon me so very suddenly, that I am at a loss for an Answer; but I don't wonder you are out of countenance at the Declaration you have made: Love is a Subject every Man of Mode is ashamed of. It has been so long exploded, that our modern Wits would no more be seen in *Cupid's* Toils than in a Church; and would as soon be persuaded to say their Prayers, as tell a Lady they love her.

Madam, *said* Alanthus, you speak of a Set of men who are best known to the World by the Names of Beaus and Coxcombs. I beg, Madam, you will not take me for one of that number, but believe me a Man of a regular Conduct, one that was never ashamed to own his Maker or to keep his Laws; and for that reason, whenever I take a Woman to my Arms, she shall come there with the best Authority that Law we live under can give us. Believe me, *Amoranda*, you are very dear to me, and I know you much better than you think I do. I think, Sir, *said* Amoranda, your Words are as mysterious as part of your Behaviour in the Wood was; I can very safely tell myself I never saw your face till then, and if you ever saw mine before, I should be obliged to you, if you would tell me where. Madam, *said he*, a very little time will draw up the Curtain and lay all open to the naked Eye; in the meantime, if you dare give yourself up into my hands, you shall find I will strive to make you very happy.

I dare say, *said* Amoranda, you do not expect any hopes from me, till I know who I give them to; or think I would bestow a Heart on one who may run away with it, and I not know where to call for it again. No, Madam, *said* Alanthus, I have a much better opinion of your good Sense, than to expect an indiscreet Action from you; but if I convince you, my Family and Estate are equal to your own, and can procure your Uncle's Consent, have you then any objection against me? Yes, *said* Amoranda, for all your plausible Pretenses and Declarations of Love, I can produce a Letter under your own hand, in which you tell me you don't love me. Then, Madam, *said he*, I'll renounce my Pretensions. *Amoranda* then pulled out the Letter which came in the Glove, and asked him if that was his hand? he said it was, but hoped he had not expressed so much Ill-manners in it.

Take it then, *said she*, and read it over. Which he did with some emotion; then said with a smile: I did not think, Madam, you would have thought this Letter worth keeping so long, but you have put a very wrong Construction upon it; and I designed it as a very great Mark of my Esteem: I sent it to put you in mind of turning the right end of the Perspective to yourself, that you might with more ease behold your own danger. I own the Obligation, Sir, *said she*, but as you have that commanding Charm of good Sense, I desire you will employ it in considering how early an Excursion I made into the World, left by Father and Mother before I understood anything but Flattery, I might have said, or loved anything but it; and had not my Uncle sent me as good an old Man as ever undertook so troublesome a Task, I might have fallen into a thousand Inconveniencies: I wish he would come home while you are here, I am sure you would like his Conversation mightily. Madam, *said* Alanthus, everything pleases me, which gives you satisfaction; and if I can but find the Art of pleasing you myself, I have no other Wishes. Just here a Footman came in with the Tea-Table and turned the Discourse; *Alanthus* drank in Love faster than Tea, and *Amoranda's* Charms were his best Repast. She on her side had not so great a command of her Eyes, but they made sometimes a discovery of her Heart, to the unspeakable inward Content of *Alanthus*. The Afternoon was now pretty far spent, and our Lover began to think of taking his leave; but first he told *Amoranda*, he would not press her farther at that time for an Assurance of his Happiness, because it was the first time he had declared himself, but hoped a few Visits more would make her forget the Ceremony and Formality of a tedious Courtship and give him a glimpse of the only Satisfaction he was capable of. He then went with unwilling steps to his Chariot, and *Amoranda* returned in with a pleased Countenance and sat down to meditate upon what had passed that afternoon; but her Soliloquies were interrupted, by hearing her Cousin *Maria* was come whom she had been expecting some hours and went to meet with that cheerfulness and good-nature, which shewed itself in all her actions.

My dearest *Maria*, said she, taking her in her arms, you have brought me what I have long wanted, a Female Friend; and now I have you, we will not part this Winter. Madam, *said Maria*, I don't want inclination to spend my whole Life with you, but I have a small Concern at home, which will hardly admit of so long an absence; however, 'tis time enough to talk of that a Month hence. Nay then, *said Amoranda*, there's a Lover in the Case. I never was in a young Girl's Company in my life, *said Maria*, but she brought in a Lover, some way or other; but Madam, I am neither young enough nor old enough to be in Love; that Passion generally takes place, when Women are in their first or second Spring, now I am past one, and not come to the other. Ah! *said Amoranda*, I fancy when the blind Boy shoots his random Arrows, wherever they hit they wound.

The best of it is, (*said Maria, laughing*) I have had the good Fortune of escaping him hitherto, and if I thought myself in any danger, would wear a Breast-plate to repel his Force. But I have heard, *said Amoranda*, Love is such a subtle thief, it finds a way to the Heart, though never so strongly guarded; besides, it is a pain we all like, though we often complain of it. You speak, Madam, *said Maria*, as if there were a good understanding betwixt you, but desire you will never introduce me into his Company; for I would always say with the old Song, *I am free, and will be so*. Well, well, *said Amoranda*, I have seen as bold Champions for Liberty as you led home at last in Chains to grace the Victor's triumph: *Cupid's* an arbitrary Prince and will allow none of his Subjects to pretend to Liberty and Property: But come, *said she*, we'll go upstairs, that you may pull off your Habit, and look like one of the Family. After they had sat a while, *Amoranda* heard *Formator's* Voice below stairs, and said to *Maria*, there's my honest Guardian come home, we'll go down to him, he is one of the best Men upon Earth. They found him in the Parlour, to whom *Amoranda* presented her Relation, and he, with his wonted good-manners, saluted and bid her welcome; then turning to *Amoranda*, said, Madam, you are dressed exceeding gay tonight, I doubt you have had a visitor, and am sure if you have, he's gone away in Fetters, for you look more than commonly engaging. Yes, *said Amoranda*, so I have, and wonder you would go out when I told you I expected him. I am sorry, *said* Formator, I was not here but did not think he would come so soon. That, *said* Amoranda, must be an affront either to him or me; for either you think my Charms are not attractive enough, or you think him an unmannerly Fellow who does not know a visit deferred is as bad as none: He told me, *Formator*, he knew me better than I thought he did, and I could have told him, I knew him better than he thought I did; but I was resolved to give him his own way, and said not a word of the matter. Why, *said* Formator, what do you know of him? I know, *said she*, he is a Marquis; that his Father is dead, that he has no Brother, and but one Sister; that——How, Madam! *said* Formator, *in the greatest surprize*, do you know all of this? did he tell you so? No *Formator, said she*, he did not tell me so, but one did, that knows as well as himself: his Sister rode by today, whom you might have seen, had you been at home; an accident happened just at our door almost, which obliged me to invite her in, and seeing her the very picture of *Alanthus*, I enquired into her Family; of which she gave me a full account without reserve and told me she had but one Brother, and his name was *Alanthus*. I see, said *Formator*, this *Alanthus* has found the way to please you, and this discovery of his Family will countenance your Choice; but, Madam, as you have found out one Secret, I must now tell you another: Your Uncle, before I left him, had provided a Husband for you, a Man of Worth, of Wealth, of Quality, and my Business was to take care you married nobody else: Now, Madam, if your Uncle's Choice be every way as good as your own, will you scruple to oblige him, when you cannot find one Objection against the Man? Why, *Formator, said she, trembling*, have you used me so cruelly, as not to tell me this sooner? Why did you let me see *Alanthus*, to whom I have given a Heart which is not in my power to recall: No *Formator, said she*, I will die to oblige my dearest Uncle, but I cannot cease to love *Alanthus*. You yourself say, my Uncle's Choice is but as good as my own; and if there be an exact equality between the Men, why am not I to be pleased, who am to spend my Days with him; and why must I be forced into the arms of a Man I never saw?

It would be cruel indeed, *said* Formator, to force you to marry a man you never saw; but Madam, you have seen him a thousand times, nay, and what is more, you love him too.

Formator, *said she, with tears in her eyes,* I did not expect this usage from you, 'tis false, by all my Love 'tis false; I never cast an eye of affection towards any of your Sex in my Life, till I saw *Alanthus,* and when I cease to love him, may I eternally lose him. And when I cease to encourage that Love, *said* Formator, may I lose your Esteem, which, Heaven knows, I value more than any earthly Good; and now, Madam, *said he,* prepare for Joy, *Alanthus* is your Uncle's Choice. *Amoranda,* was so overwhelmed with delight, at this happy discovery, that she sat for some time both speechless and motionless: At last, Formator, *said she,* you have given me the most sensible Satisfaction I am capable of, for I now find myself in a Condition to please a most indulgent, tender, kind generous Uncle, and can at the same time indulge my own inclinations: But still I am at a loss, for a meaning to some of your Words: Why do you say, if *Alanthus* be the Man, I have seen him a thousand times? Madam, *said* Formator, you know there has been all along, something mysterious in that Gentleman's Behaviour; but the next visit he makes you, will set all in a clear light, and you shall be satisfied in every particular.

Very well, *said* Maria; 'tis no wonder, Madam, you have been standing up for Love's Prerogative all this while, I see you are an excellent Subject, and will fight for your Master; they say Love's a catching Evil: I think instead of staying all the Winter, I had not best to stay all the Week. What say you Sir, *said she to* Formator, is it not infectious? Madam, *said he,* I believe Love often creates Sympathy, but I never heard it was infectious; Love is a Passion of the Mind, which most resembles Heaven, and that Heart which is not susceptible of love, is certainly filled with more inferiour Passions; but I am an old Fellow, and have now forgot both the Pleasure, Pain, and Power of it. No, Sir, *said* Maria, I am sure you have not quite forgot it, you speak with too much Energy in its behalf. I should laugh, *said* Amoranda, to see you two talk yourselves into the Passion you are so very busy about; you can't imagine, *Formator,* with what pleasure I should see you both made one. Madam, *said* Formator, the honour of being allied to you, is a sufficient reason for breaking any Resolution I have made against Matrimony; but I will certainly see your Nuptials over before I think of my own: beside, I fear this Lady will think me too old for her.

No, no, *said* Amoranda, *Maria* is not very young herself, and you may have the pleasure of going together, and no mortal take the least notice of either of you. Aye, *said* Formator, there lies the burden so heavy upon old shoulders; we do not only sink under the Infirmities of Age, but we are despised for being Old: Though the Young are very generous and willing to give us our revenge, by being content to live till that despicable time themselves. I don't think, *said* Amoranda, anybody despises a Person for having 60 Years on their backs; but because they then grow Sour, Morose, Censorious, and have so great a pique against the young, that they won't so much as remember they were ever so themselves: Tell me, Formator, *said she*, you that are free from the weakness of Age, is not my notion just? Madam, *said* Formator, your Judgment runs in too clear a Channel, to be stopped by any sediment: I have often thought old People take the most pains to make themselves disagreeable. For my part, *said* Maria, I sit and tremble to hear all this and shall do nothing tonight but study how to avoid it: I once heard of a great Person, who had one always by him, to put him in mind he was a Man, and I think it would be very convenient for us, to have somebody by us, to put us in mind we are growing old, that as he avoided Pride by one, we may Folly by the other. Nay, *said* Amoranda, we live in a very good-natured World, that will tell us our Faults without being hired to it; I'll warrant, you may meet with ten thousand, that will tell you for nothing you are an old Maid. Supper and some other Chat of this kind put an end to the Evening, and two whole days were spent without seeing or hearing from *Alanthus*; during which time, *Amoranda* was very uneasy, and *Maria*, who should have diverted herself, had seen so much in *Formator* that she grew very dull and wanted a comforter herself; by which we may see there are Charms even in Old Age, when it is dressed in the Ornament of an agreeable Temper. Formator, *said* Amoranda, you that are privy to all, will you tell me what new Mystery has introduced itself into the Behaviour of *Alanthus* now? Is there no end of his ambiguous Proceedings? And must I never see the Riddle more?

Madam, *said he*, if you never do, I am satisfied *Alanthus* will have the greatest disappointment; for I know he loves you with a Passion not to be matched in Man: but if we hear nothing from him by tomorrow, I will go myself for Intelligence. The morrow came, but still no News, and *Formator*, who read a great deal of uneasiness in *Amoranda's* Looks, told her, he would go just then, and bring her News; but as he was drawing on his Boots, a Servant from *Alanthus* brought *Amoranda* a Letter. She took the welcome Paper, and found these words:

I do not complain, dearest Amoranda, *of an Indisposition which has confined me to my Bed; but that I am robbed of all my Joy, of all my Comfort, by being kept from her I love, from her I adore.*

Oh that Amoranda had but Love enough herself to guess at mine, she would then have some notion of those Torments, which Absence, cruel Absence, creates in me: When I shall be able to throw myself at your feet, 'tis impossible for me to know; but if you would hasten my Recovery, it must be by a Line from your dear hand to
Your Burning
ALANTHUS

Amoranda's Eyes soon made a discovery of the Sentiments of her Heart, and *Formator*, who saw her Concern, told her he would go and see *Alanthus*, and bring her better news. She waited with some impatience for his Return, which was not till almost night; and then he told her, it was only a light

Fever, which his Physician had assured him would go off in a few days, and
in the meantime, he would write to her everyday, till he was in a condition
to come in Person; which accordingly he did, and every Letter gave fresh
advice of his Recovery. When *Amoranda* found her loved *Alanthus* out of danger, as all his Letters assured her he was, she began to rally poor *Maria*.
Madam, *said she*, you are grown strangely grave of late; I thought for some
time it had been occasioned by your Concern for me, but though my Gaiety
be returned, yours is quite fled, I think: Come *Formator*, *said she*, I don't know
how far you may be concerned in this Metamorphose; I assure you, I expect
a good account of this matter, and shall be very well pleased to say, Here
comes my Cousin *Formator*. Well, Madam, *said* Formator, when I see you in
the Arms of *Alanthus*, I faithfully promise, you shall dispose of *Formator* as
you please. But, madam, *said he*, have you any Commands to *Alanthus*, I left
two of his Servants at the Gate. No, no, *said she*, he's well again now; but I
leave that to you, *Formator*, send what Message you please. *Formator* went to
dismiss the Men, and then *Maria* found her tongue again. Madam, *said she*,
how will you answer this Behaviour of yours to your Good-nature? to say so
many shocking things to me, before the very Man you fancy I have an esteem
for: I declare, if I were not one of the best-natured old Maids in *Europe*, I
should resent it past forgiveness. Prithee Child, *said* Amoranda, don't be so
foolish, why I can't believe there's any difference betwixt an old Man and an
old Woman; and I dare promise, in *Formator's* name, if ever he marries, the
Woman must speak first. I don't know how it is, *said* Maria, but *Formator's*
Intellects seem to be perfectly sound; and for his Outside, there is nothing old
belonging to it but his Beard, and that, I confess, is a very queer one, as ever
I saw in my life: for I have been here above a Fortnight, and I am sure it has
never been a pin's point longer or shorter since I came. Why really, *said*
Amoranda, I have often minded his Beard myself, and I sometimes fancy the
Man was born with it; for he has never shaved it since he came here, and
one would think it might in that time have grown very well down to his
Waist: But I am glad to see you so cheerful again, prithee what was the mat-
ter with you to be so sadly in the dumps? Why, *said* Maria, if I tell you the
whole truth, it will amount to no more than you have guessed already; and
I shall make no great scruple to tell you, if I ever liked a Man in my life, 'tis
Formator. I am glad, *said* Amoranda, it will be in my power to serve you then,
for you know when I am married myself, I am to dispose of him as I please:
But what think you of the God of Love now, Mrs. *Maria*? I think of him now,
said she, as I did before, that the Distemper he flings among Men is catching;
however, he has but wounded, I am not slain: and if it were not for staying
to be your Bride-maid, I would fly for my life, and leave the Place where I saw
myself in so much danger.

But the poor Lady found herself in a much greater before the next
Morning's Dawn; for one of the careless Grooms had left a Candle in the
Stables, which set the Hay on fire, consumed the Stables, and burnt all

the Horses: and for want of a timely discovery, the Flames being very violent, they had caught hold of one end of the House; but the Family being alarmed, it was soon put out.

Formator, as soon as he heard the dreadful Cry of *Fire*, jumped out of Bed, slipped on his Night-Gown, and ran to *Amoranda's* Chamber; he found her up and in a horrible fright, but hearing *Formator* come into her Chamber, she turned to go with him out of the House, and had no sooner looked upon him, than her fear gave place to her surprize. My Lord *Alanthus! said she*, how, or when came you here? *Formator* was as much surprized to hear her ask such a question, as she was to see him there, and clapped his hand to his mouth to feel for his Beard, which in the fright and hurry he had forgot. Madam, *said he*, I fly by Instinct when you are in danger; but let me convey you hence, and in a safer place I'll tell you more. As they were going downstairs, they met several of the Servants coming to tell them the Fire was quite extinguished; upon which they returned upstairs and went into the Dining-Room. It being now fair Daylight, *Maria*, who had been all this while with them, and had had her share of the Terror which had attended the Night, seeing *Alanthus* and *Amoranda* look with some confusion in both their Senses and compare the present with the past. This *Alanthus, said she to herself*, is *Formator* in everything but the filthy Beard, on which we have so lately animadverted; but I confess, *thought she*, it made a very great alteration, and I'll try if I can to find it out: she left the two Lovers, and went, as she pretended, to see the ruined Stables. When *Amoranda* found herself alone with *Alanthus*: What, Sir, *said she*, am I to think of your being here at such an hour in perfect Health and in *Formator's* Gown, when I thought you on a languishing Bed of Sickness in your own House or Lodgings? Must I always be a Stranger to your Intentions? Sure you have a very low opinion of my Prudence, while you dare not trust me so much as with your Name or Family; and if I am acquainted with both, I owe my Intelligence to chance: your Lordship will pardon me if I resent it. Saying thus, she rose from her Seat, and was going, when *Alanthus* snatched her hand, and said, My adorable *Amoranda*, if I value myself for any Action of my Life, it is for carrying on so clean a Cheat so long a time; I have been these eight Months under your Roof and have never lain one Night abroad; have been daily conversant with you, and dined and supped at your Table, and yet you never saw me more than twice or thrice. While *Amoranda* was waiting for an Explication of what *Alanthus* had said, she saw *Maria* come laughing in with *Formator's* Beard dangling at her fingers ends: Here, Madam, *said she*, *Formator* has cast his Skin, and left it me for a Legacy; for I plainly see, 'tis all that will fall to my share of the Man. *Amoranda* looked at the Beard, and then at *Alanthus*; What, *said she*, do I see? Or what am I to believe? not my Eyes, for they have deceived me already; not *Alanthus*, for he has deceived me too. I beg, my Lord, you will disentangle my Understanding, and let me know at once who in reality you are; while you were *Formator*, I had all the value and esteem for you, which was due to a good Adviser and a careful Guardian: when I took you for Lord *Alanthus*, I looked upon you as a man of the highest Merit as well as Quality; and the additional service you did me in the Wood gave you a very good title to a Heart which I thought you greatly worthy of: But now that you are no longer *Formator*, I have done with you as a Guardian; and till I am better satisfied you are Lord *Alanthus*, I have done with you as a Lover too. *Alanthus* was very well pleased with her Caution but resolved to try her a little farther, before he gave her that satisfaction she expected. Madam, *said he*, was not the Authority I brought to introduce me sufficient? Did I not give you a Letter from your Uncle's own hand, to receive me as a Friend?

Yes, *said* Amoranda, to receive you as a Guardian, not as a Lover; to receive you as *Formator*, not as *Alanthus*: and if you could so dexterously deceive me, perhaps you have done the same by him. I fear, Madam, *said* Alanthus, you would be pleased to find me unworthy of you, and would be glad of a fair Pretence to make me a Stranger to your Favour. No, *said she*, Heaven knows, to find you anything but Lord *Alanthus*, would be the greatest disappointment I am capable of knowing; and I have made too many declarations to *Formator* of my Love for *Alanthus* to grow indifferent to him all of a sudden: but such a gross Imposition as this might prove would not only ruin my Fortune but call my Sense in question too; though, I confess there is one Circumstance, which makes me hope you are the Man I wish: and that is, the account I had from your Sister, of your Family. Nay, I have still another, which will crowd in to justify you; a Face I own you have, which says a thousand things in your behalf, and reproaches me as often for my weak suspicion of you.

Let all Disputes forever cease betwixt us, *said* Alanthus, as I will this hour give you satisfaction. He went away to his own Apartment, and when he had dressed him, returned with a Paper in his hand: Here, my *Amoranda*, *said he*, let this convince you. She took the Paper from him, which she knew to be her Uncle's hand, and found these words:

The Man, my dearest Niece, who some Months ago appeared to you as the grave, the wise, the old Formator; is now turned into the gay, the young, the accomplished Lord Marquis of W——; and whenever he thinks fit to discover himself, it is greatly my desire you use him as such. He has done me the honour to accept of me for a Friend, and promised to make you the Partner of his Bed, if he liked you when he saw you, and could find a means to win your Affections; if not, you will never know him for what he is.

When *Amoranda* had read the paper over, she re-assumed her cheerful Looks, and Pleasure diffused itself in every Muscle of her Face: But my Lord, *said she*, this discovery being made by chance, who can say you designed it should ever be made at all? I can, *said* Maria; for I was so near running away with *Formator*, that my Lord *Alanthus* would have been glad to have brought himself off at the low expense of a little Secret. Madam, *said* Alanthus, if I had designed to have lived in masquerade as long as I staid in your House, you should never have seen me as *Alanthus* at all, neither would I have staid so long with you. I came to you, disguised like an old Man, for two reasons: First, I thought the sage Advice you stood in need of would sound more natural and be better received from an old mouth than a young one; next, I thought you would be more open and free, in declaring your real Sentiments of everything to me as I was than as I am. How good an effect my Project has met with, you are not, I hope, insensible; and I beg you will give me leave to remind you of the vast difference there is betwixt your Behaviour then and now. My Lord, *said* Amoranda, I am so far from derogating from your Merit that I own, when you first took me under your Care, I was a giddy, thoughtless, inconsiderate Mortal, fit only for the Company of those Coxcombs I too frequently conversed with: but then, my Lord, you shall own in your turn, that I received all your Lectures and Admonitions with the Spirit of a willing Proselyte; that I was ready to give into all your Maxims, and took your Advice as fast, almost, as you gave it. But pray, my Lord, *said she*, (*taking the Beard*) let me once more see my good old *Formator*, let me once more behold you in that Dress, which so artfully deceived me: methinks I grieve when I tell myself I have lost the good old Man. Aye, *said* Maria, 'tis pity so good a Character should be a fictitious one; but alas for me! the Loss is mine, and if my Lord assumes the Dress again, I shall certainly lay some claim to the Man. *Alanthus* took the Beard, and dressed himself as when *Formator*. Now, my Lord, *said* Maria, you are in the height of all your Charms; the grave, sententious, grey-bearded *Formator*, had certainly Attractives which the gay, smooth-chinned Lord *Alanthus* wants. In your Eyes, *said* Amoranda; remember the Fable, the Fox complained of Acids, when he could not reach at[42] ——and yet I can't but love that Form myself, when I consider the Advantages that accrued to me under its Government, the just Rebukes, the friendly Persuasions, the kind Admonitions, the assiduous Care, to turn *Amoranda* from Folly and Madness to that Behaviour so ornamental to her Sex. Then it chastised the insolent Designs of *Callid* and repelled the rapid Force of *Biranthus*, when he shot my Coachman and would have run away with myself. Can those things die in oblivion? Can they be forgotten in a generous grateful Heart? No! *Formator's* Name shall always be dear to *Amoranda*, and shall for ever find a resting-place in her Breast. Madam, *said* Maria, you'll spend so many Raptures upon my old *Formator*, that you will leave none for your own young *Alanthus*. Yes, *said* Amoranda, I have one acknowledgement to make *Alanthus*, which is equivalent to all the rest, and that is the great Deliverance he brought me in the Wood: But now I think of it, my Lord, you promised to tell me why you left me in such exquisite Distress, when I sued for your Assistance in that dreadful Place. Madam, *said he*, you may please to remember when you suffered yourself to be drawn from your own House by

---

[42] Aesop's fable of the Fox and the Grapes. When the fox was unable to reach the grapes which he desired, he turned away complaining that they were probably sour.

those two Impostors, it was extremely against my liking; and I said as much as Modesty would admit of, to put a stop to your design: but when I found, by your excusing them, you were resolved to go, I went to my Servants, who are three Miles off, got on horseback, and with two of them rode directly to the Wood, where I knew the Scene would be acted if they had any ill design against you: I was there an hour before I met you and ranged about every part of it, till I heard some Voices, and when the base *Arentia* shrieked for her Life, I heard the Cry, and thought it had been yours: I then clapped Spurs to my Horse, and was riding towards the Sound, when I met you. How full of Joy my Heart was when I saw you safe I leave to every Heart as full of Love, to judge; but I was resolved, if possible, to cure you at once of rambling with Strangers: in order to which, I put on an Air of Cruelty, which, Heaven knows! my Heart had no hand in, and rode from you; I knew it would give you double terror, to see a prospect of relief, then find yourself abandoned; and I likewise knew, the greater your fear was then, the greater your care would be for the future, to avoid such enterprizes: but I had yet a view in favour of myself, and had reason to believe the greater your deliverance was, the greater value would you set upon your deliverer; and those considerations carried me behind a tuft of trees, where I absconded till I saw you environed in the utmost danger: Methinks, I yet behold my trembling Fair, with lift-up Hands and watery Eyes, imploring help, and striving to convince me, *Biranthus* was a Man, though some hours before, I seemed ridiculous to her for only suspecting of it.

I own, my Lord, *said* Amoranda, I owe a thousand Obligations to your generous Care, and my whole Life will be too little to thank you for them, but——No more, Madam, *said he, interrupting her*, I had a glorious return for all that Care, when at Night, as *Formator*, I heard the whole story over again, and so much in favour of the happy Stranger, as *Jove* himself would have listened to with envy; and if ever Vanity had an advantage over me, it was that pleasing Minute. This called a blush into *Amoranda's* Cheeks, who said she little thought, when she made a free confession to *Formator*, that *Alanthus* was within hearing. But I have another piece of cruelty to lay to your charge, my Lord: Since you had by your disguise found out my weakness and knew I had a value for you, why did you send me word you were in a dangerous state of Health, when at the same time you had no indisposition, but what proceeded from your Mind, in giving me pain when you had none yourself? My dearest *Amoranda*, *said he*, pardon that one trial of your Love, it was not possible for me to deny myself the exquisite pleasure I knew your kind Concern would give me; but good Heavens! how did my longing arms strive to snatch you to my bosom when you had read that Letter, that I might have sucked in the pleasing tears which dropped from your lovely Eyes. Pray, Madam, *said* Maria, will you order your Coach to carry me home again; I am resolved to go into my own Country and pick up some sweet Swain, to say a few of those fine things to me. My Lord, *continued she*, will you be pleased to oblige me with that engaging Beard of yours, that if the Man, whom Interest persuades me to, should want exteriour Charms, I may clap it on his Face and fancy him *Formator*. With all my heart, *said my Lord*, there it is, and may it contribute as much towards your Happiness, as it has done towards mine; but I believe you are the first Woman under Thirty that ever fell in love with a grey Beard. Aye, or over it either, *said* Amoranda: but pray my Lord, *said she*, now that we have set things in a little Order between our-selves, give me leave to enquire after your beautiful Sister, she promised to honour me with a few days of her Company, as she returned from Lord B——. Madam, *said* Alanthus, you saw her since I did, I have written to her several times, since you told me she was on this side of the Country, but have not seen her yet, nor does she know where to write to me. While the words were yet in their mouths, *Jenny* came running in, and said, the young Lady who had been here some time ago, was come again in Lord B——'s Coach, and was just alighting. Pray, my Lord, *said* Amoranda, put on your disguise once more, that I may have the pleasure of seeing your own Sister as much deceived as I have been. My Lord clapped on the Beard, and *Amoranda* went to meet Lady *Betty*, (*for so she was called*,) and when she had conducted her in and the common Compliments had passed, *Amoranda* told Lady *Betty*, she now claimed her promise of staying a few days with her. Madam, *said Lady* Betty, it is that promise that has brought me here now; and had I never made it, you had seen no more of me, for I own it was always my Opinion, that a Person who is not in perfect good humour should never incumber other People with their Chagrin, of which I am at Present so very full, that you must have an uncommon share of good-nature, if you can bear with my Company. Methinks, *said* Alanthus, *disguising his Voice as usual*, it is a pity so young a Lady should have so early an acquaintance with anything that could ruffle her Temper; you have likely, Madam, left a Lover behind you. Pshaw, *said Lady* Betty, you old Gentlemen always think a young Girl's Mind so set upon Lovers, that they have room for no other thoughts: though he that gives me a present uneasiness, is a Lover I hope, but he's a Brother too. I remem-ber, *said* Amoranda, *smiling*, your Ladyship spoke of an absent Brother last time I had the honour of seeing you; have you never seen him since? No, Madam, *said Lady* Betty, I fancy he's got into *Fairy-Land*, he lets me hear from him, but will not tell me how he may hear from me; 'tis a little odd, he should make his own Mother and Sister strangers to his abode. Madam, *said* Maria, has your Ladyship any Faith in *Astrology?* this old Gentleman here, is so well skilled in the occult Sciences, that he can in a quarter of an hour tell you when and where you shall see your Brother; nay, I dare be bold to affirm, he can, without stirring out of the room, show him to you in his full health and strength, without so much as raising the Devil to help him. Madam, *said Lady* Betty, I should never have taken the Gentleman for a Conjurer, he does not look like one, nor do I believe any Man upon Earth has a power of doing what you have promised in his name, unless Lord *Alanthus* be in some Closet in this

Room. No, Madam, *said* Alanthus, there is no Man in this Room, but myself, and yet I believe I could make a shift to perform all those difficulties which the Lady has told you of. *Amoranda,* who sat next to a Window which looked into the Court, saw a Coach and six come in, with Servants in her own Livery: Bless me, *Formator, said she,* who have we got here? *Alanthus* ran to the Window, and saw Mr. *Traffick* alighting. Oh! joyful Day, *said he,* Madam, here's your Uncle! They ran to meet him, and brought him in, to Lady *Betty* and *Maria,* so full of raptures and tender sentiments at the sight of his beauteous Niece that his eyes ran over with tears of joy; no less did the sight of his beloved *Alanthus* transport him: But how comes it my Lord, *said he,* that you are still *Formator?* I thought by this time, I should have met you, with the Respect due to the worthy Lord *Alanthus.* Lady *Betty,* at those words, stood like one aghast, and looking round her for interpretation, she cast her eyes on Lord *Alanthus,* who had pulled off his Beard, and whom she saw in her Brother's Form; but so far from running to him with the kind Caresses of a Sister, that she shrieked out, and fell in a Swoon. For *Amoranda* being an accidental acquaintance, and *Maria* a perfect stranger, who had just been telling her the old man was a Conjurer, and she not expecting to find her Brother there, and seeing him all of a sudden turned from an old Man, whom she had never seen before, to a Brother whom she knew not where to find; she thought herself in some enchanted Castle and all about her Fiends and Goblins. The whole Company quickly surrounded her, and brought her to herself again; when Lord *Alanthus* took her in his arms, and said, Why my dear Lady *Betty,* are you so extremely surprized? Look round you, Madam, with cheerfulness, and believe yourself in the arms of your unfeigned Brother, and among your real Friends: This, my dear Sister, is the *Fairy-Land* where I have so long lived Incognito; and there, there's the Enchantress, who, by a natural Magic, has kept me all this while in Chains of Love. Poor frighted Lady *Betty,* who had always done *Amoranda* Justice, in thinking greatly in her favour, began to hear and believe all, and when she had perfectly recovered her surprize, she turned to *Amoranda,* and said, From the first moment I saw you, lovely *Amoranda,* I had an inward impulse to love you, and how well I'm pleased with that Alliance I foresee will be betwixt us, my future Behaviour shall show; in the meantime I beg I may be let into the whole Affair, and know why Lord *Alanthus* affected the frightful Air of an old Man, rather than his own faultless Form. Madam, *said* Amoranda, I hope I need not take much time to persuade your Ladyship to believe I am very proud of your promised Friendship, and shall always, with my utmost industry, strive to deserve it; but for the Scheme of the Beard, since I had no hand in it, I leave it to be explained by those that had; Lord *Alanthus* and Mr. *Traffick* are the fittest to give your Ladyship an account, which I leave them to do, while I beg leave to go and dress me. *Amoranda* and *Maria* went to their Dressing-rooms, while the two Gentlemen entertained Lady *Betty* with the Story she desired to hear. As soon as *Amoranda* and *Maria* returned, Lord *Alanthus* went to the former, and taking her by the hand, said, I hope, my dearest *Amoranda*, you remember what a long time of Self-denial I have had, and that during *Formator's* Reign, I never dared so much as touch your Hand, though my Heart had ten thousand flutters and struggles to get to you; but as we are now bare faced, and know one another, as we have determined to make each other happy, I beg you will no longer procrastinate my Joy, but let this Day, this very Day, clap us into *Hymen's* fetters, there to remain, till Death us do part. The whole Company joined in the request of *Alanthus*, and Mr. *Traffick* added a Command, which met with no opposition. Everything was immediately prepared, and the Nuptials solemnized that afternoon, to the very great Satisfaction of all Parties, and after a Week more spent where they were, they all took Coach and went to *London*; where the Reader, if he has any Business with them, may find them.

FINIS.

FRIENDSHIP
IN
DEATH.
IN TWENTY
LETTERS
FROM THE
DEAD *to the* LIVING.

To which are added,

THOUGHTS on DEATH.

Tranſlated from the MORAL ESSAYS *of the*
Meſſieurs du Port Royal.

—— *Curæ non ipſa in Morte relinquunt.* Virg.

By Mrs. Rowe.

LONDON:
Printed for T. WORRALL, *at the* Judge's-
Head, *over againſt St.* Dunſtan's Church *in*
Fleet-Street. MDCCXXVIII.

Elizabeth Singer Rowe
(1674-1737)

ELIZABETH SINGER, the oldest daughter of a Presbyterian minister, was born in Ilchester, Somerset, on 11 September 1674, a time of rigorous persecution of Nonconformists. Her parents had met when her mother, Elizabeth Portnell, visited the religious prisoners. After another prosecution, the family moved to Frome where her father became a clothier. At age 19, her first publication appeared; it was a poem in John Dunton's *Athenian Mercury*, and this wildly eccentric bookseller would propose marriage to her in 1697. During the 1690s she published numerous poems, and collections of her works remained popular throughout the century. The four-volume *Works of Mrs. Elizabeth Rowe* were collected and published in 1770.

In 1710 she married Thomas Rowe, also the child of a Nonconformist, and moved with him to London. He died in 1715, and she moved back to Frome where she lived a literary and charitable life until her death. Her two-volume *Miscellaneous Works in Prose and Verse* (1739) included poetic tributes by Elizabeth Carter, poet, essayist, and translator of Epictetus, the Countess of Hertford, a poet and patron of poets, and others. Penelope Aubin and Anne Finch claimed friendship with her. Throughout her adult life, she had intellectual, morally serious friends, many of whom published some of the most polished writing of the period.

Friendship in Death went through at least twenty-three editions before 1816 and was praised by Isaac Watts (who became her literary executor), Matthew Prior, Samuel Johnson, James Boswell, and numerous writers of biographical sketches. She is, for instance, included in *Biographia Britannica: or the Lives of the most eminent Persons who have flourished in Great Britain and Ireland* (1760). *Friendship in Death* was dedicated to Edward Young (1683-1765), who would write *Night Thoughts* and who had already published the much-admired *Love of Fame, The Universal Passion. In Seven Characteristical Satires* in 1725. The poems she specifically mentions are his *Paraphrase of Part of the Book of Job* (1719) and *A Poem on the Last Day* (1713).

As Rowe says in her preface, her primary purpose was to 'impress' upon her readers 'the Notion of the Soul's Immortality'. Each spirit who writes to a loved one describes Heaven in ecstatic terms, and each description is somewhat different. Many of the writers have experienced easy deaths, and all compare Heaven and their present states of mind to their earthly lives. The narrative perspectives and descriptions are harmonized with individual personalities and their ages, classes, pleasures,

323

and habitual pursuits. Some manage a double perspective, as the one from the infant to the grieving mother does. In a time when no one took survival of childbirth and infancy for granted, this letter might have offered sentimental relief or religious comfort. Several of the letters recognize women's special risks. Although these tales hardly qualify as 'what oft is thought but ne'er so well expressed,' the representative selections here suggest her creative blending of popular fictions and religious ideology.

P.R.B.

Friendship in Death. In Twenty Letters from the Dead to the Living

DEDICATION

To Dr. Young.[1]

Sir,

I Have no Design in this Dedication, but to express my Gratitude, for the Pleasure and Advantage I have received from your Poem on the LAST JUDGMENT, and the *Paraphrase on Part of the Book of* JOB.[2]

The Author of these Letters is above any View of Interest, and can have no Prospect of Reputation, resolving to be concealed: But if they prove a serious Entertainment to Persons whose leisure Hours are not always innocently employed, the End is fully answered.

The greatest Infidel must own there is at least as much Probability in this Scheme, as in that of the FAIRY TALES,[3] which however Visionary, are some of them Moral, and Entertaining.

I am,

SIR,

Your most humble

Servant, Etc.

[1] *Dr. Young*: Edward Young (1683-1765), best known for *Night Thoughts*, one of the most important 'Graveyard School' poems. *Love of Fame, The Universal Passion*, a series of polished, poetic satires had been published in 1725, a few years before Rowe's book. Until Alexander Pope's 1735 *Works*, Young was considered the very best of the English satiric poets. He was also the author of several plays and of a number of respected poems. Samuel Johnson concludes his life of Young: 'he was a man of genius.'

[2] *The Last Judgment*: she means *A Poem on the Last Day* (1713), which had already been published in five editions; *A Paraphrase on part of the Book of Job* (1719) required two editions in the year of its publication and another in 1726. Both of these poems were often reprinted with *Night Thoughts*.

[3] *Fairy Tales*: probably a reference to Charles Perrault's *Histories or Tales of Past Times with Morals* (1697; trans. 1729), a collection of what we call fairy-tales, or to Marie Catherine Jumelle de Berneville, Countess d'Aulnoy's *Tales of the Fairys* (1698; trans. 1699).

324

PREFACE

The *Drift of these Letters is to impress the Notion of the Soul's Immortality*; without which, all *Virtue and Religion*, with their *Temporal and Eternal good Consequences*, must fall to the Ground.

Some who pretend to have no Scruples about the Being of a GOD, have yet their Doubts about their own Eternal Existence, though valuable Authors abound in Christian *and* Moral *Proofs of it.*

But since no Means should be left unattempted in a Point of such Importance, I hope endeavouring to make the Mind familiar with the Thoughts of our Future Existence, and contract, as it were, unawares, an Habitual Persuasion of it, by Writings built on that Foundation, and addressed to the Affections and Imagination, will not be thought improper, either as a Doctrine, or Amusement; Amusement, for which the World makes by far the largest Demand, and which generally speaking, is nothing but an Art of forgetting that Immortality, the firm Belief, and advantageous Contemplation of which, this Amusement would recommend.

Friendship in Death

LETTER I

To the Earl of R——, from Mr. ——, who had promised to appear to him after his Death.

This will find you, my Lord, confirmed in your Infidelity, by your late Disappointment. It was not in my Power to give you the Evidence of a future State, which you desired, and that I had rashly promised; but since this Engagement was a Secret to every Mortal, but ourselves, you must be assured that this comes from your deceased Friend, whose Friendship you see has reached beyond the Grave.

In my last Sickness, we fixed on the Time and Place of my Appearance; you were punctual to the Appointment: For tho' I was not permitted to make myself visible, I had the Curiosity to know if you had the Resolution to attend the Solemnity of a Visit from the Dead. The Hour was come, the Clock from a neighbouring Steeple struck One, no human Voice was heard to break the awful Silence, the Moon and Stars shone clear in their Midnight Splendor and glimmered through the Trees, which in lofty Rows led to the Centre of a Grove, where I was engaged to meet you.

I saw you enter the Walks with a careless incredulous Air, not the least Concern or Expectation appeared in your Looks, as if you came there only in regard to your own Word, and a sort of respect to my Memory: However, the Calmness of the Night induced you to walk 'till the Morning began to break, when you retired, singing an Idle Song you had got out of the *Fairy Tales*. By the Gaiety of your Temper you seemed pleased, my Lord, with a new Proof against a Future Life, and happy to find yourself (as you concluded) on a level with the Beasts that perish. A glorious Advantage! and worthy of your Triumph.

But we have so often discoursed on this Subject that I would not tire you with the Repetition of any thing past; only once more to make way to your Reason, by moving your Passions, in recollecting the Manner of your Brother's Death, which was all a Demonstration of the Immortality of the Soul; and to what Heights of Fortitude that Prospect could raise the Heart of Man at the Hour of Terror and in the Jaws of Death.

With what a ready Composure did he endure the Violence of his Distemper! With what Conviction and full Assurance expect the Reward of his Piety! With what Calmness, with what a graceful Resignation did he receive the Sentence of Death, when (at his Importunity) the Physicians told him there were no Hopes of his Recovery. *Then I have but a few weary Steps*, he replied, *and the Journey of Life will be finished.*

This was not a time for Affectation; all was open undissembled Goodness and a true Greatness of Mind: Nothing else could have supported him, when every Circumstance of Life conspired to allure him back to Life, to deepen the Shadows of the Grave, and make the King of Terrors more terrible.

There was not, my Lord, among the Race of Men, a more lovely and agreeable Person than your Brother; his Marriage was just concluded with the charming *Cleora*, he had just finished a noble Seat[4] and fine Gardens to receive her: When he was near Death, she came at his Request to take a last and sad farewell: Angels might have sorrowed to see Tears in the brightest Eyes on Earth, while her Tenderness for you would have disguised her Anguish. This, with the Sight of a fond young Sister, fainting in her Woman's Arms; your aged Father sitting near, silent and stupid with his Grief. What could support the Mind of Man in such complicated Distress! The accomplished Youth, who had all that was gentle and human in his Disposition, must have betrayed some Weakness, if he had not been assisted by a Power superior to Nature. But how equal, how steady was his Mind! how becoming, how graceful his whole Behaviour! Never was the last, the closing part of Life, performed with more Decency and Grandeur. His Reason was clear and elevated, and his Words were the very Language of Immortality, and excited at the same time, both *Pity* and *Envy* in those that were near him.

When the cold Sweats hung on his Brows, and his Breath and Speech failed, Joy struggled through the Decay of Nature, and a heavenly Smile sat on his Face; a Smile that at once compelled our Tears and accused us of Weakness in them.

You, my Lord, attended him to the last Moment of Life, and when I pressed this Argument of a future State, you confessed, that though you thought Religion a Delusion, it was the most agreeable Delusion in the world, and the

---

[4] *Seat*: large home on a country estate.

Men who flattered themselves with those gay Visions, had much the Advantage of those that saw nothing before them but a gloomy Uncertainty, or the dreadful Hope of an Annihilation.

From this Uncertainty I was very solicitous to draw you, while I was in a mortal State; but I have now a more ardent Desire to convince you, though I cannot obtain the Permission to give you that Evidence you requested: However, this Letter may satisfy you that I am in a State of Existence; nor is an Apparition from the Dead a greater Miracle than a Variety of Objects that daily surround you and owe the Loss of their *Effect* to your Familiarity with them.

Happy Minds in this superior State are still concerned for the Welfare of Mortals and make a Thousand kind Visits to their Friends; to whom, if the Laws of the Immaterial Worlds did not forbid, it would be easy to make themselves visible, by the Splendor of their own Vehicles, and the Command they have on the Powers of material Things, and the Organs of Sight: It often seems a Miracle to us that you do not perceive us; for we are not absent from you by *Places*, but by the different Conditions of the *States* we are in.

You'll find this in your Closet, and may be assured it comes from

Your constant

And immortal Friend

CLERIMONT.

LETTER III

To the Countess *of* ***, *from her only Son, who died when he was* two *Years old.*

Your Grief is an Allay to my Happiness. The only Sentiment my Infant State was conscious of, was a Fondness for you, which was then pure Instinct and natural Sympathy, but is now Gratitude and filial Affection. As soon as my Spirit was released from its uneasy Confinement, I found myself an active and reasonable Being. I was transported at the Advantage and superior manner of my Existence. The first Reflection I made was on my lovely Benefactor, for I knew you in that Relation in my Infant State: But I was surprized to see you weeping over the little breathless Form from which I thought myself so happily delivered, as if you had lamented my Escape. The fair Proportion, the Agility, the Splendor of the new Vehicle, that my Spirit now informed, was so blest an Exchange that I wondered at your Grief; for I was so little acquainted with the Difference of material and immaterial Bodies, that I thought myself as visible to your Sight as you were to mine. I was exceedingly moved at your Tears, but was ignorant why, unless because yours was the most beautiful Face next my Guardian Angel, I had ever seen, and that you resembled some of the gay Forms that used to recreate my guiltless Slumbers, and smile on me in gentle Dreams. I was then ignorant of your maternal Relation to me, but remembered that you had been my Refuge in all the little Distresses of which I had but a faint Notion. I left you unwillingly in the Height of your Calamity to follow my radiant Guide to a Place of Tranquility and Joy, where I met thousands of happy Spirits of my own Order, who informed me of the History of my native World, for whose Inhabitants I have a peculiar Benevolence, and can't help interesting myself in their Welfare: But as I never discerned between Good and Evil, nor experienced the Motives that governed the Race of Men, I am, I confess, astonished at their Conduct, and find their Joys and Sorrows to be all strange and unaccountable. I have made Visits to the lower World since my Decease; the first that I made was from a tender Curiosity to know if you was satisfied with the Disposal of Heaven in my early Fate; but I was surprized to find after several Months were past, your Grief oppressed every Thought, and clouded all the Joys of your Life, which made me very inquisitive into my own History. I asked the Celestial who was your Attendant, why I was so much lamented, and of what Consequence my Life would have been to the Public or my own Family, since those fair Eyes were yet drowned in Tears for one that had made such a short and insignificant Appearance below.

As for the Public, the gentle Minister told me there was a Hazard, I might have proved a Blessing or Curse; but that I was the only Hope of an illustrious Family, and Heir to a vast Estate and distinguished Title; and pointing to a Coat of Arms, told me that was the Badge of my Dignity, and the noble Seat we had in View, with the Gardens, Fields, the Woods and Parks that surrounded it were all my entailed Possession.[5]

A goodly Possession! I replied, and proper for the four-footed Animals that I beheld feeding on the verdant Pasture; but of what use these Fields and Woods had been to one that had an immortal Spirit I cannot conceive: And for a Title, what Happiness could an airy Syllable, an empty Sound, bring with it? The Coat of Arms I took for such a Toy, that if Burlesque had not been beneath the Dignity of an Angel, I should have thought the mentioning it a Ridicule on mortal Men. I cannot conceive wherein the Charm, the Gratification of these things consist. If I were possessed of the whole earthly Globe, what use could I make of this gross Element; the Dregs of the Creation? I have no dependance on Water or Fire, or Earth or Air. 'Tis unintelligible to me that Hills and Valleys, Trees and Rivers, the Mines and Caverns under their Feet, any more than the Clouds that fly over their Heads, should be the wealth of reasonable Creatures. They may keep their Possessions unenvied by me: I am glad I did not live long enough to make so wrong a Judgment, not to acquire a Relish for such low Enjoyments. I am so little concerned for the Loss of such an Inheritance, that if the black Prince of the airy Regions claimed my Share, I would not dispute his Title, tho' he is my Aversion, and your Foe.

[5] *entailed Possession*: an estate that could be inherited only by a specific person and the heirs of his body.

So superior, Madam, are my present Circumstances to that of the greatest Monarch under the Sun that all earthly Grandeur is Pageantry and Farce, compared to the real, the innate Dignity which I now possess. I am advanced to celestial Glory, and triumph in the Heights of immortal Life and Pleasure, whence Pity falls on the Kings of the Earth.

If you could conceive my Happiness, instead of the mournful Solemnity with which you interred me, you would have celebrated my Funeral Rites with Songs and Festivals: Instead of the thoughtless thing you lately smiled on and caressed, I am now in the Perfection of my Being, in the Elevation of Reason: Instead of a little Extent of Land, and the Propriety of so much Space to breathe in, I tread the starry Pavement, make the Circuit of the Skies, and breathe the Air of Paradise. I am secure of eternal Duration, and independent but on the Almighty, whom I love and adore, as the Fountain of my Being and Blessedness.

Pardon me, Madam, 'tis you now seem the Infant, and I repay you that superior Regard and Tenderness which you lately bestowed on me.

NARCISSUS.

LETTER IV

*To my Lord ****, from a young Lady who was in a Convent in* Florence,

My Lord, finding Materials in your Closet, I took the Opportunity of your Absence to give you this Intelligence of my Death: The Hand will convince you that it comes from your once loved *Ethelinda.*

I lived but a few Weeks after you left Italy, such was the Excess of my Grief, tho' a strict Modesty still forced me to conceal my unhappy Passion from the most intimate Companion I had. After I had discovered it to you, I dared confess the guilty Secret to none but the compassionate and forgiving Powers above, who assisted my Weakness and confirmed my Resolution never to comply with any of those Schemes you proposed to free me from my Confinement. You had indeed convinced me that the Vows I had made were rash and uncommanded; but oh! 'twas past; Saints and Angels heard it, the all-seeing Skies were invoked to witness the chaste Engagement; 'twas sealed above, and entered in the Records of Heaven. Thus hopeless was my Passion; Perjury and Sacrilege stood in all their Horrors before me, Ruin and eternal Perdition were betwixt us: And yet that I loved you, my Lord, I had too often subscribed to that soft Confession to leave you any doubt of it; nor was the tender Frailty without Excuse, if all the Merit Man could boast, if every Grace that Nature could give or gentle Art improve deserved Distinction, it had been a Crime to have been insensible in any Circumstance but mine. Strange Circumstance! that could make it *Virtue* to look coldly on you.

There was the Emphasis of my Misery, mine was a Heart devoted to superior Ardours, and sacred to Heaven alone; that Heaven which is my

329

impartial Judge and Witness how sincerely I strove to blot you from my Soul. But neither Reason nor the nicest Sense of Honour, nor even Devotion could assist me; still you returned on my Imagination triumphant in all your Charms. Hopeless of the Conquest, I gave myself up to Grief and Despair, resolving never to attempt my Escape from the Holy Retreat to which my Vows had confined me, but rather to fall a Victim to the sacred Names of Chastity and Truth. Heaven accepted the Sacrifice, and Death my kind Deliverer, at once released me from Misery and Mortality. The crystal Gates opened a spacious Entrance, and the blest Immortals received me to the Mansions of Life and Bliss.

Whatever was feigned of *Elysian* Fields and *Cyprian* Groves,[6] is here without Delusion surpassed: These are the Imperial Seats, the native Dominions of Love: Here His holy Torch flames out with propitious Splendor, and His golden Shafts are dipped in immortal Joys. Here are no Vows that tear us from our Wishes, no Conflict 'twixt Passion and Virtue; what we like we admire, what we admire we enjoy, nor is it more our Happiness than Commendation so to do.

That unhappy Passion which was my Torment and Crime is now my Glory and my Boast. Nothing selfish or irregular, nothing that needs Restraint or Disguise mingles with the noble Ardour. 'Tis all calm and beneficent, becoming the Dignity of Reason and the Grandeur of an immortal Mind, and is as lasting as its Essence. When the Lamps of Heaven are quenched, when the Sun has burnt out its Splendor, this Divine Principle shall shine with undiminished Lustre, the Joy and Triumph of the Heavenly Nations: The Substance of Love, my Lord, dwells in Heaven, its Shadow only is to be found upon Earth.

ETHELINDA.

LETTER IX

To Sylvia.

From the fragrant Bowers, the ever-blooming Fields, and light-some Regions of the Morning Star, I wish Health and every Blessing to the charming *Sylvia*! the Blessing of the Earth.

I have a Secret to reveal to you of the greatest Importance to your present and future Happiness. You are as much a Stranger to your own Rank and Circumstances as I was to mine, 'till I came here, where I met a fair Spirit, who informed me, that when she was a Mortal, I was her Son, and not the Heir of the Earl of ****, as was supposed; and that the Lord *** is your own Brother. 'Tis necessary that you should know and discover this to him, which will prevent that innocent Fondness, which he now indulges for you, from growing into a guilty Passion.

---

[6] *Elysian Fields and Cyprian Groves*: in Greek mythology, the souls of the virtuous went to the Elysian Fields and experienced complete happiness; the Cyprian groves were sacred to the worship of Aphrodite, goddess of love.

You have been educated only as a Dependent on the noble Family you are in, and as a Companion to the young Ladies, who are really your Sisters. The Mystery is this: My Lord, your Father, had several Daughters successively by the Countess your Mother, but no lawful Heir, which made him fond of a natural Son that he had by a Mistress. His Affection for him was so extravagant, that he contrived to settle his Estate on him: This gave your Mother such Anxiety, that her Jealousy and Aversion to the Youth, put her on this rash Design, when she was with Child to exchange it, if it proved a Daughter. My Mother, who was married out of her Service,[7] and in whom she could entirely confide, was with Child of me at the same time. Their time of Delivery was very near together; my Mother had a Son, and you proved a Daughter. The Affair was managed with such Dexterity, that I was exchanged, and passed without Suspicion for the Countess's Son, and you were received by my Mother, and were supposed to be her Daughter: But within a Year the Countess had really a Son, but she dying as soon as she was delivered, the Secret was undiscovered.

I lived a Guiltless Impostor 'till I was ten Years old, when a sudden Decay withered my tender Bloom; but as I had been bred in the strictest Notions of Piety and Truth, without any childish Prejudices or lavish Fears, I expected my approaching End, whilst Death made his Advances armed with a golden headed Dart. I had no Notions of Misery, all my Expectations were bright, tho' imperfect, of some Paradise beyond the Grave; and closing my Eyes, I fell asleep, and waked to immortal Life and Happiness. All that was past looked like a Dream, like an airy Image, of I know not what. Some Notion I had of a God, and my Dependence on him; but how different from the Illumination that broke in on my Soul, the Moment it threw off its mortal Veil. 'Twas then I began to live and reflect: 'Twas then I found myself a rational Being, and looked back with Contempt, on the insignificant Part I had been acting. The Memory of my original Follies, the childish Baubles and Toys that had just before been my Diversion, would have given me some Confusion, if my Case had been singular; but I met thousands of gay Spirits newly released, who had performed their short Task, and finished their trifling Farces of Life; at the same time transported at their present superior Circumstances, they made the most agreeable Reflections on their past State. What Grandeur, what Vivacity, what Enlargement of their intellectual Powers! How sparkling, how resembling the Angels of God their Forms! While a perfect Consciousness, and exact Remembrance of what they were but a few Moments past, raised their Joy and Gratitude to the Height, and recommended Heaven itself.

There was one Circumstance in my early Death, that makes me look on it as a peculiar Favour, in that I was removed by the just Dispensation of Heaven, from the Possession of what is, in the strictest Equity, your Brother's

---

[7] *out of her Service:* she had stopped working as a maid when she married.

Right. This Reflection, from a Principle of Justice and Truth, gave me an Ineffable Satisfaction; since if I had lived, I had been the unhappy, tho' innocent Usurper of a Rank and Inheritance to which I had not the least real Title. This, with a thousand other Advantages, makes me bless the Period that freed me from Mortality; that happy Moment that delivered me from Ignorance and Vanity; from the Errors, the Guilt, the Miseries of human Life; of which, tho' I had but little Experience, I am now fully informed of the State of my Fellow Creatures, and with what Toil and Hazard a longer Course of Years had been attended.

I remember no Engagement to the World, but my Affection for you; nor has Death effaced the tender Impression, but what was then a natural Sympathy is now a rational Esteem. I view with Pleasure your growing Virtue, and frequent my native World for your sake. There was something perfectly engaging in the guiltless Sorrow you expressed in my Sickness; and when my Eyes were closed in Death, you would have watched the breathless Clay, in hopes to wake me from the fatal Slumbers again; nor could the gloomy Solemnity of a Room of State deter you from paying your Visits to the silent Relics. If any thing could have tempted me to wish myself a Mortal again, it would have been the tender Tears you shed for me. The only Intervals of human Life I review with pleasure are the Hours I spent with you: This gentle Passion was the Stamp of Heaven on my Soul, the first soft Impression it received, and it gains new Energy in these happy Regions of pure Beneficence and Love. This gives me a constant Solicitude, while I see you on the Borders of such a Temptation. You are yet perfectly guiltless, and have done nothing unbecoming the Sanctity of Nature and the chaste Affection of a Sister for a Brother; but you are on the very Limits of Danger, a Step farther, the least Advance, involves you in Sin and Destruction. I know this Discovery will give you a secret Horror, and quench every kindling Desire. The Purity of your Virtue will start at the enchanting Error that might have led you on to certain Perdition; for young as you are, the contagious Spark is ready to kindle, and the lovely Boy appears more alluring. Your mutual Conversation, and the early Dawning of superior Merit in both, endeared you to each other, by such Sentiments, as only noble and virtuous Minds experience. But as a more late Discovery might have been fatal to your Innocence and Peace, I impatiently attended an Opportunity and Method to make you sensible of your Danger. I know (tho' I have been dead for Years) you still remember me, and I have often heard you name me, and seen you with Delight gazing on my Picture; this made me resolve to appear to you when I saw you. The first Opportunity that pleased me, you were sitting, gazing at your own Reflection, and sticking Flowers in your Hair, to adorn it for your young Lover. I knew you had read of Fairies and looked at painted *Cupids* with delight: In such a Poetical Form I thought you would have heard my Story and been pleased with my Figure.

While youthful Splendor lightened in my Eyes,
Clear as the smiling Glory of the Skies;
Sprinkled with radiant Gold, a Purple Hue
My Wings displayed, my Robe celestial Blue:
More white than Flax my curling Tresses flowed,
My dimpled Cheeks with rosy Beauty glowed.[8]

I could not have believed a form more gay than those that glittered on your
Fan could have discomposed you; but to my Surprize, I saw you faint away,
before I had begun to speak to you. You soon recovered from the Swoon, and
returning to the House, told a Story, which you found no Body believed; so
wise is the Age in which you live, as not to be imposed on. You easily persuaded yourself 'twas no more than a Dream. However, I dared attempt your
Courage no more; but give you this important Information this way; which
if you should not credit, you are undone. In this Admonition your Guardian
Angel joins with

ALEXIS.

LETTER XIV

To

My dear Sister, I have often, since I left the World, had the Privilege to supply the Place of your Guardian Angel. I have been an invisible Witness of your
Tears for my Death; and to allay the Excess of your Grief for me, I have been
at last permitted to let you know that I am happy.

I can give you no Account how my soul was released: I fell asleep in per-
fect Health, with an unusual Serenity of Mind, and from the gentlest Slumbers
of Innocence and Peace, awaked in immortal Bliss. (How common is sudden
Death?) I found myself in a moment got above the Stars, and out-shining the
Sun in its Meridian Splendor. Corruption had put on Incorruption, and
Mortality was swallowed up of Life and Immortality. O Death! I cried in the
Exaltation of my Thoughts, O Death! where is thy Conquest?[9] O King of
Terrors! where is thy boasted Victory? where is thy Scepter and Imperial
Horrors, thy gloomy State, and dreadful Attendants? where are thy vast
Dominions, the cheerless and formless Darkness, the Shade and the
Emptiness, the Seats of Corruption and Decay?

The Spell is broken! the Enchantment is dissolved! the Shadows, the
Phantoms, the visionary Terrors fly! the celestial Morning dawns, and charm-
ing Scenes arise: But oh! how boundless! how various! how transporting the
Prospect!

Still lost in Joy and Wonder, tell me, I said, ye Angels, ye smiling Forms
that surround me, what easy Passage has my Spirit found from its mortal

---

[8] Rowe's *Farewell to Love: A Pindaric to the Athenian Society.*
[9] *O Death! Where is thy Conquest?*: Rowe echoes 1 Corinthians 15: 54–5.

Prison? What gentle Hand has unlocked my earthly Fetters, and brought me out of Darkness and Confinement into immense Light and Liberty? Who was the kind Messenger that conveyed the welcome Invitation to my Ear? What melodious Voice called me away from yonder cold Tempestuous Regions to these soft and peaceful Habitations? How have I found my Passage through the tractless Ether and gained the Summit of the everlasting Hills? Am I awake? Do I dream? Is this a gay, a flattering Vision? Oh no! 'tis all blissful and transporting Certainty; I see, I hear Things unutterable, such as never entered into the Heart of mortal Man to conceive. Read and believe; believe and be happy.

You see, my dear Sister, how blindly you repine at the Decrees of Heaven, and how unreasonably you lament what you call my early and untimely Fate. Could I be happy too soon?

I left the World indeed, in the full Pride of my youthful Years, in the Height of Greatness and Reputation, surrounded with the Blandishments and Flatteries of Pleasure. But these Advantages might have been fatal Snares to my Virtue in a longer Trial: 'Twas indulgent in Heaven, after a short Probation, to crown me with the Rewards of Victory. 'Tis past the Toil, the Danger, and all to come is endless Peace and Triumph.

If you could see as far into Futurity now, and think as justly of it as you will certainly do on your Death-bed, this Letter from me had been superfluous; I only can *design* it beneficial, you may *make* it so.

Bibliography

BACKSCHEIDER, PAULA R., *Spectacular Politics: Theatrical Power and Mass Culture in Early Modern England*. Baltimore and London: Johns Hopkins University Press, 1993.

BALLASTER, ROS, *Seductive Forms: Women's Amatory Fiction from 1684 to 1740*. Oxford: Clarendon Press, 1992.

CASTLE, TERRY, *Masquerade and Civilization: The Carnivalesque in Eighteenth-Century English Culture and Fiction*. Stanford: Stanford University Press, 1986.

CRAFT-FAIRCHILD, CATHERINE, *Masquerade and Gender: Disguise and Female Identity in Eighteenth-Century Fictions by Women*. University Park: Pennsylvania State University Press, 1993.

DAVIS, LENNARD, *Factual Fictions: The Origins of the English Novel*. New York: Columbia University Press, 1983.

DAY, ROBERT ADAMS, *Told in Letters: Epistolary Fiction Before Richardson*. Ann Arbor: University of Michigan Press, 1966.

GALLAGHER, CATHERINE, *Nobody's Story: The Vanishing Acts of Women Writers in the Marketplace, 1670–1820*. Berkeley and Los Angeles: University of California Press, 1994.

HUNTER, J. PAUL, *Before Novels: The Cultural Contexts of Eighteenth-Century English Fiction*. New York: W. W. Norton, 1990.

McKEON, MICHAEL, *The Origins of the English Novel 1600–1740*. Baltimore: Johns Hopkins University Press, 1987.

McKILLOP, A. D., *The Early Masters of English Fiction*. Lawrence: University Press of Kansas, 1956.

PEARSON, JACQUELINE, *The Prostituted Muse: Images of Women and Women Dramatists, 1642–1737*. New York: St Martin's Press, 1988.

PERRY, RUTH, *Women, Letters and the Novel*. New York: AMS Press, 1980.

RICHETTI, JOHN, *Popular Fiction before Richardson: Narrative Patterns 1700–1739*. Oxford: Clarendon Press, 1969; repr. with a new introduction by the author, 1992.

—— 'Popular Narrative in the Early Eighteenth Century: Formats and Formulas,' in *The First English Novelists: Essays in Understanding, Tennessee Studies in Literature*, 29 (1985), 3–39.

ROSS, DEBORAH, *The Excellence of Falsehood: Romance, Realism, and Women's Contribution to the Novel*. Lexington: University Press of Kentucky, 1991.

SAAR, DOREEN A. and MARY ANN SCHOFIELD, *Eighteenth-Century Anglo-American Women Novelists: A Critical Reference Guide*. New York: G. K. Hall, 1996.

SCHOFIELD, MARY ANN, *Masking and Unmasking the Female Mind*: *Disguising Romances in Feminine Fiction: 1713-1799*. Newark: University of Delaware Press, 1990.

SCHOFIELD, MARY ANN, and CECILIA MACHESKI (eds.), *Fetter'd or Free? British Women Novelists, 1670-1815*. Athens: Ohio University Press, 1985.

SPENCER, JANE, *The Rise of the Woman Novelist: From Aphra Behn to Jane Austen*. Oxford: Basil Blackwell, 1986.

TODD, JANET (ed.), *Aphra Behn Studies*. Cambridge: Cambridge University Press, 1996.

TODD, JANET, *The Secret Life of Aphra Behn*. London: Andre Deutsch, 1996.

TODD, JANET, *The Sign of Angellica: Women, Writing and Fiction, 1660-1800*. New York: Columbia University Press, 1989.

WATT, IAN, *The Rise of the Novel: Studies in Defoe, Richardson, and Fielding*. Berkeley and Los Angeles: University of California Press, 1957.

WILLIAMSON, MARILYN, *Raising Their Voices, 1650-1750*. Detroit: Wayne State University Press, 1990.